HOLDER!

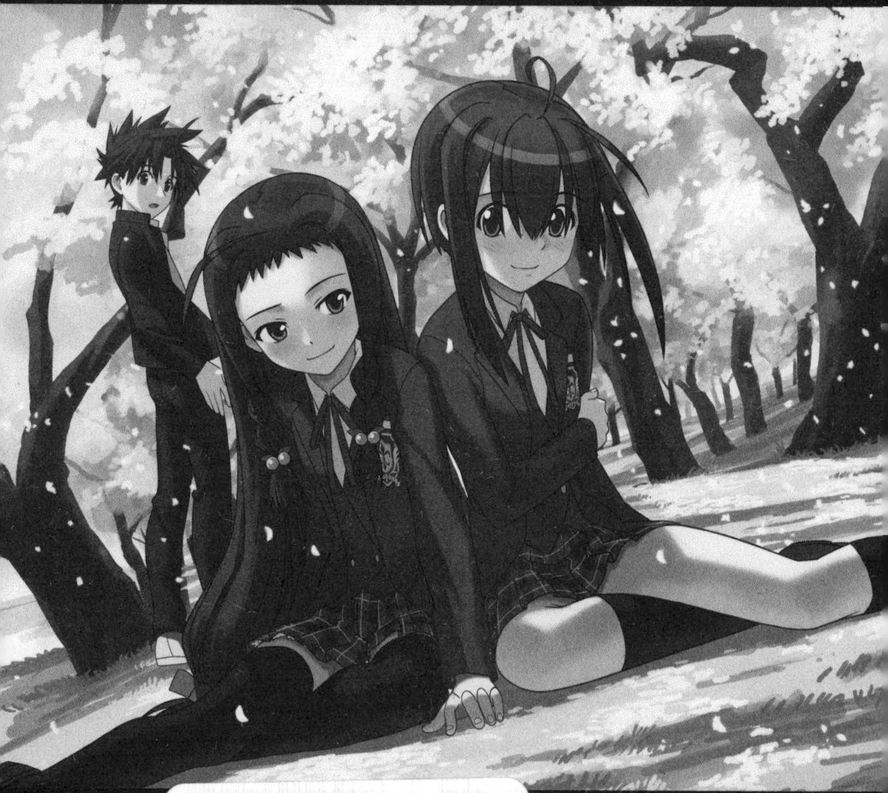

KEN AKAMATSU

vol.15

CHARACTERS

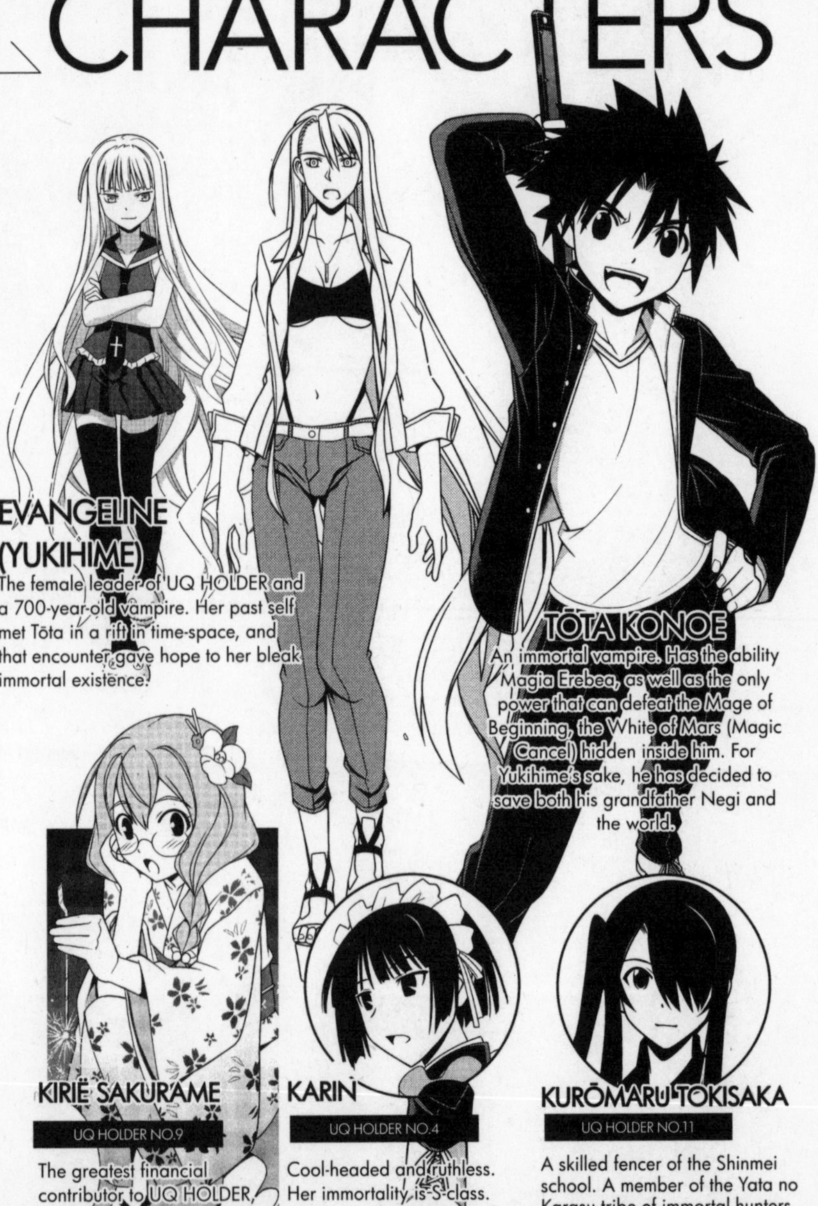

EVANGELINE (YUKIHIME)

The female leader of UQ HOLDER and a 700-year-old vampire. Her past self met Tōta in a rift in time-space, and that encounter gave hope to her bleak immortal existence.

TŌTA KONOE

An immortal vampire. Has the ability Magia Erebea, as well as the only power that can defeat the Mage of Beginning, the White of Mars (Magic Cancel) hidden inside him. For Yukihime's sake, he has decided to save both his grandfather Negi and the world.

KIRIË SAKURAME

UQ HOLDER NO.9

The greatest financial contributor to UQ HOLDER, who constantly calls Tōta incompetent. She can stop time by kissing Tōta.

KARIN

UQ HOLDER NO.4

Cool-headed and ruthless. Her immortality is S-class. Also known as the Saintess of Steel.

KURŌMARU TOKISAKA

UQ HOLDER NO.11

A skilled fencer of the Shinmei school. A member of the Yata no Karasu tribe of immortal hunters, he will be neither male nor female until his coming-of-age ceremony at age 16.

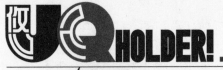

UQ HOLDER!...

Ken Akamatsu Presents

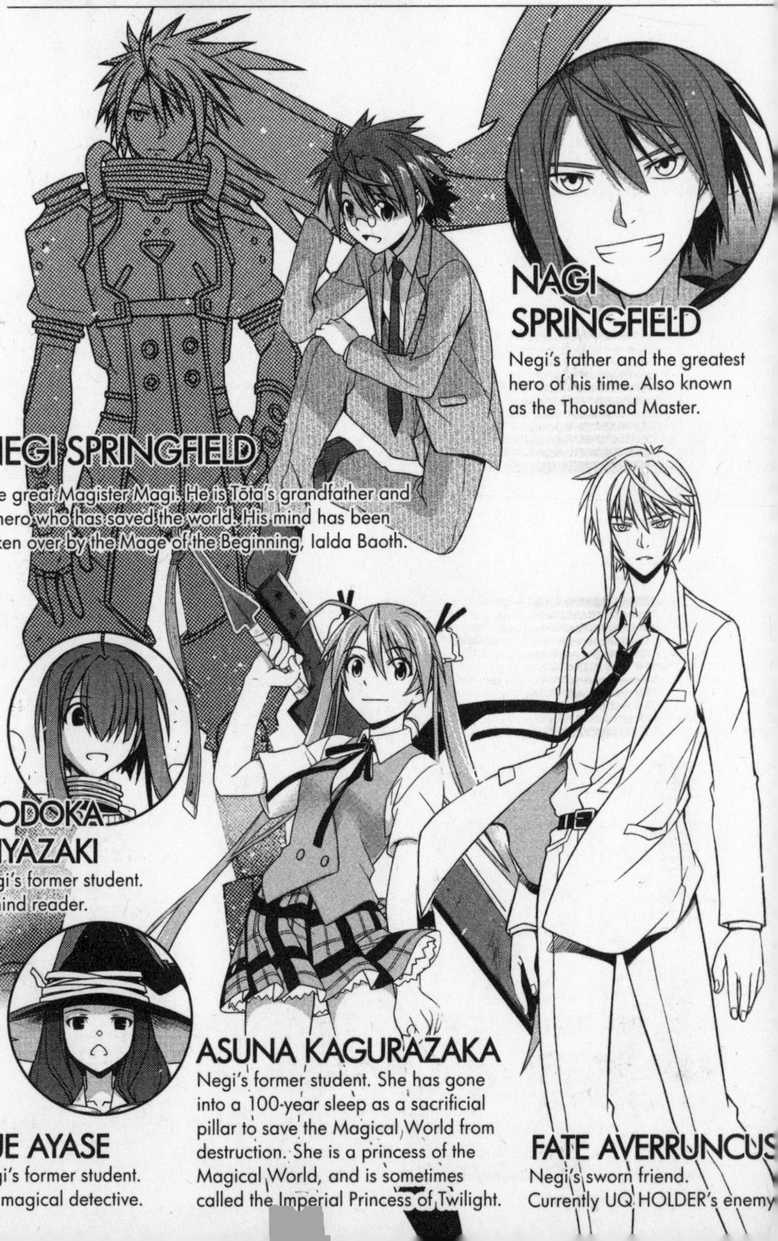

NAGI SPRINGFIELD

Negi's father and the greatest hero of his time. Also known as the Thousand Master.

NEGI SPRINGFIELD

The great Magister Magi. He is Tōta's grandfather and a hero who has saved the world. His mind has been taken over by the Mage of the Beginning, Ialda Baoth.

NODOKA MIYAZAKI

Negi's former student. A mind reader.

YUE AYASE

Negi's former student. The magical detective.

ASUNA KAGURAZAKA

Negi's former student. She has gone into a 100-year sleep as a sacrificial pillar to save the Magical World from destruction. She is a princess of the Magical World, and is sometimes called the Imperial Princess of Twilight.

FATE AVERRUNCUS

Negi's sworn friend. Currently UQ HOLDER's enemy.

THE STORY SO FAR

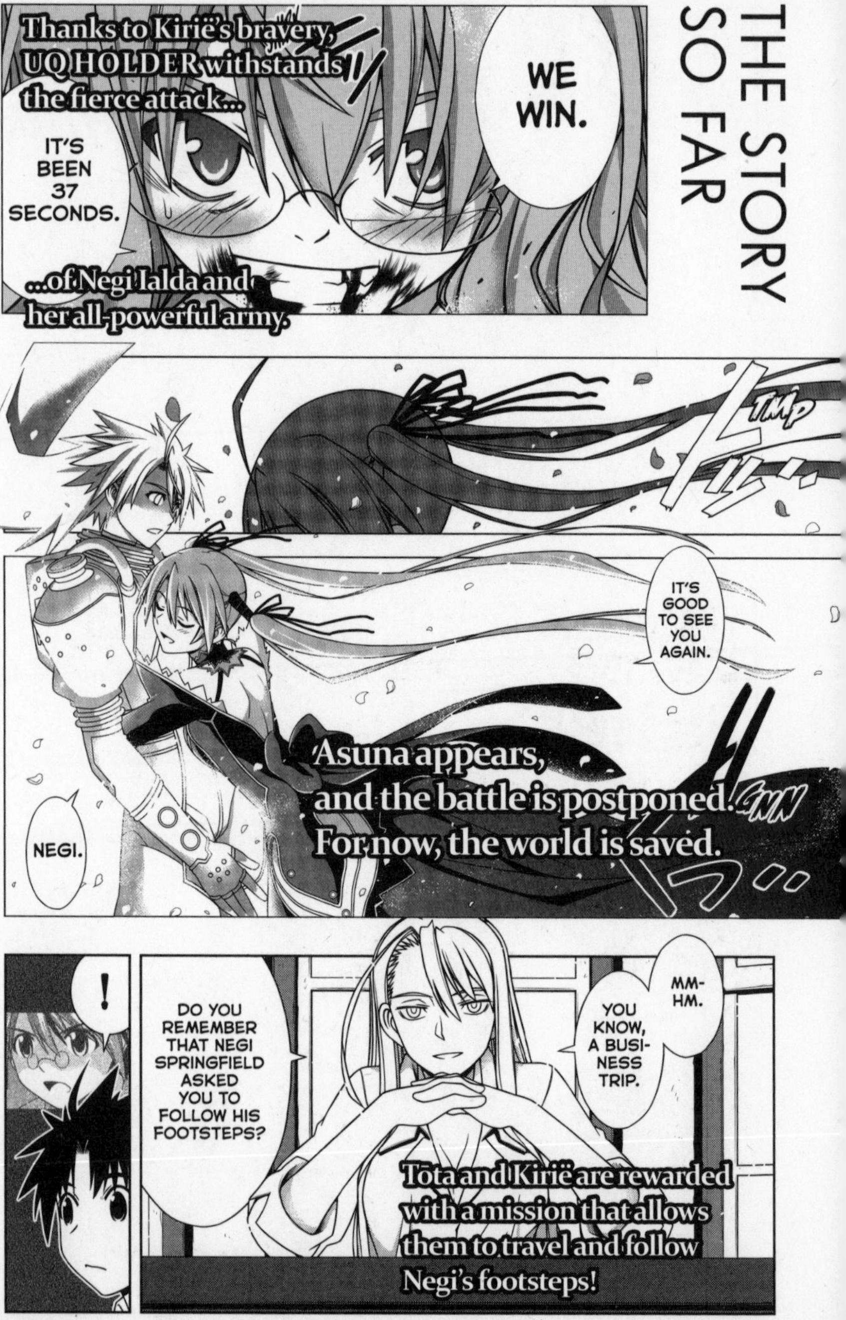
WE WIN.
Thanks to Kiriё's bravery, UQ HOLDER withstands the fierce attack...
IT'S BEEN 37 SECONDS.
...of Negi Ialda and her all-powerful army.
TMP
IT'S GOOD TO SEE YOU AGAIN.
Asuna appears, and the battle is postponed. For now, the world is saved.
GNN
NEGI.
MM-HM.
YOU KNOW, A BUSI-NESS TRIP.
DO YOU REMEMBER THAT NEGI SPRINGFIELD ASKED YOU TO FOLLOW HIS FOOTSTEPS?
Tōta and Kiriё are rewarded with a mission that allows them to travel and follow Negi's footsteps!
!

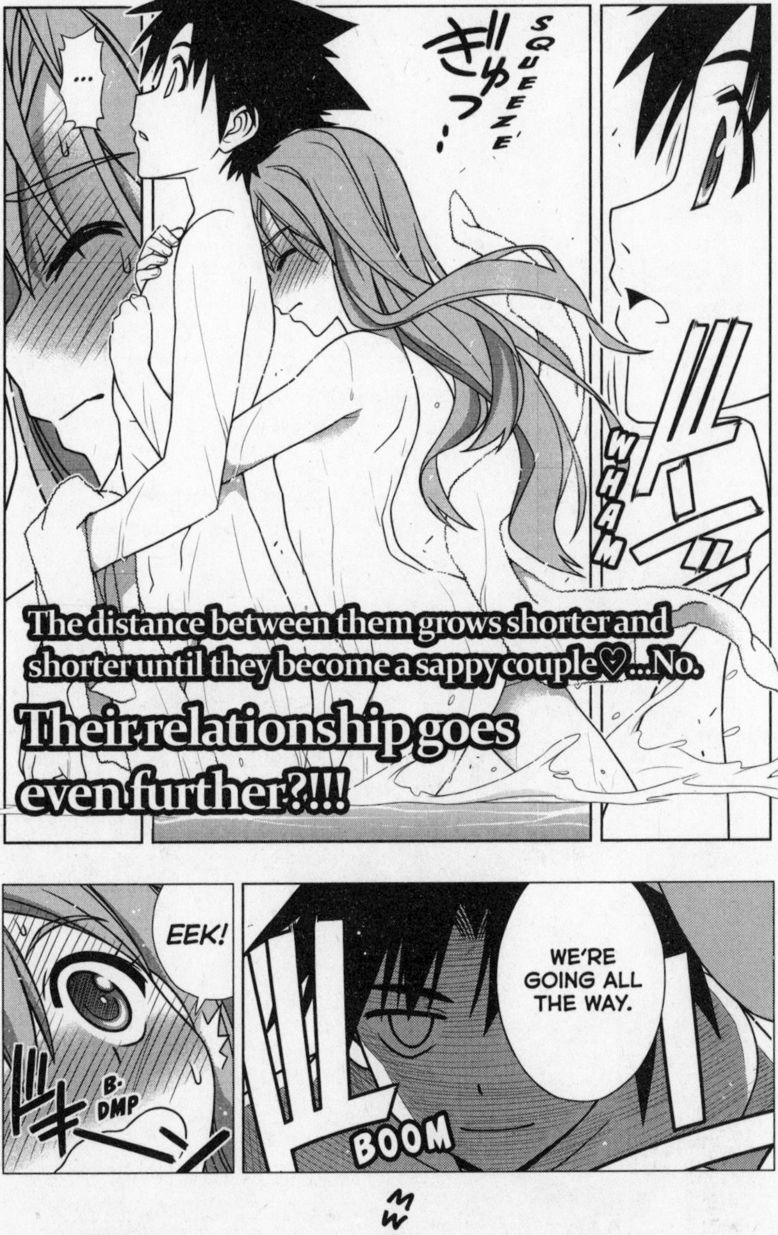
WHAM
SQUEEZE
The distance between them grows shorter and shorter until they become a sappy couple♡...No.
Their relationship goes even further?!!!
...
WE'RE GOING ALL THE WAY.
BOOM
EEK!
B-DMP

By the way, what are MWAH♡ Negi's footsteps?

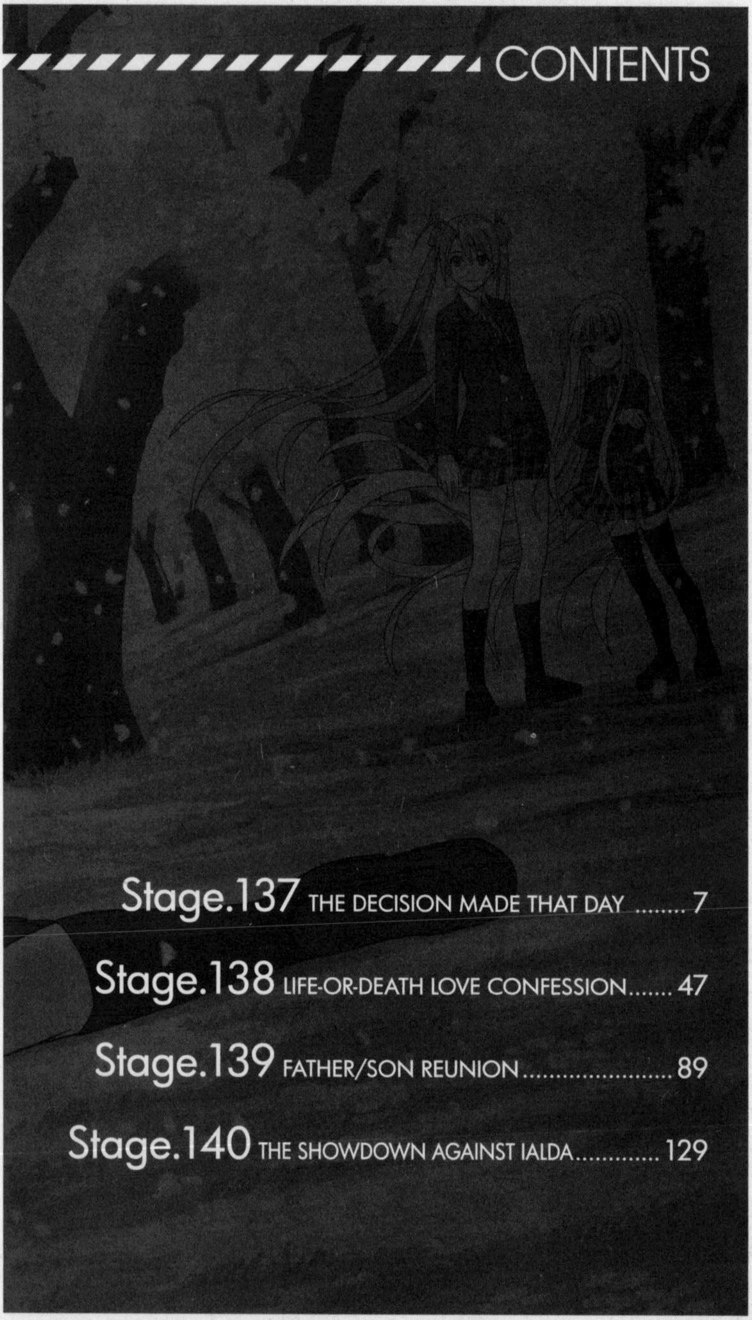

CONTENTS

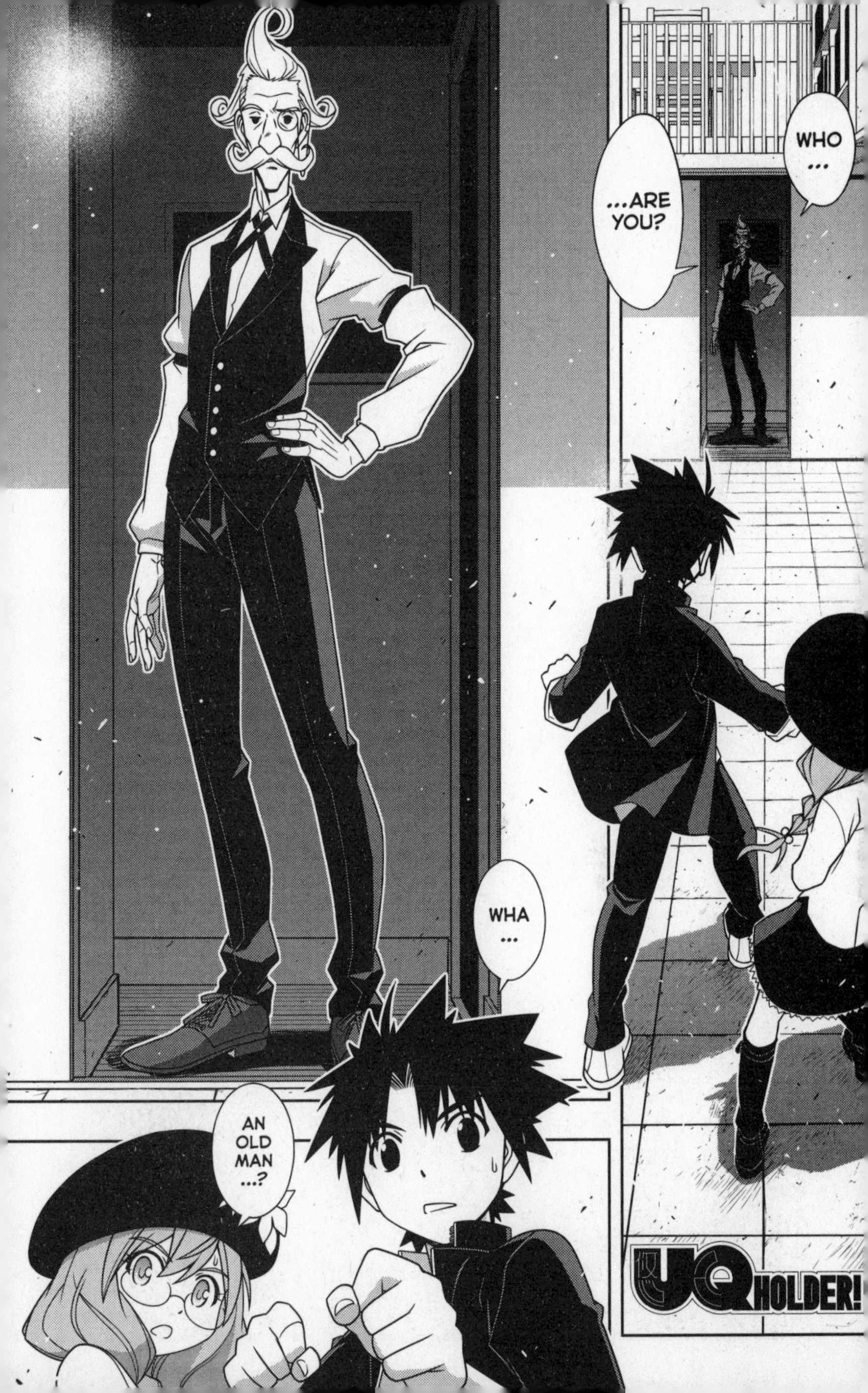
WHO ...
...ARE YOU?
WHA ...
AN OLD MAN ...?

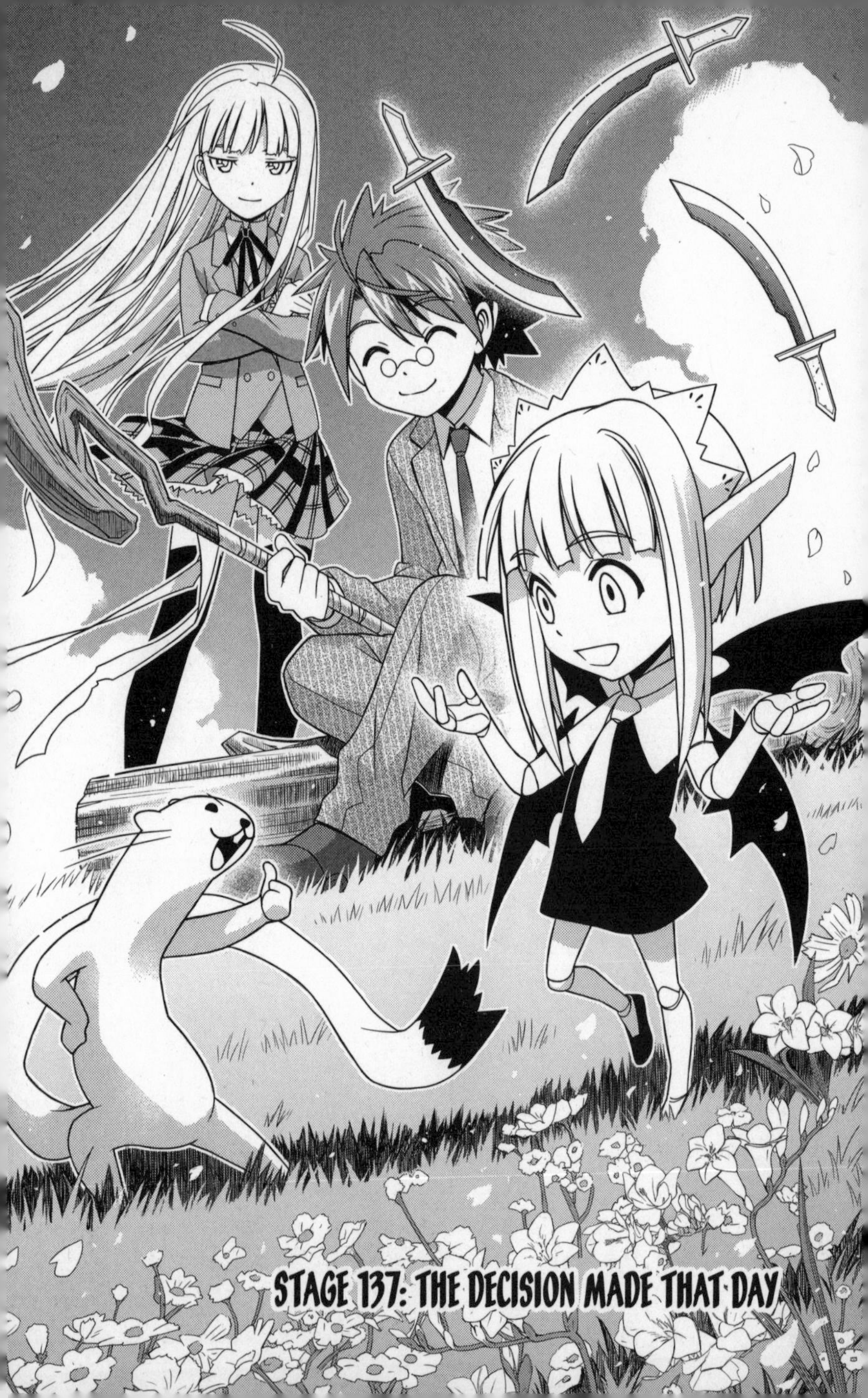
STAGE 137: THE DECISION MADE THAT DAY

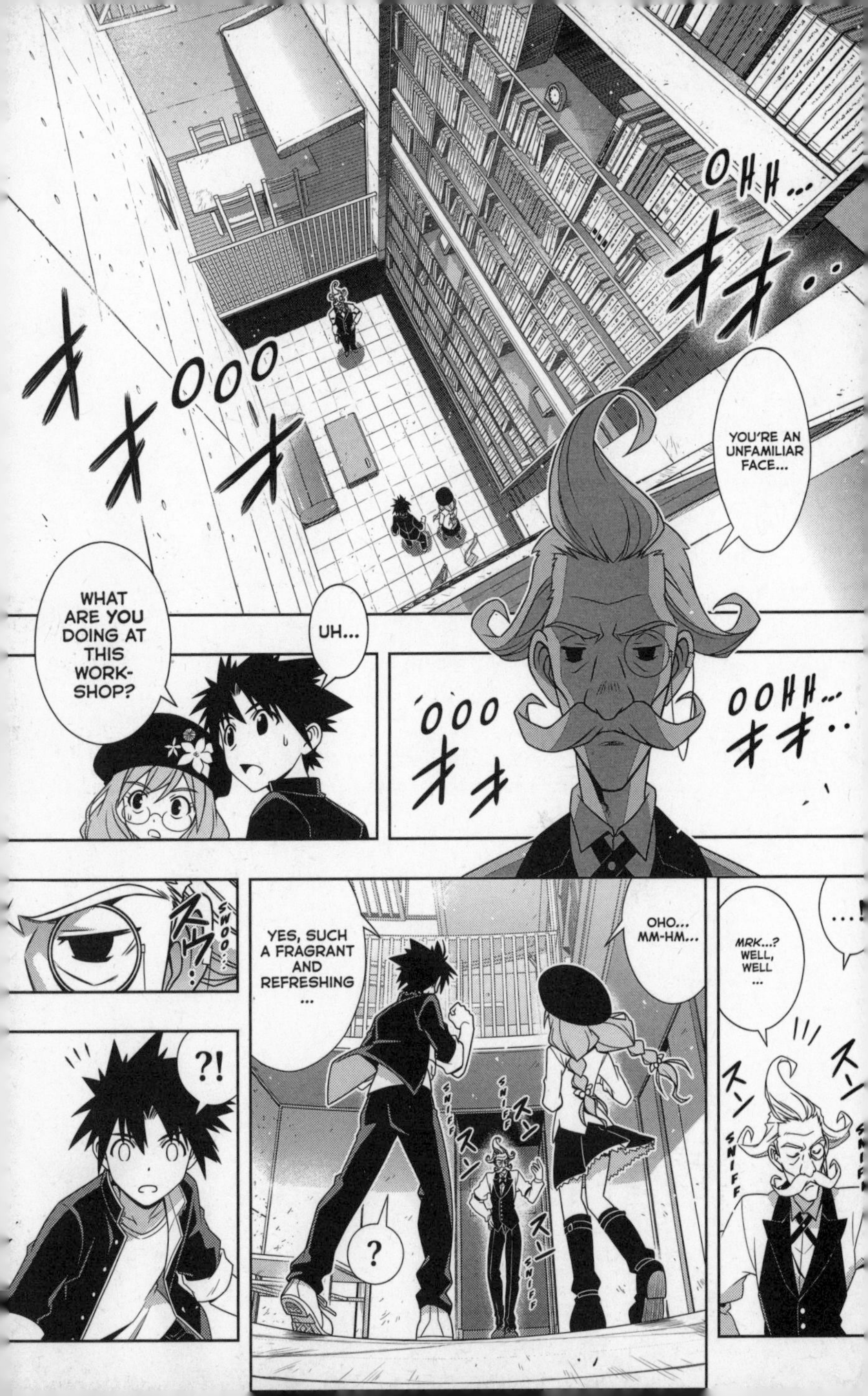
OHHH...
オオ..
OOO
オオオ
YOU'RE AN UNFAMILIAR FACE...
OOHHH...
オオ..
OOO
オオ
UH...
WHAT ARE YOU DOING AT THIS WORK-SHOP?
...!
MRK...? WELL, WELL ...
スン
SNIFF
OHO... MM-HM...
YES, SUCH A FRAGRANT AND REFRESHING ...
SNIFF
スン
?
SWOO...
?!

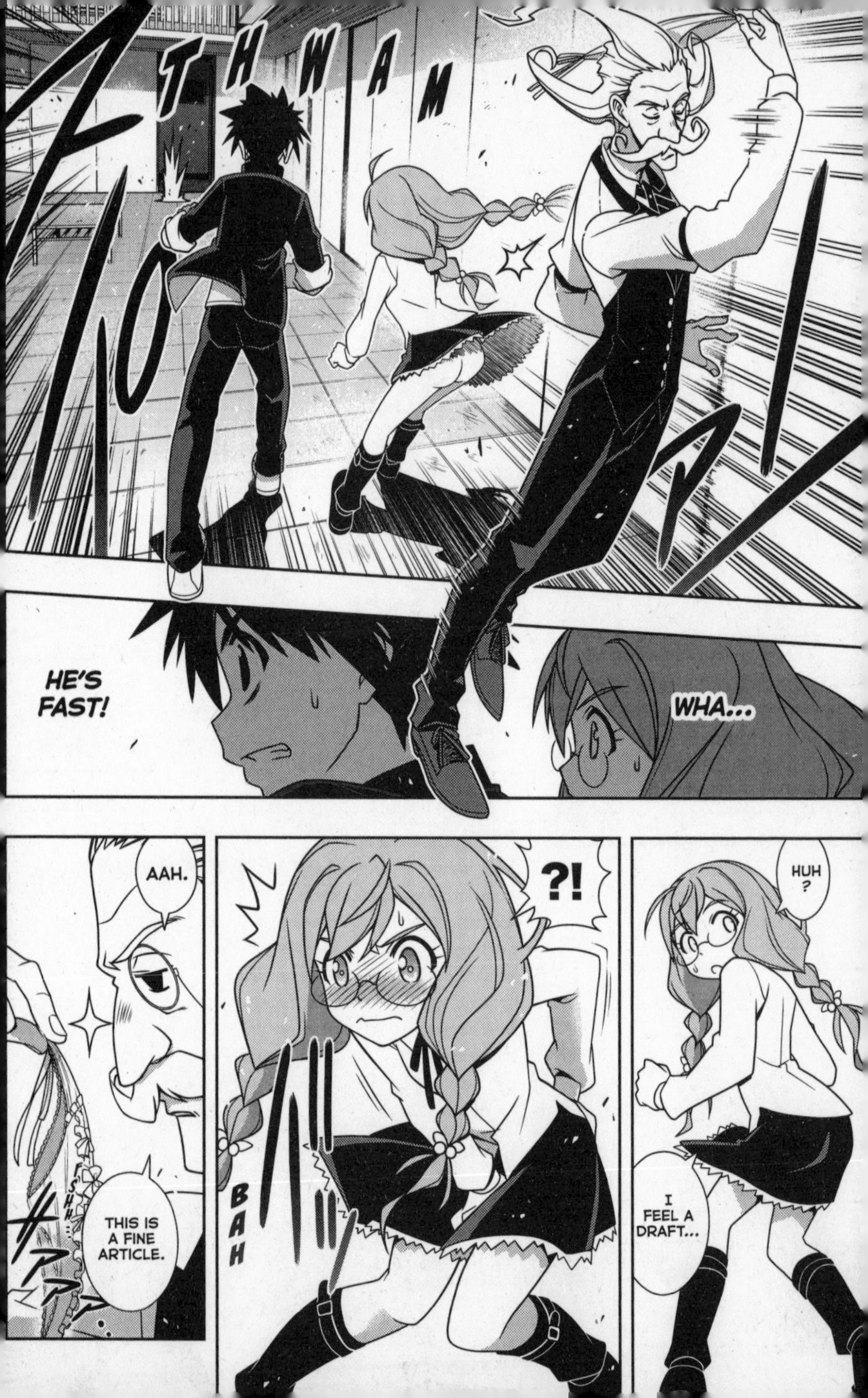
THWAM
WHA...
HE'S FAST!
HUH ?
I FEEL A DRAFT...
?!
BAH
AAH.
THIS IS A FINE ARTICLE.

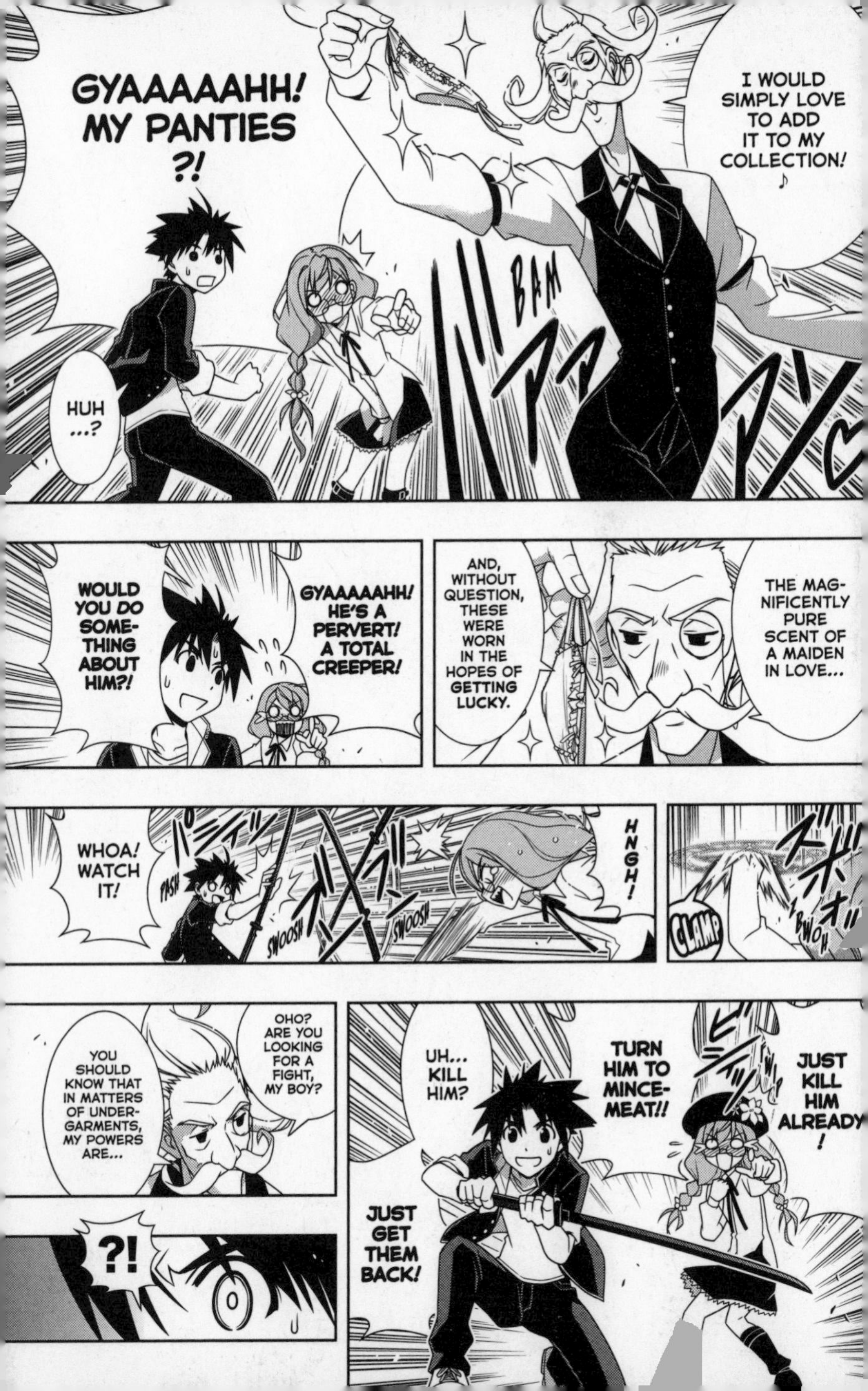
I WOULD SIMPLY LOVE TO ADD IT TO MY COLLECTION! ♪
BAM
GYAAAAAHH! MY PANTIES ?!
HUH ...?
THE MAG-NIFICENTLY PURE SCENT OF A MAIDEN IN LOVE...
AND, WITHOUT QUESTION, THESE WERE WORN IN THE HOPES OF GETTING LUCKY.
GYAAAAAHH! HE'S A PERVERT! A TOTAL CREEPER!
WOULD YOU DO SOME-THING ABOUT HIM?!
BWOH
CLAMP
HNGH!
SWOOSH
SWOOSH
PASH
WHOA! WATCH IT!
JUST KILL HIM ALREADY!
TURN HIM TO MINCE-MEAT!!
UH... KILL HIM?
JUST GET THEM BACK!
OHO? ARE YOU LOOKING FOR A FIGHT, MY BOY?
YOU SHOULD KNOW THAT IN MATTERS OF UNDER-GARMENTS, MY POWERS ARE...
?!

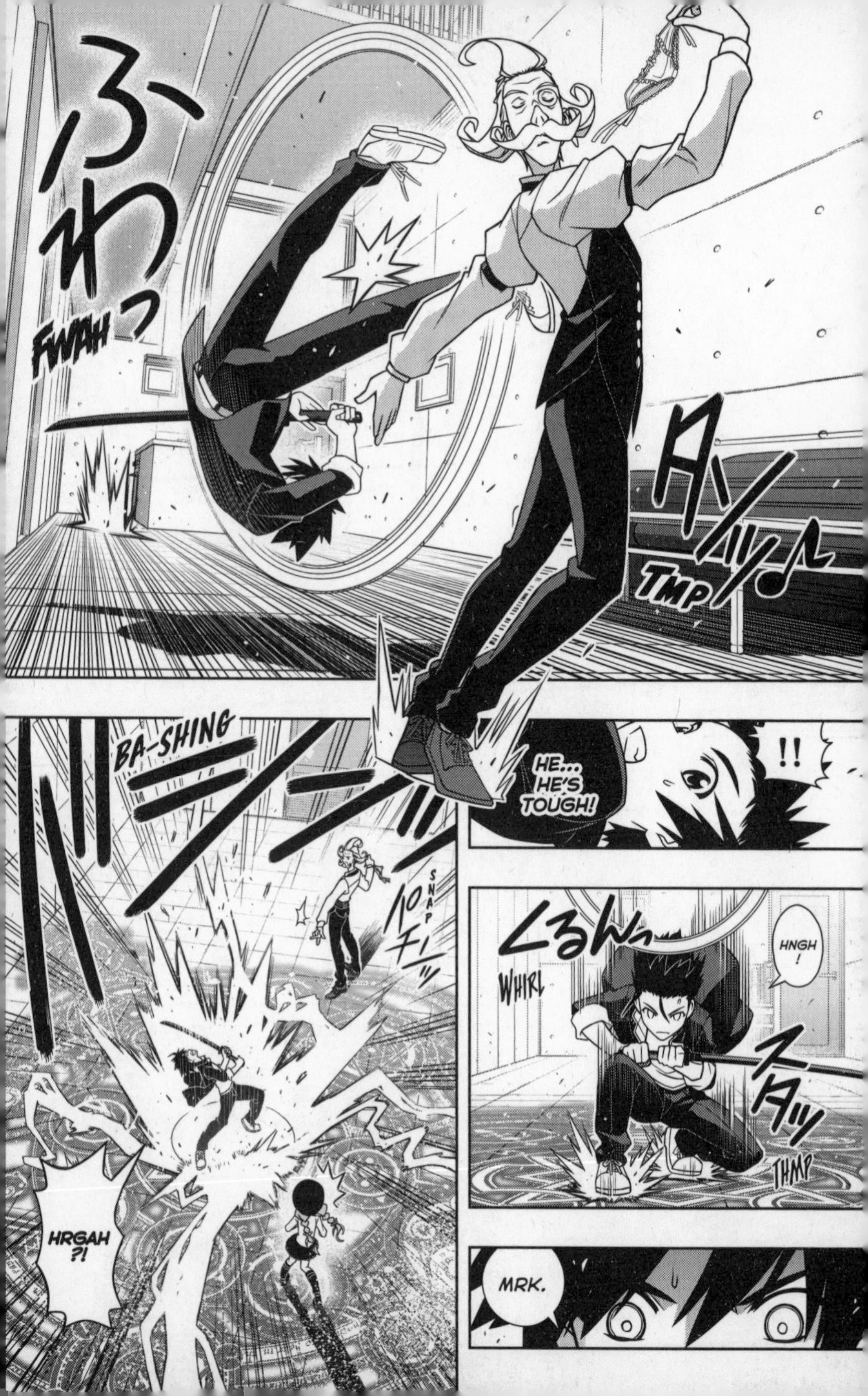

ふわっ
FWAH
タンッ♪
TMP
!!
HE... HE'S TOUGH!
HNGH!
くるんっ
WHIRL
スタッ
THMP
MRK.
BA-SHING
SNAP
HRGAH?!

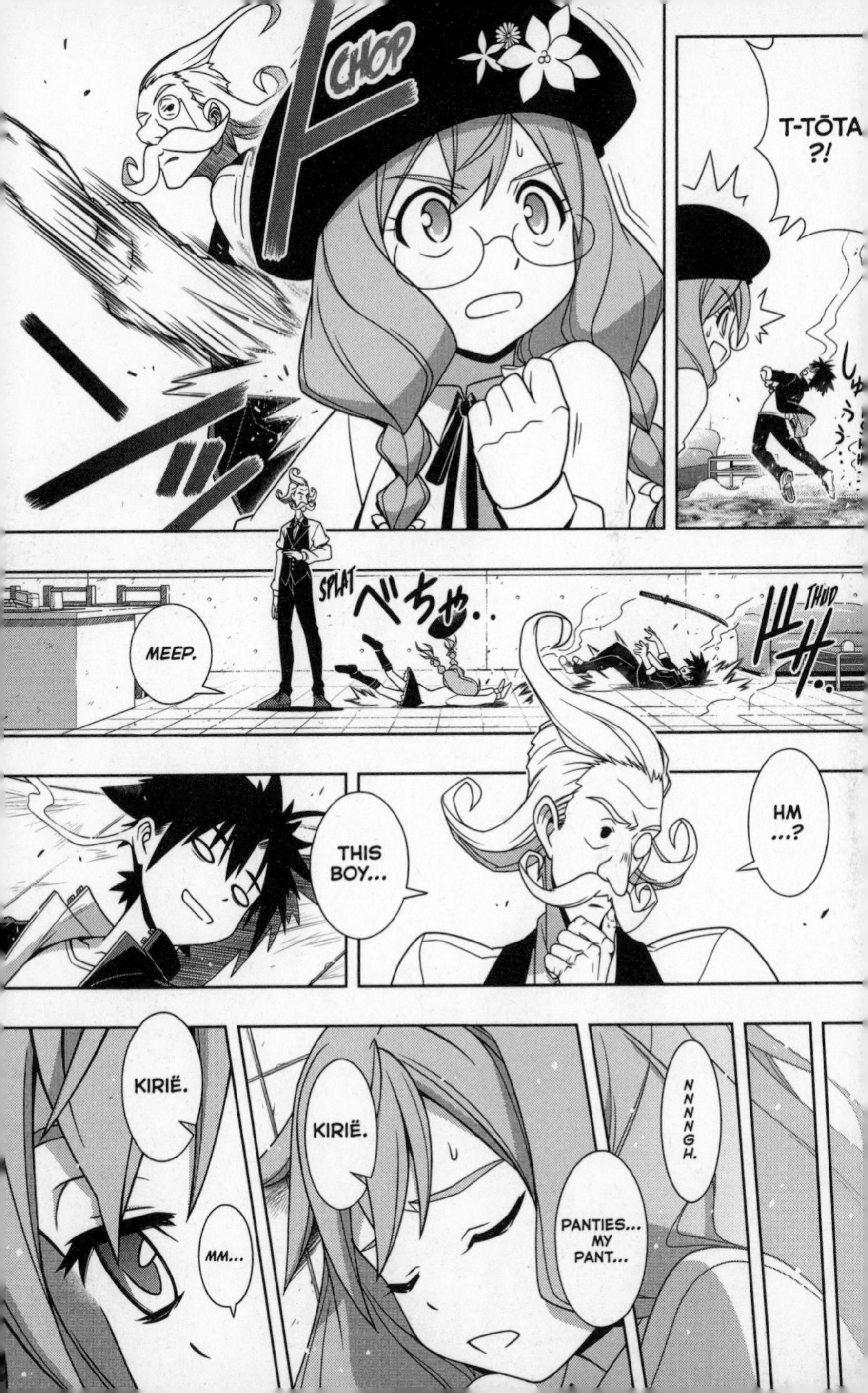
T-TŌTA ?!
CHOP
THUD
SPLAT
べちゃ
MEEP.
HM ...?
THIS BOY...
NNNNGH.
PANTIES... MY PANT...
KIRIË.
KIRIË.
MM...

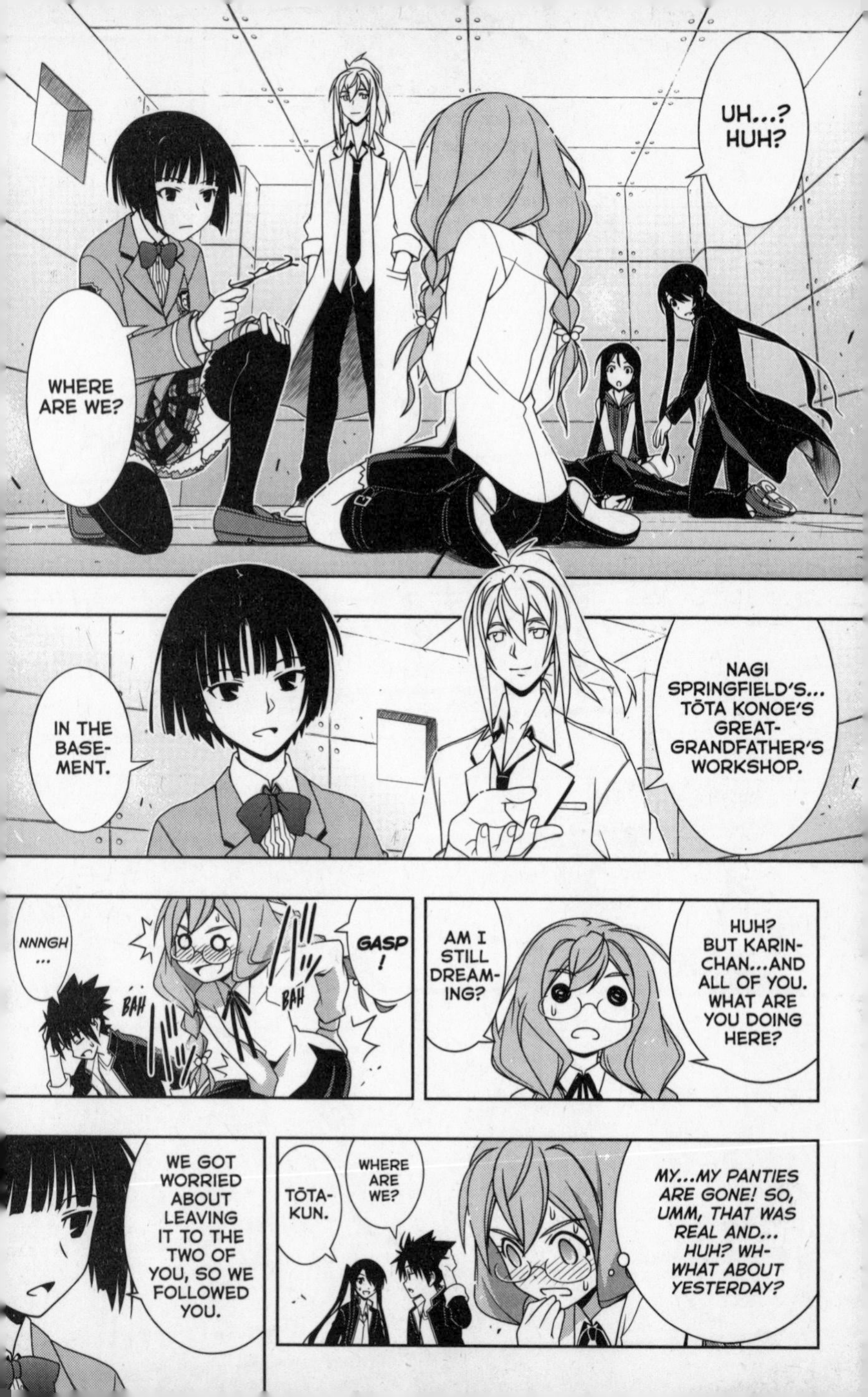
UH...? HUH?
WHERE ARE WE?
NAGI SPRINGFIELD'S... TŌTA KONOE'S GREAT-GRANDFATHER'S WORKSHOP.
IN THE BASEMENT.
HUH? BUT KARIN-CHAN...AND ALL OF YOU. WHAT ARE YOU DOING HERE?
AM I STILL DREAMING?
GASP!
BAH
BAH
NNNGH...
MY...MY PANTIES ARE GONE! SO, UMM, THAT WAS REAL AND... HUH? WH-WHAT ABOUT YESTERDAY?
WHERE ARE WE?
TŌTA-KUN.
WE GOT WORRIED ABOUT LEAVING IT TO THE TWO OF YOU, SO WE FOLLOWED YOU.

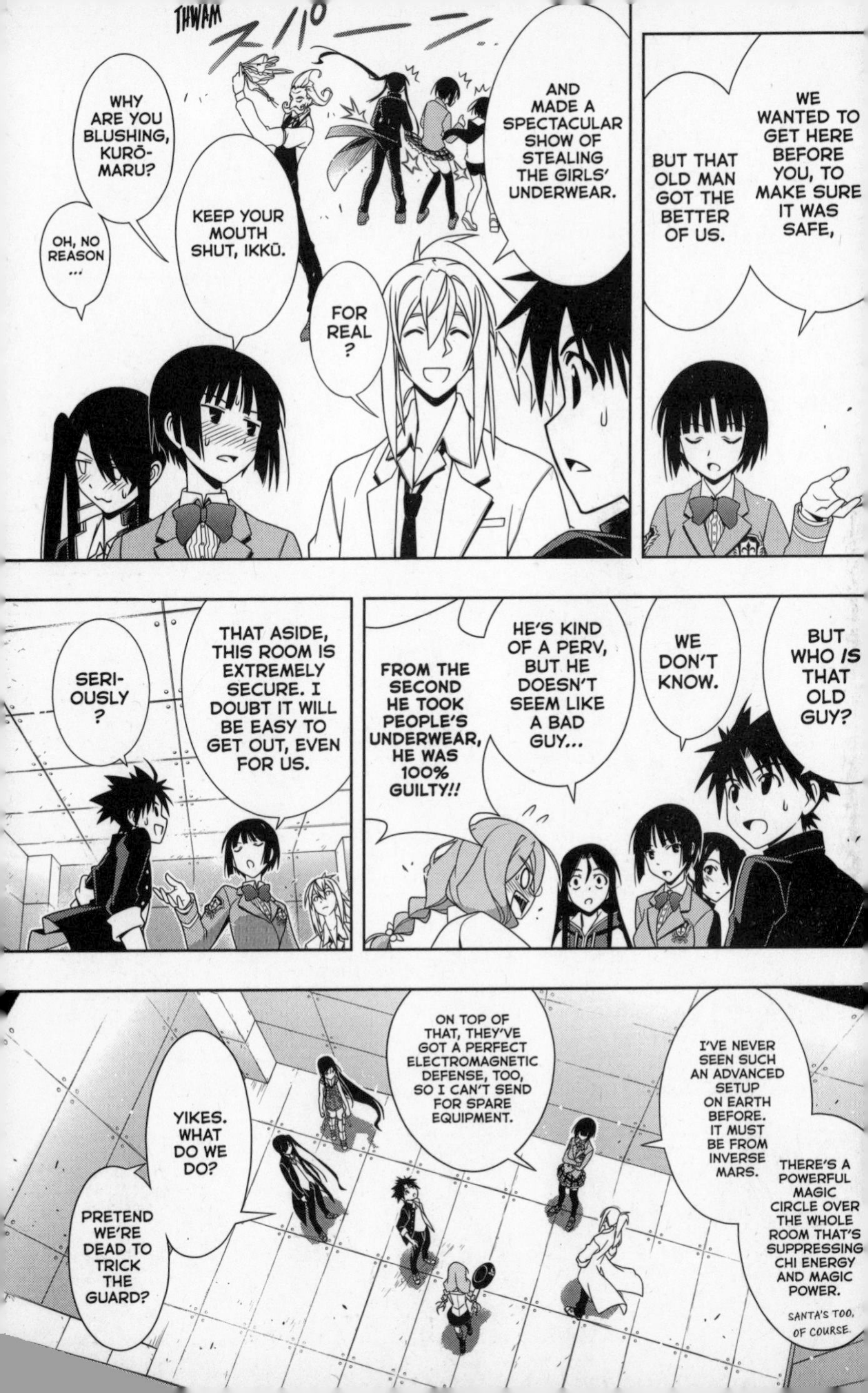
WE WANTED TO GET HERE BEFORE YOU, TO MAKE SURE IT WAS SAFE,
BUT THAT OLD MAN GOT THE BETTER OF US.
AND MADE A SPECTACULAR SHOW OF STEALING THE GIRLS' UNDERWEAR.
THWAM
FOR REAL?
WHY ARE YOU BLUSHING, KURŌ-MARU?
KEEP YOUR MOUTH SHUT, IKKŪ.
OH, NO REASON...
BUT WHO IS THAT OLD GUY?
WE DON'T KNOW.
HE'S KIND OF A PERV, BUT HE DOESN'T SEEM LIKE A BAD GUY...
FROM THE SECOND HE TOOK PEOPLE'S UNDERWEAR, HE WAS 100% GUILTY!!
THAT ASIDE, THIS ROOM IS EXTREMELY SECURE. I DOUBT IT WILL BE EASY TO GET OUT, EVEN FOR US.
SERIOUSLY?
I'VE NEVER SEEN SUCH AN ADVANCED SETUP ON EARTH BEFORE. IT MUST BE FROM INVERSE MARS.
THERE'S A POWERFUL MAGIC CIRCLE OVER THE WHOLE ROOM THAT'S SUPPRESSING CHI ENERGY AND MAGIC POWER.
SANTA'S TOO, OF COURSE.
ON TOP OF THAT, THEY'VE GOT A PERFECT ELECTROMAGNETIC DEFENSE, TOO, SO I CAN'T SEND FOR SPARE EQUIPMENT.
YIKES. WHAT DO WE DO?
PRETEND WE'RE DEAD TO TRICK THE GUARD?

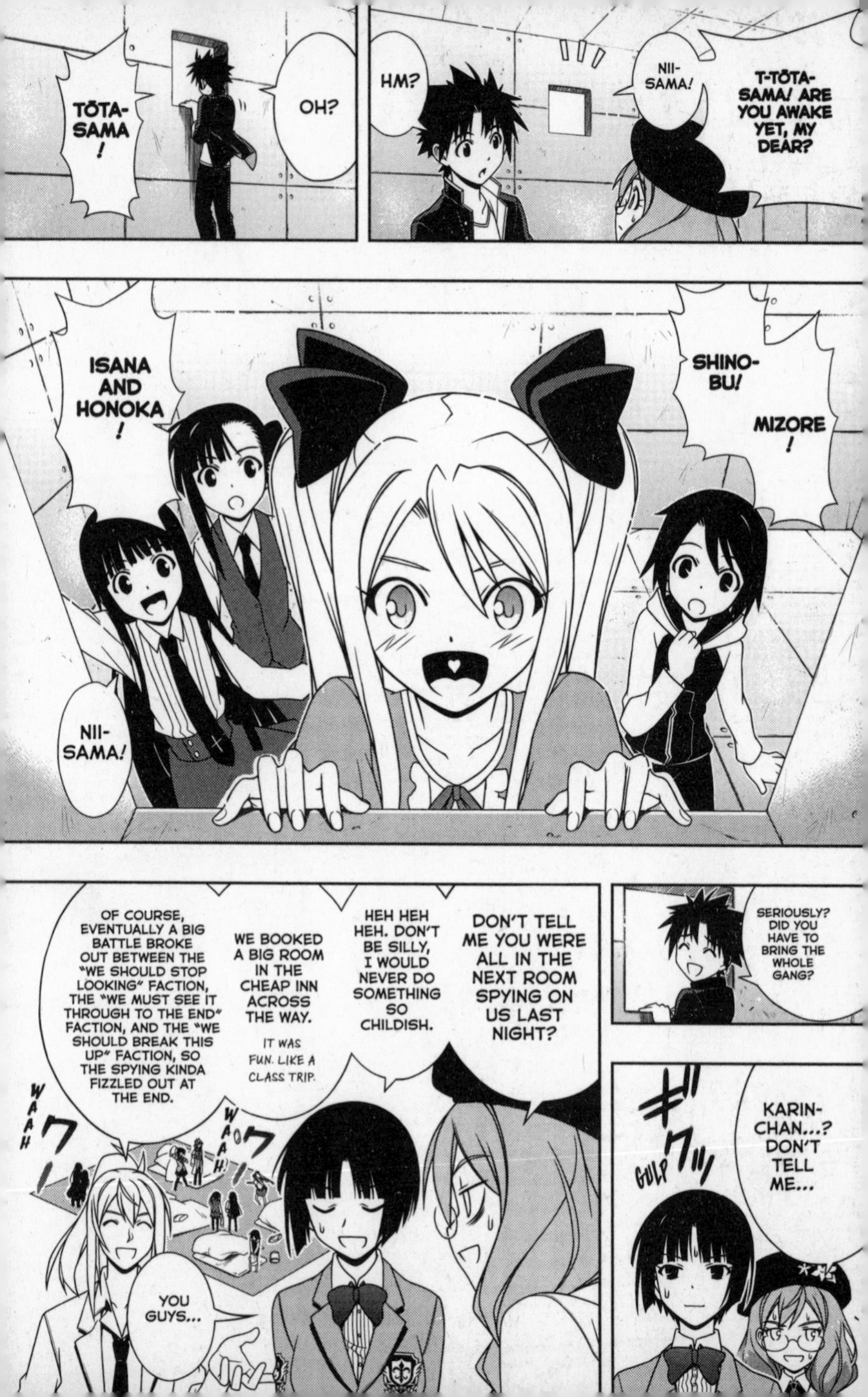
T-TŌTA-SAMA! ARE YOU AWAKE YET, MY DEAR?
NII-SAMA!
HM?
OH?
TŌTA-SAMA!
SHINO-BU!
MIZORE!
ISANA AND HONOKA!
NII-SAMA!
SERIOUSLY? DID YOU HAVE TO BRING THE WHOLE GANG?
KARIN-CHAN...? DON'T TELL ME...
GULP
DON'T TELL ME YOU WERE ALL IN THE NEXT ROOM SPYING ON US LAST NIGHT?
HEH HEH HEH. DON'T BE SILLY, I WOULD NEVER DO SOMETHING SO CHILDISH.
WE BOOKED A BIG ROOM IN THE CHEAP INN ACROSS THE WAY.
IT WAS FUN. LIKE A CLASS TRIP.
OF COURSE, EVENTUALLY A BIG BATTLE BROKE OUT BETWEEN THE "WE SHOULD STOP LOOKING" FACTION, THE "WE MUST SEE IT THROUGH TO THE END" FACTION, AND THE "WE SHOULD BREAK THIS UP" FACTION, SO THE SPYING KINDA FIZZLED OUT AT THE END.
WAAH
WAAH
YOU GUYS...

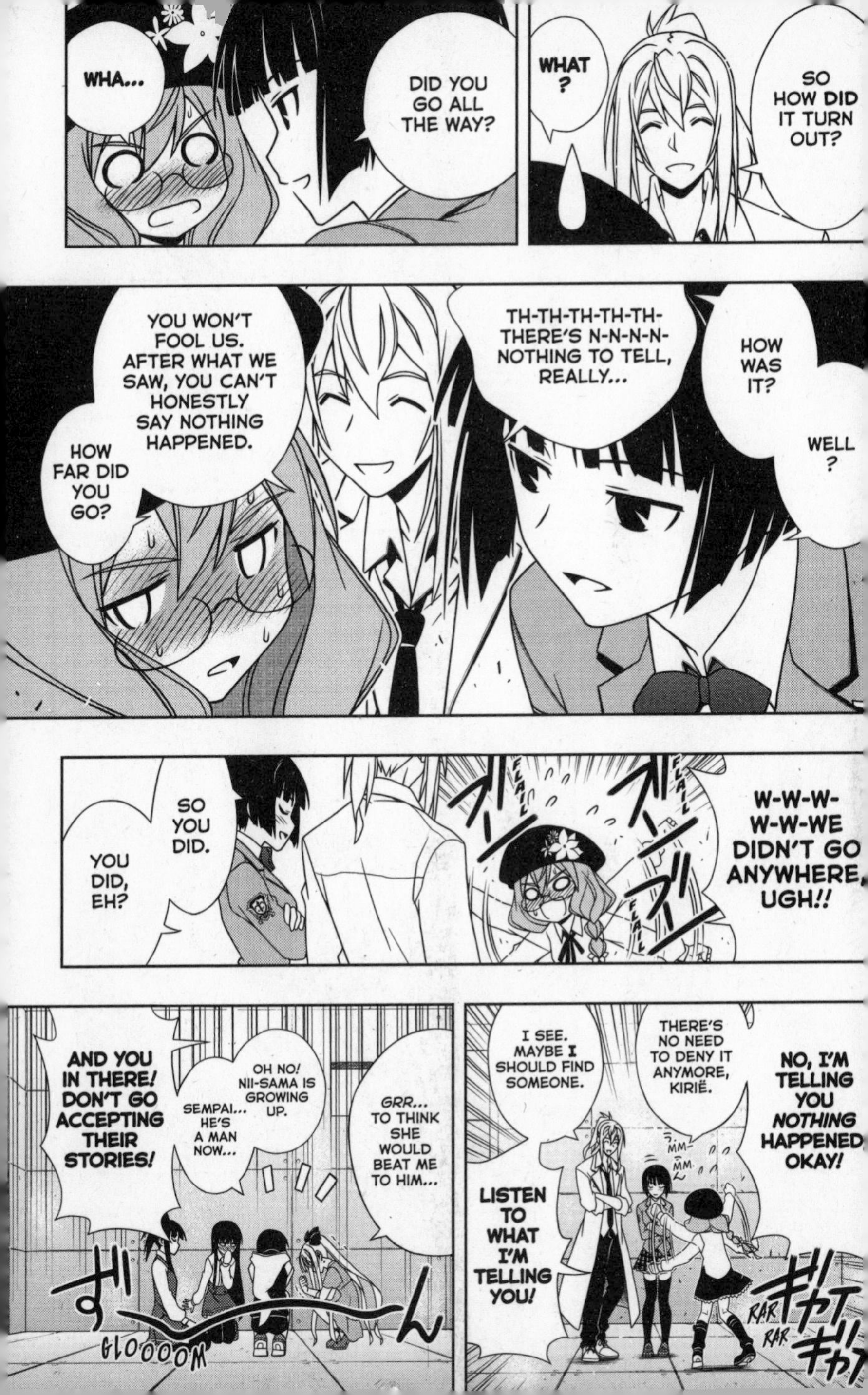

SO HOW DID IT TURN OUT?
WHAT?
DID YOU GO ALL THE WAY?
WHA...
HOW WAS IT?
WELL?
TH-TH-TH-TH-TH-THERE'S N-N-N-N-NOTHING TO TELL, REALLY...
YOU WON'T FOOL US. AFTER WHAT WE SAW, YOU CAN'T HONESTLY SAY NOTHING HAPPENED.
HOW FAR DID YOU GO?
W-W-W-W-W-WE DIDN'T GO ANYWHERE, UGH!!
FLAIL
FLAIL
FLAIL
SO YOU DID.
YOU DID, EH?
NO, I'M TELLING YOU *NOTHING* HAPPENED OKAY!
THERE'S NO NEED TO DENY IT ANYMORE, KIRIË.
I SEE. MAYBE I SHOULD FIND SOMEONE.
MM-MM.
LISTEN TO WHAT I'M TELLING YOU!
RAR RAR
GRR... TO THINK SHE WOULD BEAT ME TO HIM...
OH NO! NII-SAMA IS GROWING UP.
SEMPAI... HE'S A MAN NOW...
AND YOU IN THERE! DON'T GO ACCEPTING THEIR STORIES!
GLOOOOM

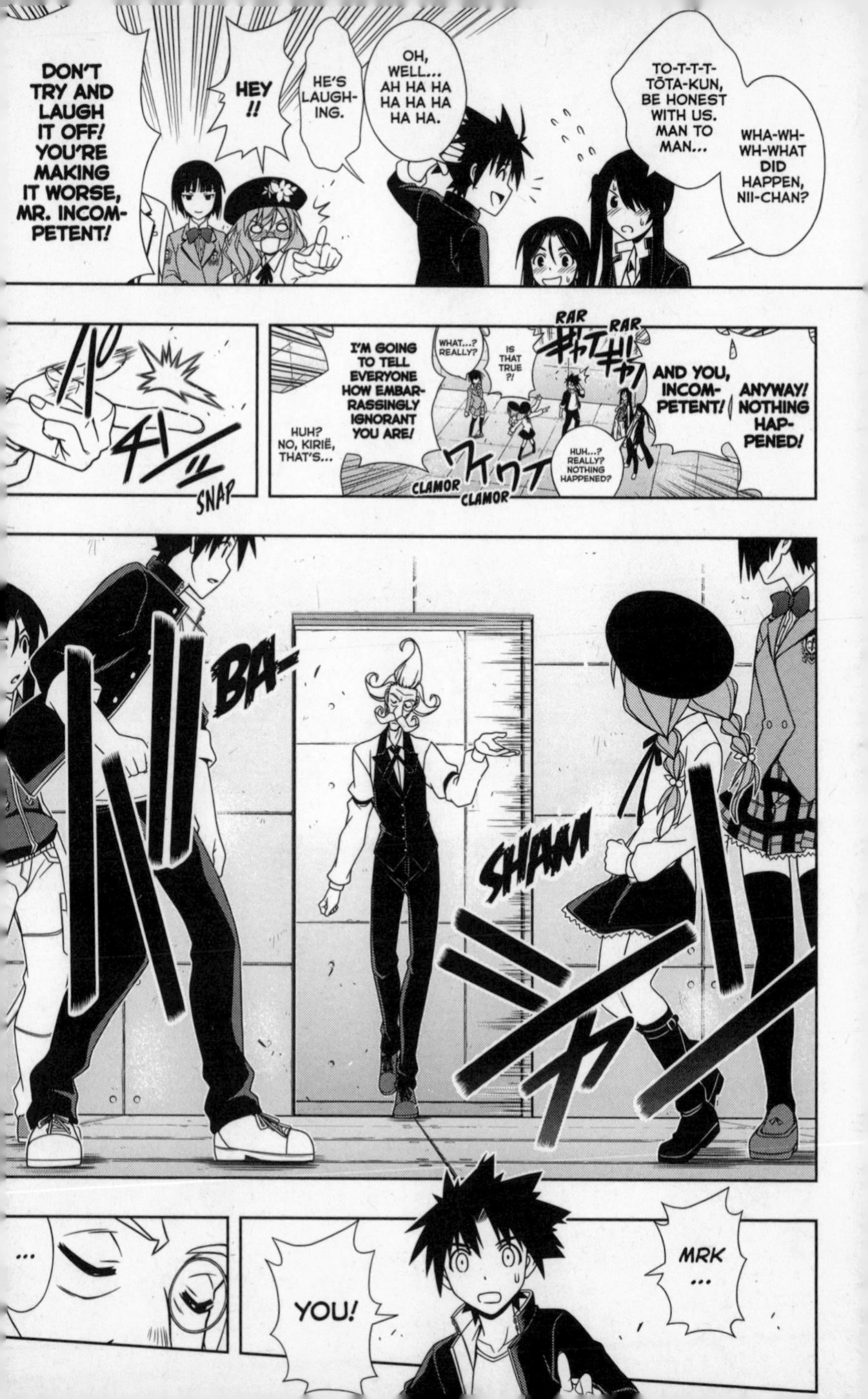
TO-T-T-T- TŌTA-KUN, BE HONEST WITH US. MAN TO MAN...
WHA-WH-WH-WHAT DID HAPPEN, NII-CHAN?
OH, WELL... AH HA HA HA HA HA HA HA.
HE'S LAUGH-ING.
HEY!!
DON'T TRY AND LAUGH IT OFF! YOU'RE MAKING IT WORSE, MR. INCOM-PETENT!
ANYWAY! NOTHING HAP-PENED!
AND YOU, INCOM-PETENT!
RAR
RAR
IS THAT TRUE?!
WHAT...? REALLY?
I'M GOING TO TELL EVERYONE HOW EMBAR-RASSINGLY IGNORANT YOU ARE!
HUH...? REALLY? NOTHING HAPPENED?
HUH? NO, KIRIË, THAT'S...
CLAMOR
CLAMOR
SNAP
SHAM
BA-
MRK ...
YOU!
...

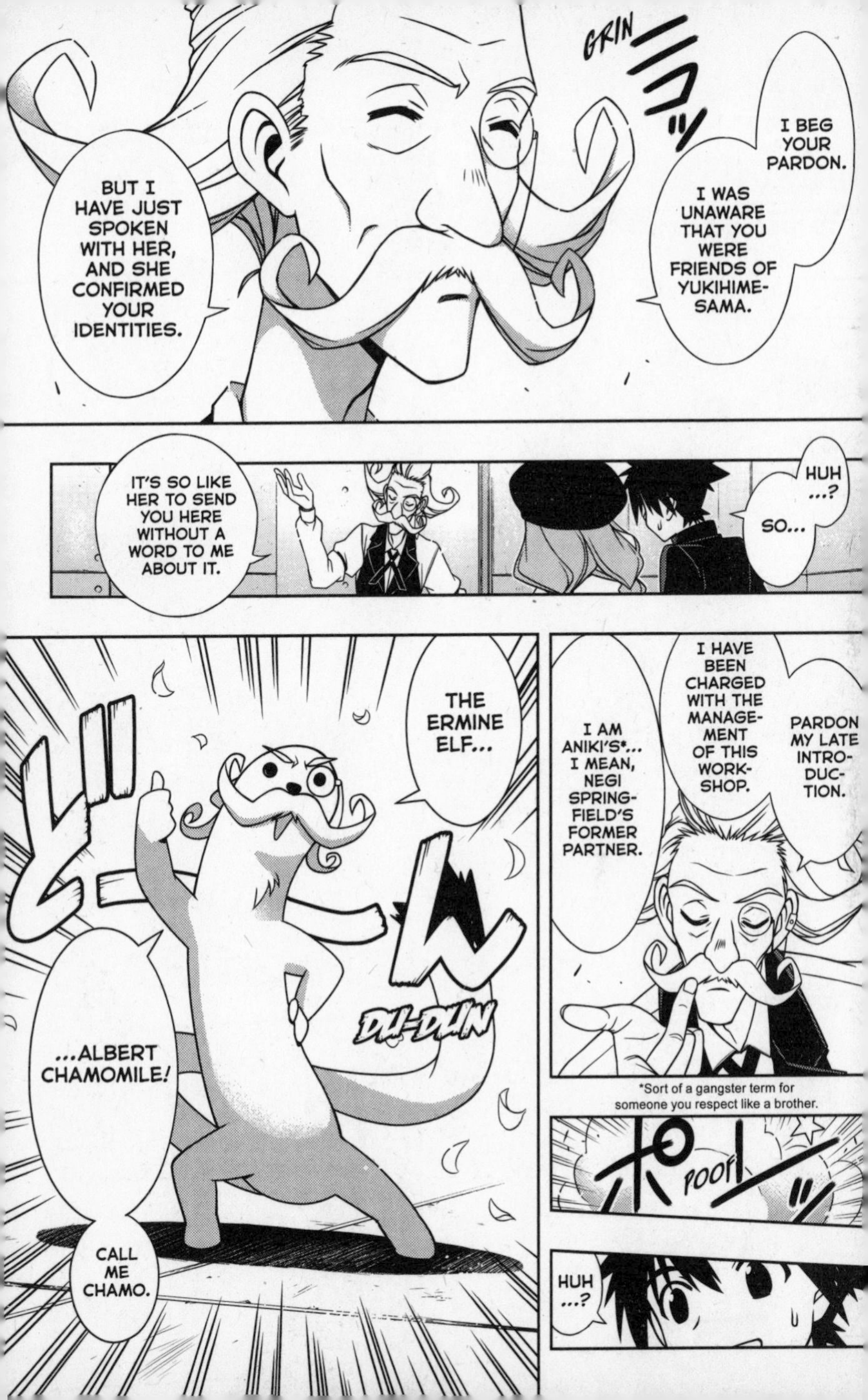
GRIN
I BEG YOUR PARDON.
I WAS UNAWARE THAT YOU WERE FRIENDS OF YUKIHIME-SAMA.
BUT I HAVE JUST SPOKEN WITH HER, AND SHE CONFIRMED YOUR IDENTITIES.
HUH ...?
SO...
IT'S SO LIKE HER TO SEND YOU HERE WITHOUT A WORD TO ME ABOUT IT.
PARDON MY LATE INTRODUCTION.
I HAVE BEEN CHARGED WITH THE MANAGEMENT OF THIS WORKSHOP.
I AM ANIKI'S*... I MEAN, NEGI SPRINGFIELD'S FORMER PARTNER.
*Sort of a gangster term for someone you respect like a brother.
POOF
HUH ...?
THE ERMINE ELF...
...ALBERT CHAMOMILE!
DU-DUN
CALL ME CHAMO.

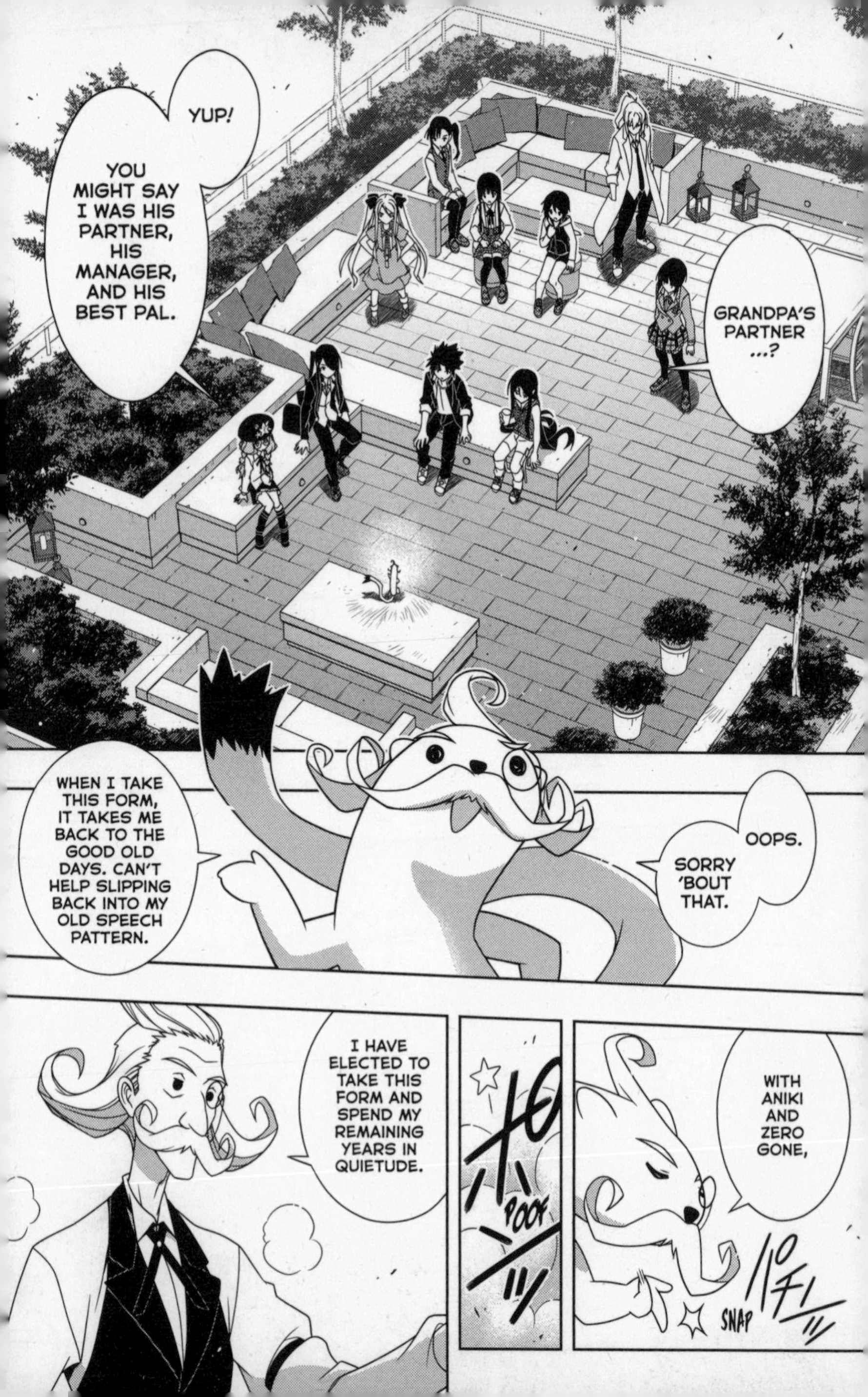
GRANDPA'S PARTNER ...?
YUP!
YOU MIGHT SAY I WAS HIS PARTNER, HIS MANAGER, AND HIS BEST PAL.
OOPS.
SORRY 'BOUT THAT.
WHEN I TAKE THIS FORM, IT TAKES ME BACK TO THE GOOD OLD DAYS. CAN'T HELP SLIPPING BACK INTO MY OLD SPEECH PATTERN.
WITH ANIKI AND ZERO GONE,
SNAP
POOF
I HAVE ELECTED TO TAKE THIS FORM AND SPEND MY REMAINING YEARS IN QUIETUDE.

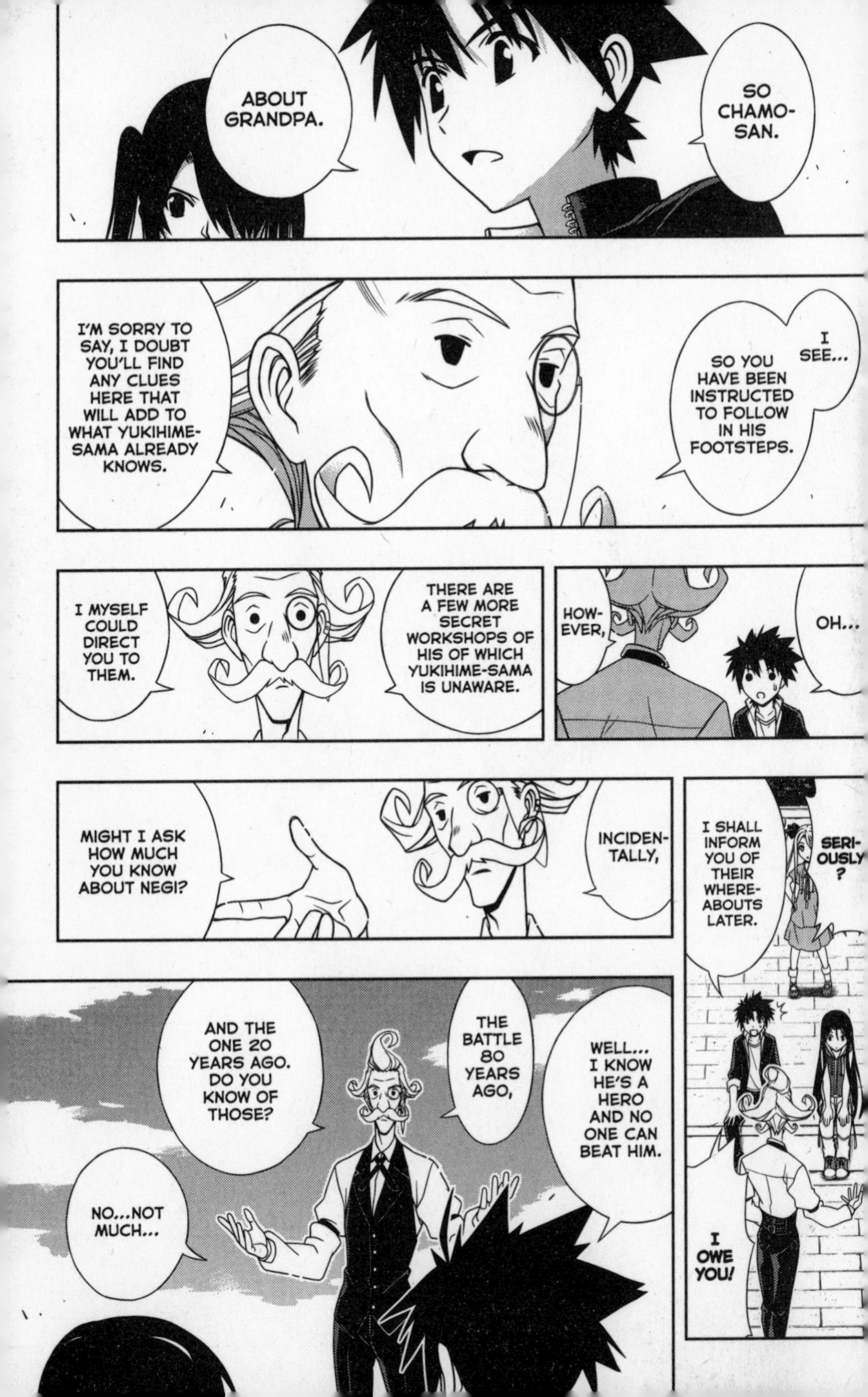
SO CHAMO-SAN.
ABOUT GRANDPA.
I SEE...
SO YOU HAVE BEEN INSTRUCTED TO FOLLOW IN HIS FOOTSTEPS.
I'M SORRY TO SAY, I DOUBT YOU'LL FIND ANY CLUES HERE THAT WILL ADD TO WHAT YUKIHIME-SAMA ALREADY KNOWS.
OH...
HOW-EVER,
THERE ARE A FEW MORE SECRET WORKSHOPS OF HIS OF WHICH YUKIHIME-SAMA IS UNAWARE.
I MYSELF COULD DIRECT YOU TO THEM.
SERI-OUSLY?
I SHALL INFORM YOU OF THEIR WHERE-ABOUTS LATER.
I OWE YOU!
INCIDEN-TALLY,
MIGHT I ASK HOW MUCH YOU KNOW ABOUT NEGI?
WELL... I KNOW HE'S A HERO AND NO ONE CAN BEAT HIM.
THE BATTLE 80 YEARS AGO,
AND THE ONE 20 YEARS AGO. DO YOU KNOW OF THOSE?
NO...NOT MUCH...

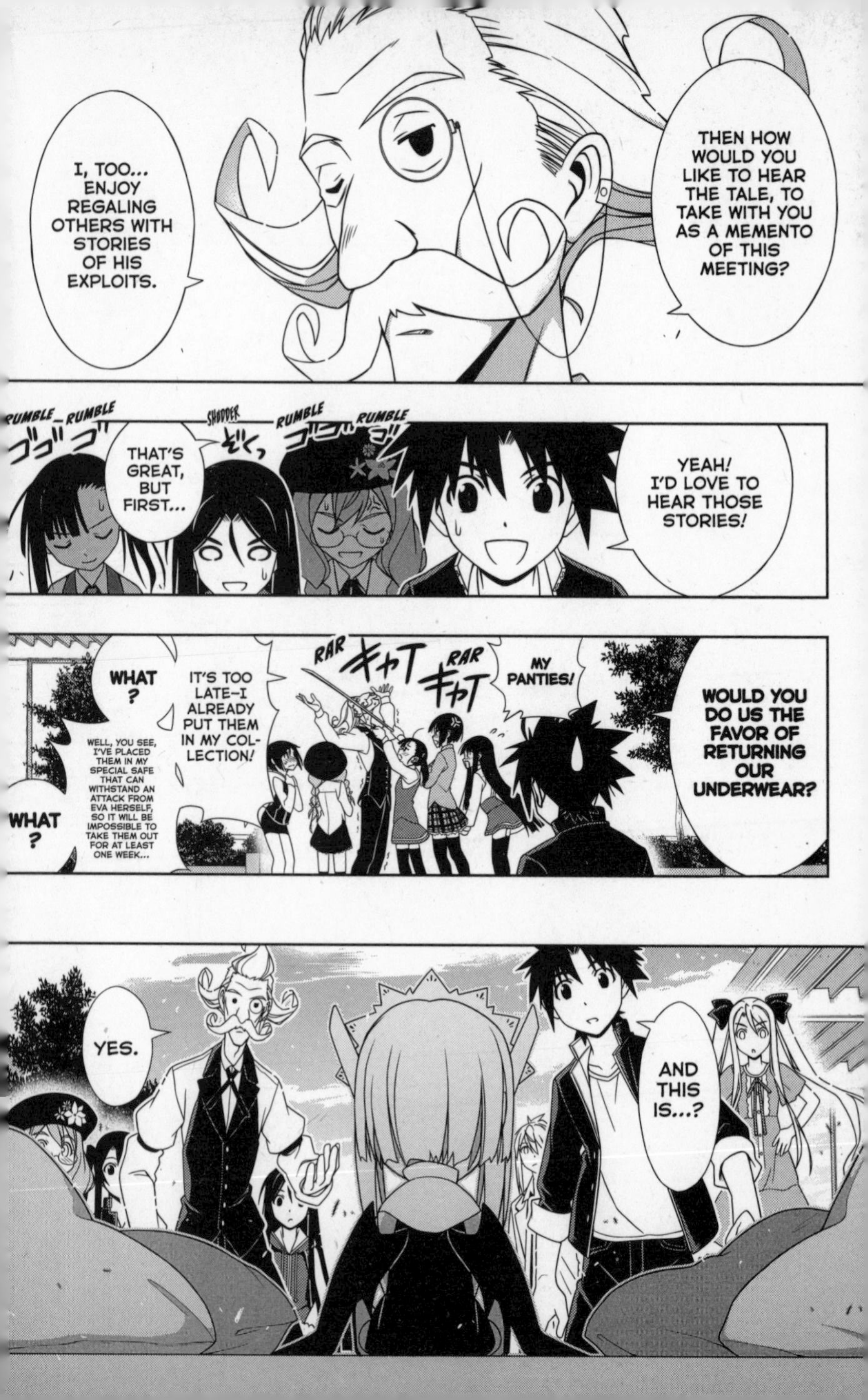
THEN HOW WOULD YOU LIKE TO HEAR THE TALE, TO TAKE WITH YOU AS A MEMENTO OF THIS MEETING?
I, TOO... ENJOY REGALING OTHERS WITH STORIES OF HIS EXPLOITS.
YEAH! I'D LOVE TO HEAR THOSE STORIES!
RUMBLE
RUMBLE
SHUDDER
THAT'S GREAT, BUT FIRST...
RUMBLE
RUMBLE
WOULD YOU DO US THE FAVOR OF RETURNING OUR UNDERWEAR?
MY PANTIES!
RAR
RAR
IT'S TOO LATE—I ALREADY PUT THEM IN MY COLLECTION!
WHAT?
WELL, YOU SEE, I'VE PLACED THEM IN MY SPECIAL SAFE THAT CAN WITHSTAND AN ATTACK FROM EVA HERSELF, SO IT WILL BE IMPOSSIBLE TO TAKE THEM OUT FOR AT LEAST ONE WEEK...
WHAT?
AND THIS IS...?
YES.

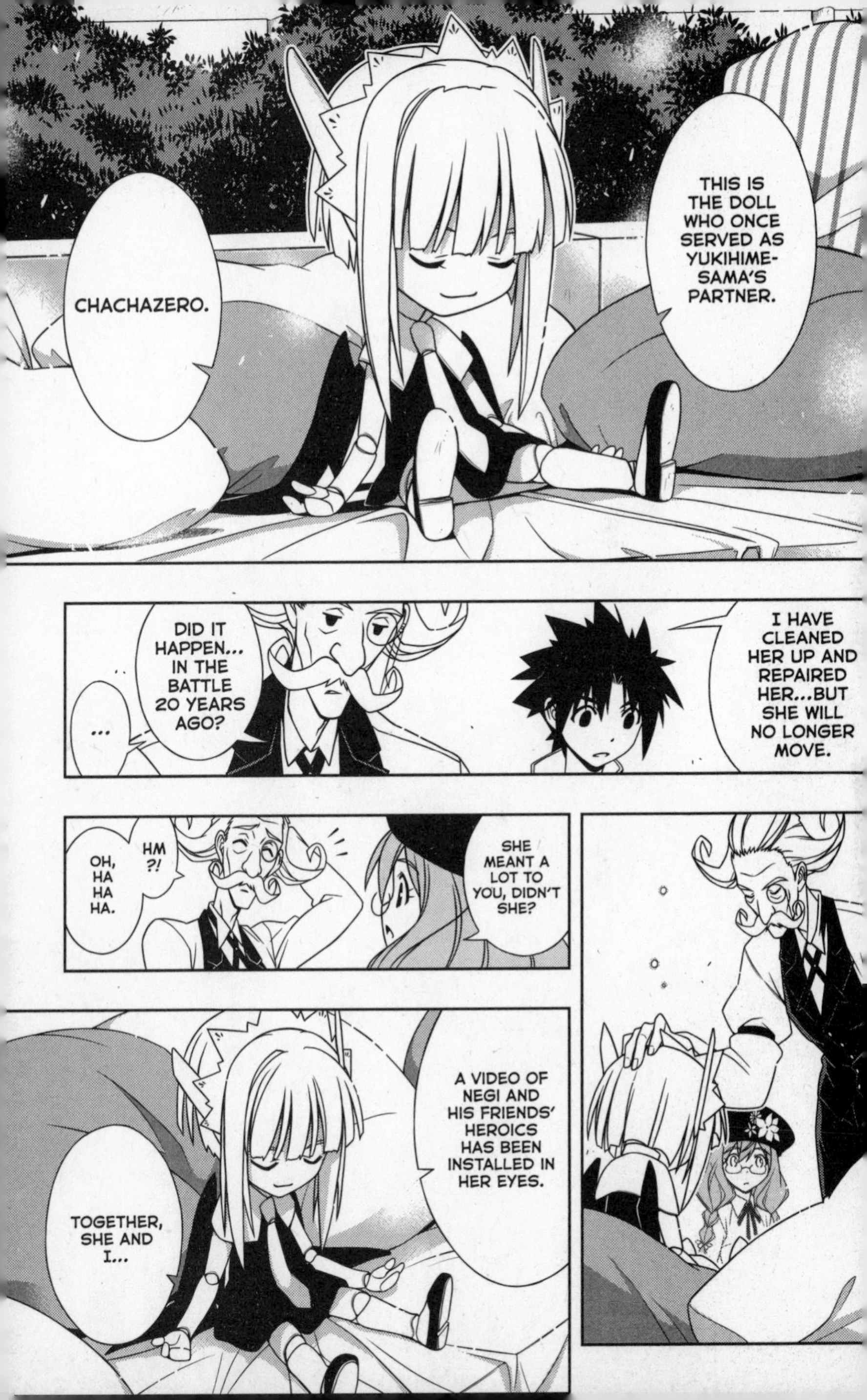
THIS IS THE DOLL WHO ONCE SERVED AS YUKIHIME-SAMA'S PARTNER.
CHACHAZERO.
I HAVE CLEANED HER UP AND REPAIRED HER...BUT SHE WILL NO LONGER MOVE.
DID IT HAPPEN... IN THE BATTLE 20 YEARS AGO?
...
SHE MEANT A LOT TO YOU, DIDN'T SHE?
HM ?!
OH, HA HA HA.
A VIDEO OF NEGI AND HIS FRIENDS' HEROICS HAS BEEN INSTALLED IN HER EYES.
TOGETHER, SHE AND I...

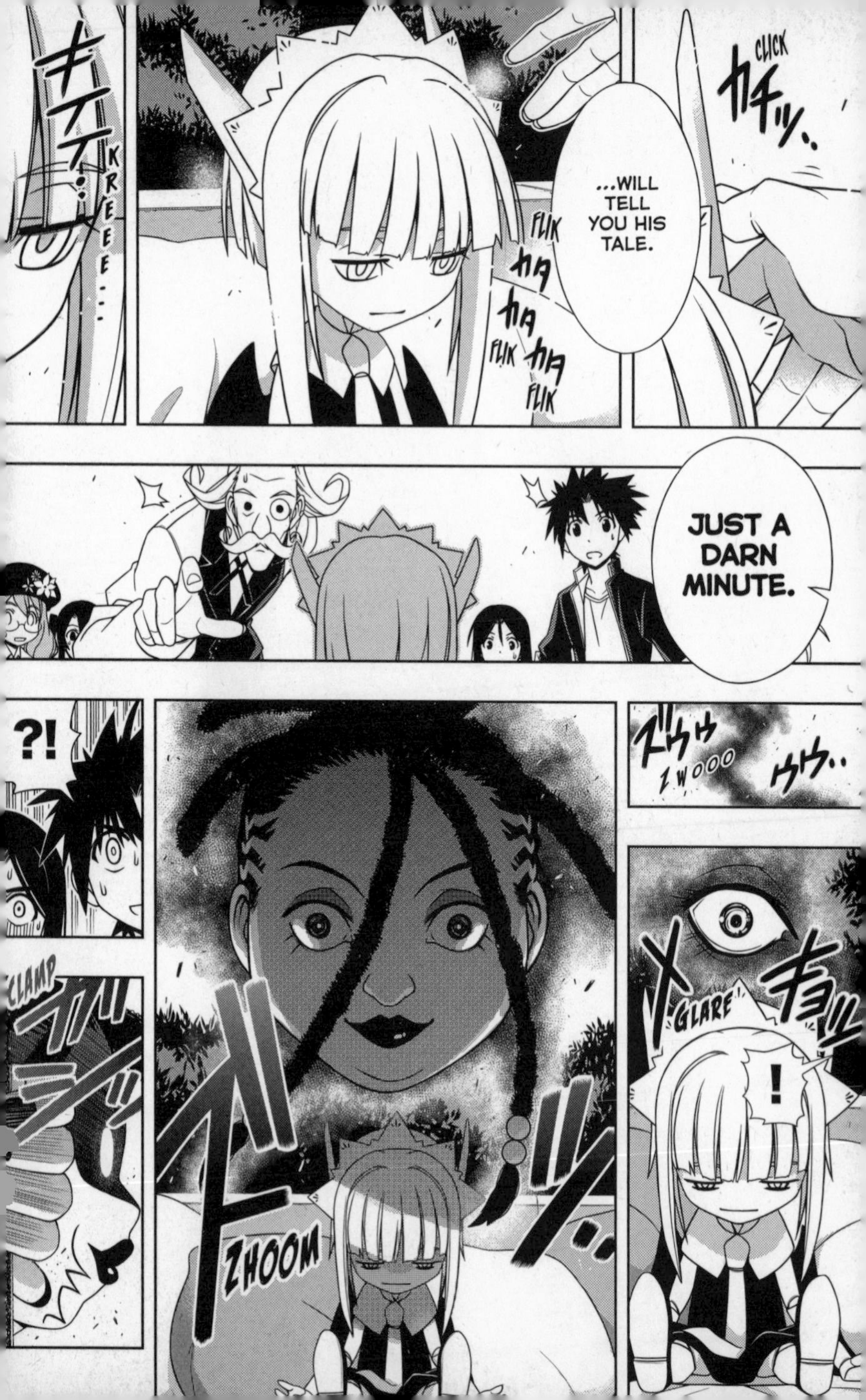
CLICK
カチッ..
...WILL TELL YOU HIS TALE.
FLIK カタ カタ FLIK カタ FLIK
キィィ...
KREEEE...
JUST A DARN MINUTE.
ズウゥ ウウ..
ZWOOO
?!
メキョッ
GLARE
!
ズドッ
ZHOOM
CLAMP

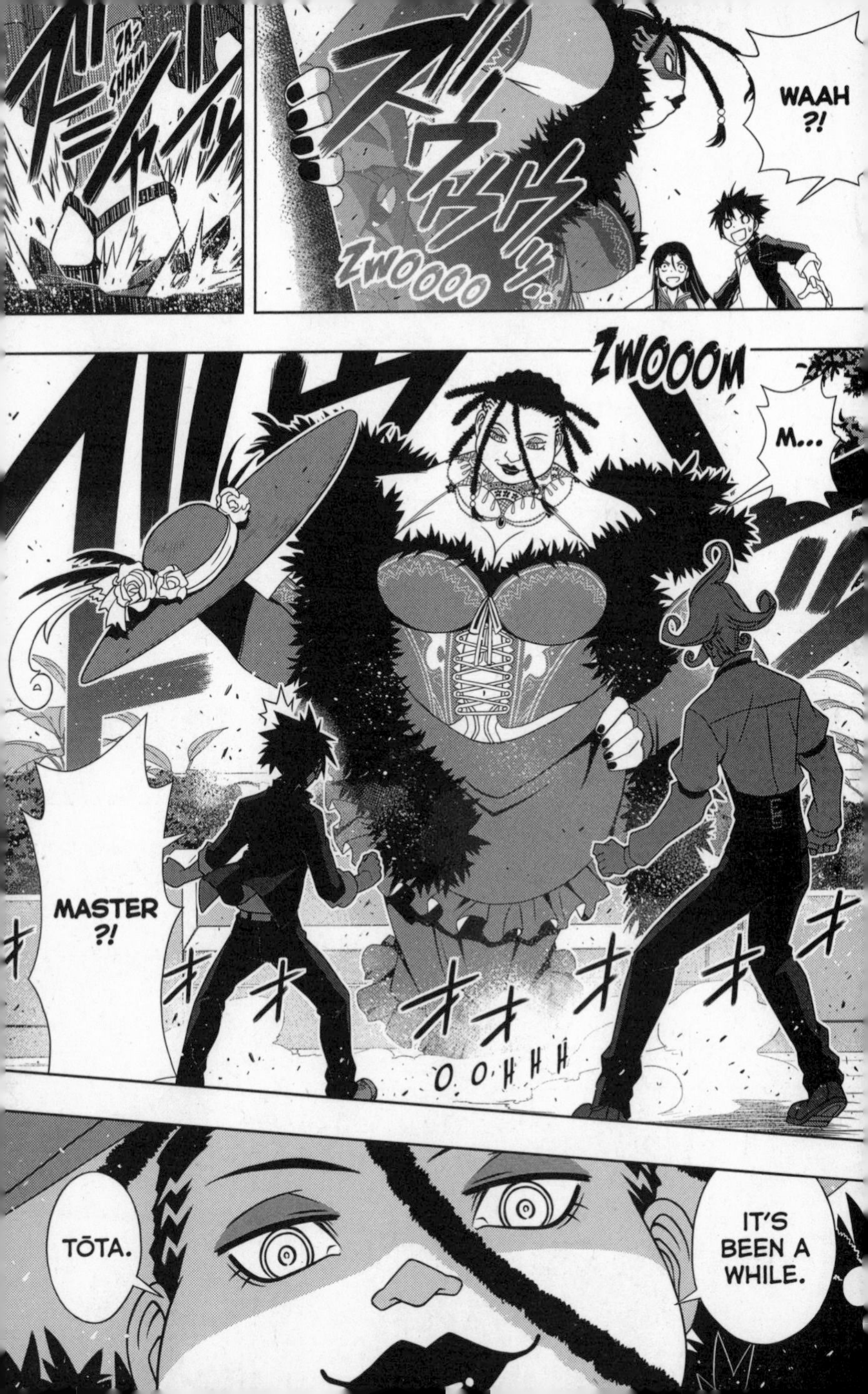
WAAH ?!
ZWOOOO
ZA-SHAM
ZWOOOM
M...
MASTER ?!
OOHHH
IT'S BEEN A WHILE.
TŌTA.

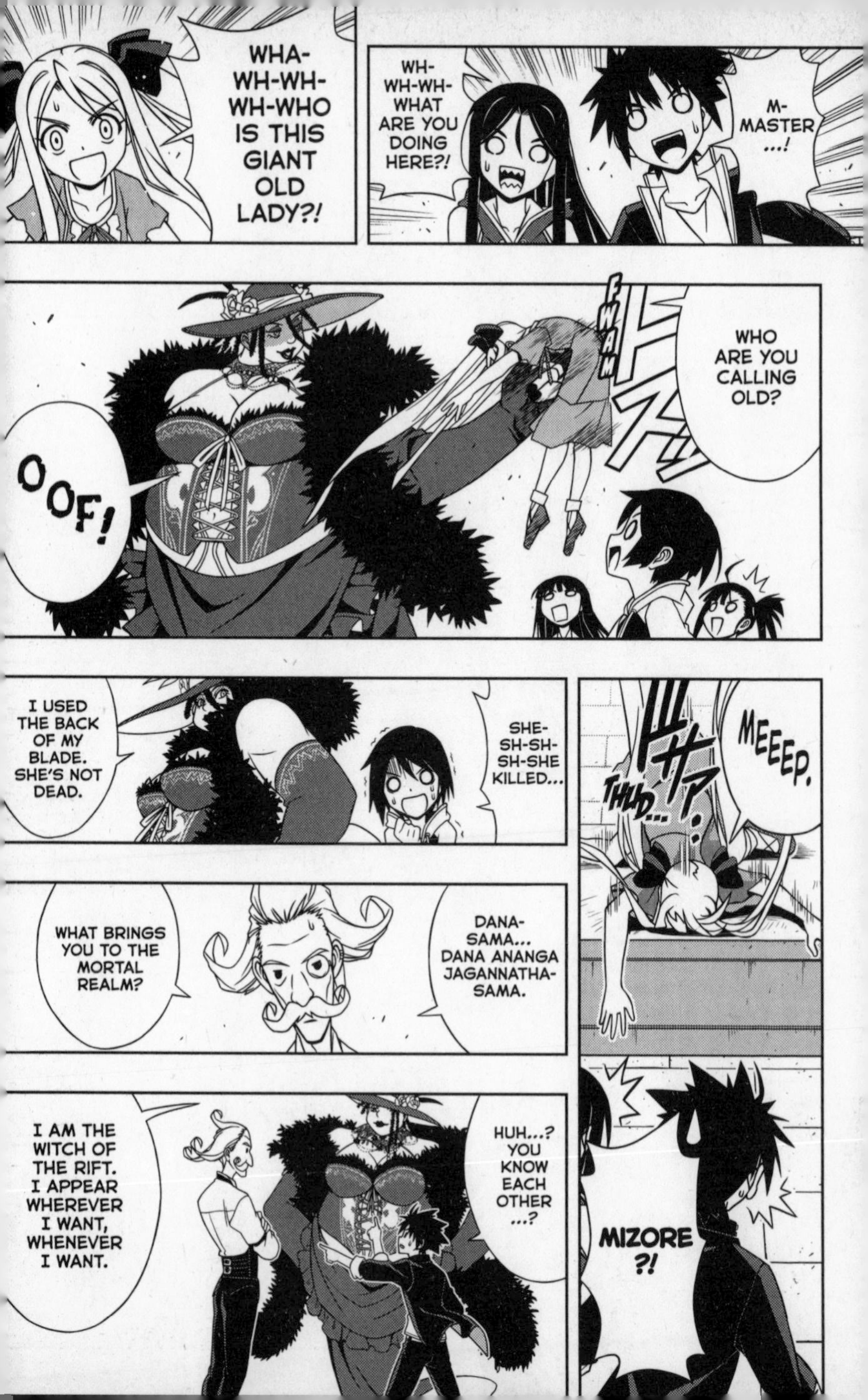
M-MASTER...!
WH-WH-WH-WHAT ARE YOU DOING HERE?!
WHA-WH-WH-WH-WHO IS THIS GIANT OLD LADY?!
WHO ARE YOU CALLING OLD?
FWAM
OOF!
MEEEP.
THUD...
SHE-SH-SH-SH-SHE KILLED...
I USED THE BACK OF MY BLADE. SHE'S NOT DEAD.
DANA-SAMA... DANA ANANGA JAGANNATHA-SAMA.
WHAT BRINGS YOU TO THE MORTAL REALM?
MIZORE?!
HUH...? YOU KNOW EACH OTHER...?
I AM THE WITCH OF THE RIFT. I APPEAR WHEREVER I WANT, WHENEVER I WANT.

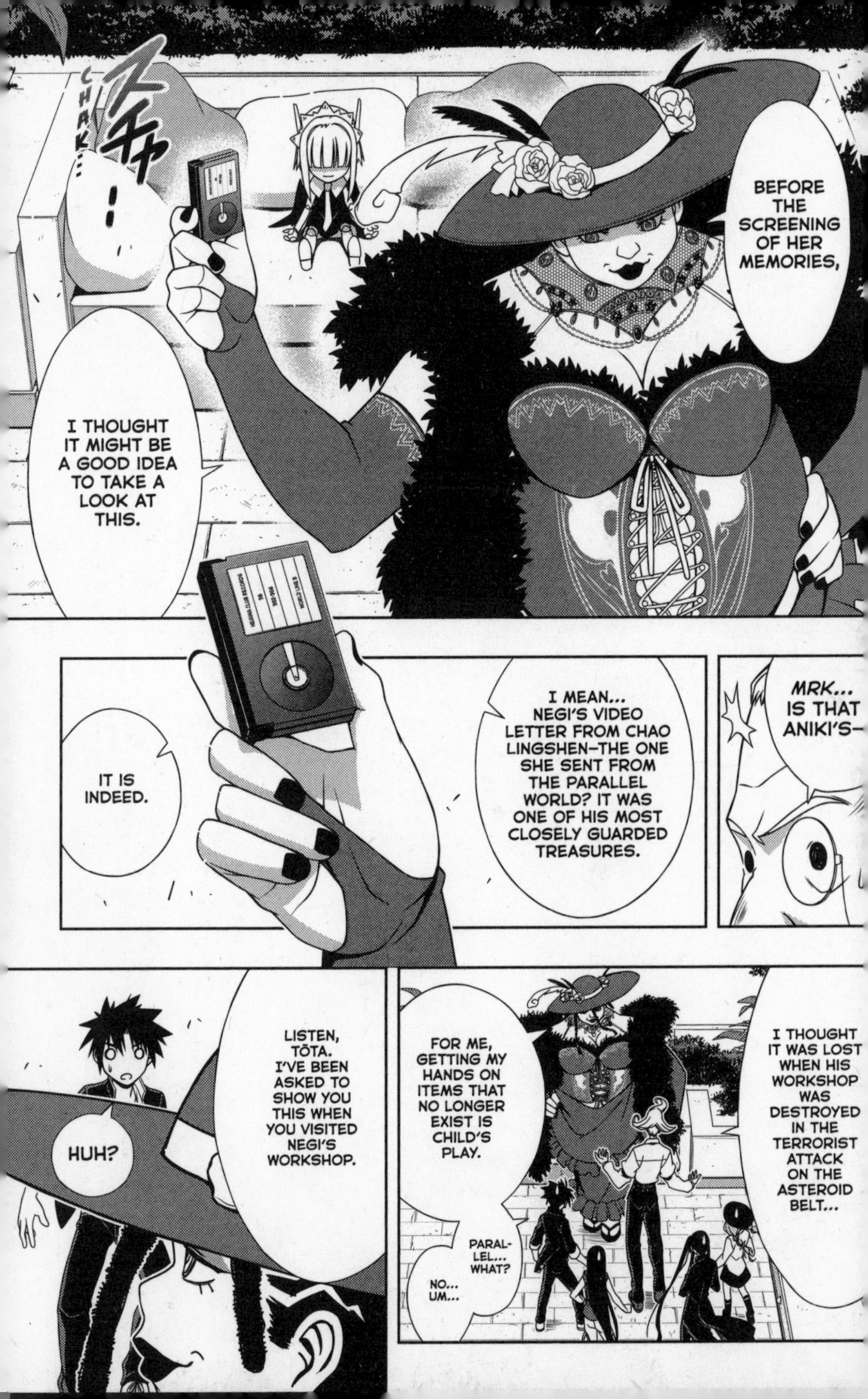
スチャ
CHAK...
!
BEFORE THE SCREENING OF HER MEMORIES,
I THOUGHT IT MIGHT BE A GOOD IDEA TO TAKE A LOOK AT THIS.
MRK... IS THAT ANIKI'S—
I MEAN... NEGI'S VIDEO LETTER FROM CHAO LINGSHEN—THE ONE SHE SENT FROM THE PARALLEL WORLD? IT WAS ONE OF HIS MOST CLOSELY GUARDED TREASURES.
IT IS INDEED.
I THOUGHT IT WAS LOST WHEN HIS WORKSHOP WAS DESTROYED IN THE TERRORIST ATTACK ON THE ASTEROID BELT...
FOR ME, GETTING MY HANDS ON ITEMS THAT NO LONGER EXIST IS CHILD'S PLAY.
PARAL-LEL... WHAT?
NO... UM...
LISTEN, TŌTA. I'VE BEEN ASKED TO SHOW YOU THIS WHEN YOU VISITED NEGI'S WORKSHOP.
HUH?

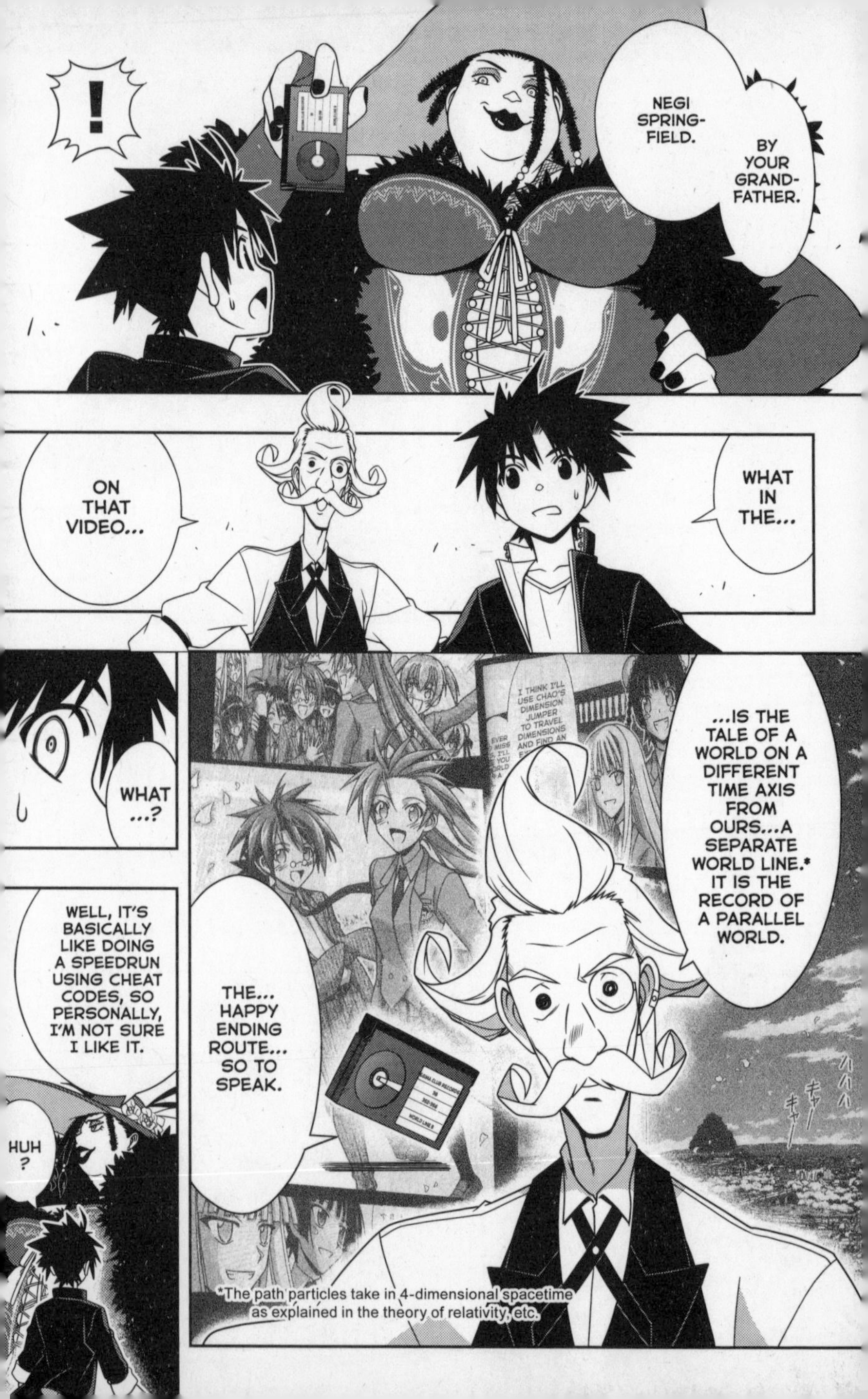

NEGI SPRING-FIELD.
BY YOUR GRAND-FATHER.
!
WHAT IN THE...
ON THAT VIDEO...
...IS THE TALE OF A WORLD ON A DIFFERENT TIME AXIS FROM OURS...A SEPARATE WORLD LINE.* IT IS THE RECORD OF A PARALLEL WORLD.
THE... HAPPY ENDING ROUTE... SO TO SPEAK.
WHAT ...?
WELL, IT'S BASICALLY LIKE DOING A SPEEDRUN USING CHEAT CODES, SO PERSONALLY, I'M NOT SURE I LIKE IT.
HUH ?

*The path particles take in 4-dimensional spacetime as explained in the theory of relativity, etc.

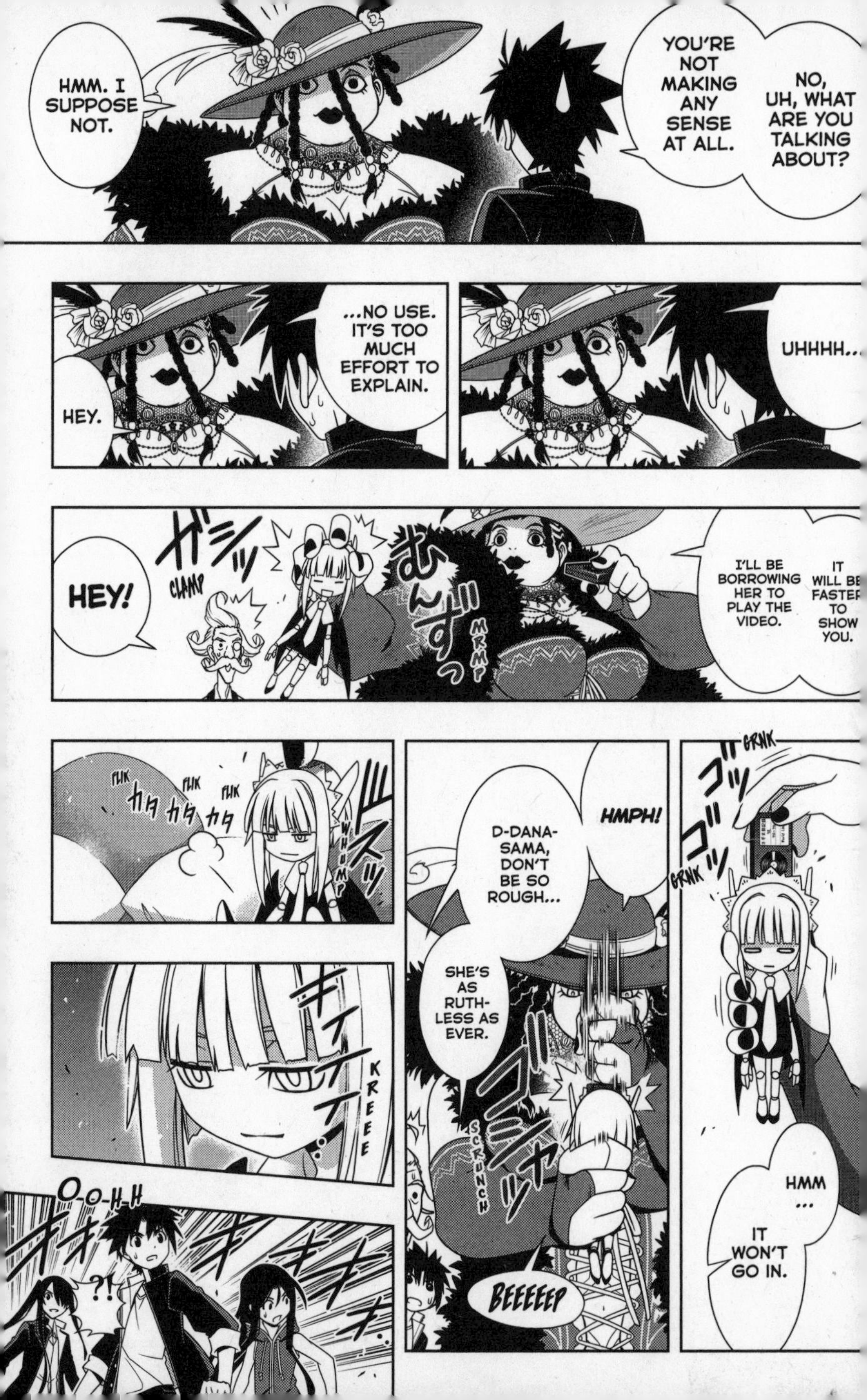
NO, UH, WHAT ARE YOU TALKING ABOUT?
YOU'RE NOT MAKING ANY SENSE AT ALL.
HMM. I SUPPOSE NOT.
UHHHH...
...NO USE. IT'S TOO MUCH EFFORT TO EXPLAIN.
HEY.
IT WILL BE FASTER TO SHOW YOU.
I'LL BE BORROWING HER TO PLAY THE VIDEO.
むんずっ
MRMP
ガシッ
CLAMP
HEY!
ゴッ
GRNK
ゴッ
GRNK
HMM... IT WON'T GO IN.
HMPH!
D-DANA-SAMA, DON'T BE SO ROUGH...
SHE'S AS RUTHLESS AS EVER.
ゴシャッ
SCRUNCH
BEEEEEP
ドスッ
WHUMP
カタ
FLIK
カタ
FLIK
カタ
FLIK
キイイイ
KREEE
オオオオ
O-O-H-H
?!

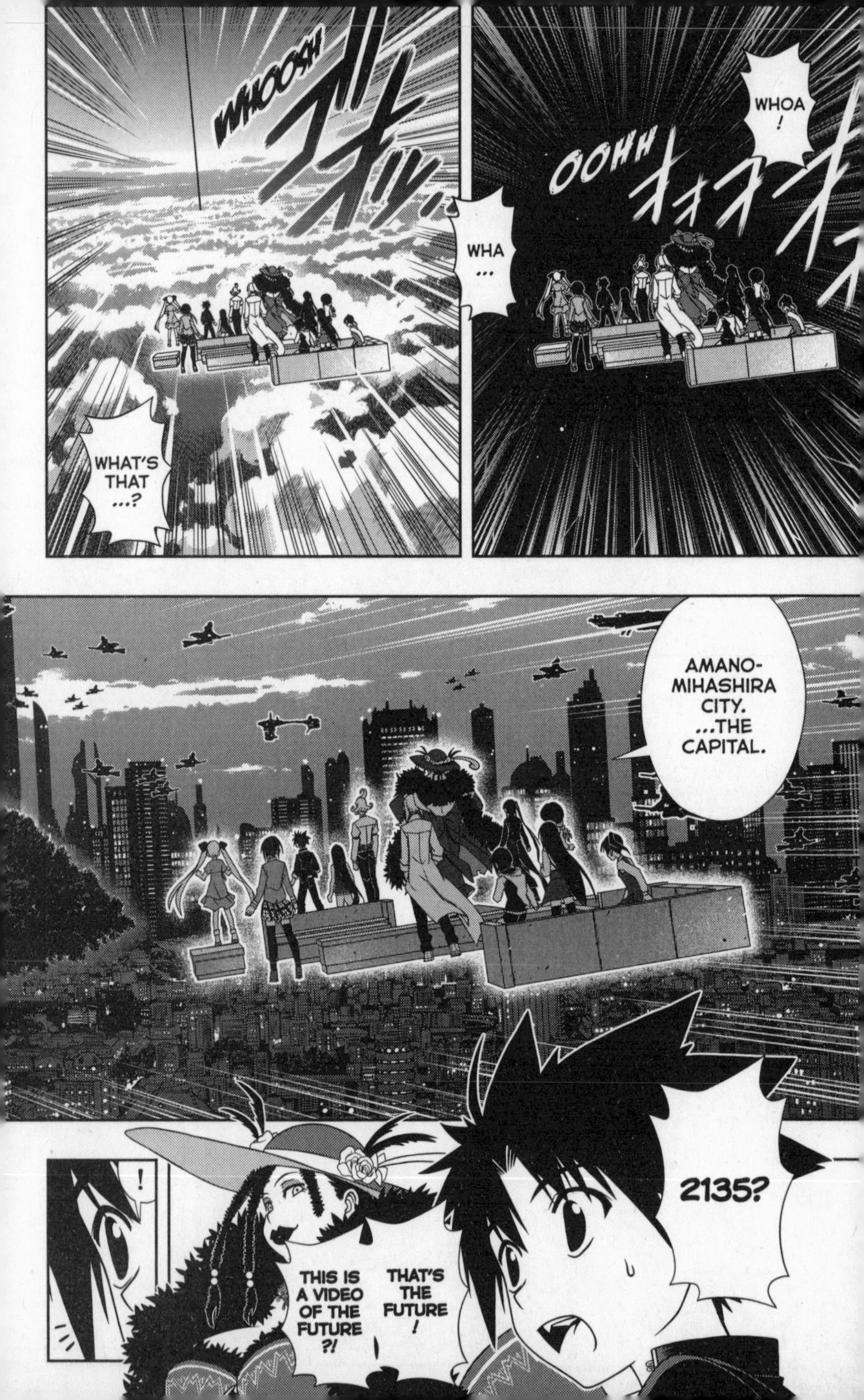
WHOA!
OOHH
WHA...
WHOOSH
WHAT'S THAT...?
AMANO-MIHASHIRA CITY. ...THE CAPITAL.
2135?
THAT'S THE FUTURE!
THIS IS A VIDEO OF THE FUTURE?!
!

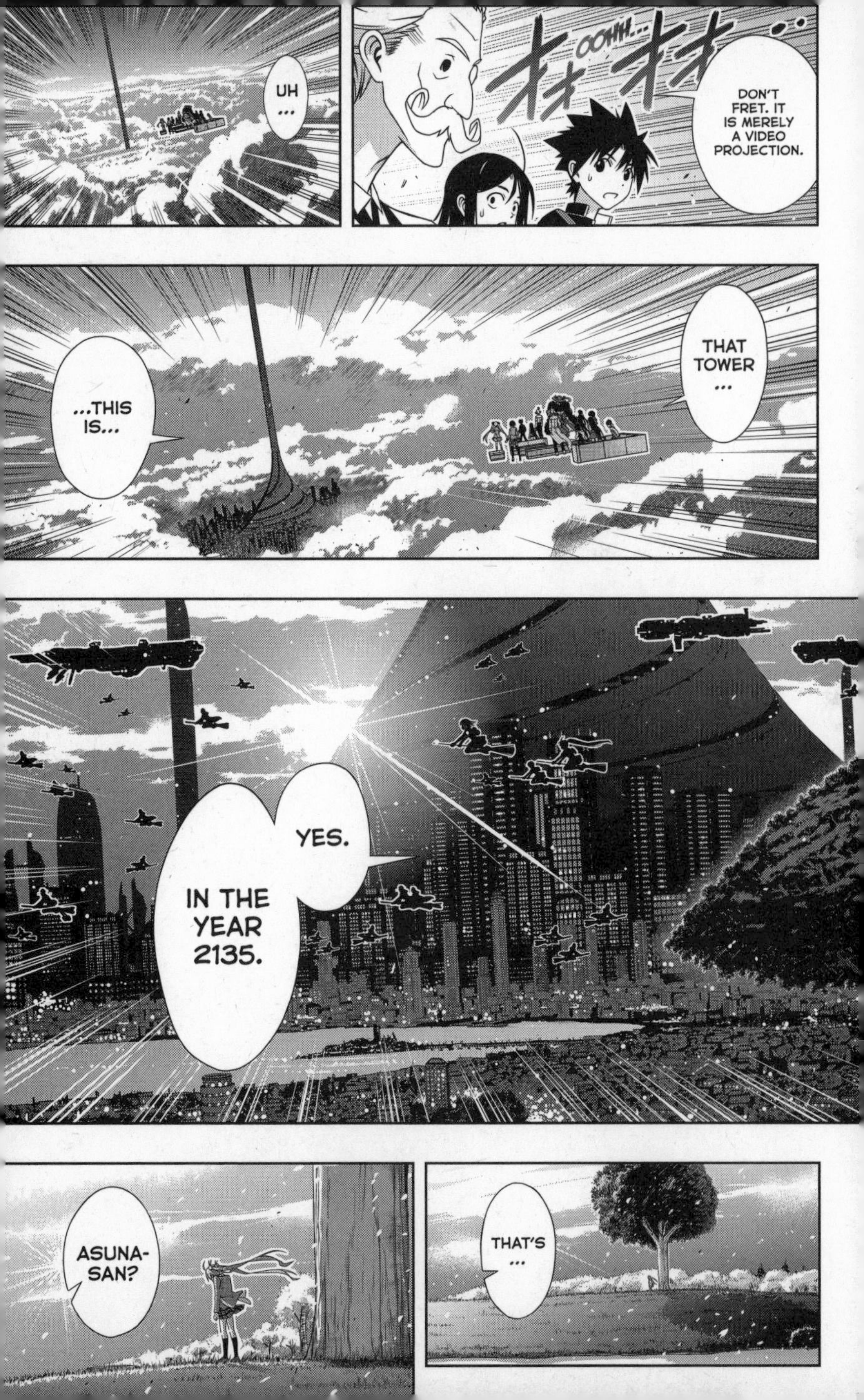
OOHH...
DON'T FRET. IT IS MERELY A VIDEO PROJECTION.
UH ...
THAT TOWER ...
...THIS IS...
YES.
IN THE YEAR 2135.
THAT'S ...
ASUNA-SAN?

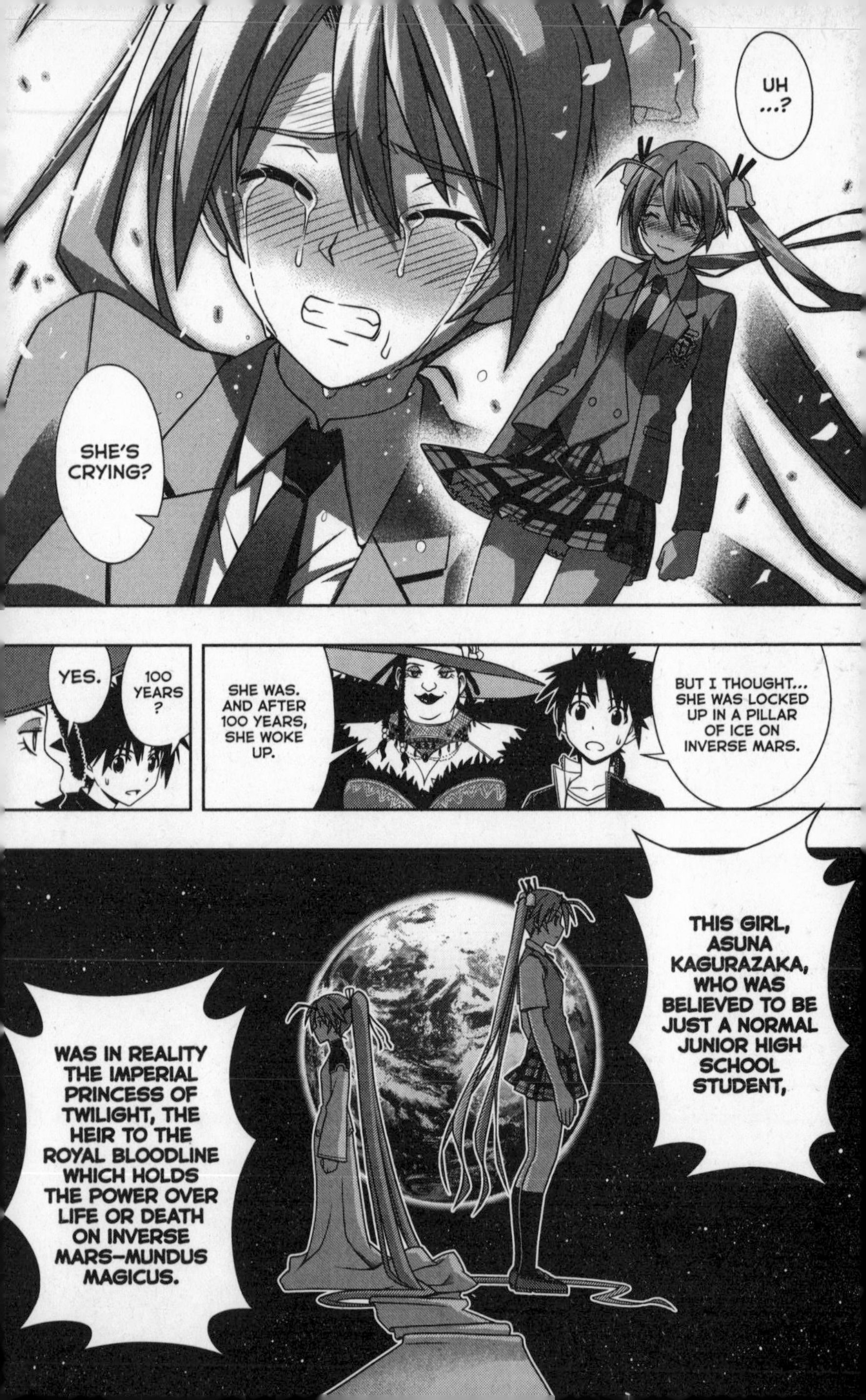
UH ...?
SHE'S CRYING?
BUT I THOUGHT... SHE WAS LOCKED UP IN A PILLAR OF ICE ON INVERSE MARS.
SHE WAS. AND AFTER 100 YEARS, SHE WOKE UP.
100 YEARS ?
YES.
THIS GIRL, ASUNA KAGURAZAKA, WHO WAS BELIEVED TO BE JUST A NORMAL JUNIOR HIGH SCHOOL STUDENT,
WAS IN REALITY THE IMPERIAL PRINCESS OF TWILIGHT, THE HEIR TO THE ROYAL BLOODLINE WHICH HOLDS THE POWER OVER LIFE OR DEATH ON INVERSE MARS—MUNDUS MAGICUS.

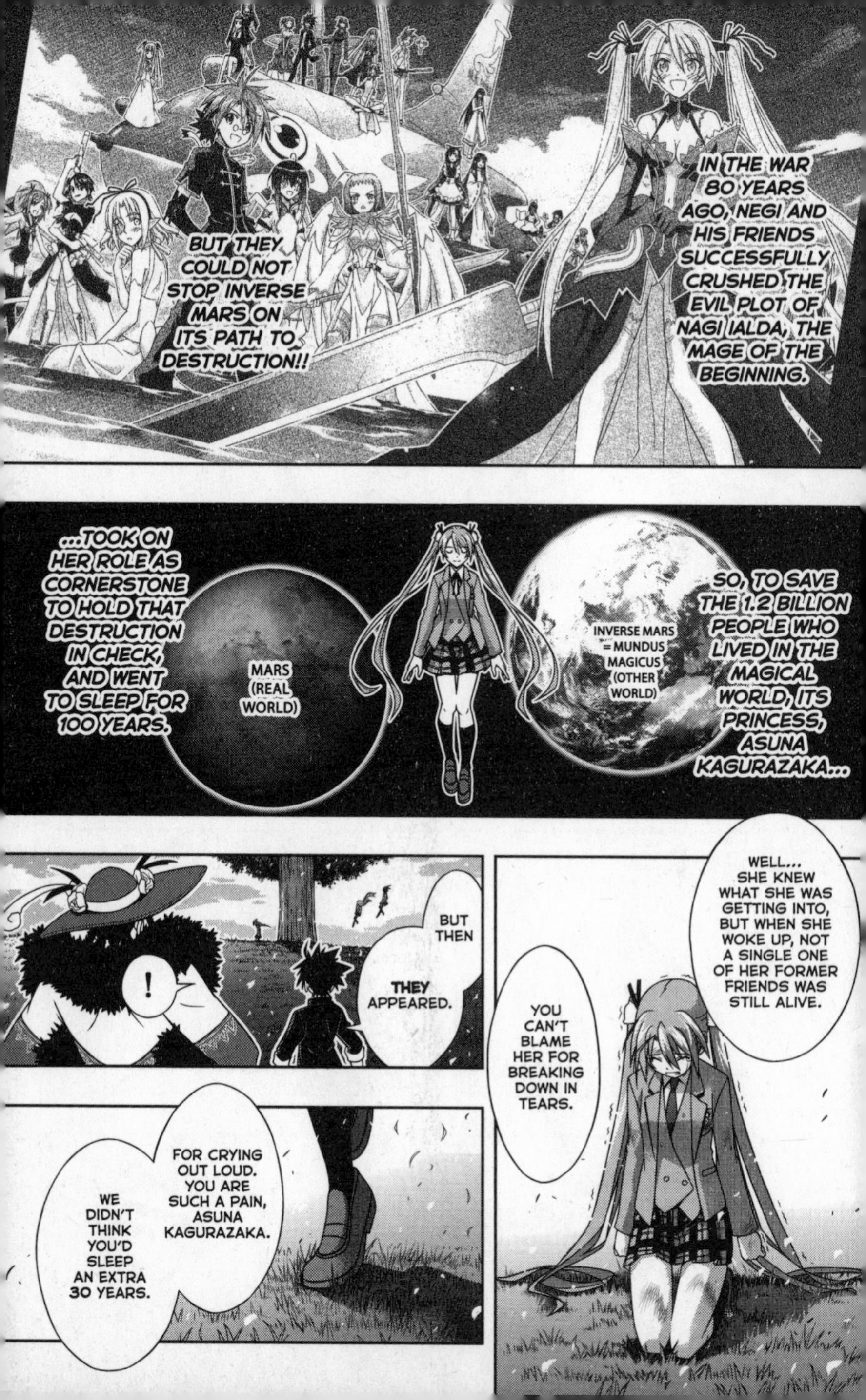
IN THE WAR 80 YEARS AGO, NEGI AND HIS FRIENDS SUCCESSFULLY CRUSHED THE EVIL PLOT OF NAGI IALDA, THE MAGE OF THE BEGINNING.
BUT THEY COULD NOT STOP INVERSE MARS ON ITS PATH TO DESTRUCTION!!
SO, TO SAVE THE 1.2 BILLION PEOPLE WHO LIVED IN THE MAGICAL WORLD, ITS PRINCESS, ASUNA KAGURAZAKA...
INVERSE MARS = MUNDUS MAGICUS (OTHER WORLD)
MARS (REAL WORLD)
...TOOK ON HER ROLE AS CORNERSTONE TO HOLD THAT DESTRUCTION IN CHECK, AND WENT TO SLEEP FOR 100 YEARS.
WELL... SHE KNEW WHAT SHE WAS GETTING INTO, BUT WHEN SHE WOKE UP, NOT A SINGLE ONE OF HER FORMER FRIENDS WAS STILL ALIVE.
YOU CAN'T BLAME HER FOR BREAKING DOWN IN TEARS.
BUT THEN THEY APPEARED.
!
FOR CRYING OUT LOUD. YOU ARE SUCH A PAIN, ASUNA KAGURAZAKA.
WE DIDN'T THINK YOU'D SLEEP AN EXTRA 30 YEARS.

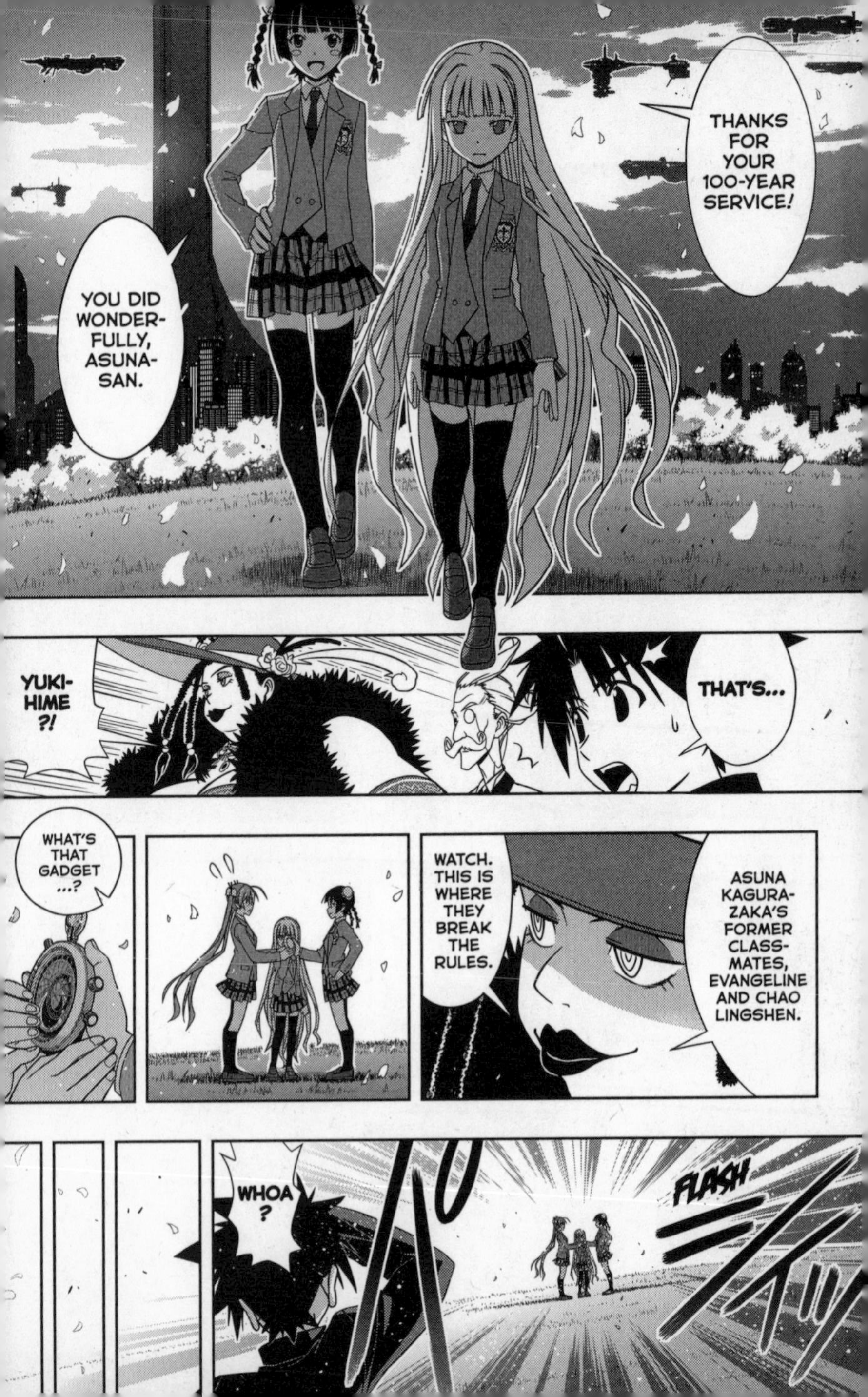
THANKS FOR YOUR 100-YEAR SERVICE!
YOU DID WONDERFULLY, ASUNA-SAN.
THAT'S...
YUKI-HIME ?!
ASUNA KAGURAZAKA'S FORMER CLASSMATES, EVANGELINE AND CHAO LINGSHEN.
WATCH. THIS IS WHERE THEY BREAK THE RULES.
WHAT'S THAT GADGET ...?
FLASH
WHOA ?

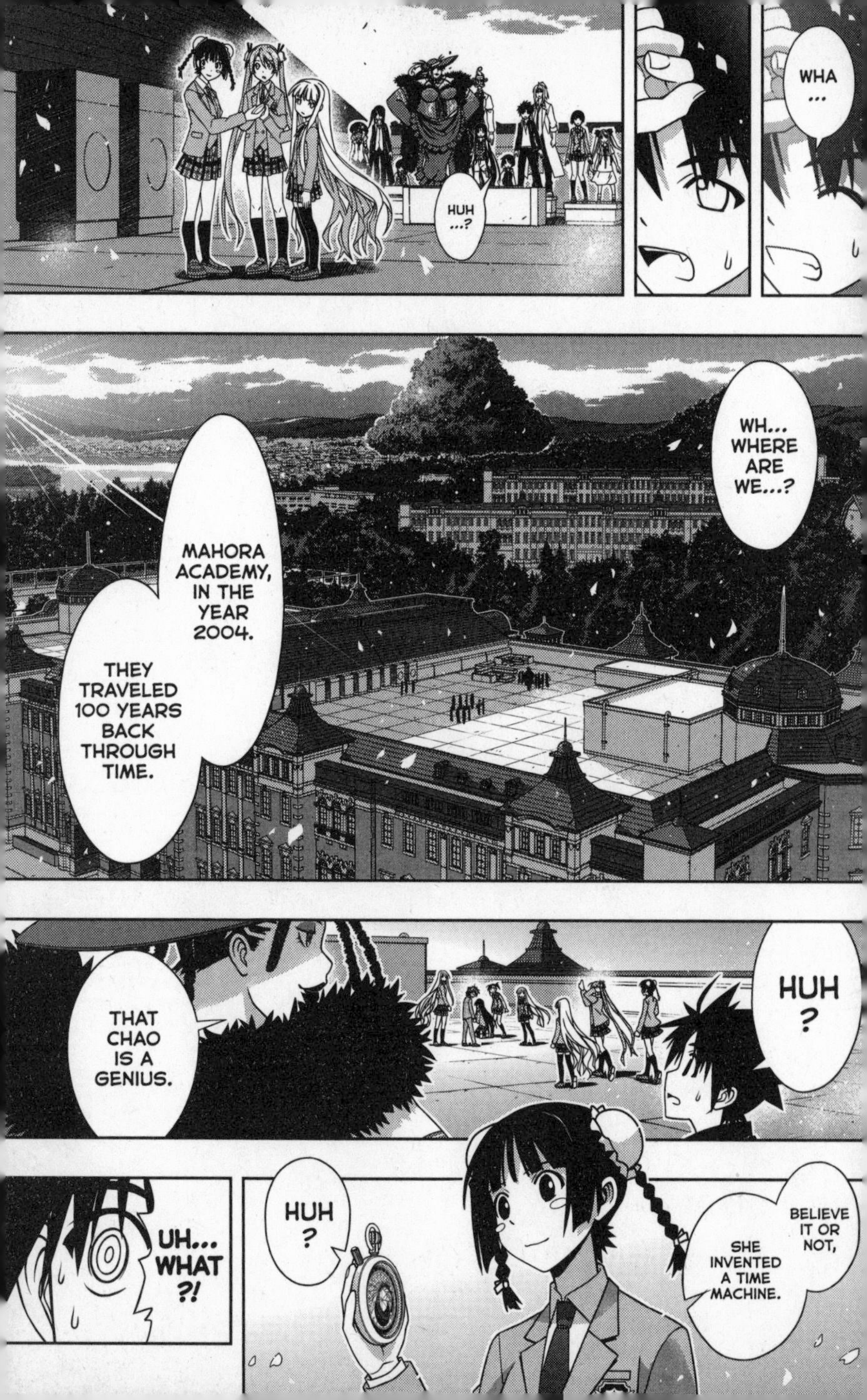
WHA...
HUH...?
WH... WHERE ARE WE...?
MAHORA ACADEMY, IN THE YEAR 2004.
THEY TRAVELED 100 YEARS BACK THROUGH TIME.
HUH?
THAT CHAO IS A GENIUS.
BELIEVE IT OR NOT,
SHE INVENTED A TIME MACHINE.
HUH?
UH... WHAT?!

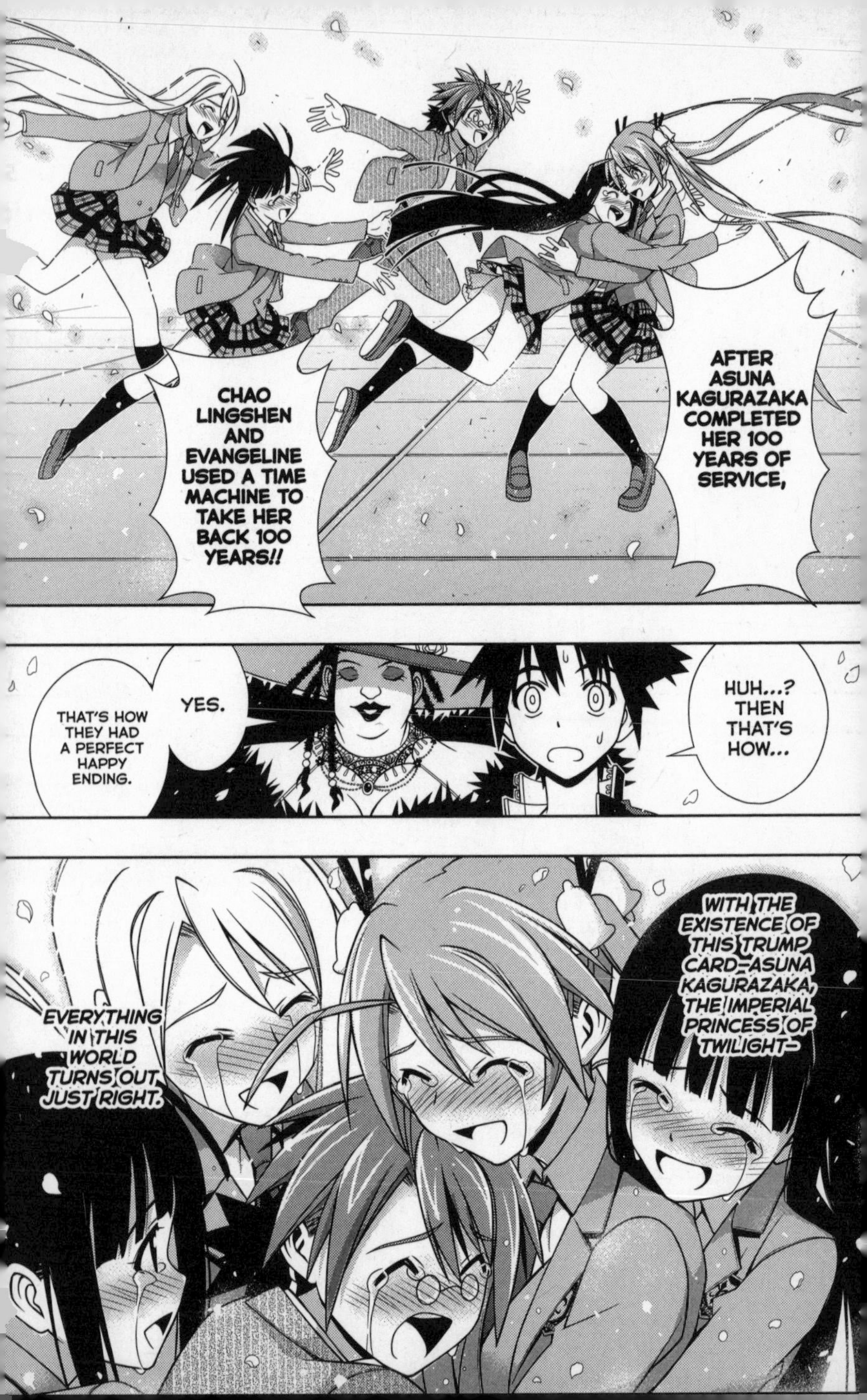
AFTER ASUNA KAGURAZAKA COMPLETED HER 100 YEARS OF SERVICE,
CHAO LINGSHEN AND EVANGELINE USED A TIME MACHINE TO TAKE HER BACK 100 YEARS!!
HUH...? THEN THAT'S HOW...
YES.
THAT'S HOW THEY HAD A PERFECT HAPPY ENDING.
WITH THE EXISTENCE OF THIS TRUMP CARD–ASUNA KAGURAZAKA, THE IMPERIAL PRINCESS OF TWILIGHT–
EVERYTHING IN THIS WORLD TURNS OUT JUST RIGHT.

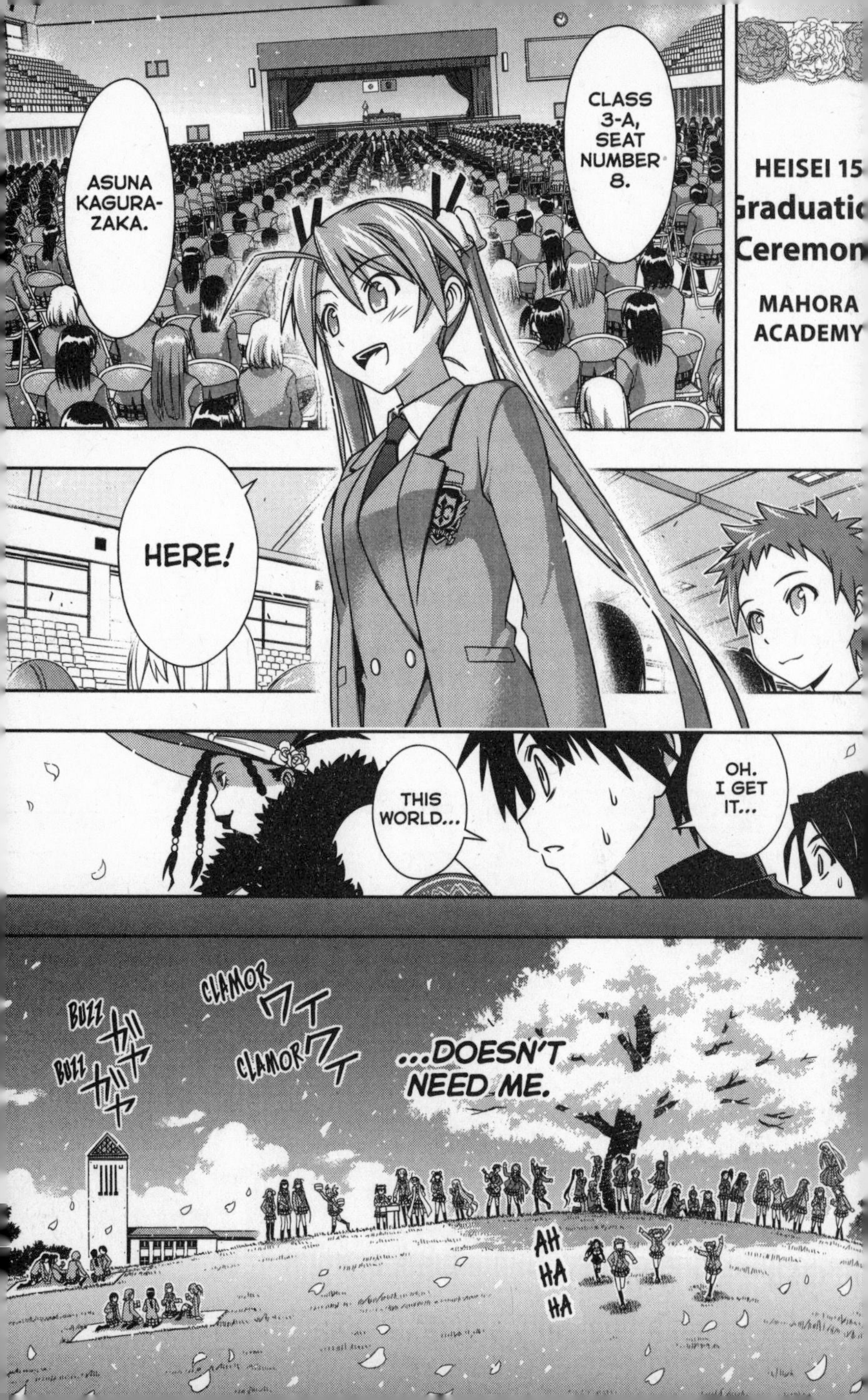

HEISEI 15
Graduatio
Ceremon
MAHORA ACADEMY
CLASS 3-A, SEAT NUMBER 8.
ASUNA KAGURAZAKA.
HERE!
OH. I GET IT...
THIS WORLD...
...DOESN'T NEED ME.
CLAMOR ワイ
CLAMOR ワイ
BUZZ ガヤ
BUZZ ガヤ
AH HA HA

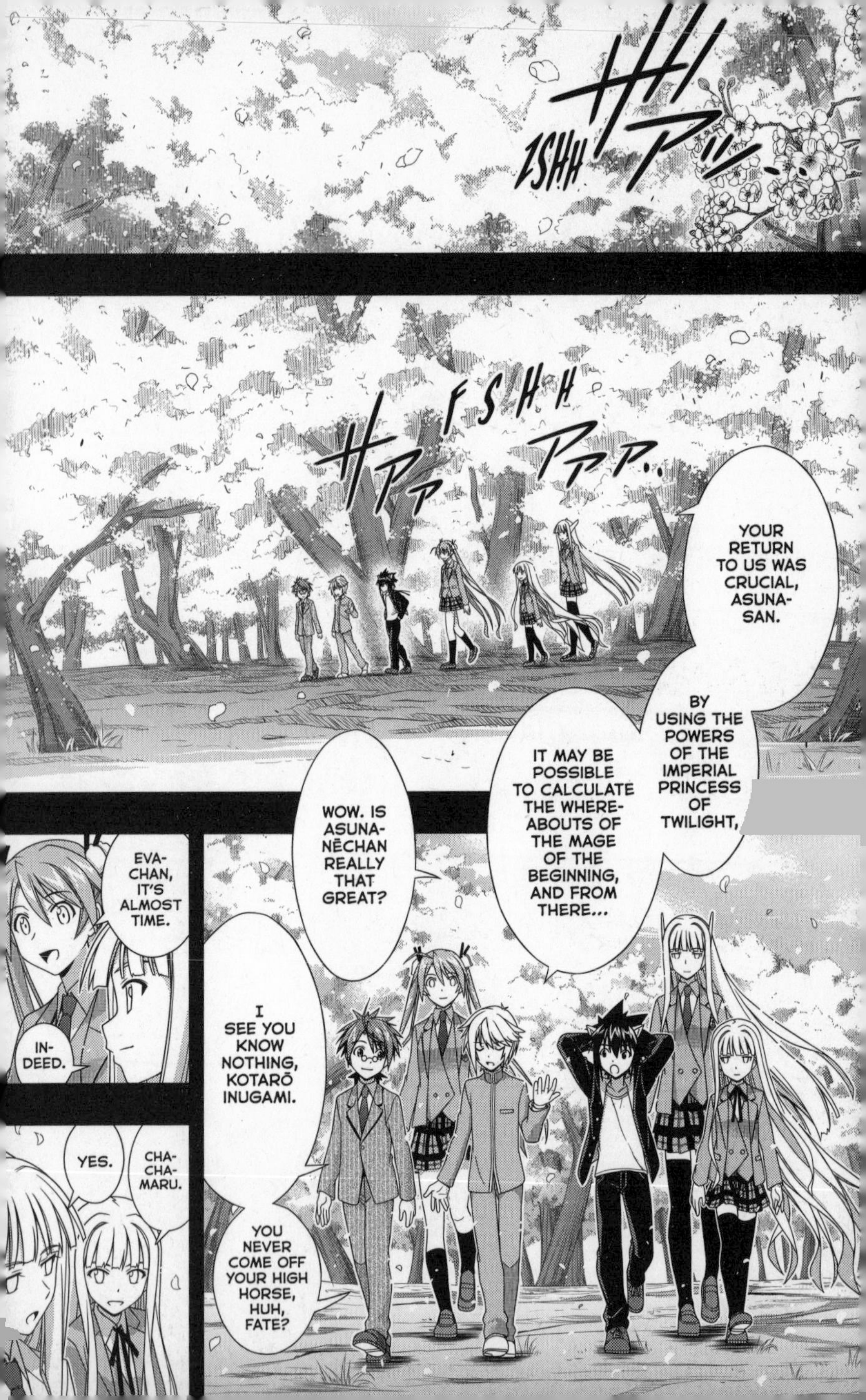
ZSHH
FSHH
YOUR RETURN TO US WAS CRUCIAL, ASUNA-SAN.
BY USING THE POWERS OF THE IMPERIAL PRINCESS OF TWILIGHT,
IT MAY BE POSSIBLE TO CALCULATE THE WHEREABOUTS OF THE MAGE OF THE BEGINNING, AND FROM THERE...
WOW. IS ASUNA-NĒCHAN REALLY THAT GREAT?
I SEE YOU KNOW NOTHING, KOTARŌ INUGAMI.
YOU NEVER COME OFF YOUR HIGH HORSE, HUH, FATE?
EVA-CHAN, IT'S ALMOST TIME.
INDEED.
CHACHAMARU.
YES.

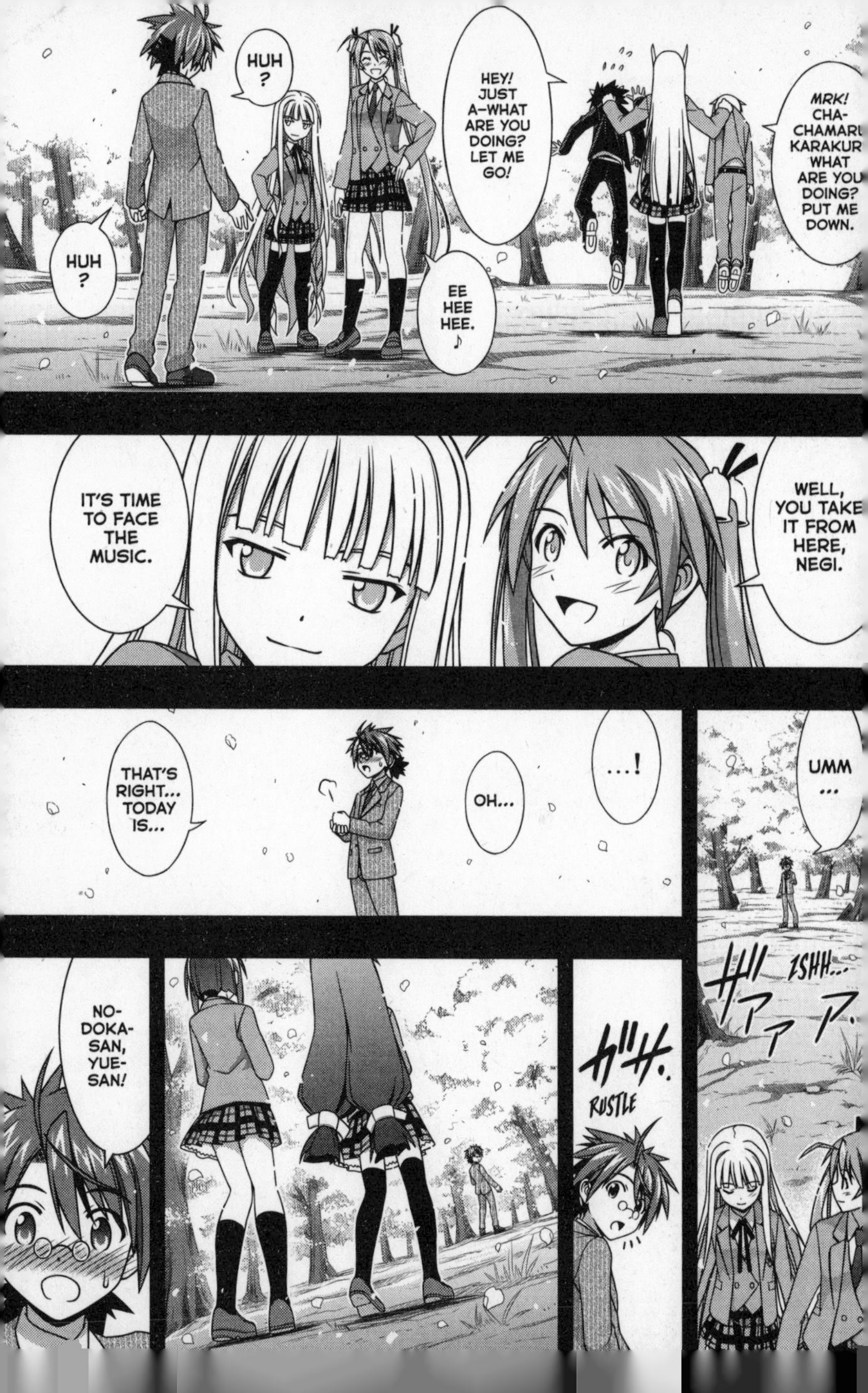
MRK! CHA-CHAMARU KARAKURI WHAT ARE YOU DOING? PUT ME DOWN.
HEY! JUST A-WHAT ARE YOU DOING? LET ME GO!
EE HEE HEE. ♪
HUH ?
HUH ?
WELL, YOU TAKE IT FROM HERE, NEGI.
IT'S TIME TO FACE THE MUSIC.
UMM ...
ZSHH...
...!
OH...
THAT'S RIGHT... TODAY IS...
RUSTLE
NO-DOKA-SAN, YUE-SAN!

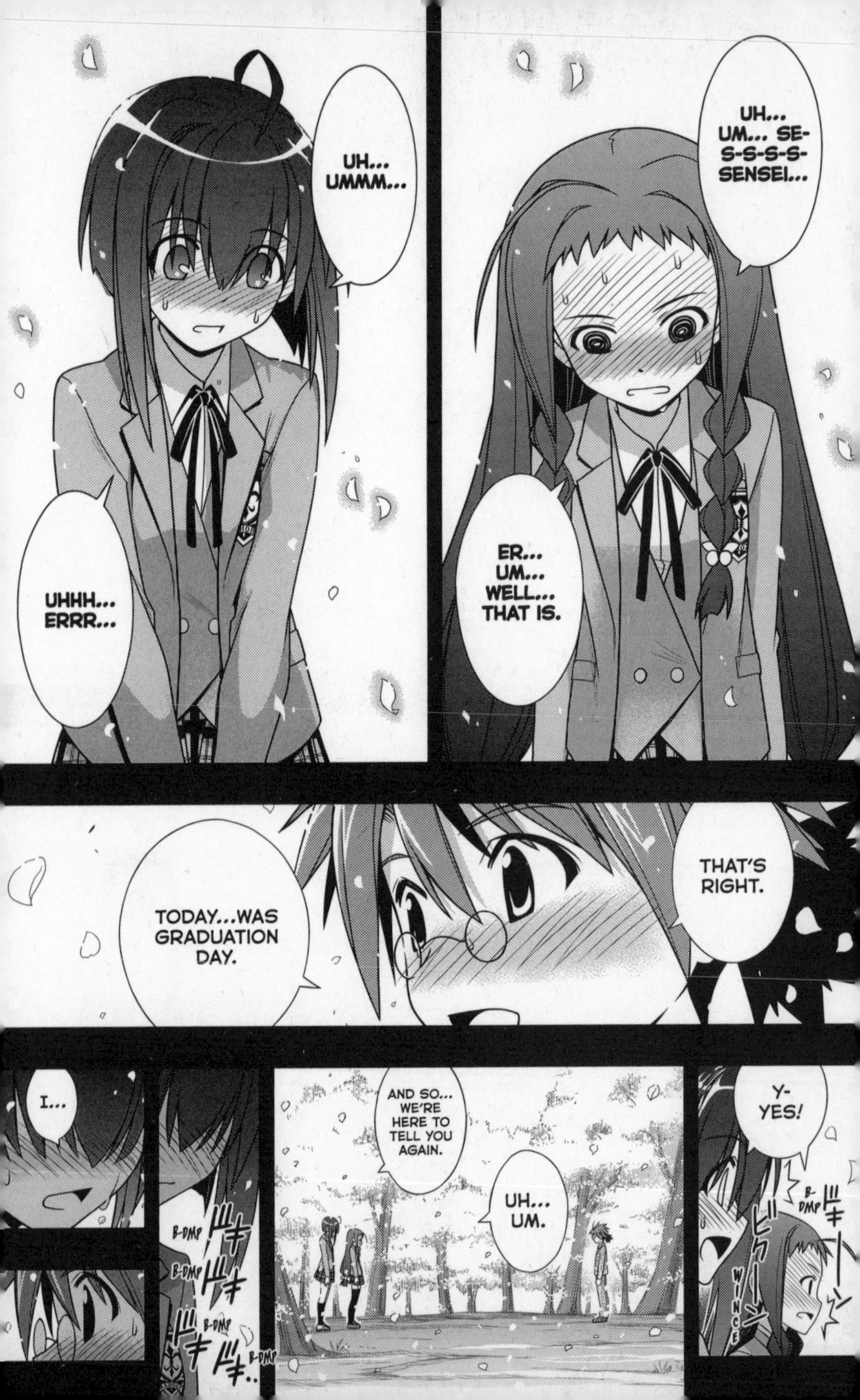
UH... UM... SE-S-S-S-S-SENSEI...
ER... UM... WELL... THAT IS.
UH... UMMM...
UHHH... ERRR...
THAT'S RIGHT.
TODAY...WAS GRADUATION DAY.
Y-YES!
B-DMP
WINCE
AND SO... WE'RE HERE TO TELL YOU AGAIN.
UH... UM.
I...
B-DMP
B-DMP
B-DMP
B-DMP

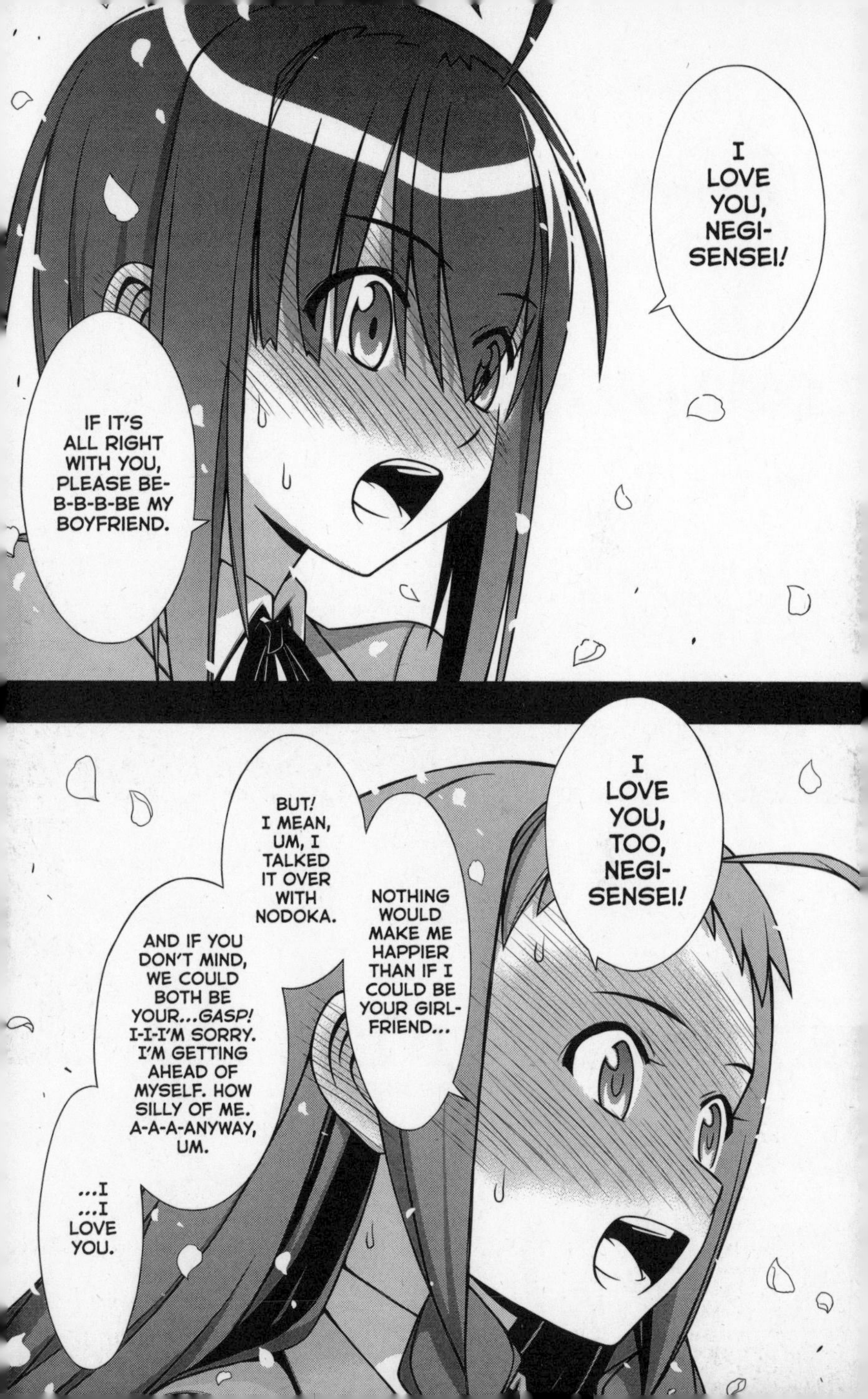
I LOVE YOU, NEGI-SENSEI!
IF IT'S ALL RIGHT WITH YOU, PLEASE BE-B-B-B-BE MY BOYFRIEND.
I LOVE YOU, TOO, NEGI-SENSEI!
NOTHING WOULD MAKE ME HAPPIER THAN IF I COULD BE YOUR GIRL-FRIEND...
BUT! I MEAN, UM, I TALKED IT OVER WITH NODOKA.
AND IF YOU DON'T MIND, WE COULD BOTH BE YOUR...*GASP!* I-I-I'M SORRY. I'M GETTING AHEAD OF MYSELF. HOW SILLY OF ME. A-A-A-ANYWAY, UM.
...I ...I LOVE YOU.

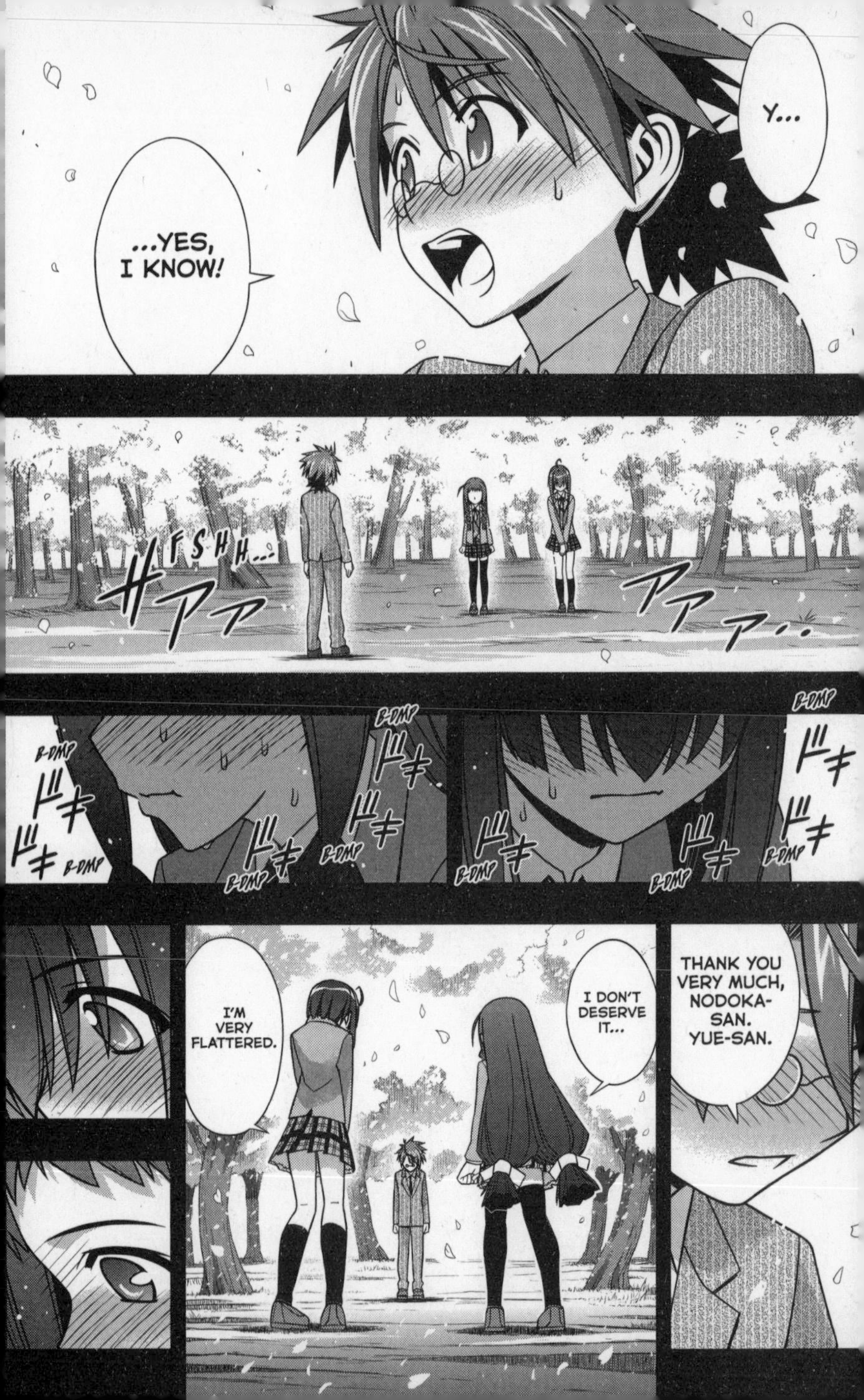
Y...
...YES, I KNOW!
FSHH...
ザアア
アア・・
B-DMP
ドキ
ドキ
B-DMP
ドキ
B-DMP
ドキ
B-DMP
B-DMP
ドキ
ドキ
B-DMP
ドキ
ドキ
B-DMP
B-DMP
THANK YOU VERY MUCH, NODOKA-SAN. YUE-SAN.
I DON'T DESERVE IT...
I'M VERY FLATTERED.

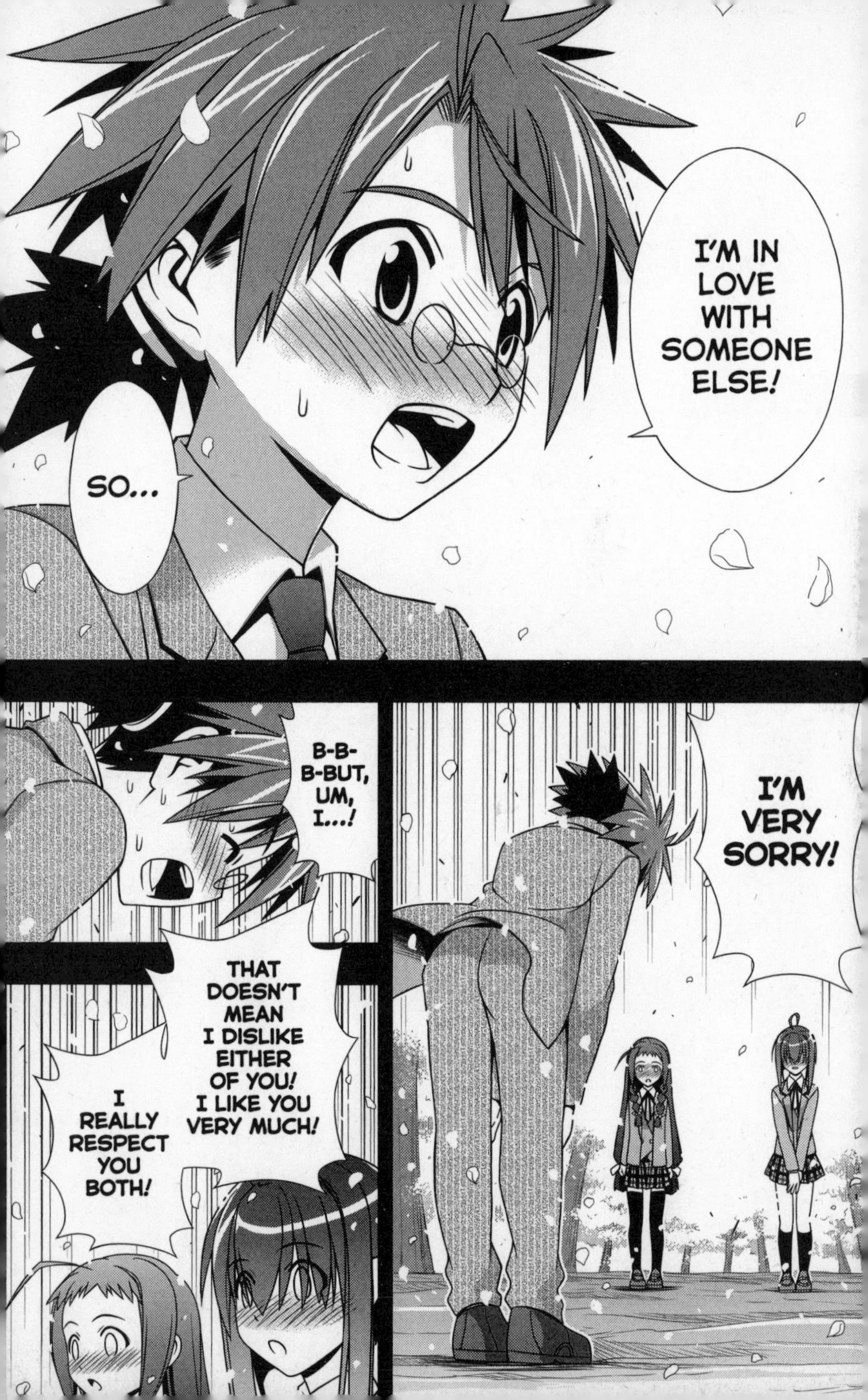
I'M IN LOVE WITH SOMEONE ELSE!
SO...
I'M VERY SORRY!
B-B-B-BUT, UM, I...!
THAT DOESN'T MEAN I DISLIKE EITHER OF YOU! I LIKE YOU VERY MUCH!
I REALLY RESPECT YOU BOTH!

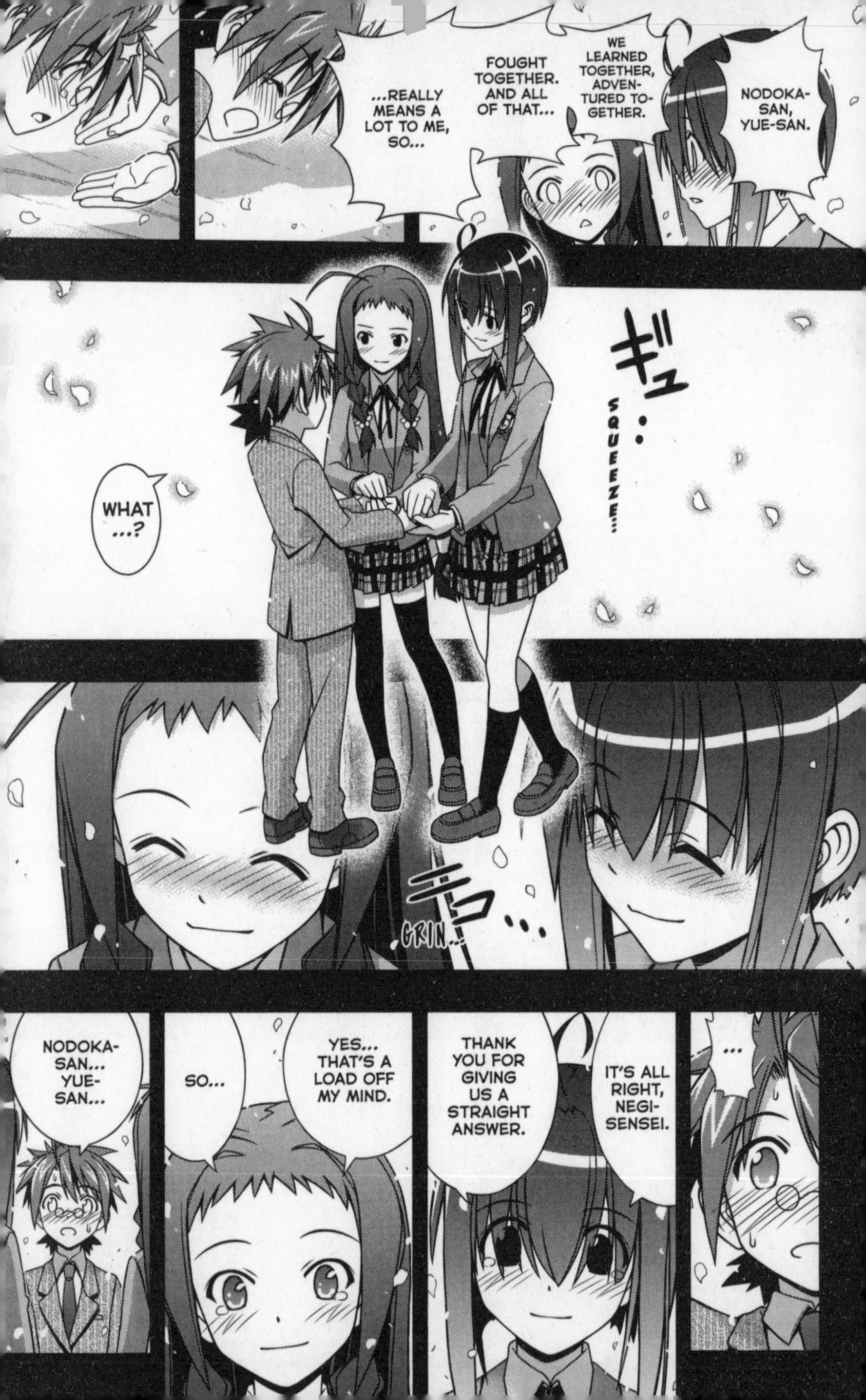
NODOKA-SAN, YUE-SAN.
WE LEARNED TOGETHER, ADVEN-TURED TO-GETHER.
FOUGHT TOGETHER. AND ALL OF THAT...
...REALLY MEANS A LOT TO ME, SO...
ギュ
SQUEEZE...
WHAT ...?
ニコ...
GRIN...
...
IT'S ALL RIGHT, NEGI-SENSEI.
THANK YOU FOR GIVING US A STRAIGHT ANSWER.
YES... THAT'S A LOAD OFF MY MIND.
SO...
NODOKA-SAN... YUE-SAN...

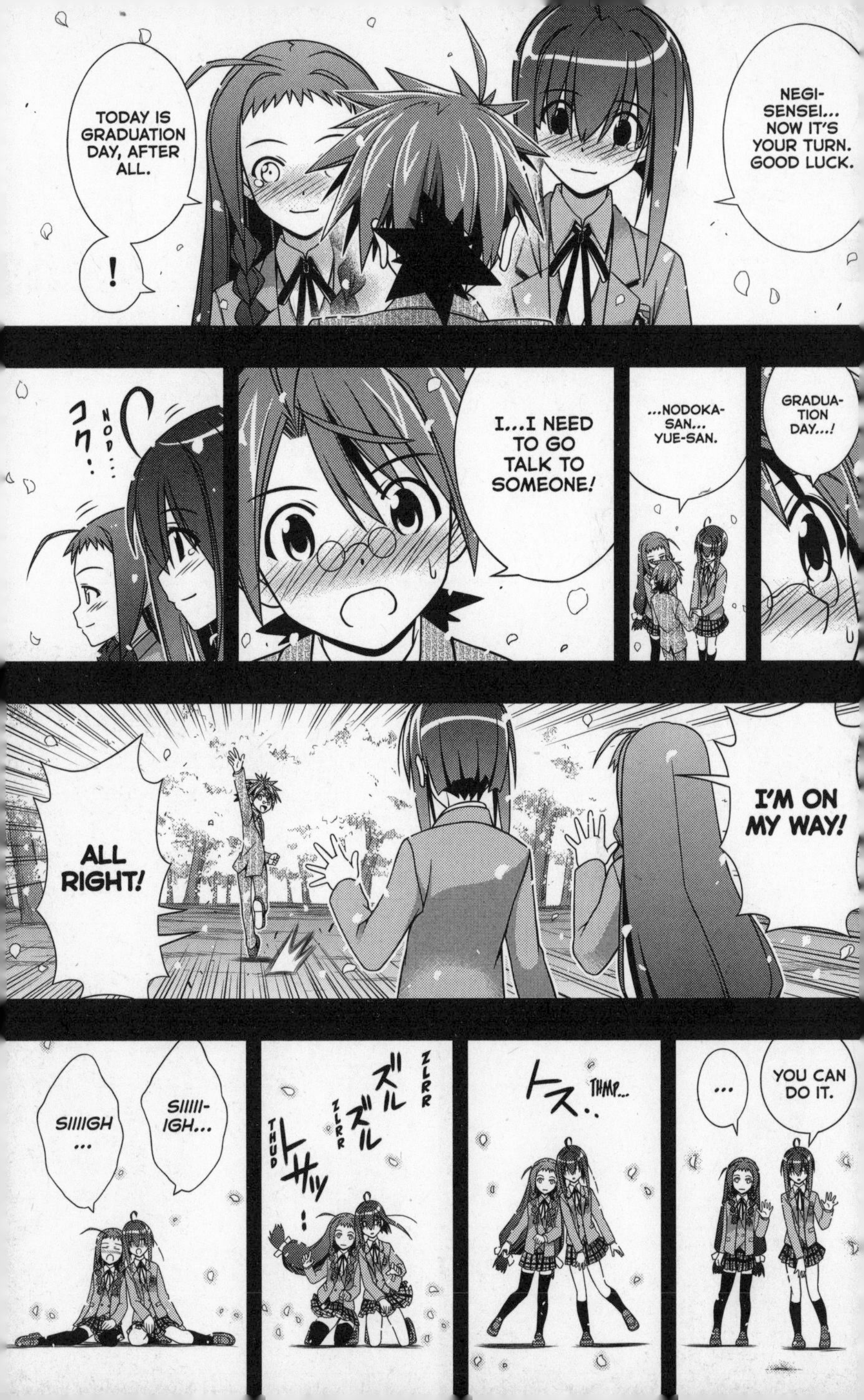
NEGI-SENSEI... NOW IT'S YOUR TURN. GOOD LUCK.
TODAY IS GRADUATION DAY, AFTER ALL.
!
GRADUA-TION DAY...!
...NODOKA-SAN... YUE-SAN.
I...I NEED TO GO TALK TO SOMEONE!
コク
NOD...
I'M ON MY WAY!
ALL RIGHT!
YOU CAN DO IT.
...
トス..
THMP...
ズル
ZLRR
ズル
ZLRR
トサッ
THUD
SIIIII-IGH...
SIIIIGH ...

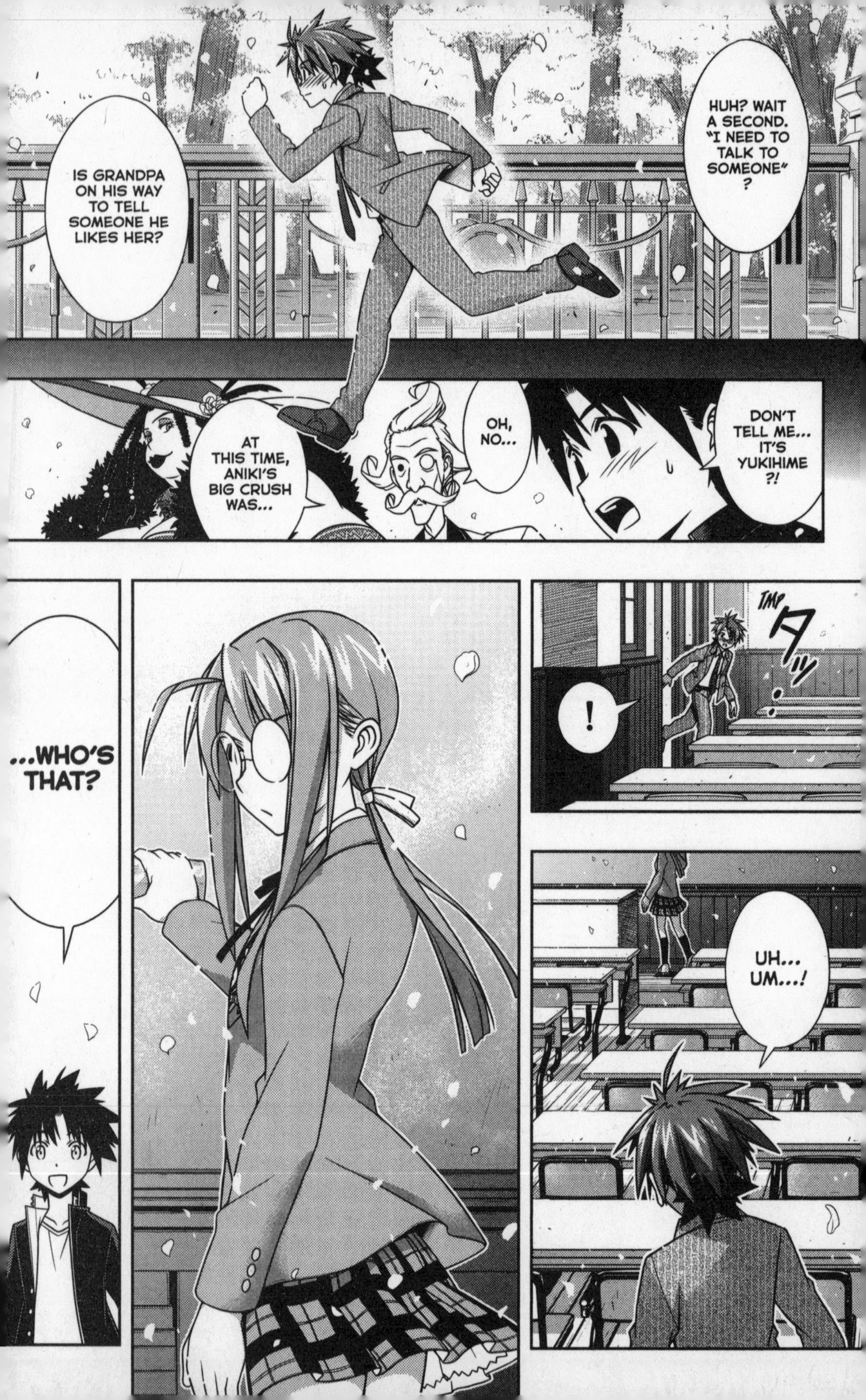
HUH? WAIT A SECOND. "I NEED TO TALK TO SOMEONE"?
IS GRANDPA ON HIS WAY TO TELL SOMEONE HE LIKES HER?
DON'T TELL ME... IT'S YUKIHIME?!
OH, NO...
AT THIS TIME, ANIKI'S BIG CRUSH WAS...
TMP
!
UH... UM...!
...WHO'S THAT?

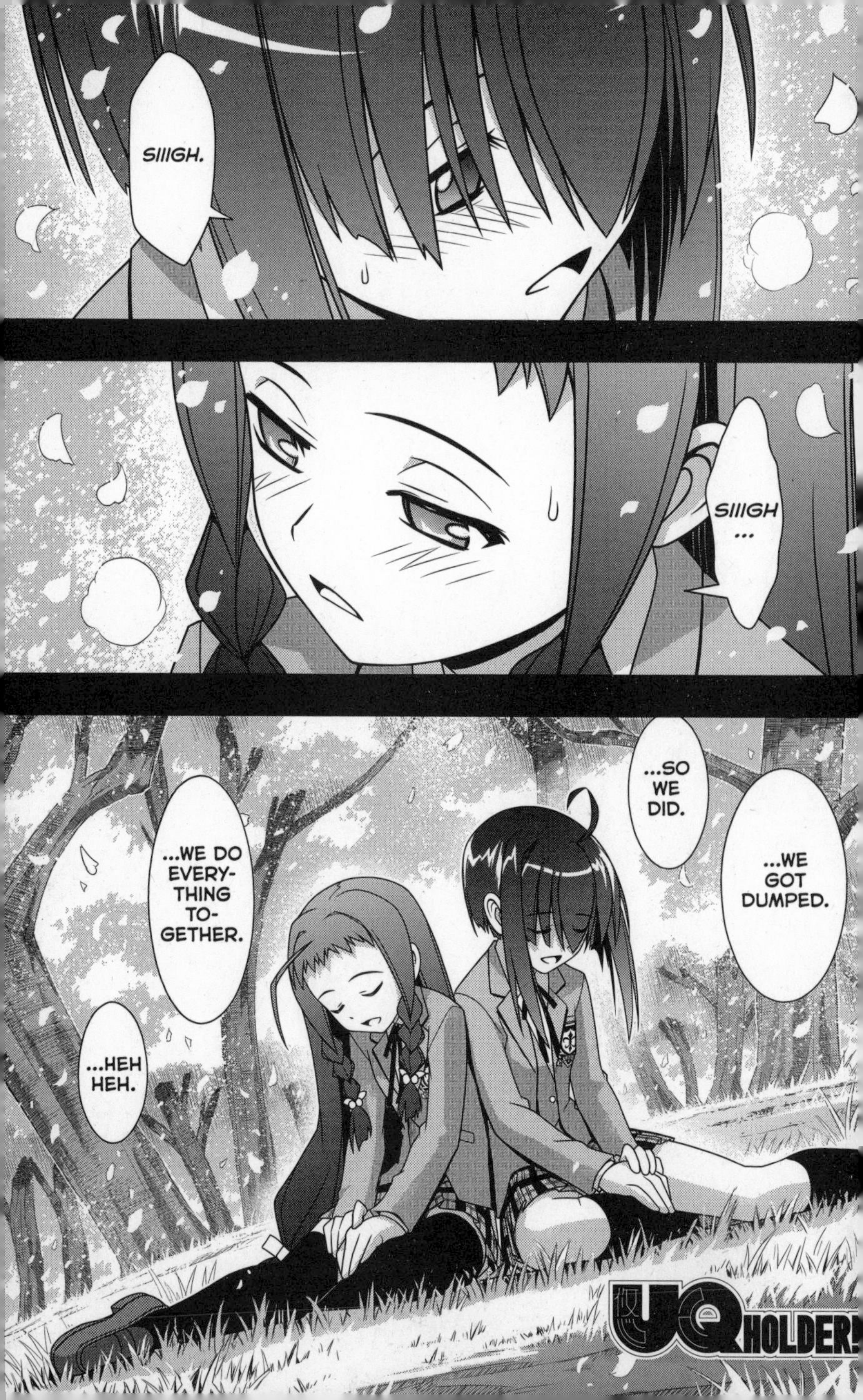
SIIIGH.
SIIIGH ...
...WE GOT DUMPED.
...SO WE DID.
...WE DO EVERY-THING TO-GETHER.
...HEH HEH.
UQ HOLDER!

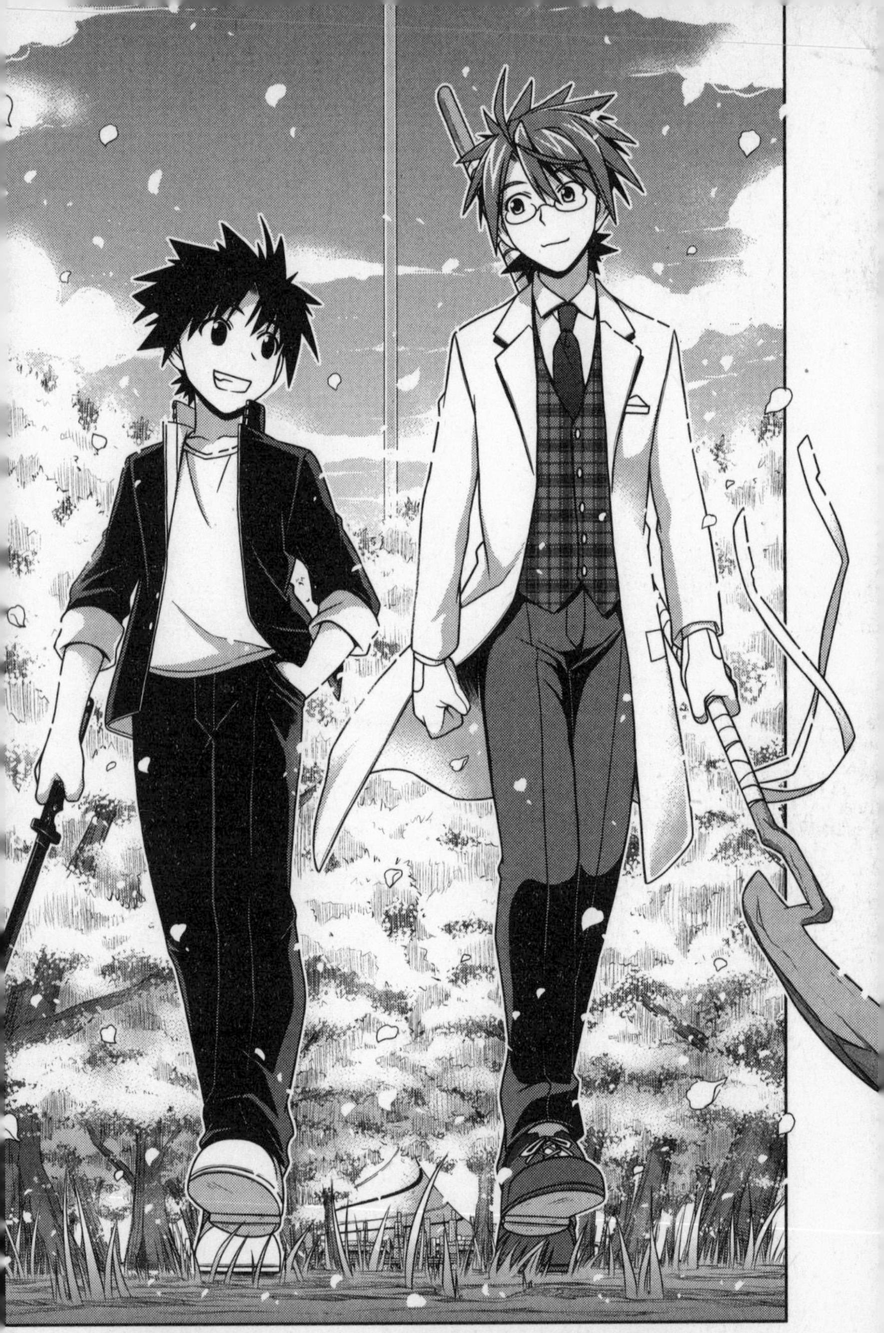

STAGE 138: LIFE-OR-DEATH LOVE CONFESSION

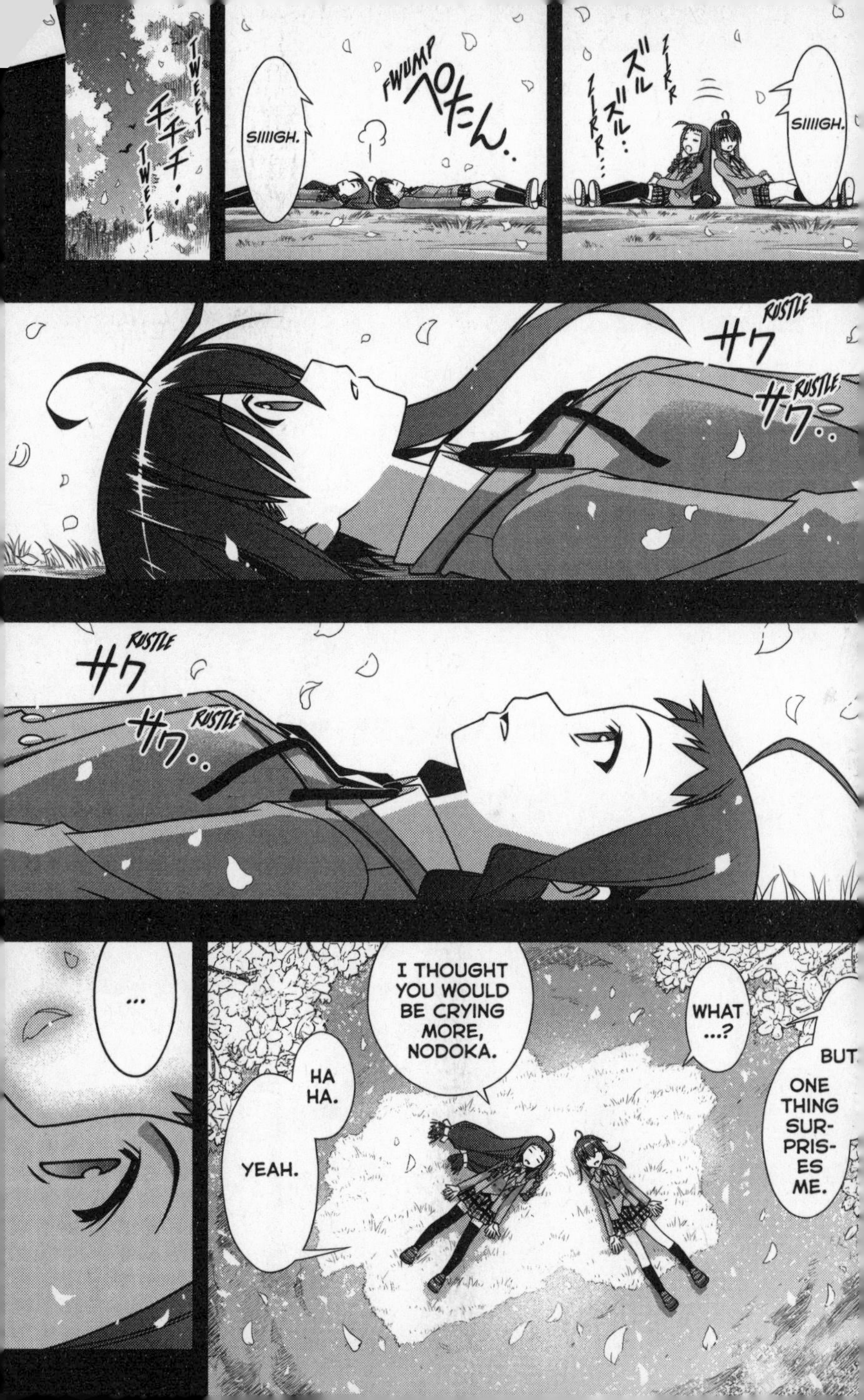
SIIIGH.
ZURR ズル
ZURR ズル...
FWUMP ぺたん..
SIIIGH.
TWEET チチチ.
TWEET
RUSTLE サワ
RUSTLE サワ..
RUSTLE サワ
RUSTLE サワ..
BUT ONE THING SURPRISES ME.
WHAT ...?
I THOUGHT YOU WOULD BE CRYING MORE, NODOKA.
HA HA.
YEAH.
...

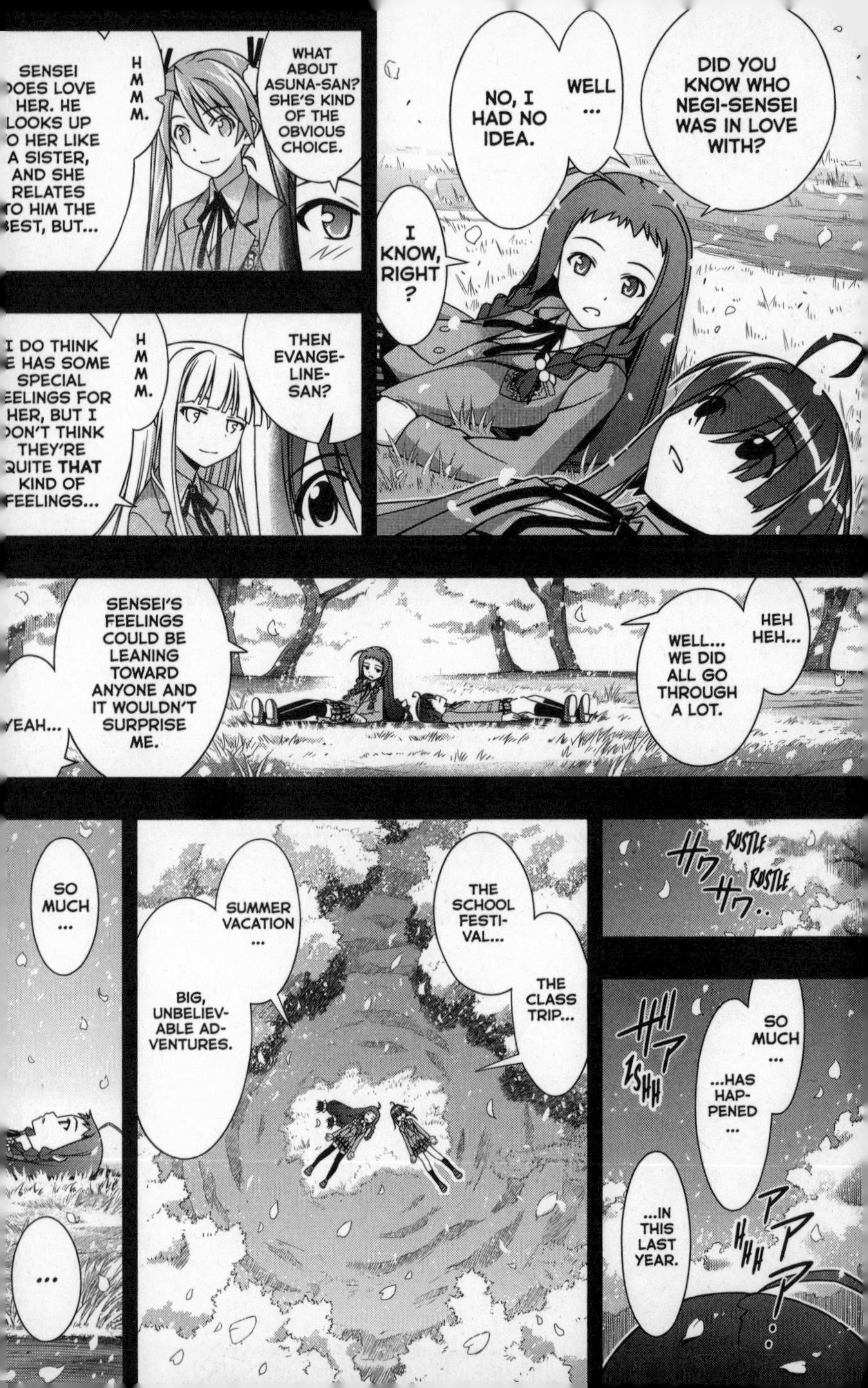
DID YOU KNOW WHO NEGI-SENSEI WAS IN LOVE WITH?
WELL ...
NO, I HAD NO IDEA.
I KNOW, RIGHT?
WHAT ABOUT ASUNA-SAN? SHE'S KIND OF THE OBVIOUS CHOICE.
HMMM.
SENSEI OES LOVE HER. HE LOOKS UP O HER LIKE A SISTER, AND SHE RELATES O HIM THE EST, BUT...
THEN EVANGE-LINE-SAN?
HMMM.
I DO THINK E HAS SOME SPECIAL EELINGS FOR HER, BUT I ON'T THINK THEY'RE UITE THAT KIND OF EELINGS...
HEH HEH...
WELL... WE DID ALL GO THROUGH A LOT.
SENSEI'S FEELINGS COULD BE LEANING TOWARD ANYONE AND IT WOULDN'T SURPRISE ME.
EAH...
サワ RUSTLE サワ.. RUSTLE
ザァ ZSHH
SO MUCH ...
...HAS HAP-PENED ...
...IN THIS LAST YEAR.
アアア HHH
THE SCHOOL FESTI-VAL...
THE CLASS TRIP...
SUMMER VACATION ...
BIG, UNBELIEV-ABLE AD-VENTURES.
SO MUCH ...
...

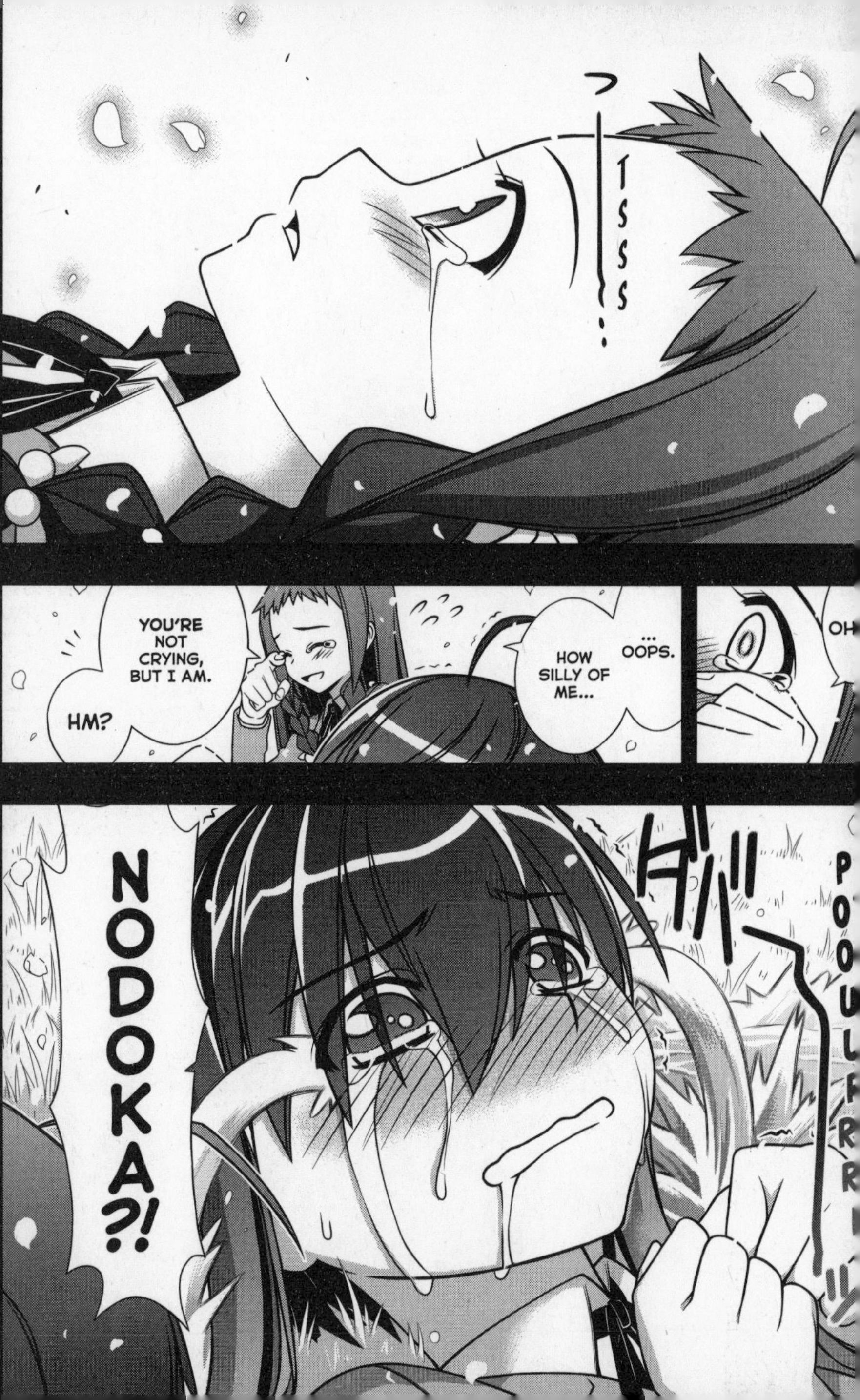
TSSS
OH
... OOPS.
HOW SILLY OF ME...
YOU'RE NOT CRYING, BUT I AM.
HM?
POOULFRRR
NODOKA?!

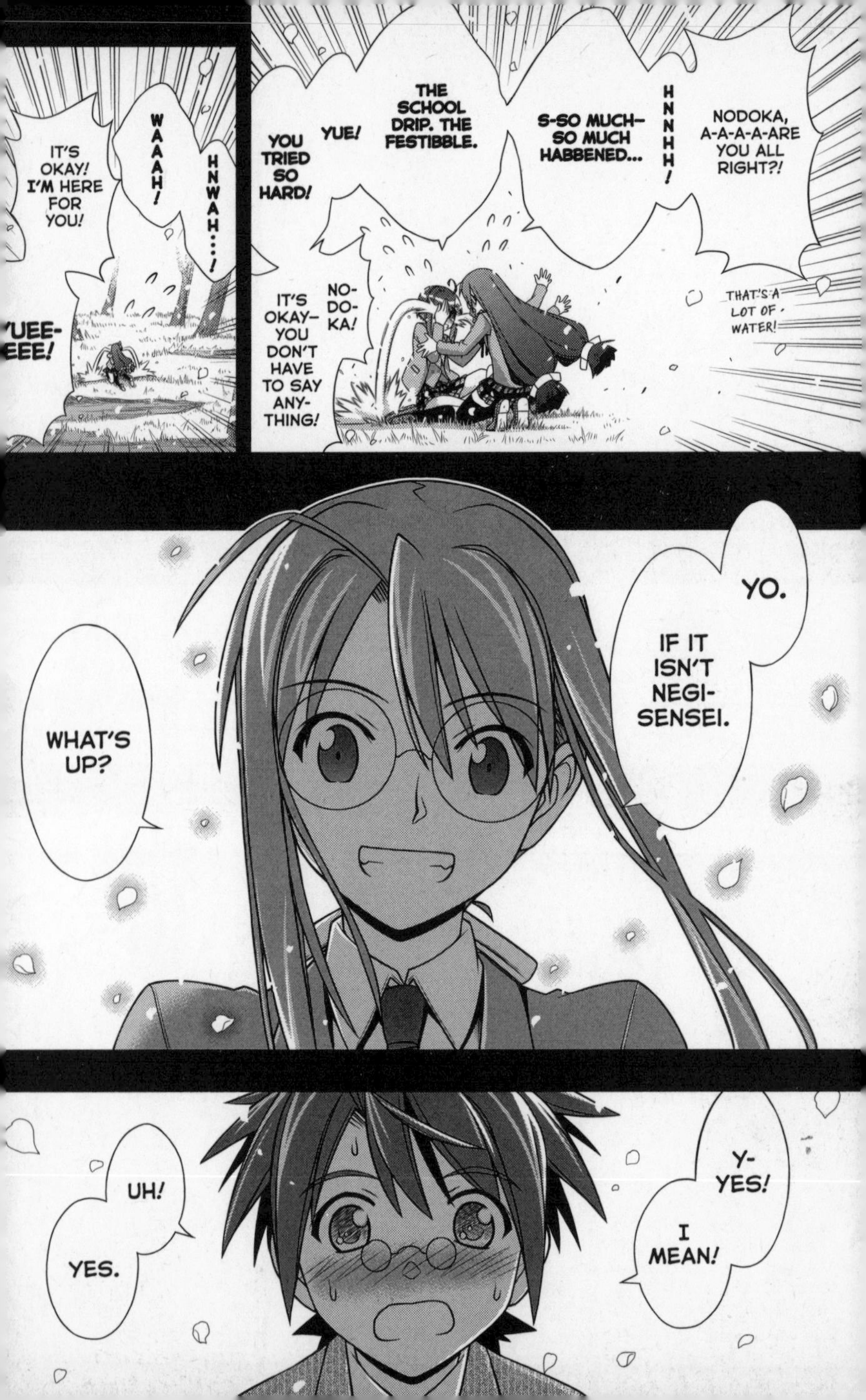
NODOKA, A-A-A-A-ARE YOU ALL RIGHT?!
HNNHH!
S-SO MUCH— SO MUCH HABBENED...
THE SCHOOL DRIP. THE FESTIBBLE.
YUE!
YOU TRIED SO HARD!
THAT'S A LOT OF WATER!
NO-DO-KA!
IT'S OKAY— YOU DON'T HAVE TO SAY ANYTHING!
HNWAH...!
WAAAAH!
IT'S OKAY! I'M HERE FOR YOU!
UEE-EEE!
YO.
IF IT ISN'T NEGI-SENSEI.
WHAT'S UP?
Y-YES!
I MEAN!
UH!
YES.

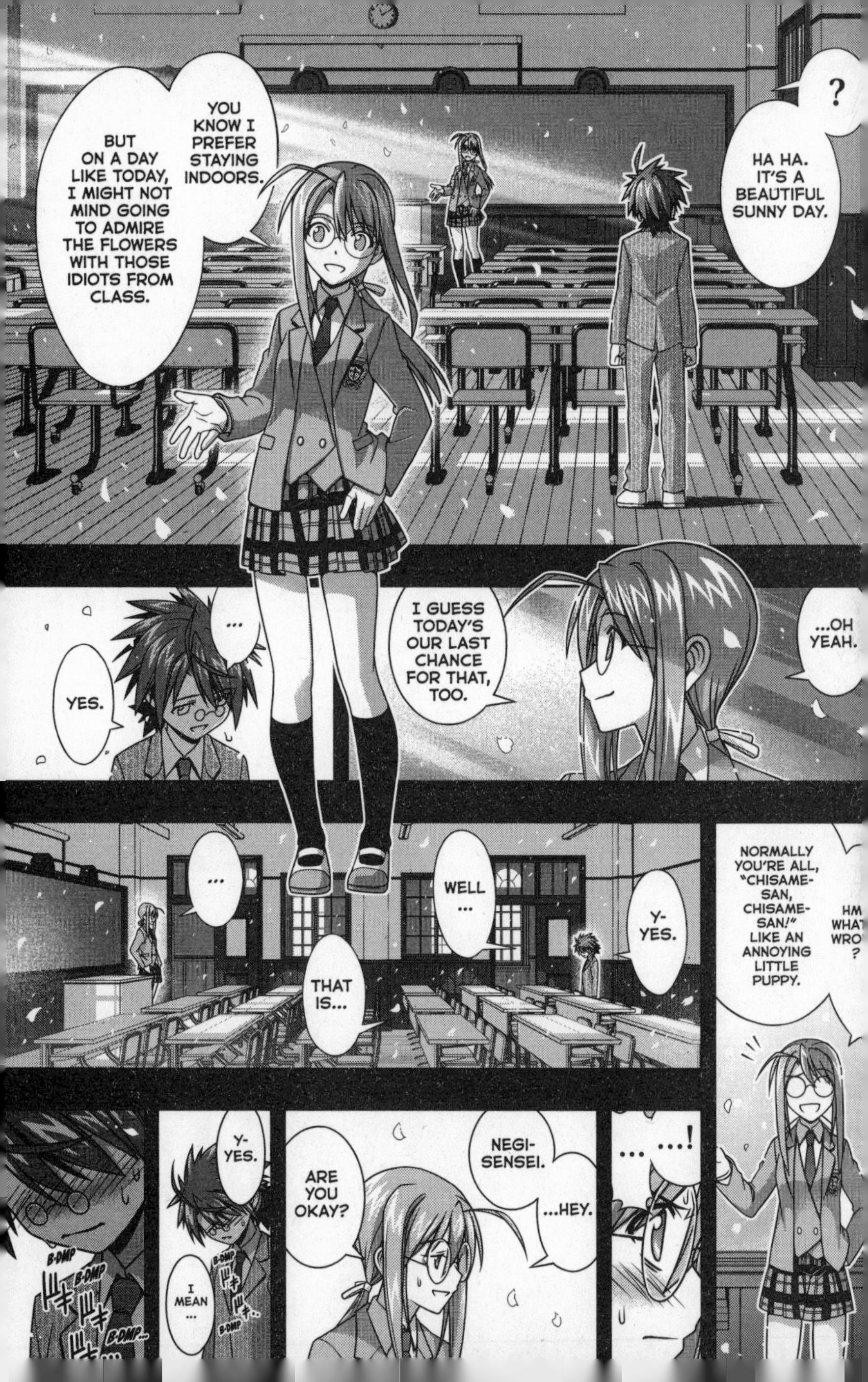
?
HA HA. IT'S A BEAUTIFUL SUNNY DAY.
YOU KNOW I PREFER STAYING INDOORS.
BUT ON A DAY LIKE TODAY, I MIGHT NOT MIND GOING TO ADMIRE THE FLOWERS WITH THOSE IDIOTS FROM CLASS.
...OH YEAH.
I GUESS TODAY'S OUR LAST CHANCE FOR THAT, TOO.
...
YES.
NORMALLY YOU'RE ALL, "CHISAME-SAN, CHISAME-SAN!" LIKE AN ANNOYING LITTLE PUPPY.
HM WHAT WRO ?
Y-YES.
WELL...
THAT IS...
...
... ...!
NEGI-SENSEI.
...HEY.
ARE YOU OKAY?
Y-YES.
I MEAN...
B-DMP
B-DMP
B-DMP
B-DMP
B-DMP...

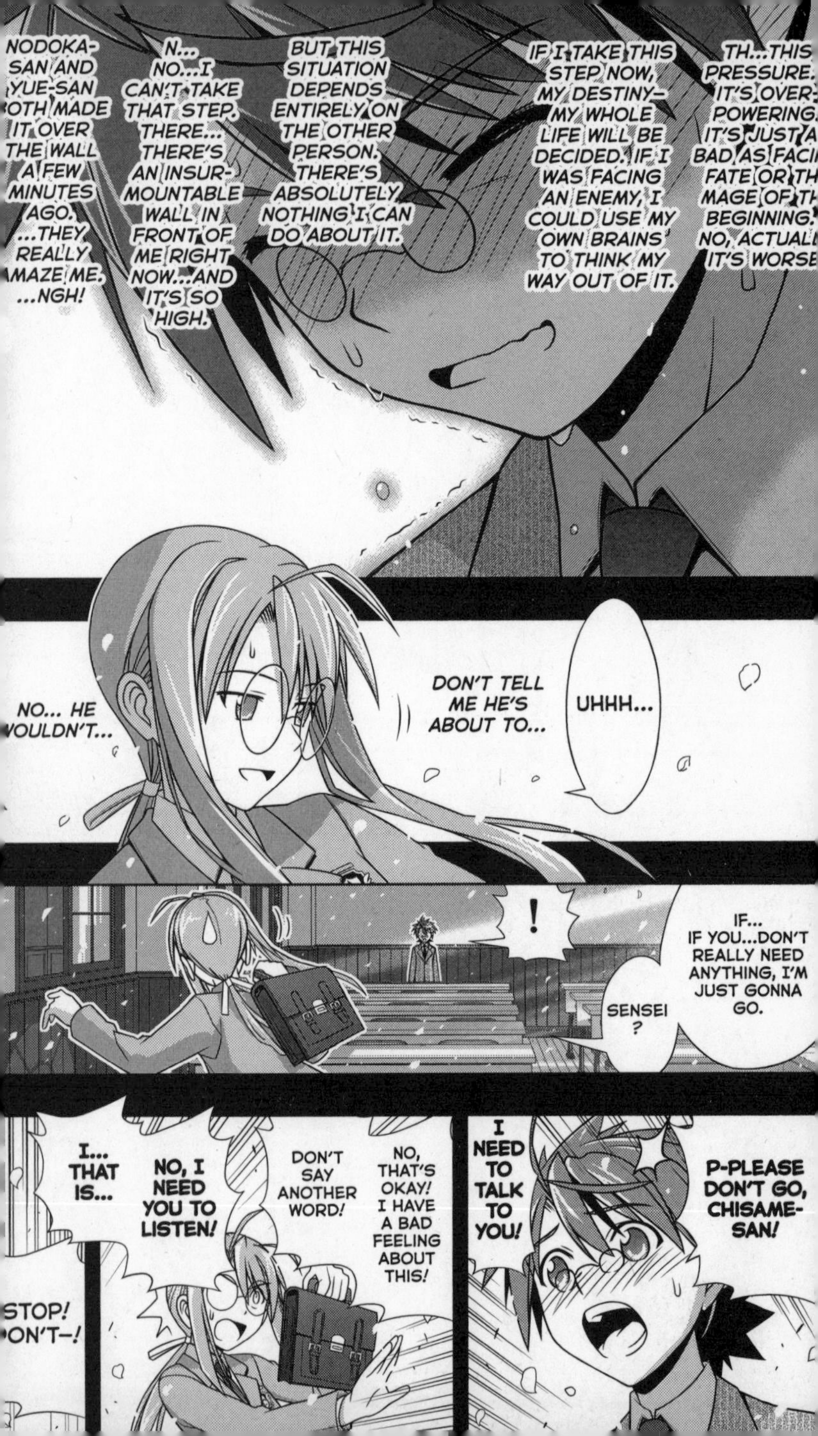
TH...THIS PRESSURE. IT'S OVER-POWERING. IT'S JUST A BAD AS FACI FATE OR TH MAGE OF TH BEGINNING. NO, ACTUALL IT'S WORSE
IF I TAKE THIS STEP NOW, MY DESTINY— MY WHOLE LIFE WILL BE DECIDED. IF I WAS FACING AN ENEMY, I COULD USE MY OWN BRAINS TO THINK MY WAY OUT OF IT.
BUT THIS SITUATION DEPENDS ENTIRELY ON THE OTHER PERSON. THERE'S ABSOLUTELY NOTHING I CAN DO ABOUT IT.
N... NO...I CAN'T TAKE THAT STEP. THERE... THERE'S AN INSUR-MOUNTABLE WALL IN FRONT OF ME RIGHT NOW...AND IT'S SO HIGH.
NODOKA-SAN AND YUE-SAN OTH MADE IT OVER THE WALL A FEW MINUTES AGO. ...THEY REALLY MAZE ME. ...NGH!
UHHH...
DON'T TELL ME HE'S ABOUT TO...
NO... HE OULDN'T...
IF... IF YOU...DON'T REALLY NEED ANYTHING, I'M JUST GONNA GO.
SENSEI ?
!
P-PLEASE DON'T GO, CHISAME-SAN!
I NEED TO TALK TO YOU!
NO, THAT'S OKAY! I HAVE A BAD FEELING ABOUT THIS!
DON'T SAY ANOTHER WORD!
NO, I NEED YOU TO LISTEN!
I... THAT IS...
STOP! ON'T–!

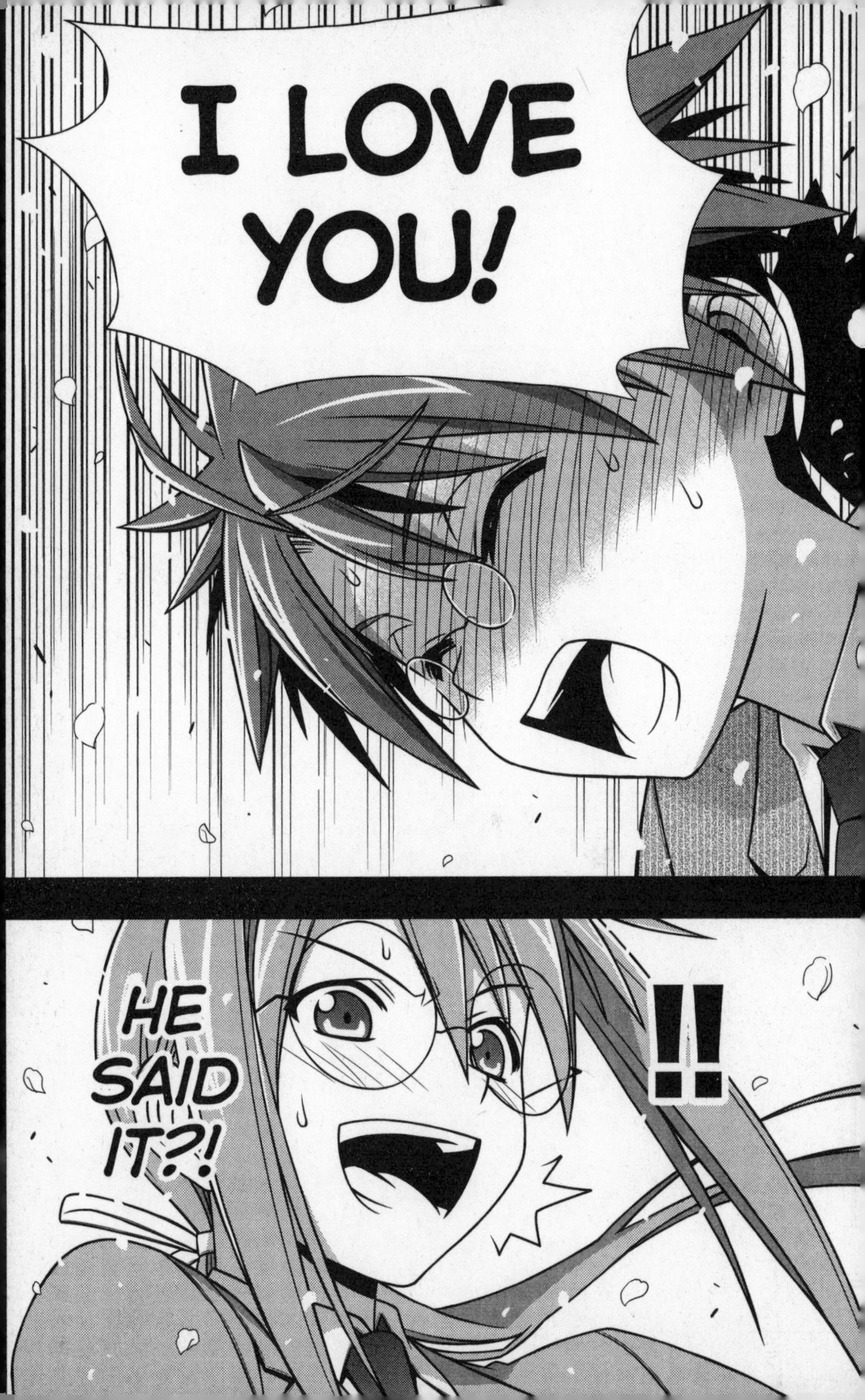
I LOVE YOU!
HE SAID IT?!
!!

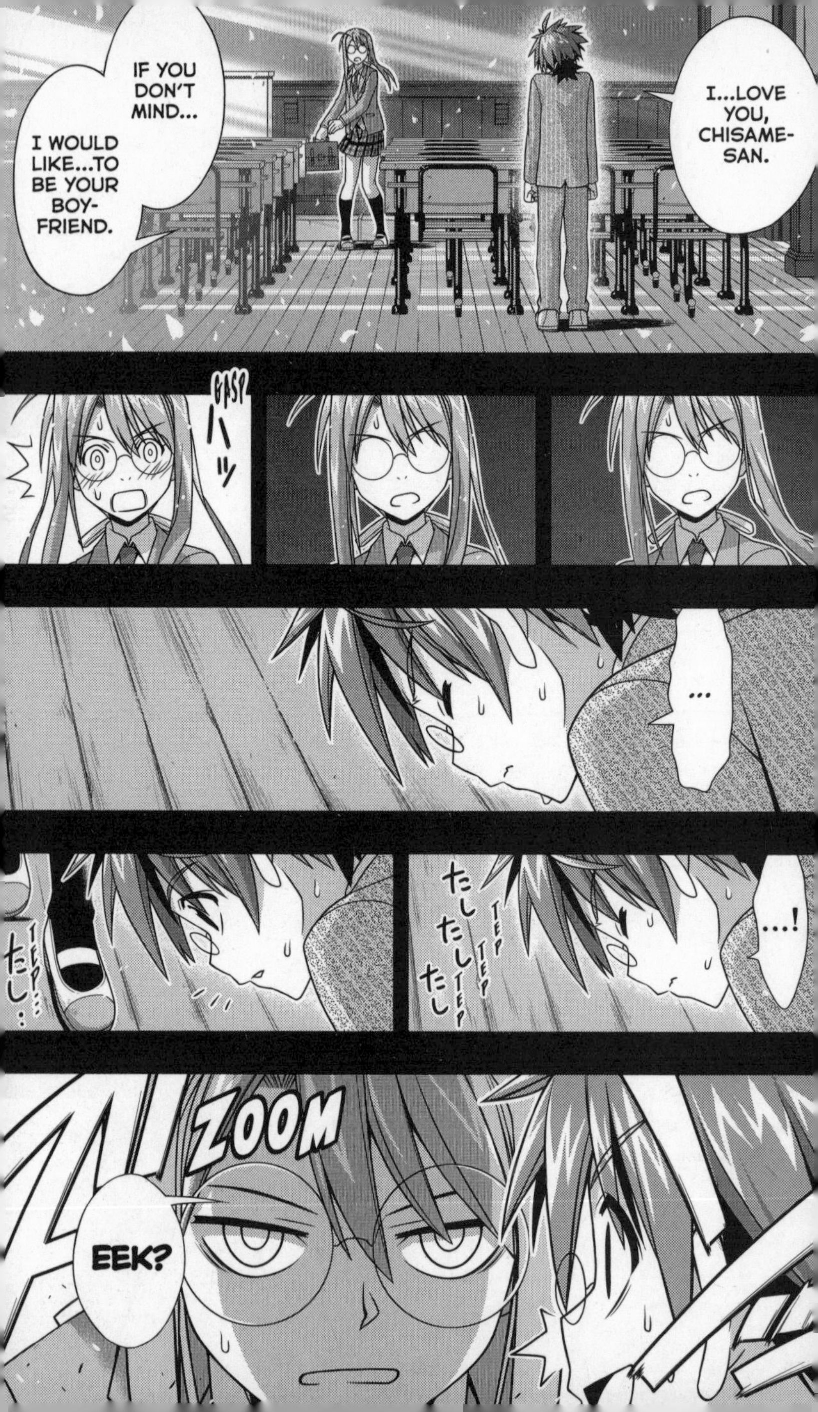
I...LOVE YOU, CHISAME-SAN.
IF YOU DON'T MIND...
I WOULD LIKE...TO BE YOUR BOY-FRIEND.
GASP
ハッ
...
...!
たし たし たし
TEP TEP TEP
たし...
TEP...
ZOOM
EEK?

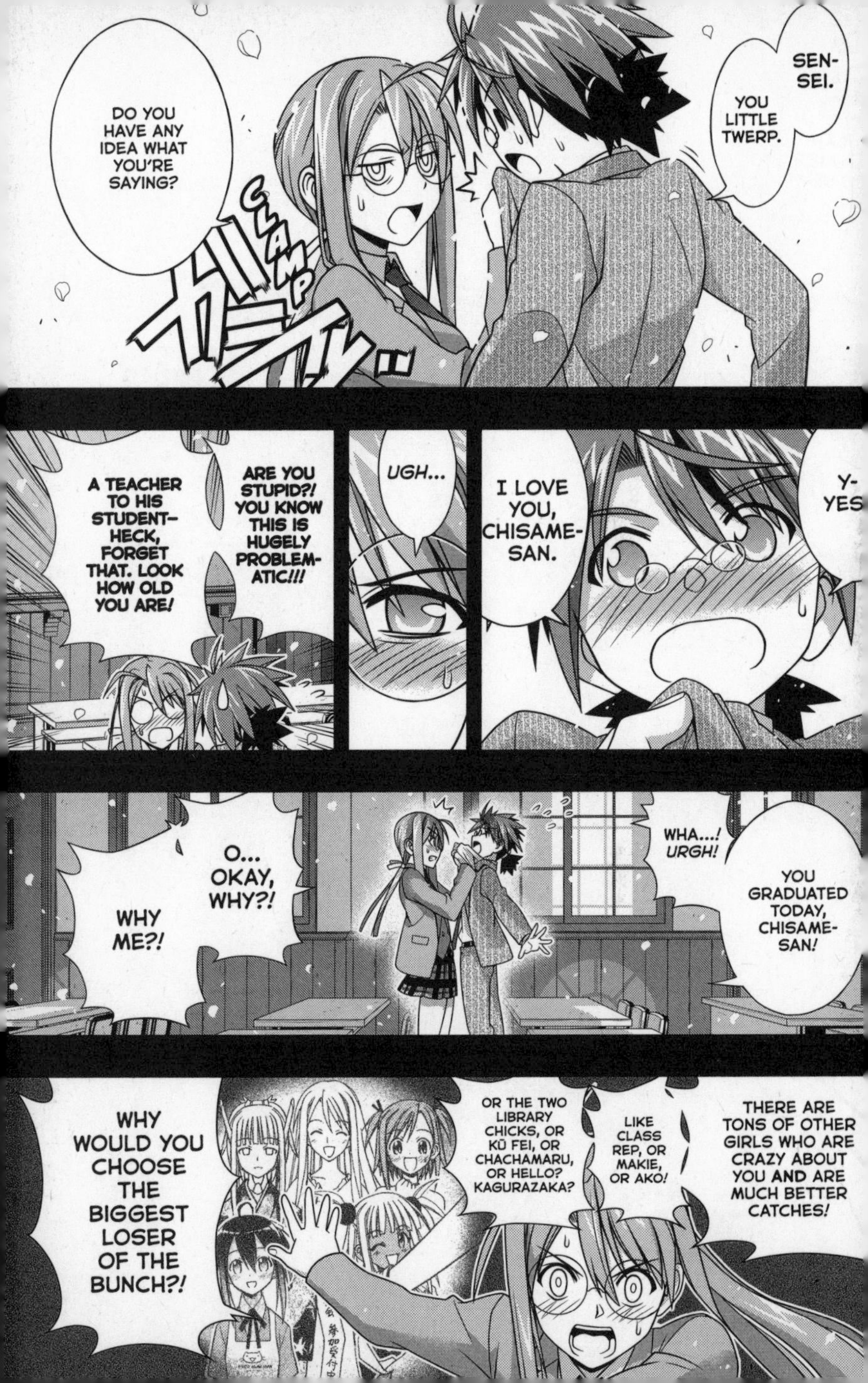

SEN-SEI.
YOU LITTLE TWERP.
CLAMP
DO YOU HAVE ANY IDEA WHAT YOU'RE SAYING?
Y-YES
I LOVE YOU, CHISAME-SAN.
UGH...
ARE YOU STUPID?! YOU KNOW THIS IS HUGELY PROBLEM-ATIC!!!
A TEACHER TO HIS STUDENT—HECK, FORGET THAT. LOOK HOW OLD YOU ARE!
YOU GRADUATED TODAY, CHISAME-SAN!
WHA...! URGH!
O... OKAY, WHY?!
WHY ME?!
THERE ARE TONS OF OTHER GIRLS WHO ARE CRAZY ABOUT YOU AND ARE MUCH BETTER CATCHES!
LIKE CLASS REP, OR MAKIE, OR AKO!
OR THE TWO LIBRARY CHICKS, OR KŪ FEI, OR CHACHAMARU, OR HELLO? KAGURAZAKA?
WHY WOULD YOU CHOOSE THE BIGGEST LOSER OF THE BUNCH?!

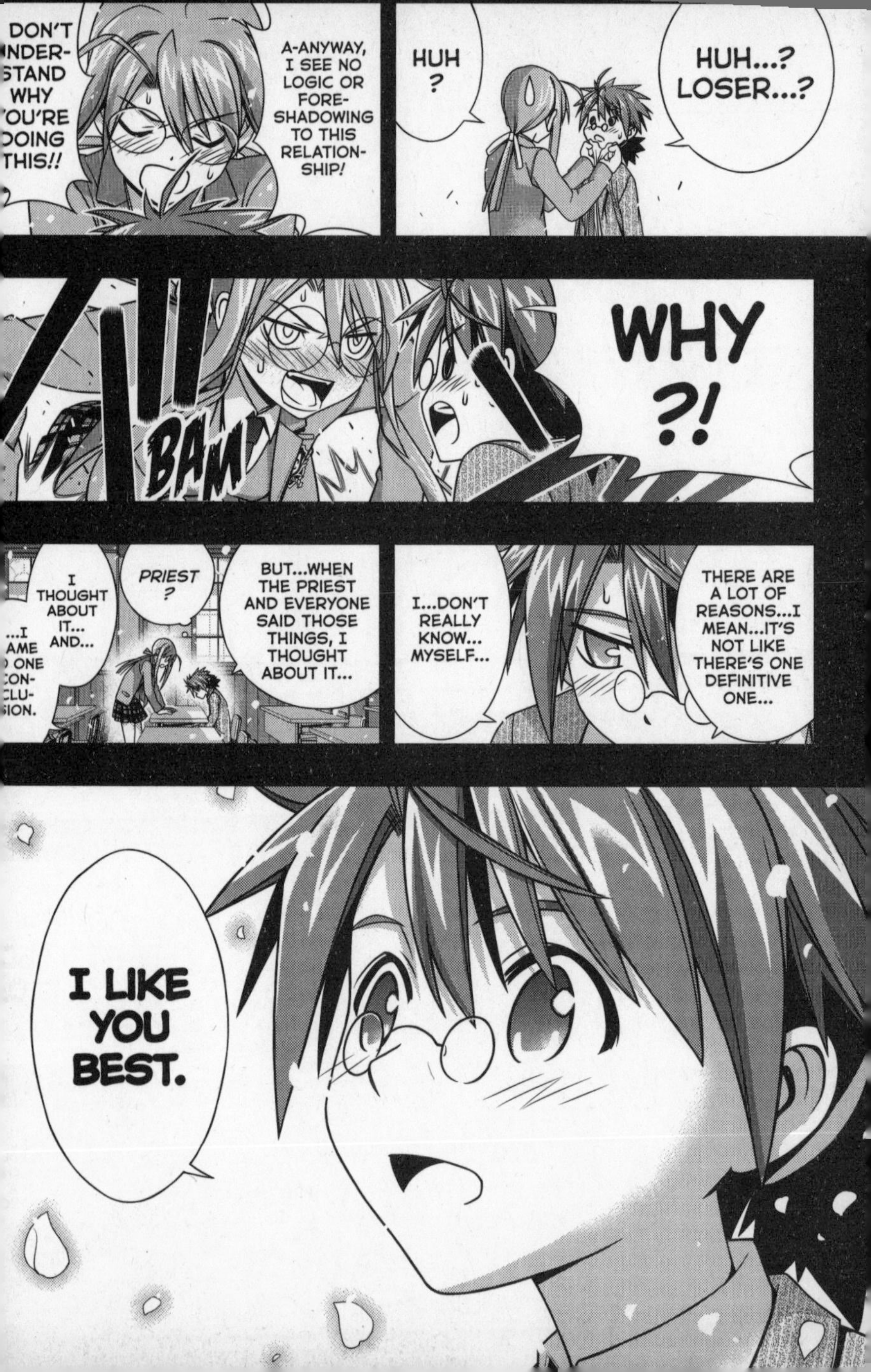
HUH...? LOSER...?
HUH ?
A-ANYWAY, I SEE NO LOGIC OR FORE-SHADOWING TO THIS RELATION-SHIP!
DON'T NDER-STAND WHY OU'RE OING THIS!!
WHY ?!
BAM
THERE ARE A LOT OF REASONS...I MEAN...IT'S NOT LIKE THERE'S ONE DEFINITIVE ONE...
I...DON'T REALLY KNOW... MYSELF...
BUT...WHEN THE PRIEST AND EVERYONE SAID THOSE THINGS, I THOUGHT ABOUT IT...
PRIEST ?
I THOUGHT ABOUT IT... AND...
...I AME ONE CON-CLU-ION.
I LIKE YOU BEST.

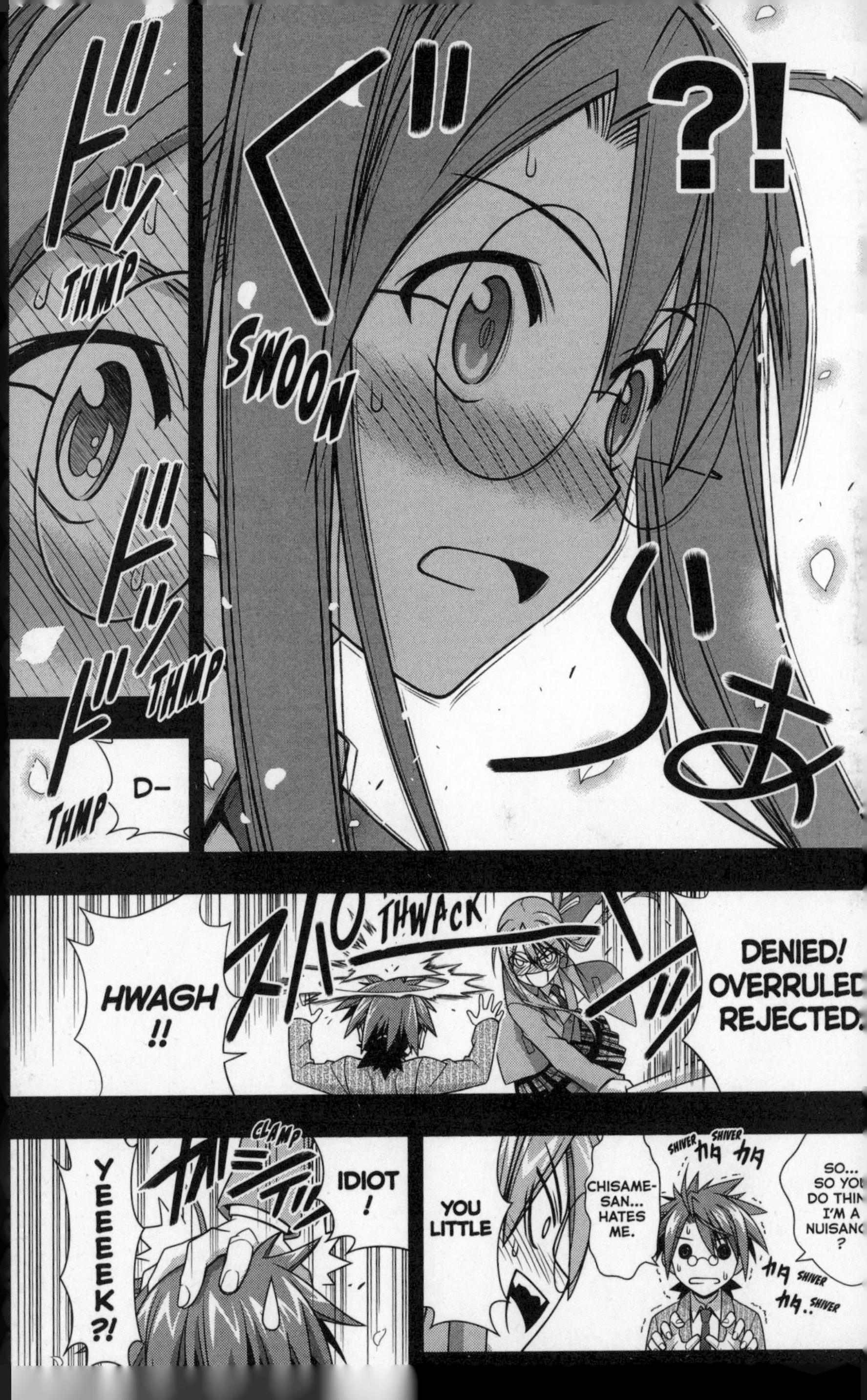
?!
SWOON
THMP
THMP
THMP
D-
DENIED! OVERRULED REJECTED.
THWACK
HWAGH!!
SO... SO YOU DO THIN I'M A NUISANC ?
SHIVER SHIVER
SHIVER SHIVER
CHISAME-SAN... HATES ME.
YOU LITTLE
IDIOT!
CLAMP
YEEEEK?!

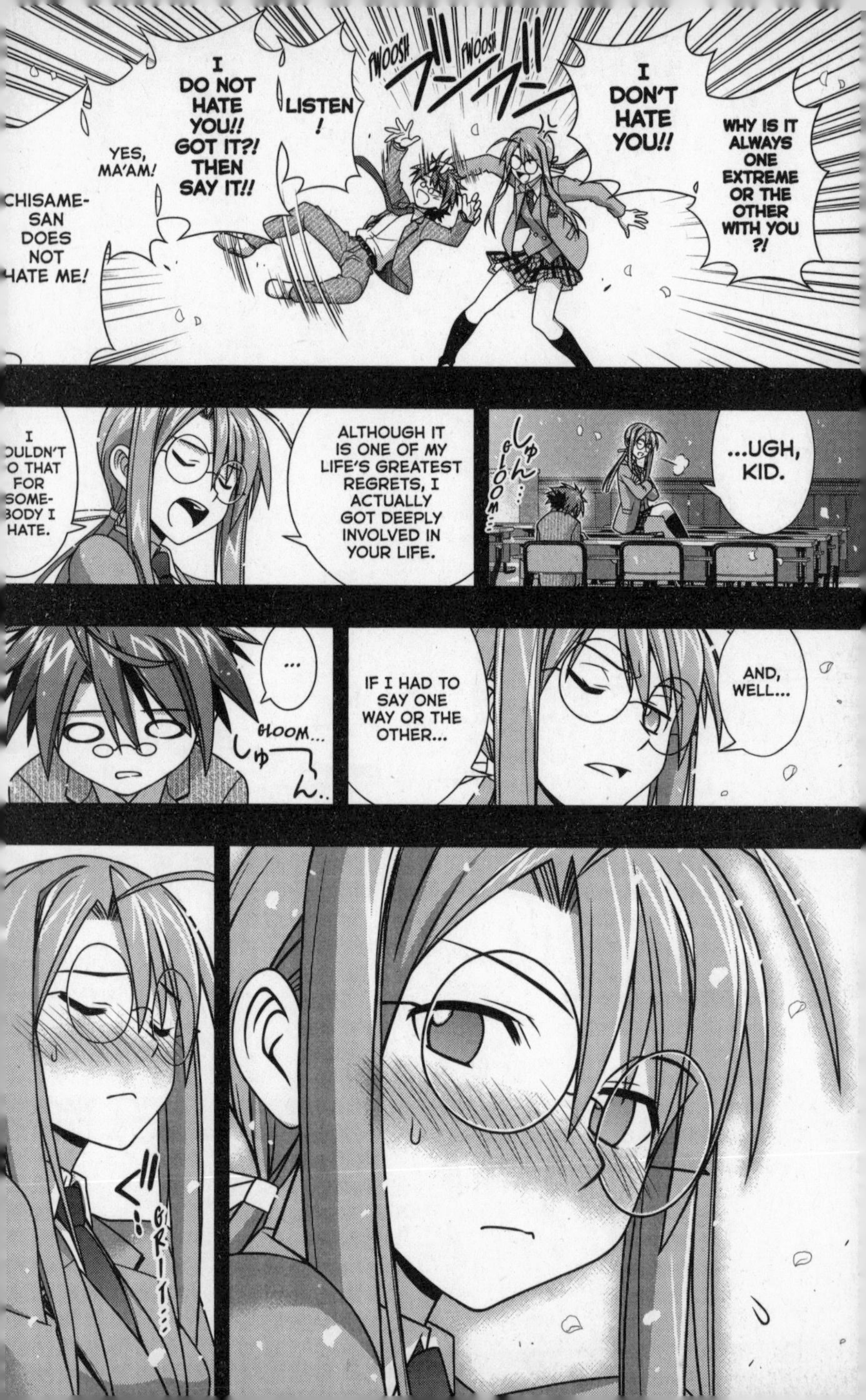
WHY IS IT ALWAYS ONE EXTREME OR THE OTHER WITH YOU?!
I DON'T HATE YOU!!
FWOOSH
FWOOSH
LISTEN!
I DO NOT HATE YOU!! GOT IT?! THEN SAY IT!!
YES, MA'AM!
CHISAME-SAN DOES NOT HATE ME!
...UGH, KID.
GLOOM...
ALTHOUGH IT IS ONE OF MY LIFE'S GREATEST REGRETS, I ACTUALLY GOT DEEPLY INVOLVED IN YOUR LIFE.
I OULDN'T O THAT FOR SOMEBODY I HATE.
AND, WELL...
IF I HAD TO SAY ONE WAY OR THE OTHER...
...
GLOOM...
GRIT...

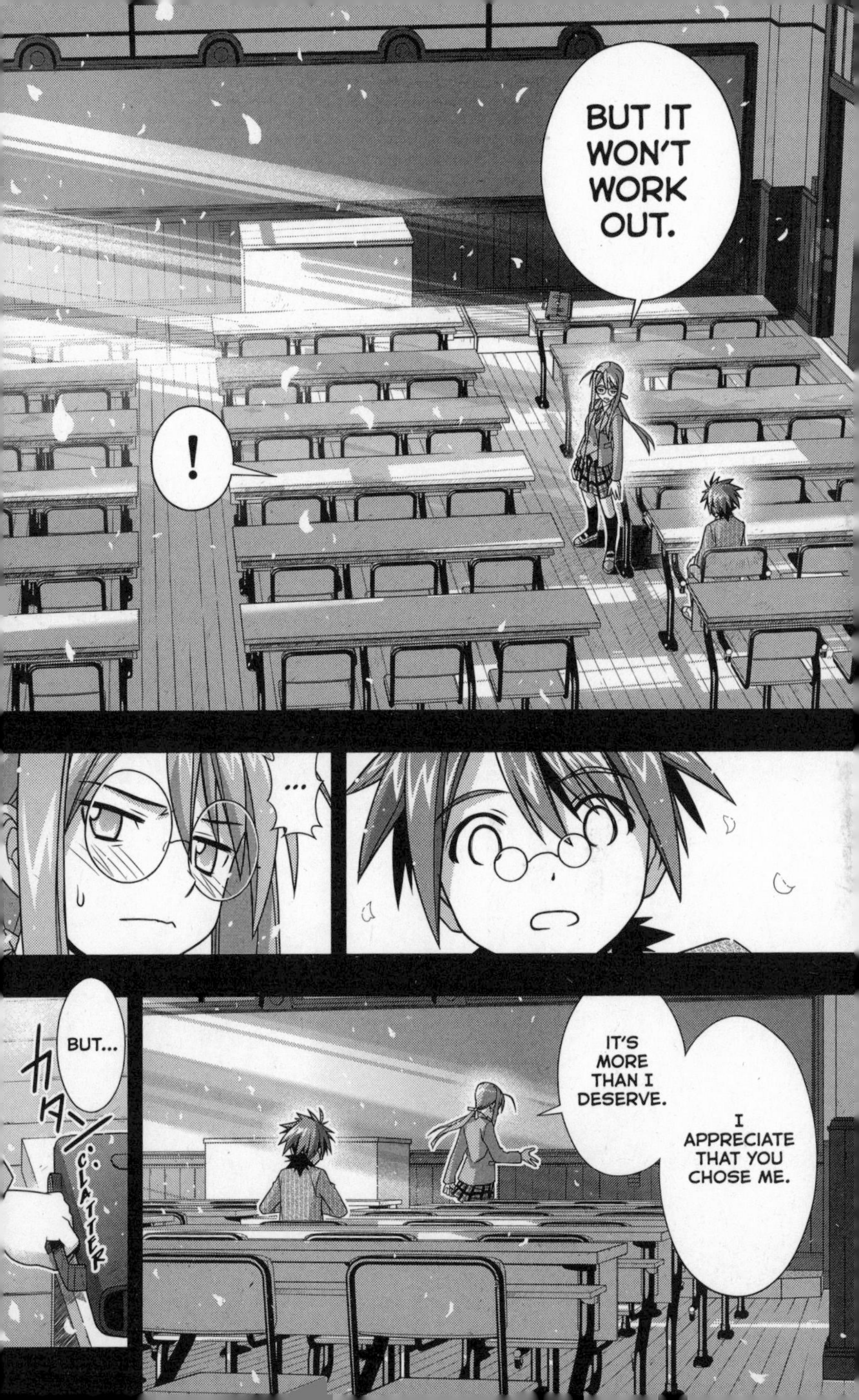
BUT IT WON'T WORK OUT.
!
...
IT'S MORE THAN I DESERVE.
I APPRECIATE THAT YOU CHOSE ME.
BUT...
カタン
CLATTER

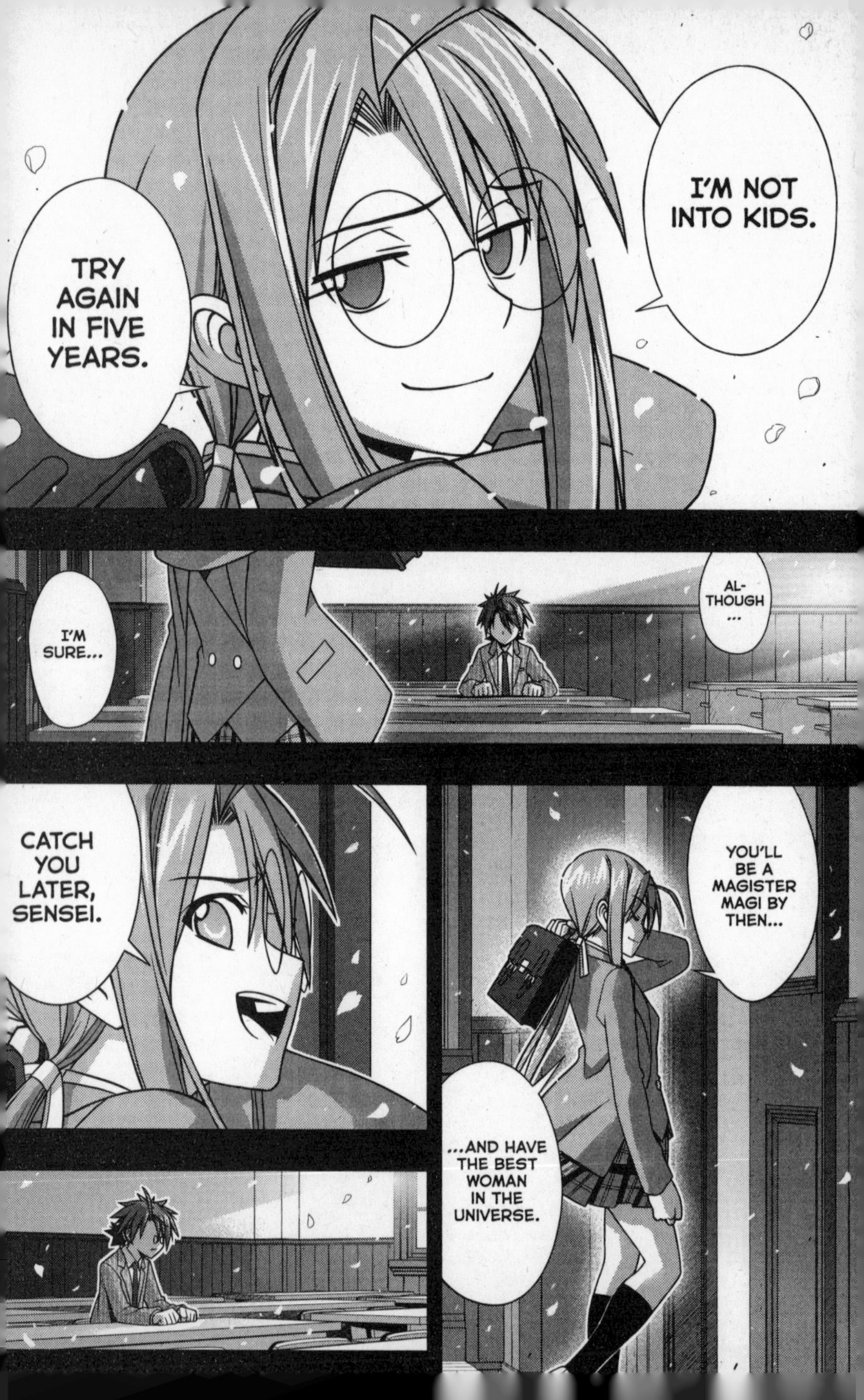
I'M NOT INTO KIDS.
TRY AGAIN IN FIVE YEARS.
ALTHOUGH...
I'M SURE...
YOU'LL BE A MAGISTER MAGI BY THEN...
...AND HAVE THE BEST WOMAN IN THE UNIVERSE.
CATCH YOU LATER, SENSEI.

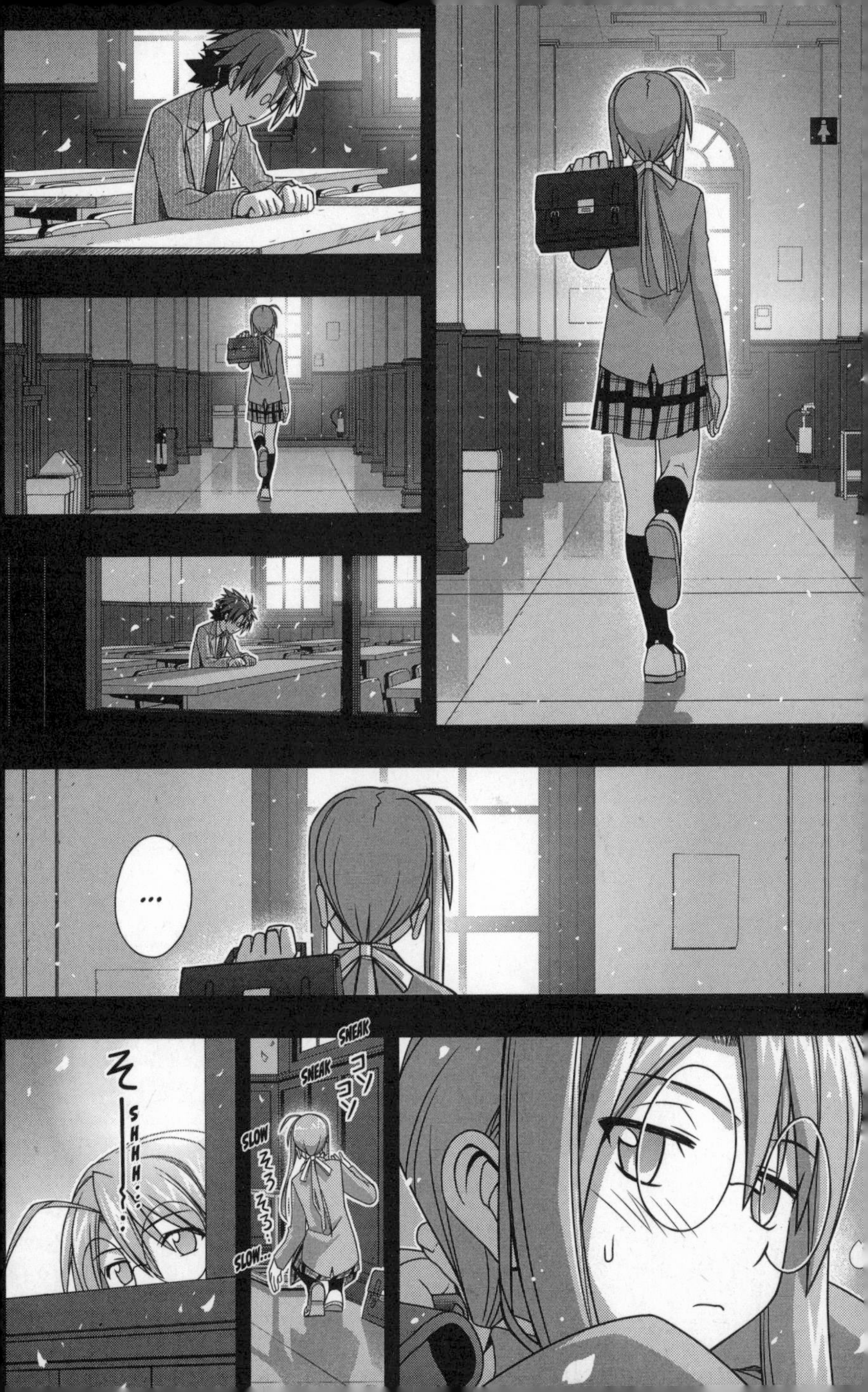
...
SNEAK
コソ コソ
SNEAK
SLOW
そろ そろ...
SLOW...
ス—
SHHH...

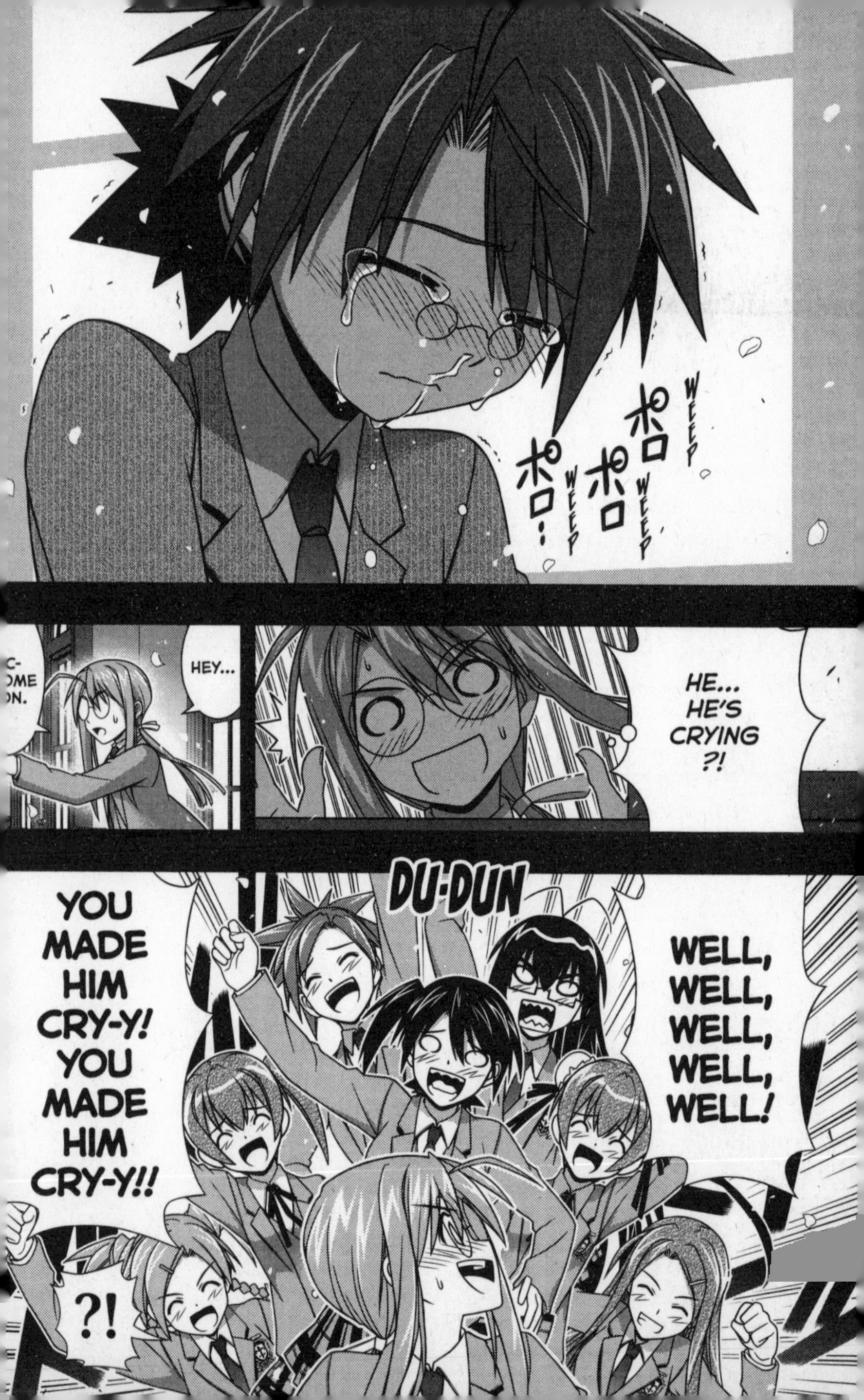
ポロ
WEEP
ポロ
WEEP
ポロ…
WEEP
HE... HE'S CRYING ?!
HEY...
C- OME ON.
DU-DUN
WELL, WELL, WELL, WELL, WELL!
YOU MADE HIM CRY-Y! YOU MADE HIM CRY-Y!!
?!

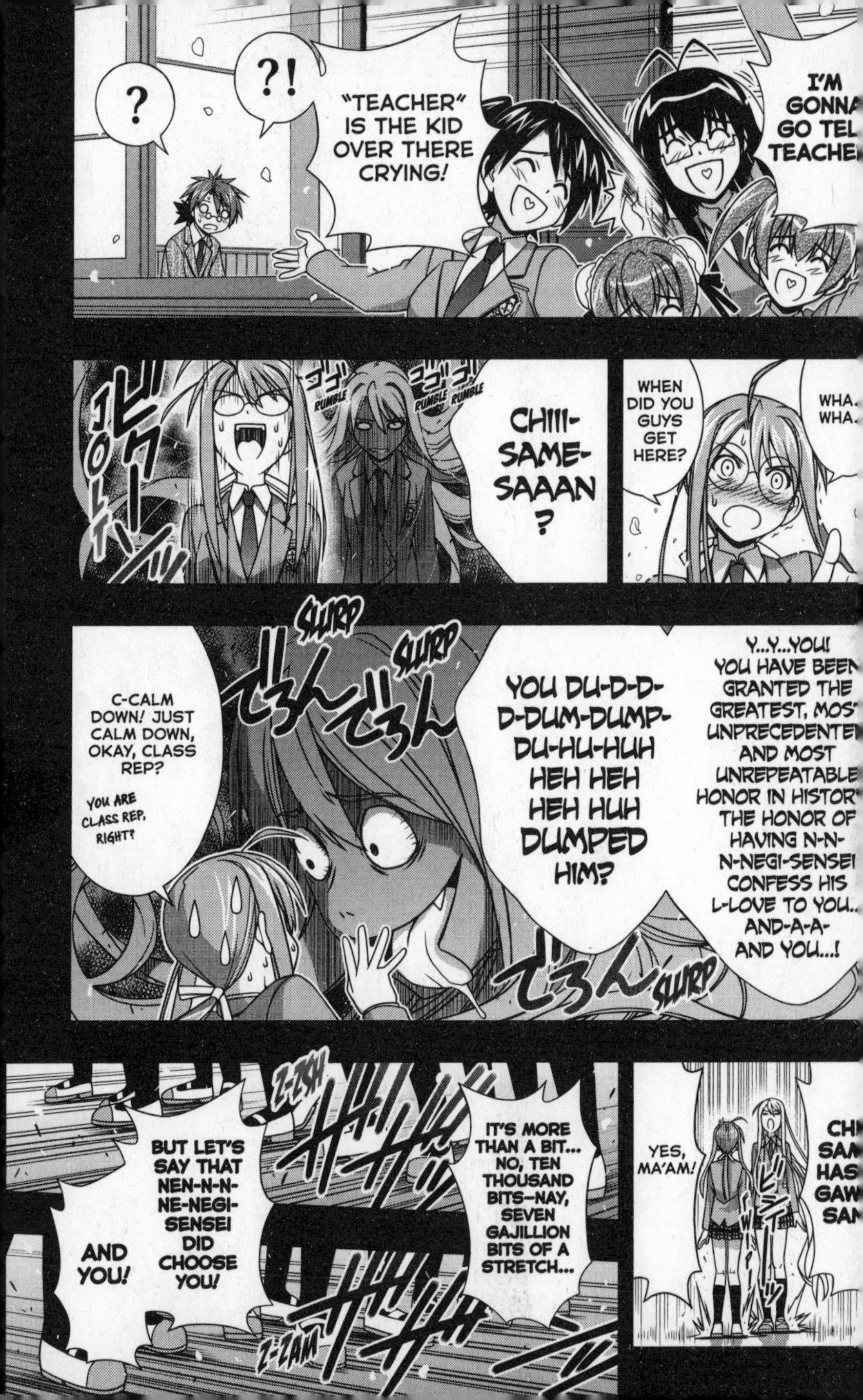
I'M GONNA GO TEL TEACHE
"TEACHER" IS THE KID OVER THERE CRYING!
?!
?
WHA.. WHA..
WHEN DID YOU GUYS GET HERE?
CHIIII-SAME-SAAAN?
RUMBLE
RUMBLE
RUMBLE
JOLT
Y...Y...YOU! YOU HAVE BEEN GRANTED THE GREATEST, MOST UNPRECEDENTE AND MOST UNREPEATABLE HONOR IN HISTOR THE HONOR OF HAVING N-N-N-NEGI-SENSEI CONFESS HIS L-LOVE TO YOU... AND-A-A-AND YOU...!
YOU DU-D-D-D-DUM-DUMP-DU-HU-HUH HEH HEH HEH HUH DUMPED HIM?
SLURP
SLURP
SLURP
C-CALM DOWN! JUST CALM DOWN, OKAY, CLASS REP?
YOU ARE CLASS REP, RIGHT?
CH SAM HAS GAW SAN
YES, MA'AM!
WHIP
IT'S MORE THAN A BIT... NO, TEN THOUSAND BITS--NAY, SEVEN GAJILLION BITS OF A STRETCH...
BUT LET'S SAY THAT NEN-N-N-NE-NEGI-SENSEI DID CHOOSE YOU!
AND YOU!
Z-ZSH
Z-ZAM

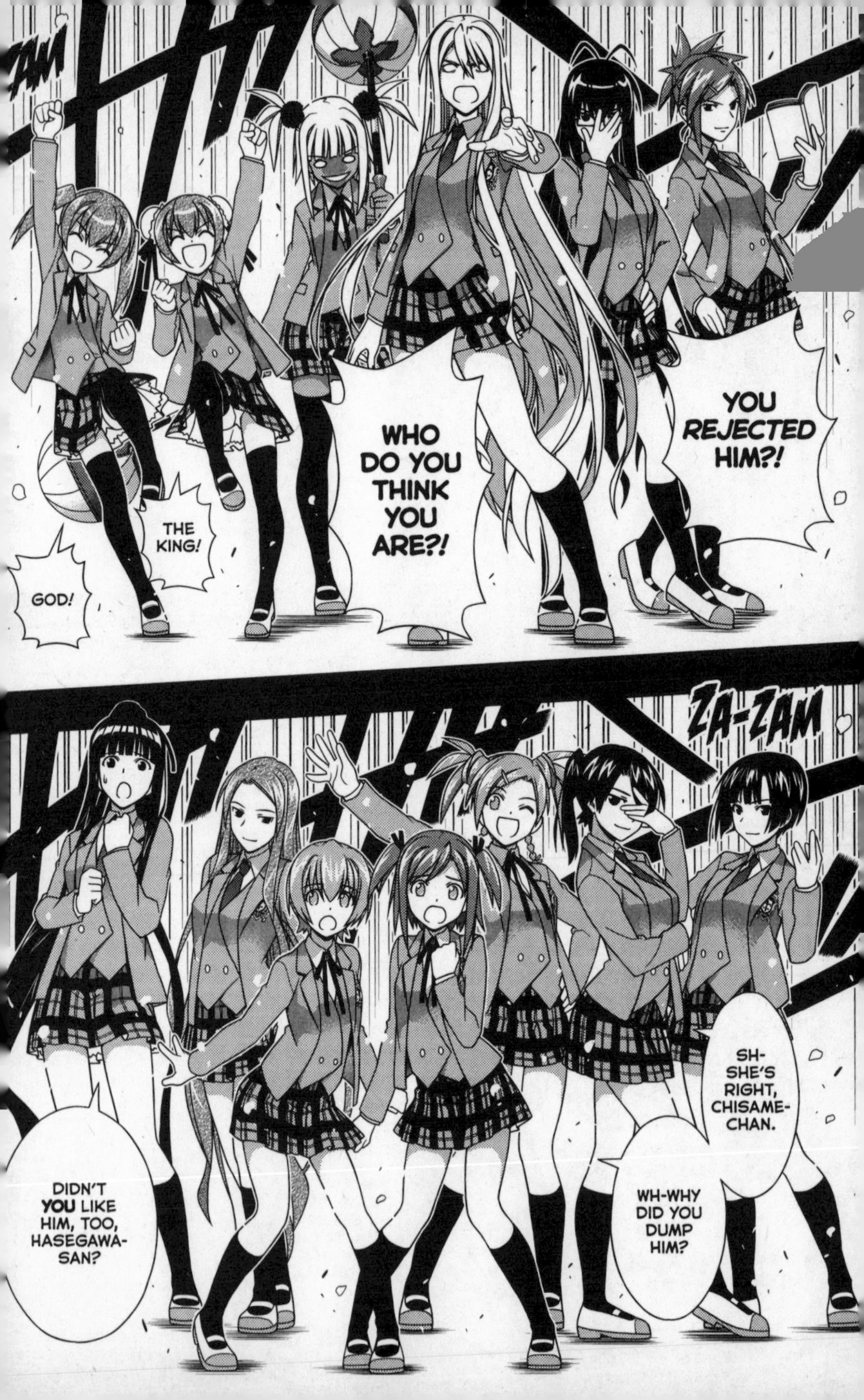
YOU REJECTED HIM?!
WHO DO YOU THINK YOU ARE?!
THE KING!
GOD!
ZAM
ZA-ZAM
SH-SHE'S RIGHT, CHISAME-CHAN.
WH-WHY DID YOU DUMP HIM?
DIDN'T **YOU** LIKE HIM, TOO, HASEGAWA-SAN?

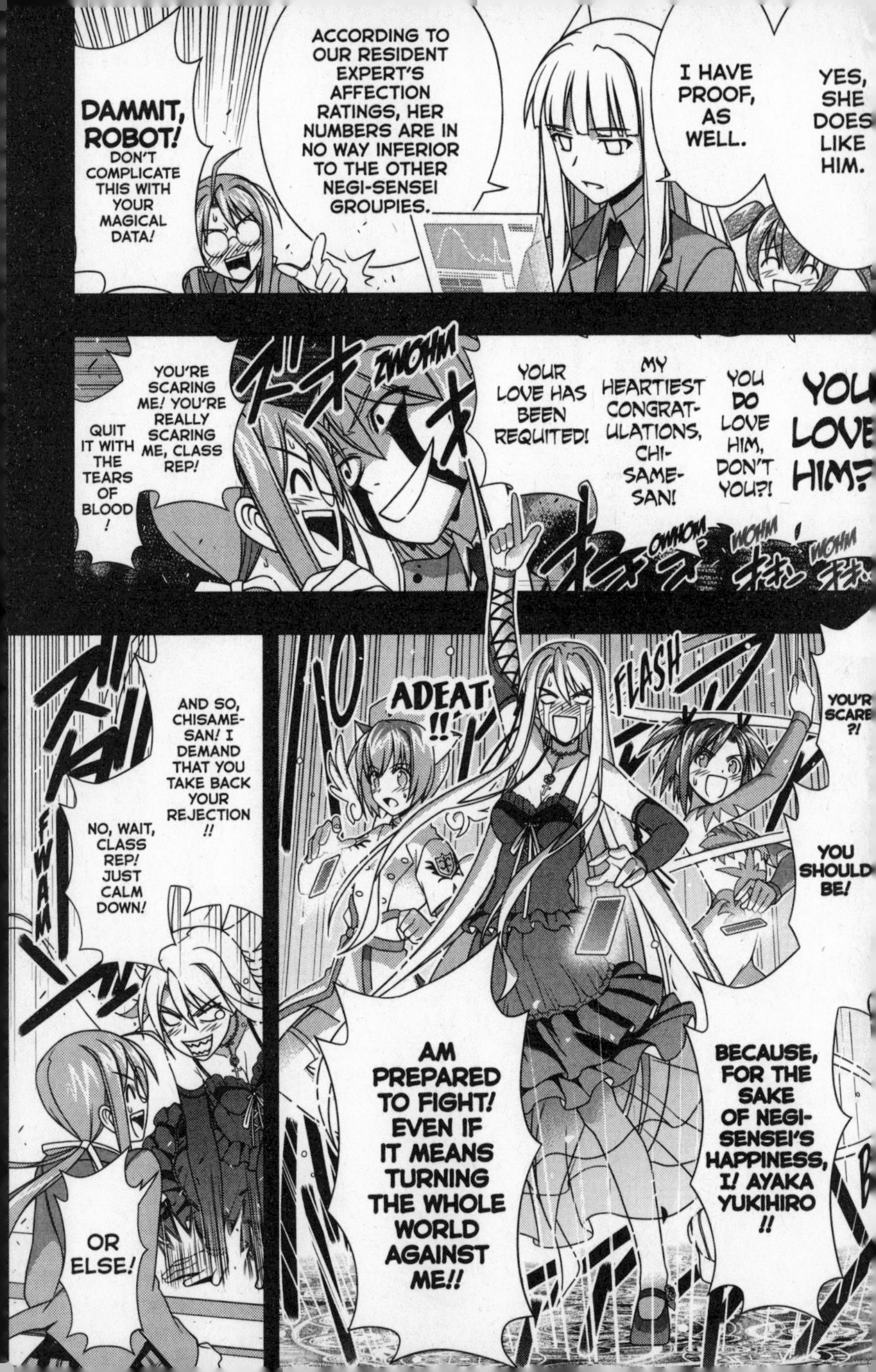
YES, SHE DOES LIKE HIM.
I HAVE PROOF, AS WELL.
ACCORDING TO OUR RESIDENT EXPERT'S AFFECTION RATINGS, HER NUMBERS ARE IN NO WAY INFERIOR TO THE OTHER NEGI-SENSEI GROUPIES.
DAMMIT, ROBOT! DON'T COMPLICATE THIS WITH YOUR MAGICAL DATA!
YOU LOVE HIM?
YOU DO LOVE HIM, DON'T YOU?!
MY HEARTIEST CONGRAT-ULATIONS, CHI-SAME-SAN!
YOUR LOVE HAS BEEN REQUITED!
ZWOHM
YOU'RE SCARING ME! YOU'RE REALLY SCARING ME, CLASS REP!
QUIT IT WITH THE TEARS OF BLOOD!
WOHM
WOHM
OWHOM
YOU SHOULD BE!
FLASH
ADEAT!!
BECAUSE, FOR THE SAKE OF NEGI-SENSEI'S HAPPINESS, I! AYAKA YUKIHIRO!!
AM PREPARED TO FIGHT! EVEN IF IT MEANS TURNING THE WHOLE WORLD AGAINST ME!!
AND SO, CHISAME-SAN! I DEMAND THAT YOU TAKE BACK YOUR REJECTION!!
NO, WAIT, CLASS REP! JUST CALM DOWN!
FWAM
OR ELSE!

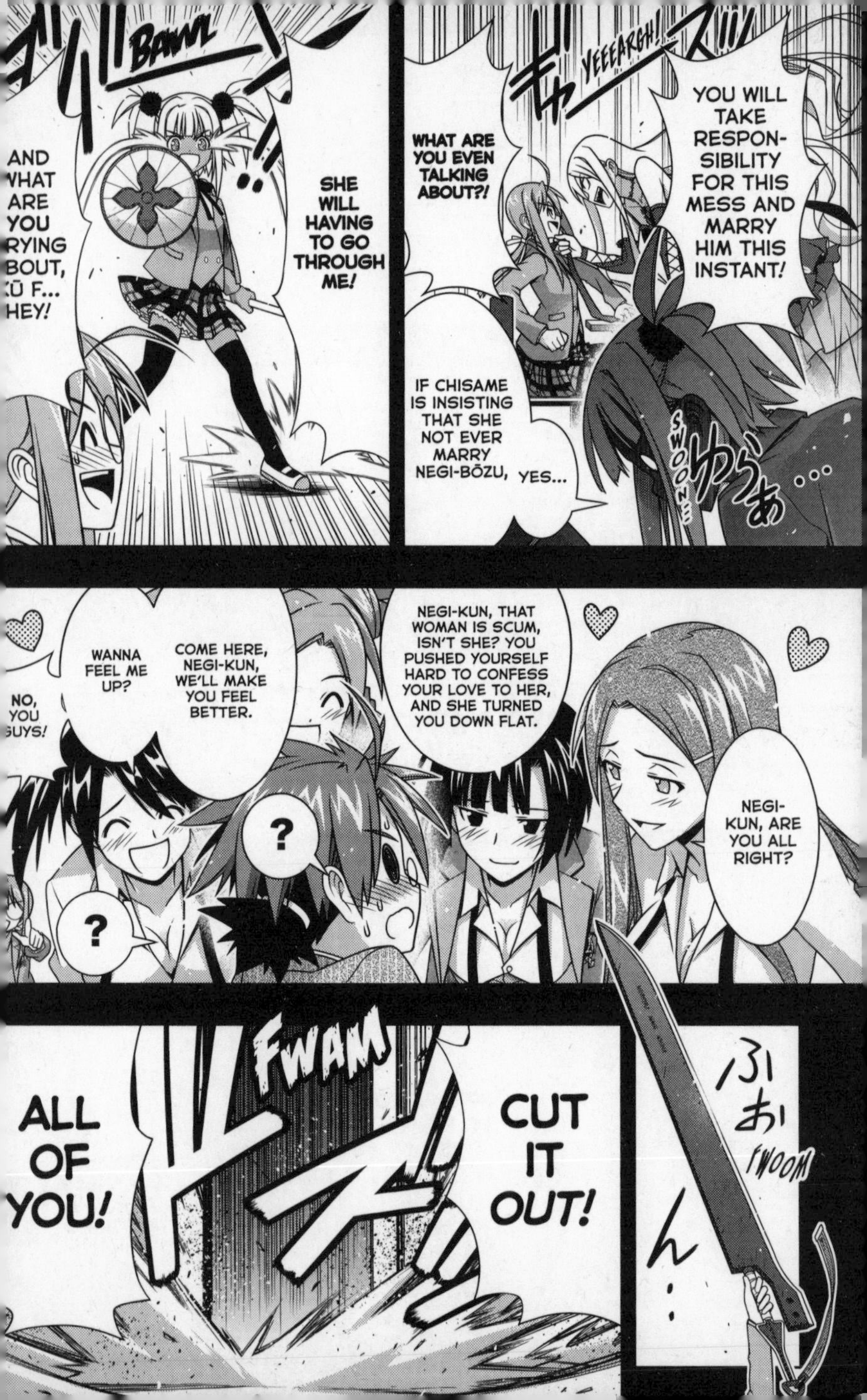
YEEEARGH!!
YOU WILL TAKE RESPON-SIBILITY FOR THIS MESS AND MARRY HIM THIS INSTANT!
WHAT ARE YOU EVEN TALKING ABOUT?!
IF CHISAME IS INSISTING THAT SHE NOT EVER MARRY NEGI-BŌZU, YES...
SWOON
ゆらぁ...
BAWI
SHE WILL HAVING TO GO THROUGH ME!
AND WHAT ARE YOU RYING BOUT, Ū F... HEY!
NEGI-KUN, ARE YOU ALL RIGHT?
NEGI-KUN, THAT WOMAN IS SCUM, ISN'T SHE? YOU PUSHED YOURSELF HARD TO CONFESS YOUR LOVE TO HER, AND SHE TURNED YOU DOWN FLAT.
COME HERE, NEGI-KUN, WE'LL MAKE YOU FEEL BETTER.
WANNA FEEL ME UP?
NO, YOU UYS!
?
?
ふぉん..
FWOOM
FWAM
CUT IT OUT!
ALL OF YOU!

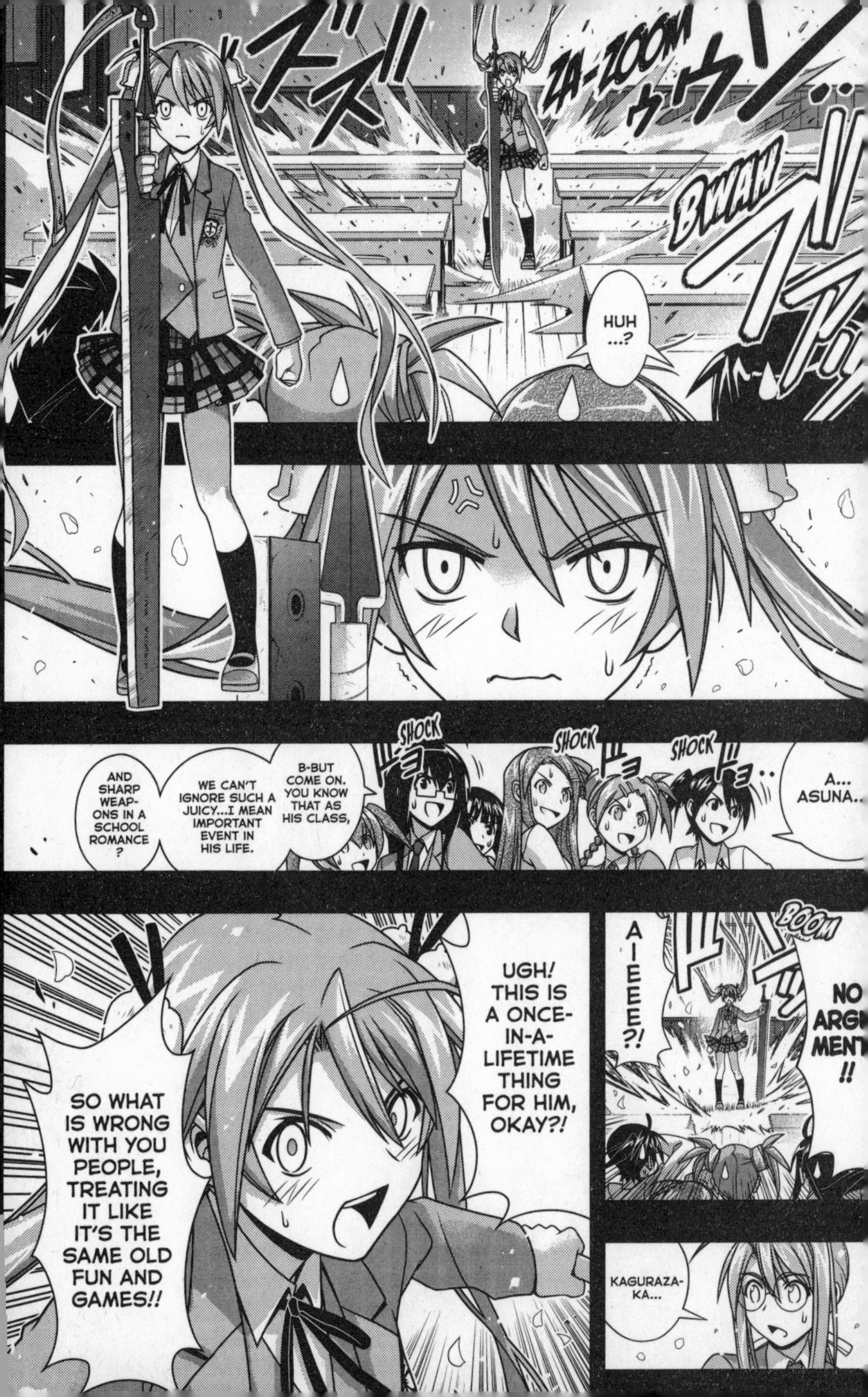
ZA-ZOOM
BWAH
HUH ...?
A... ASUNA..
SHOCK
SHOCK
SHOCK
B-BUT COME ON. YOU KNOW THAT AS HIS CLASS,
WE CAN'T IGNORE SUCH A JUICY...I MEAN IMPORTANT EVENT IN HIS LIFE.
AND SHARP WEAP-ONS IN A SCHOOL ROMANCE ?
BOOM
NO ARGU MENT !!
AIEEE?!
KAGURAZA-KA...
UGH! THIS IS A ONCE-IN-A-LIFETIME THING FOR HIM, OKAY?!
SO WHAT IS WRONG WITH YOU PEOPLE, TREATING IT LIKE IT'S THE SAME OLD FUN AND GAMES!!

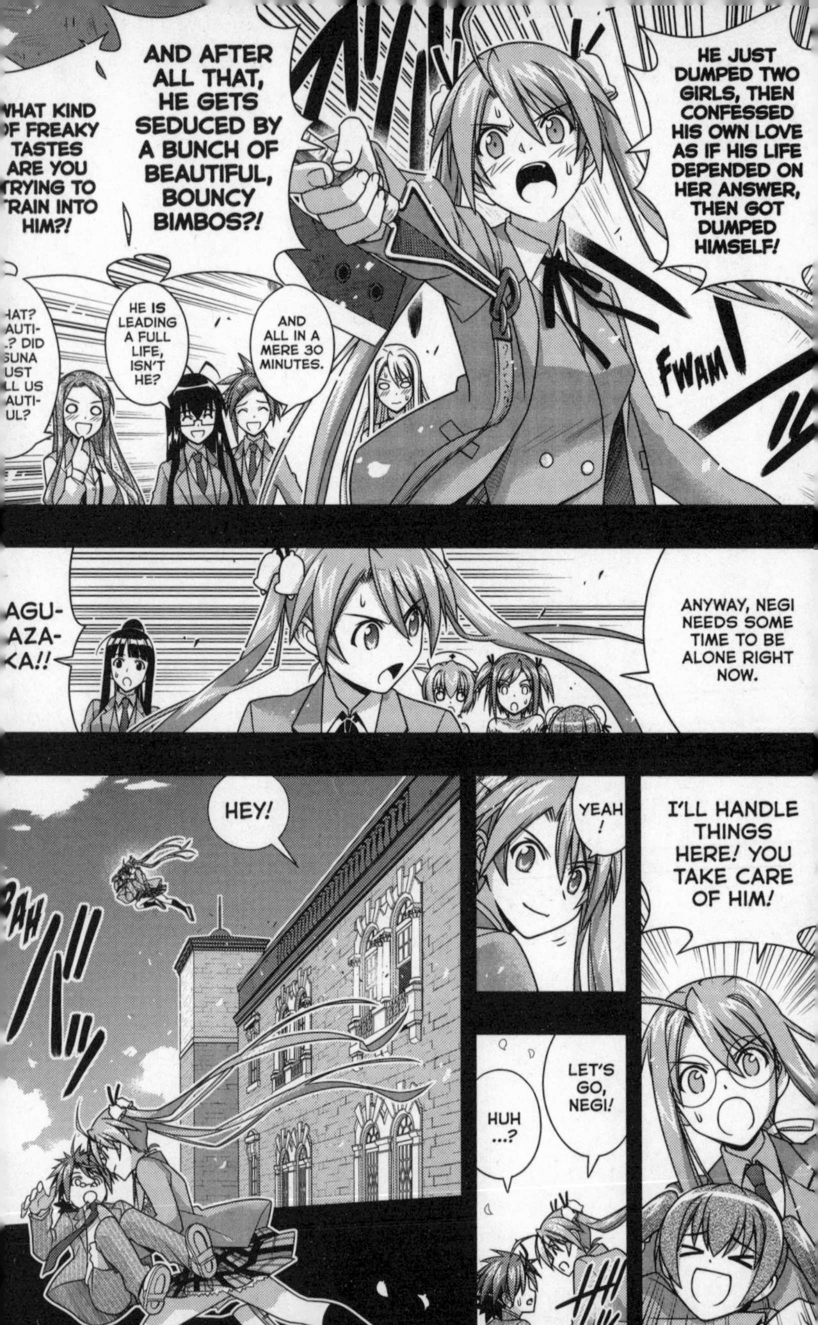
HE JUST DUMPED TWO GIRLS, THEN CONFESSED HIS OWN LOVE AS IF HIS LIFE DEPENDED ON HER ANSWER, THEN GOT DUMPED HIMSELF!
AND AFTER ALL THAT, HE GETS SEDUCED BY A BUNCH OF BEAUTIFUL, BOUNCY BIMBOS?!
WHAT KIND OF FREAKY TASTES ARE YOU TRYING TO TRAIN INTO HIM?!
FWAM
AND ALL IN A MERE 30 MINUTES.
HE IS LEADING A FULL LIFE, ISN'T HE?
HAT? AUTI- ..? DID SUNA UST LL US AUTI- UL?
ANYWAY, NEGI NEEDS SOME TIME TO BE ALONE RIGHT NOW.
AGU- AZA- KA!!
I'LL HANDLE THINGS HERE! YOU TAKE CARE OF HIM!
YEAH!
LET'S GO, NEGI!
HUH ...?
HEY!

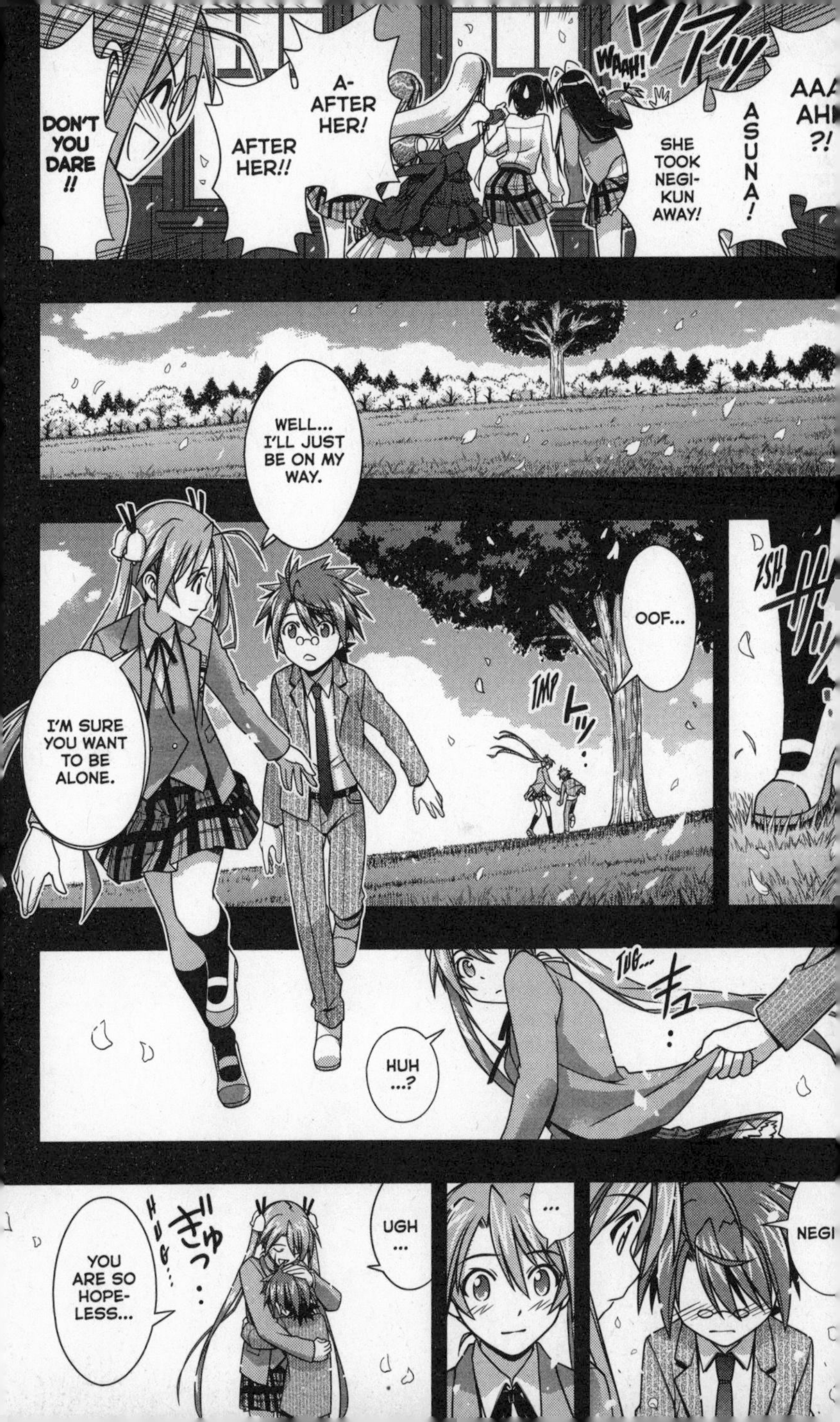
AAA AH ?!
ASUNA!
SHE TOOK NEGI-KUN AWAY!
WAAAH!
A- AFTER HER!
AFTER HER!!
DON'T YOU DARE!!
WELL... I'LL JUST BE ON MY WAY.
ZSH
OOF...
TMP
I'M SURE YOU WANT TO BE ALONE.
TUG...
HUH ...?
NEGI
...
UGH ...
HUG...
YOU ARE SO HOPE-LESS...

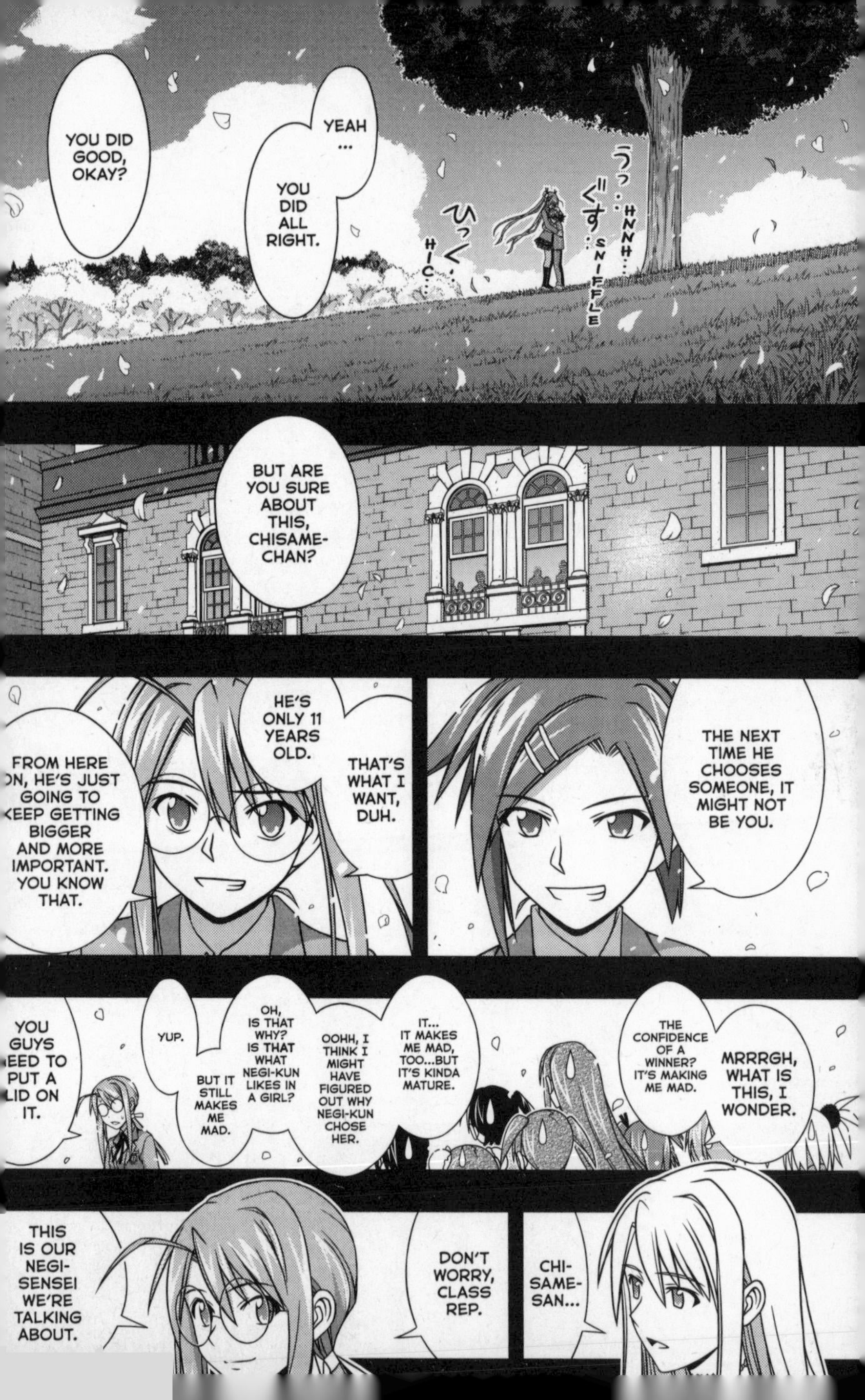
うっ.. HNNH...
ぐすっ SNIFFLE
ひっく HIC...
YEAH... YOU DID ALL RIGHT.
YOU DID GOOD, OKAY?
BUT ARE YOU SURE ABOUT THIS, CHISAME-CHAN?
THE NEXT TIME HE CHOOSES SOMEONE, IT MIGHT NOT BE YOU.
THAT'S WHAT I WANT, DUH.
HE'S ONLY 11 YEARS OLD.
FROM HERE ON, HE'S JUST GOING TO KEEP GETTING BIGGER AND MORE IMPORTANT. YOU KNOW THAT.
MRRRGH, WHAT IS THIS, I WONDER.
THE CONFIDENCE OF A WINNER? IT'S MAKING ME MAD.
IT... IT MAKES ME MAD, TOO...BUT IT'S KINDA MATURE.
OOHH, I THINK I MIGHT HAVE FIGURED OUT WHY NEGI-KUN CHOSE HER.
OH, IS THAT WHY? IS THAT WHAT NEGI-KUN LIKES IN A GIRL?
YUP.
BUT IT STILL MAKES ME MAD.
YOU GUYS NEED TO PUT A LID ON IT.
CHI-SAME-SAN...
DON'T WORRY, CLASS REP.
THIS IS OUR NEGI-SENSEI WE'RE TALKING ABOUT.

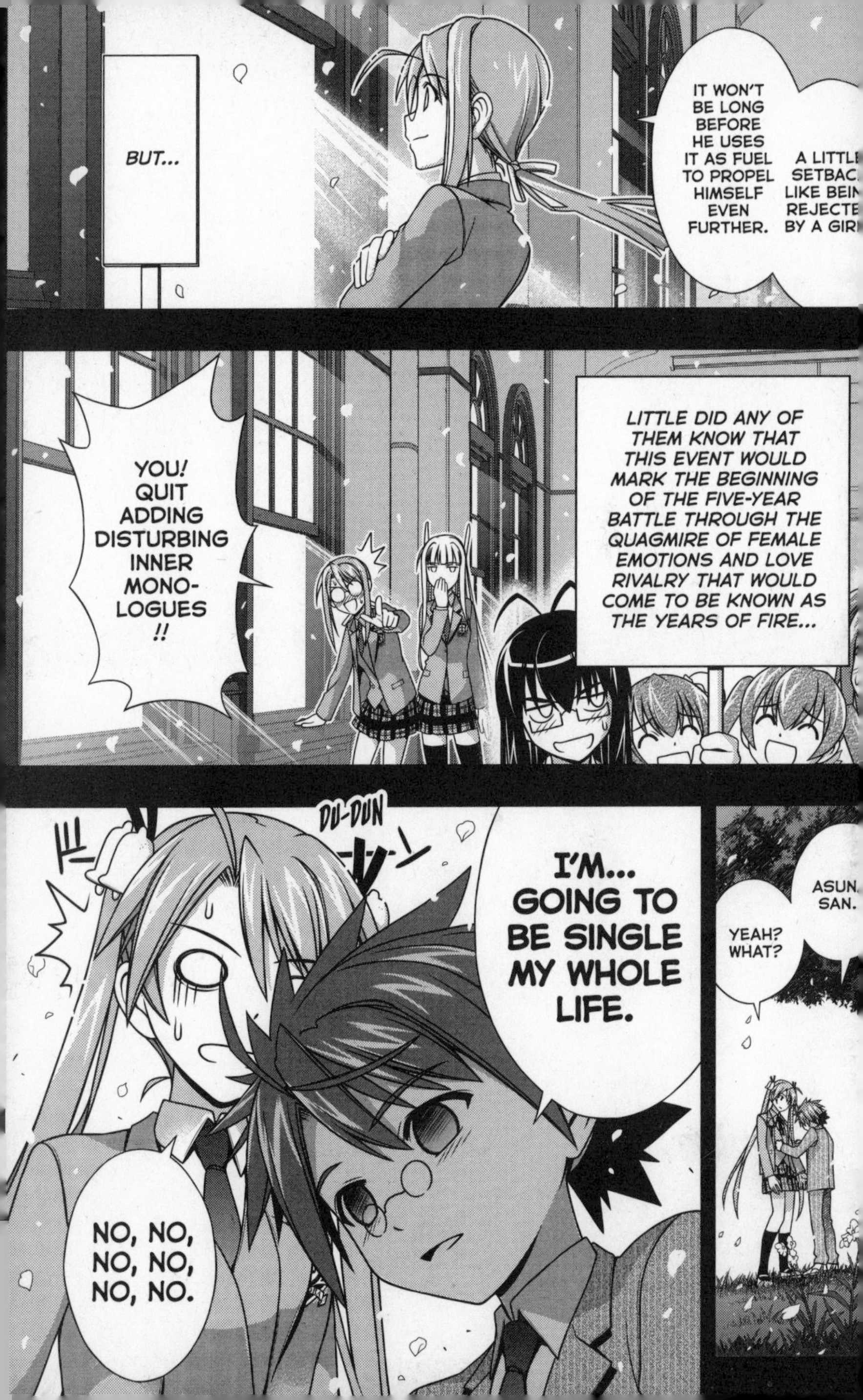
A LITTL SETBAC LIKE BEIN REJECTE BY A GIR
IT WON'T BE LONG BEFORE HE USES IT AS FUEL TO PROPEL HIMSELF EVEN FURTHER.
BUT...
LITTLE DID ANY OF THEM KNOW THAT THIS EVENT WOULD MARK THE BEGINNING OF THE FIVE-YEAR BATTLE THROUGH THE QUAGMIRE OF FEMALE EMOTIONS AND LOVE RIVALRY THAT WOULD COME TO BE KNOWN AS THE YEARS OF FIRE...
YOU! QUIT ADDING DISTURBING INNER MONO-LOGUES !!
ASUN SAN.
YEAH? WHAT?
I'M... GOING TO BE SINGLE MY WHOLE LIFE.
DU-DUN
NO, NO, NO, NO, NO, NO.

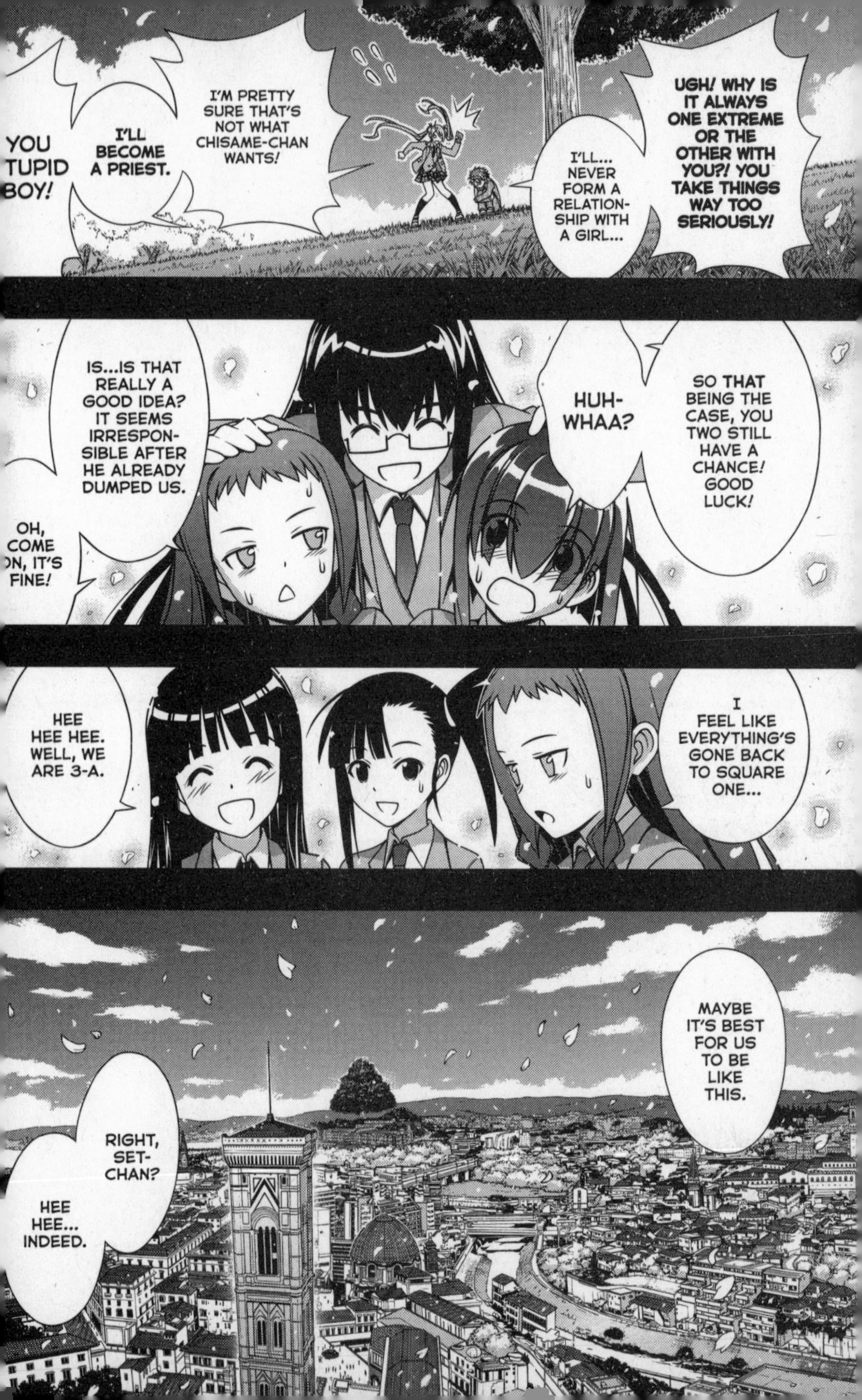

UGH! WHY IS IT ALWAYS ONE EXTREME OR THE OTHER WITH YOU?! YOU TAKE THINGS WAY TOO SERIOUSLY!
I'LL... NEVER FORM A RELATIONSHIP WITH A GIRL...
I'M PRETTY SURE THAT'S NOT WHAT CHISAME-CHAN WANTS!
I'LL BECOME A PRIEST.
YOU TUPID BOY!
SO THAT BEING THE CASE, YOU TWO STILL HAVE A CHANCE! GOOD LUCK!
HUH-WHAA?
IS...IS THAT REALLY A GOOD IDEA? IT SEEMS IRRESPONSIBLE AFTER HE ALREADY DUMPED US.
OH, COME ON, IT'S FINE!
I FEEL LIKE EVERYTHING'S GONE BACK TO SQUARE ONE...
HEE HEE HEE. WELL, WE ARE 3-A.
MAYBE IT'S BEST FOR US TO BE LIKE THIS.
RIGHT, SET-CHAN?
HEE HEE... INDEED.

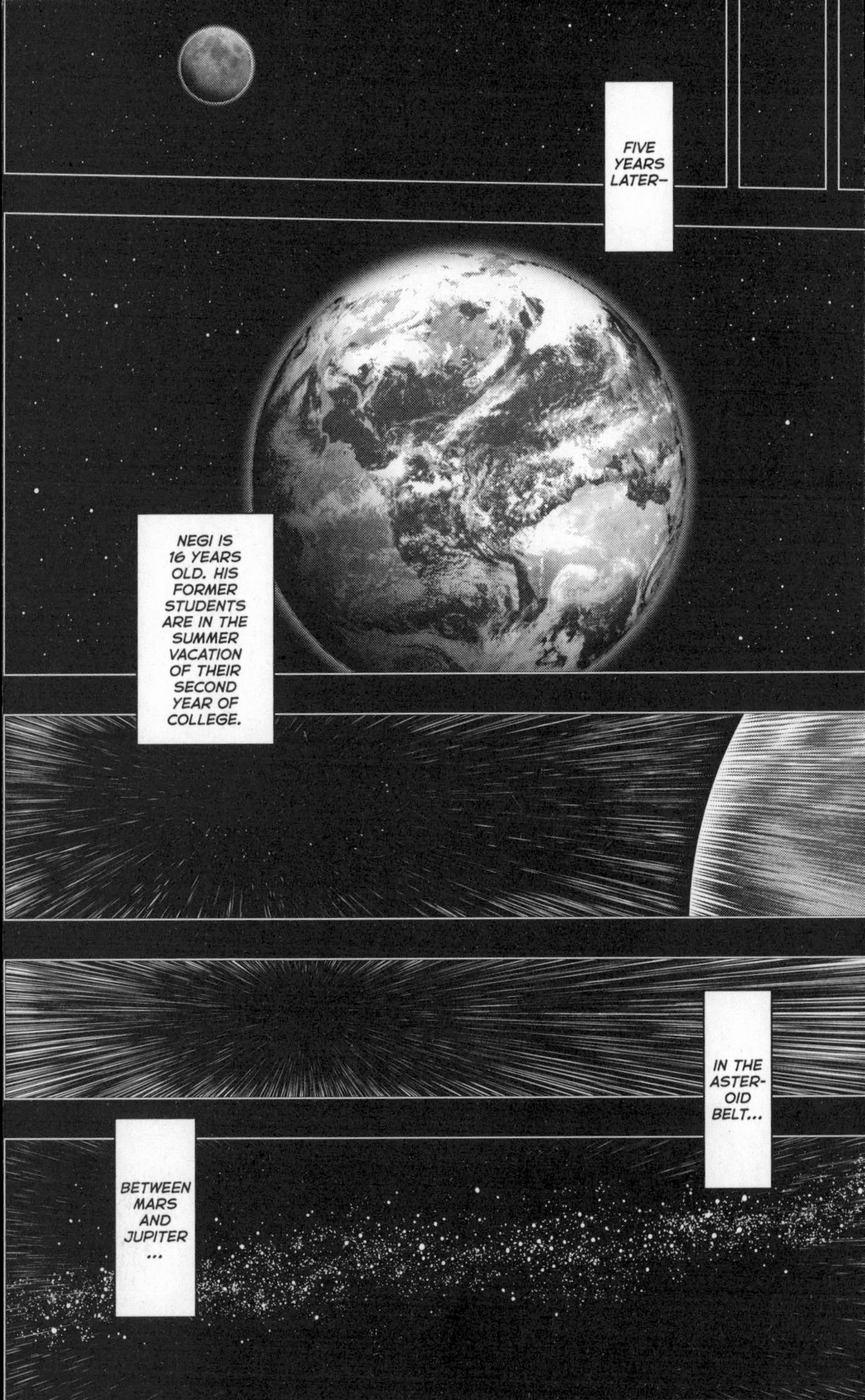
FIVE YEARS LATER–
NEGI IS 16 YEARS OLD. HIS FORMER STUDENTS ARE IN THE SUMMER VACATION OF THEIR SECOND YEAR OF COLLEGE.
IN THE ASTER-OID BELT...
BETWEEN MARS AND JUPITER ...

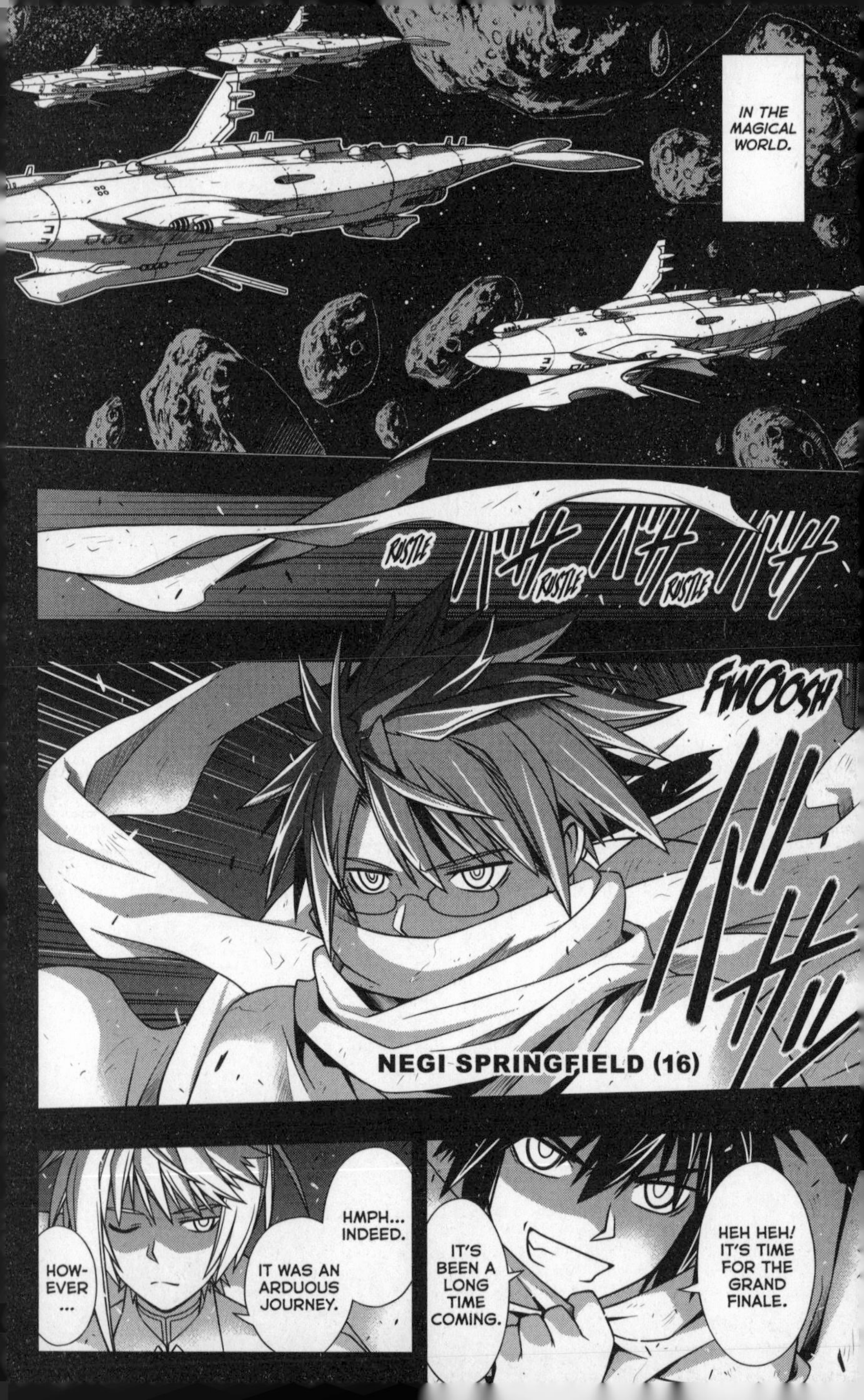
IN THE MAGICAL WORLD.
RUSTLE
RUSTLE
RUSTLE
FWOOSH
NEGI SPRINGFIELD (16)
HEH HEH! IT'S TIME FOR THE GRAND FINALE.
IT'S BEEN A LONG TIME COMING.
HMPH... INDEED.
IT WAS AN ARDUOUS JOURNEY.
HOW-EVER...

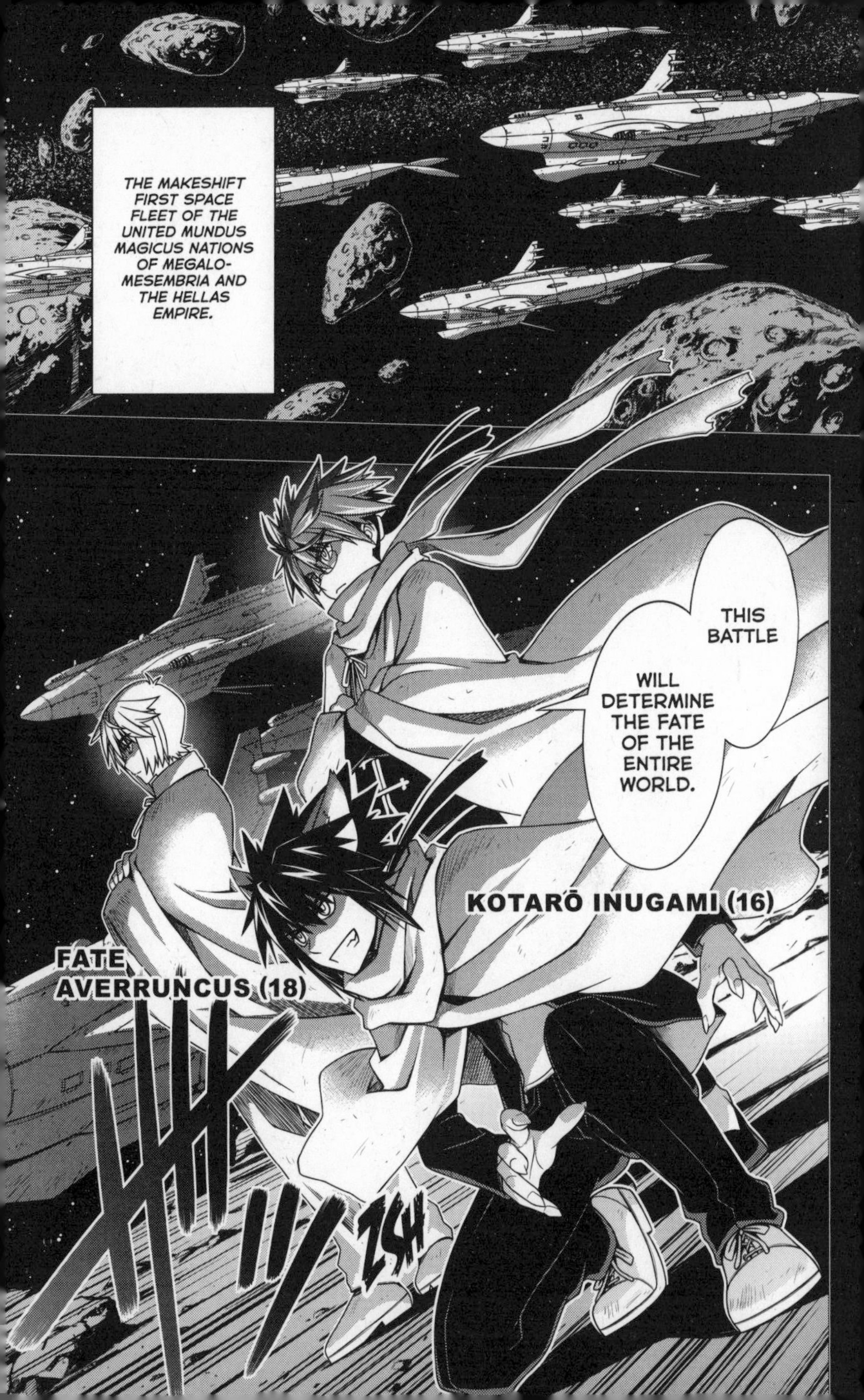
THE MAKESHIFT FIRST SPACE FLEET OF THE UNITED MUNDUS MAGICUS NATIONS OF MEGALO-MESEMBRIA AND THE HELLAS EMPIRE.
THIS BATTLE
WILL DETERMINE THE FATE OF THE ENTIRE WORLD.
KOTARŌ INUGAMI (16)
FATE AVERRUNCUS (18)
ZSH

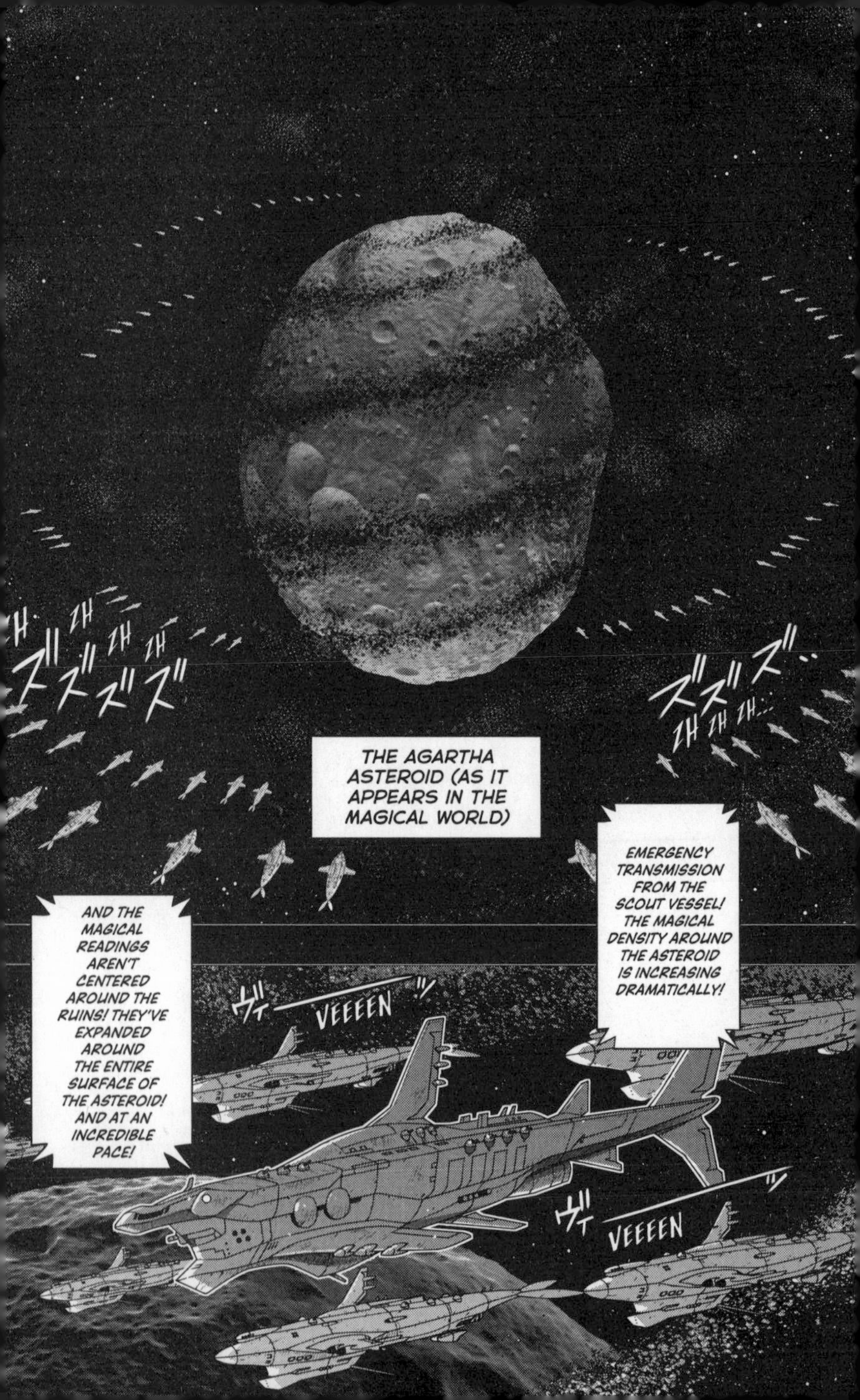

ZH ZH ZH...
ZH ZH ZH ZH
THE AGARTHA ASTEROID (AS IT APPEARS IN THE MAGICAL WORLD)
EMERGENCY TRANSMISSION FROM THE SCOUT VESSEL! THE MAGICAL DENSITY AROUND THE ASTEROID IS INCREASING DRAMATICALLY!
AND THE MAGICAL READINGS AREN'T CENTERED AROUND THE RUINS! THEY'VE EXPANDED AROUND THE ENTIRE SURFACE OF THE ASTEROID! AND AT AN INCREDIBLE PACE!
VEEEEN
VEEEEN

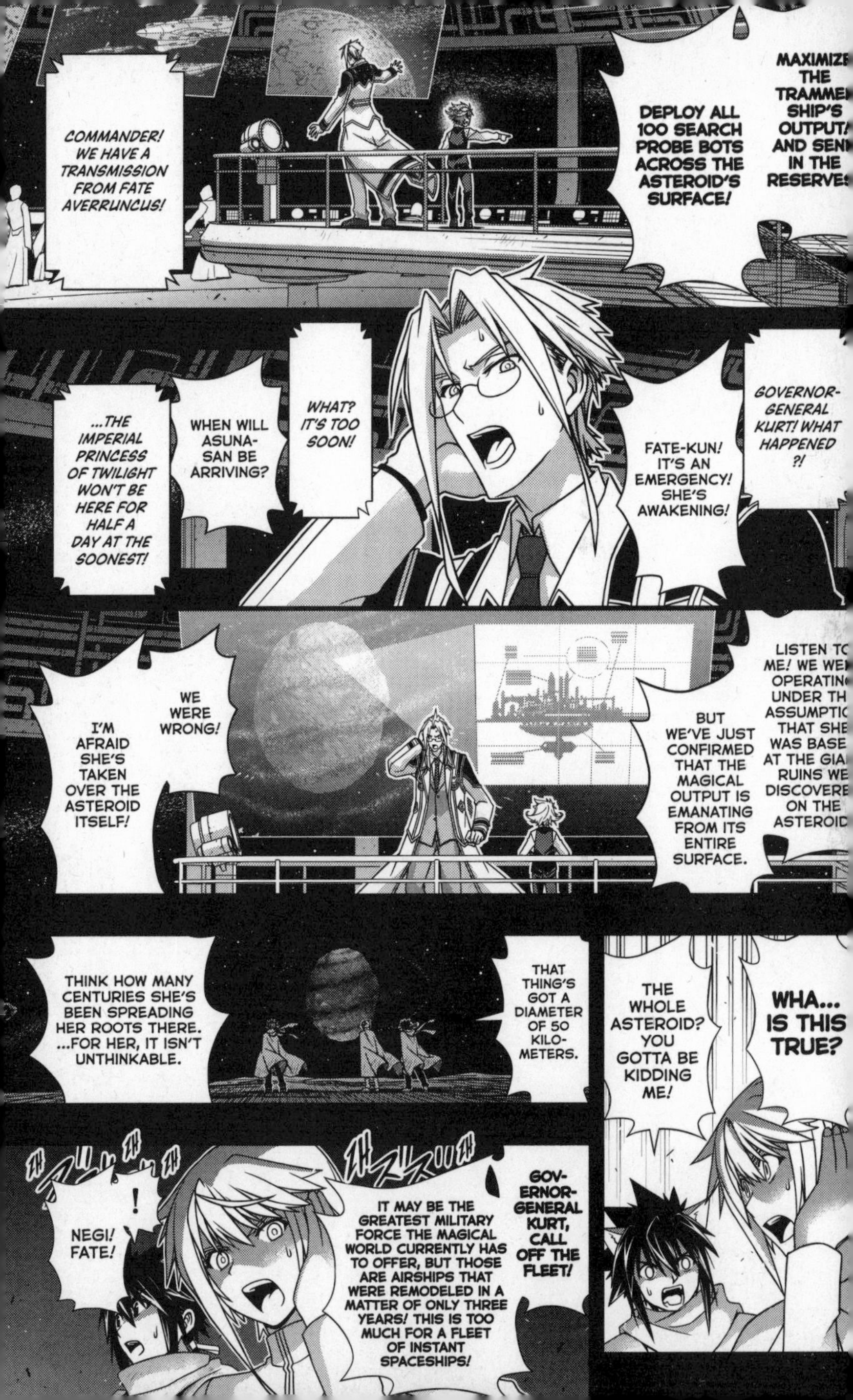
MAXIMIZE THE TRAMME SHIP'S OUTPU AND SEN IN THE RESERVES
DEPLOY ALL 100 SEARCH PROBE BOTS ACROSS THE ASTEROID'S SURFACE!
COMMANDER! WE HAVE A TRANSMISSION FROM FATE AVERRUNCUS!
GOVERNOR-GENERAL KURT! WHAT HAPPENED ?!
FATE-KUN! IT'S AN EMERGENCY! SHE'S AWAKENING!
WHAT? IT'S TOO SOON!
WHEN WILL ASUNA-SAN BE ARRIVING?
...THE IMPERIAL PRINCESS OF TWILIGHT WON'T BE HERE FOR HALF A DAY AT THE SOONEST!
LISTEN TO ME! WE WE OPERATIN UNDER TH ASSUMPTIC THAT SHE WAS BASE AT THE GIA RUINS WE DISCOVERE ON THE ASTEROID
BUT WE'VE JUST CONFIRMED THAT THE MAGICAL OUTPUT IS EMANATING FROM ITS ENTIRE SURFACE.
WE WERE WRONG!
I'M AFRAID SHE'S TAKEN OVER THE ASTEROID ITSELF!
WHA... IS THIS TRUE?
THE WHOLE ASTEROID? YOU GOTTA BE KIDDING ME!
THAT THING'S GOT A DIAMETER OF 50 KILO-METERS.
THINK HOW MANY CENTURIES SHE'S BEEN SPREADING HER ROOTS THERE. ...FOR HER, IT ISN'T UNTHINKABLE.
GOV-ERNOR-GENERAL KURT, CALL OFF THE FLEET!
IT MAY BE THE GREATEST MILITARY FORCE THE MAGICAL WORLD CURRENTLY HAS TO OFFER, BUT THOSE ARE AIRSHIPS THAT WERE REMODELED IN A MATTER OF ONLY THREE YEARS! THIS IS TOO MUCH FOR A FLEET OF INSTANT SPACESHIPS!
!
NEGI! FATE!

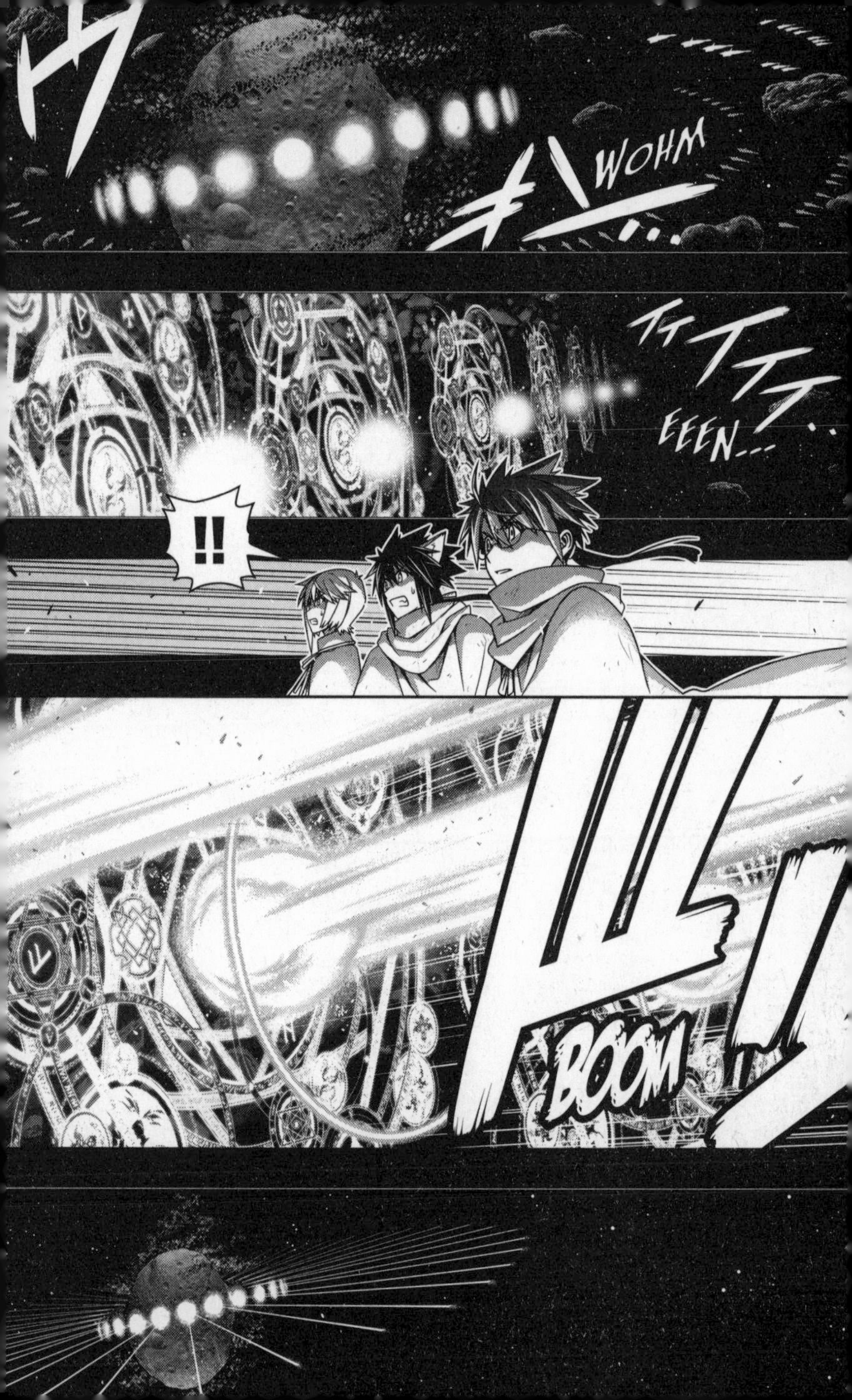
WOHM
EEEN...
!!
BOOM

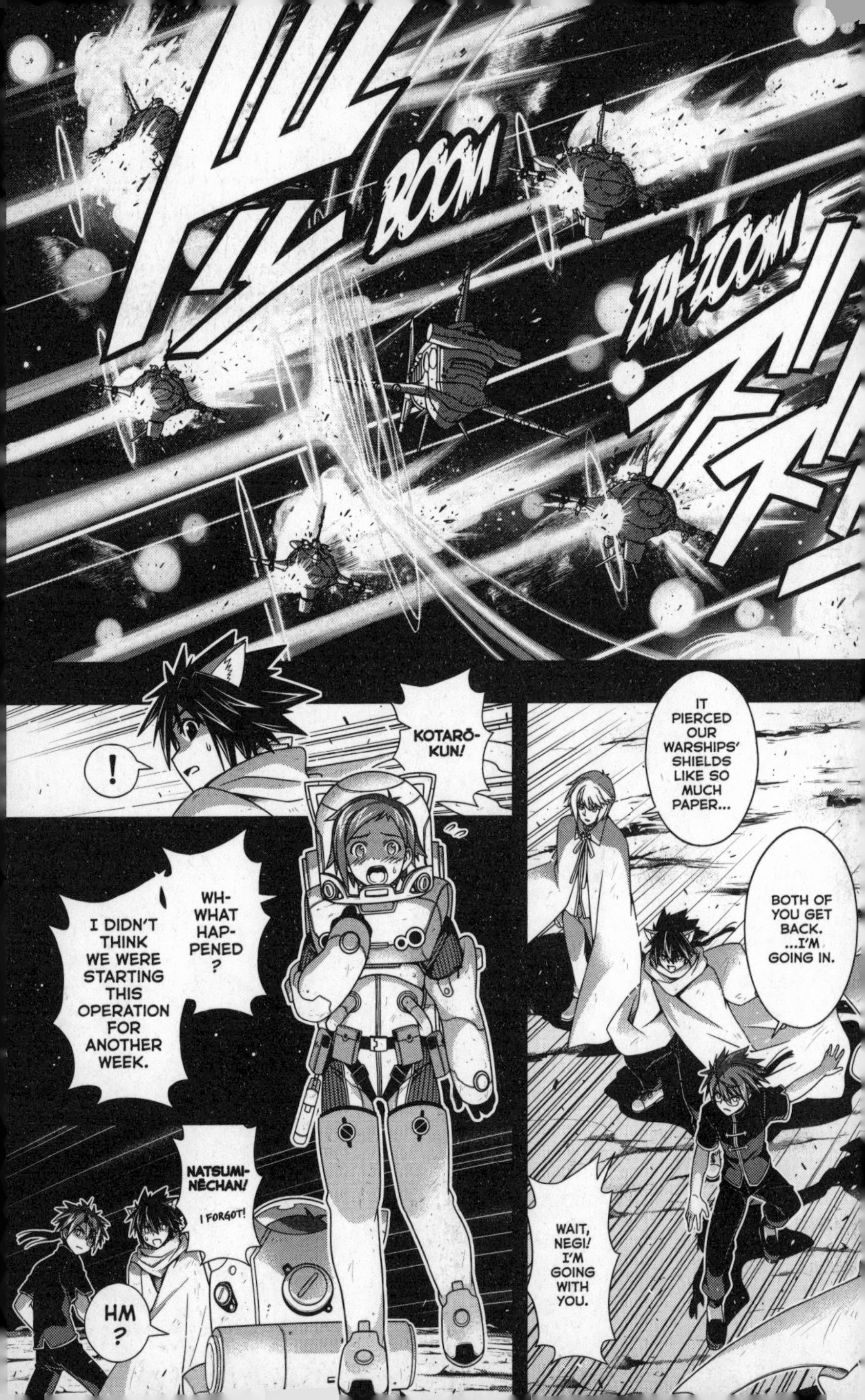
BOOM
ZA-ZOOM
IT PIERCED OUR WARSHIPS' SHIELDS LIKE SO MUCH PAPER...
BOTH OF YOU GET BACK. ...I'M GOING IN.
WAIT, NEGI! I'M GOING WITH YOU.
KOTARŌ-KUN!
!
WH-WHAT HAPPENED?
I DIDN'T THINK WE WERE STARTING THIS OPERATION FOR ANOTHER WEEK.
NATSUMI-NĒCHAN!
I FORGOT!
HM?

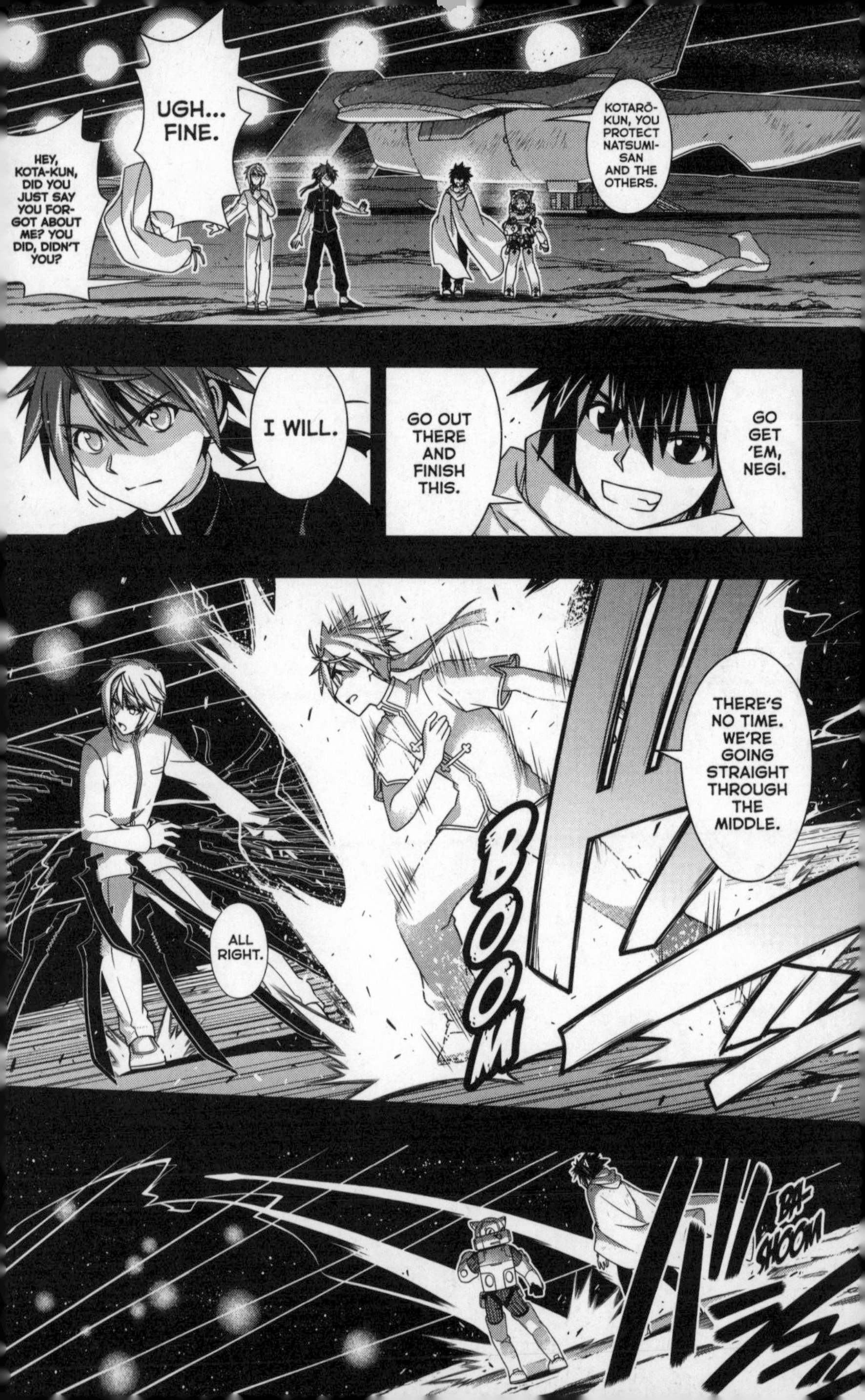
KOTARŌ-KUN, YOU PROTECT NATSUMI-SAN AND THE OTHERS.
UGH... FINE.
HEY, KOTA-KUN, DID YOU JUST SAY YOU FORGOT ABOUT ME? YOU DID, DIDN'T YOU?
GO GET 'EM, NEGI.
GO OUT THERE AND FINISH THIS.
I WILL.
THERE'S NO TIME. WE'RE GOING STRAIGHT THROUGH THE MIDDLE.
BOOM
ALL RIGHT.
BA-SHOOM

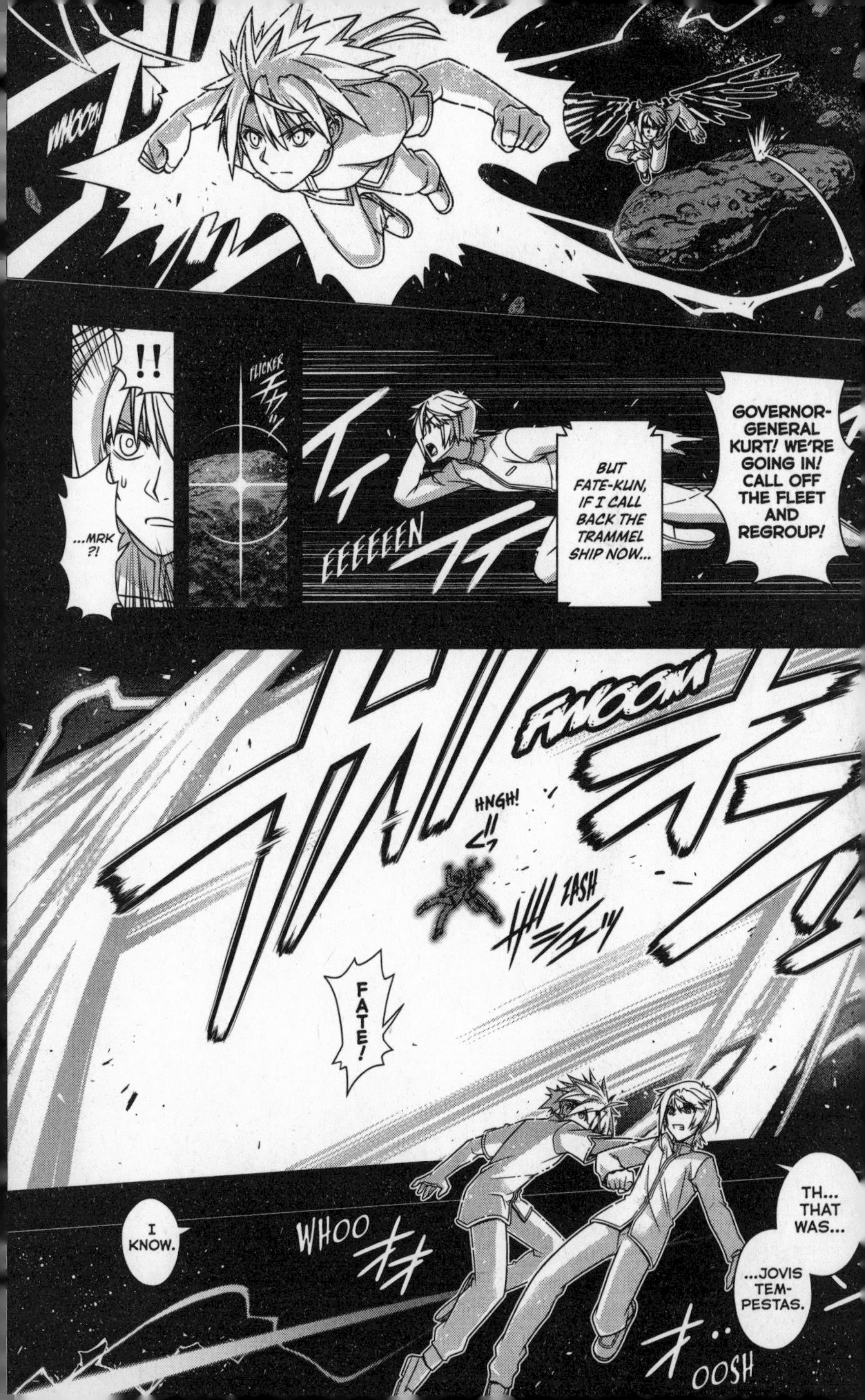

WHOOOSH
GOVERNOR-GENERAL KURT! WE'RE GOING IN! CALL OFF THE FLEET AND REGROUP!
BUT FATE-KUN, IF I CALL BACK THE TRAMMEL SHIP NOW...
EEEEEEN
FLICKER
!!
...MRK ?!
FWOOM
ZASH
HNGH!
FATE!
TH... THAT WAS...
...JOVIS TEMPESTAS.
OOSH
WHOO
I KNOW.

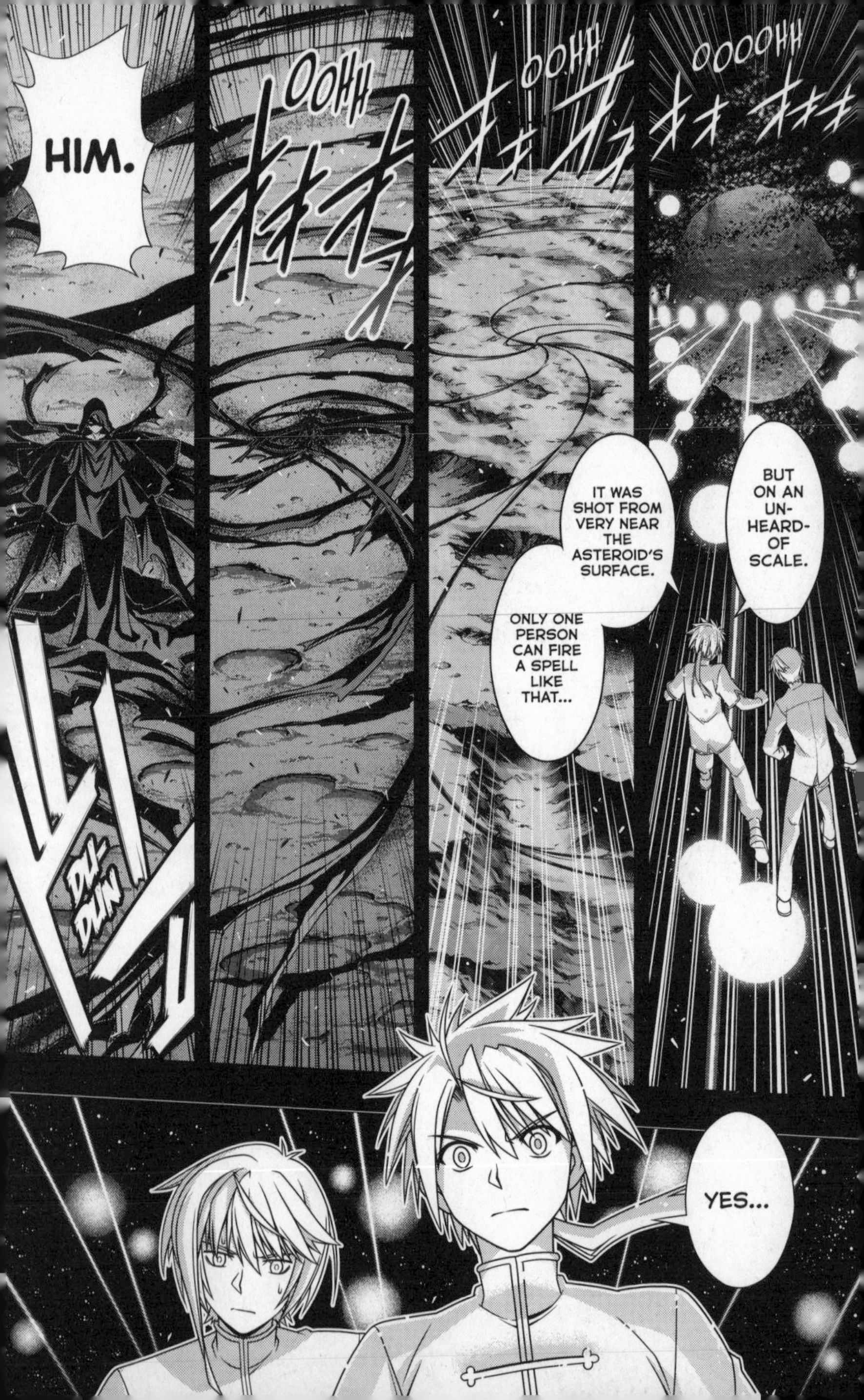
OOOOHH
IT WAS SHOT FROM VERY NEAR THE ASTEROID'S SURFACE.
BUT ON AN UN-HEARD-OF SCALE.
ONLY ONE PERSON CAN FIRE A SPELL LIKE THAT...
OOHH
OOHH
HIM.
DU-DUN
YES...

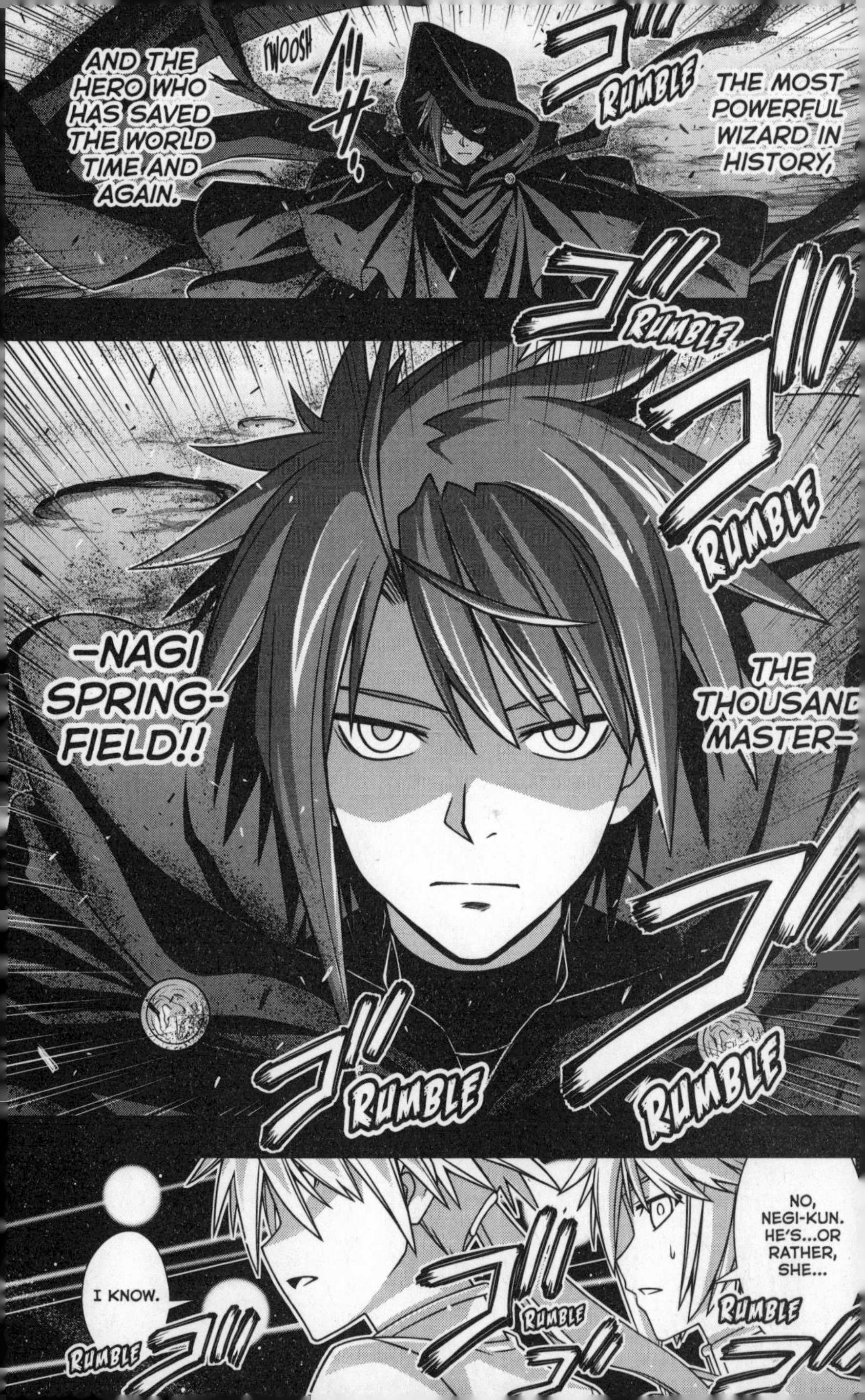
RUMBLE
THE MOST POWERFUL WIZARD IN HISTORY,
FWOOSH
AND THE HERO WHO HAS SAVED THE WORLD TIME AND AGAIN.
RUMBLE
RUMBLE
THE THOUSAND MASTER—
—NAGI SPRINGFIELD!!
RUMBLE
RUMBLE
NO, NEGI-KUN. HE'S...OR RATHER, SHE...
RUMBLE
RUMBLE
I KNOW.
RUMBLE

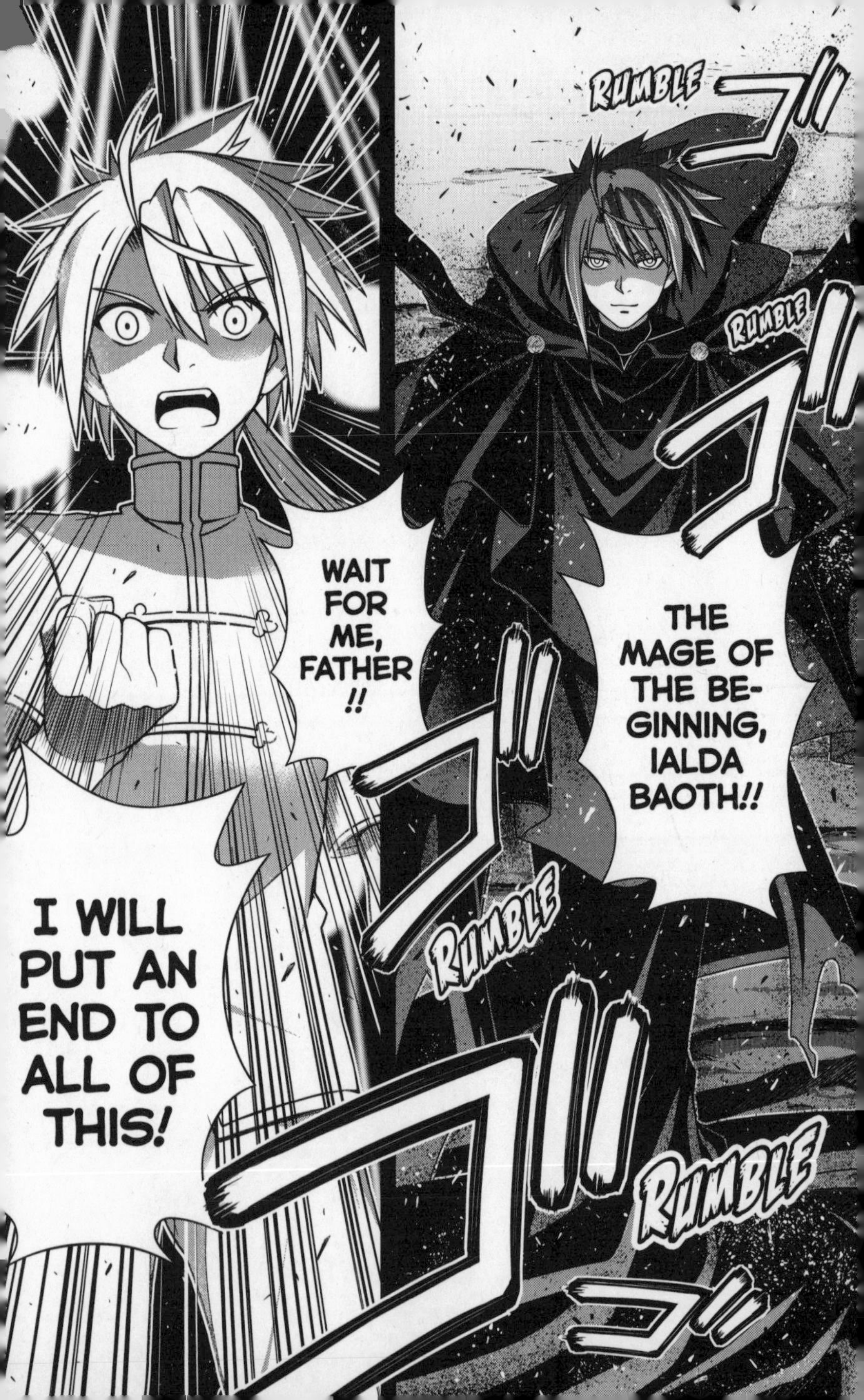
RUMBLE
RUMBLE
THE MAGE OF THE BEGINNING, IALDA BAOTH!!
RUMBLE
RUMBLE
WAIT FOR ME, FATHER!!
I WILL PUT AN END TO ALL OF THIS!

UQ HOLDER!

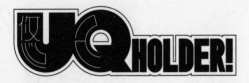

UQ HOLDER!

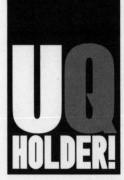

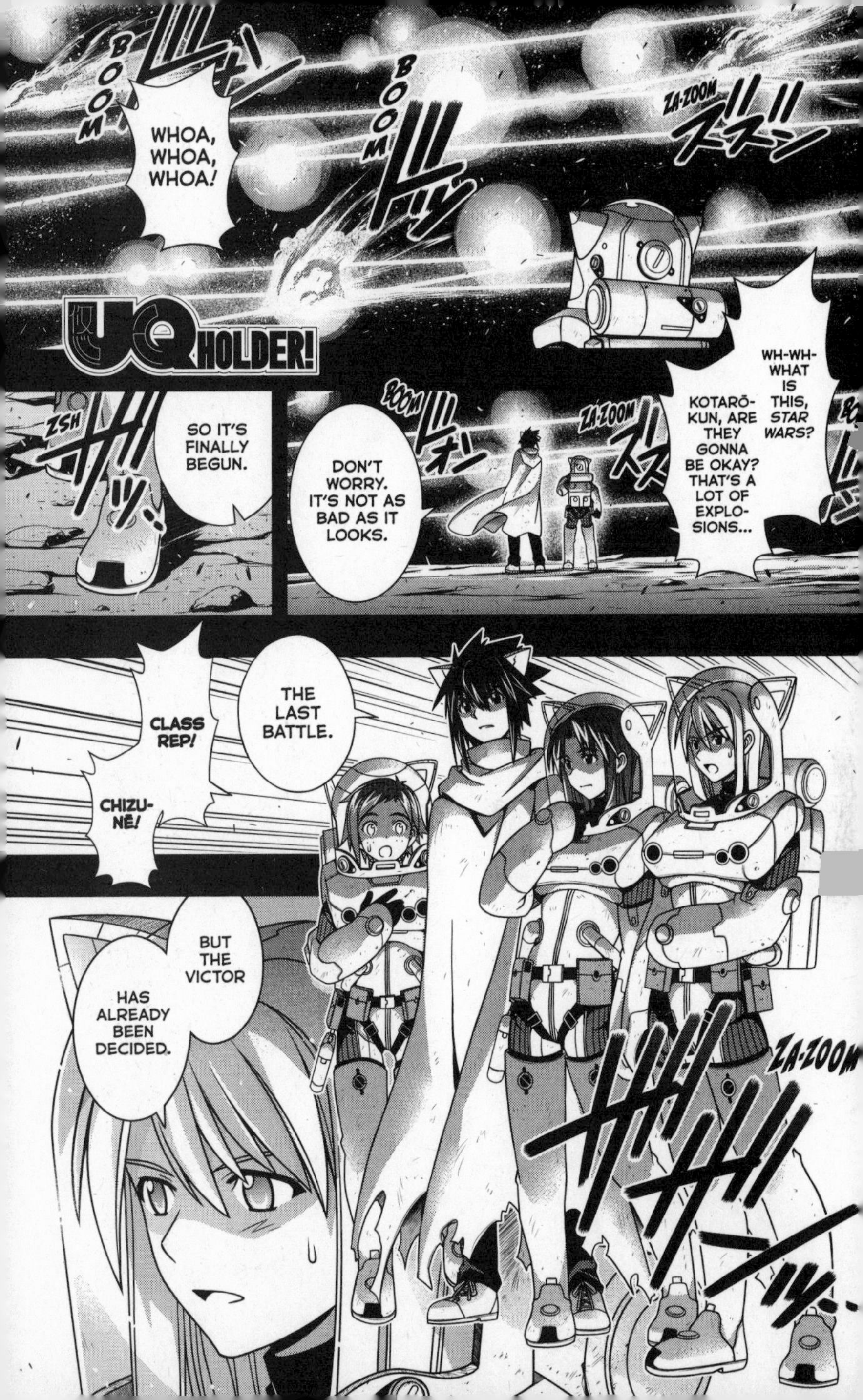
ZA-ZOOM
BOOM
WHOA, WHOA, WHOA!
BOOM
UQ HOLDER!
WH-WH-WHAT IS THIS, *STAR WARS*?
KOTARŌ-KUN, ARE THEY GONNA BE OKAY? THAT'S A LOT OF EXPLOSIONS...
ZA-ZOOM
BOOM
DON'T WORRY. IT'S NOT AS BAD AS IT LOOKS.
ZSH
SO IT'S FINALLY BEGUN.
THE LAST BATTLE.
CLASS REP!
CHIZUNĒ!
BUT THE VICTOR HAS ALREADY BEEN DECIDED.
ZA-ZOOM

STAGE 139: FATHER/SON REUNION

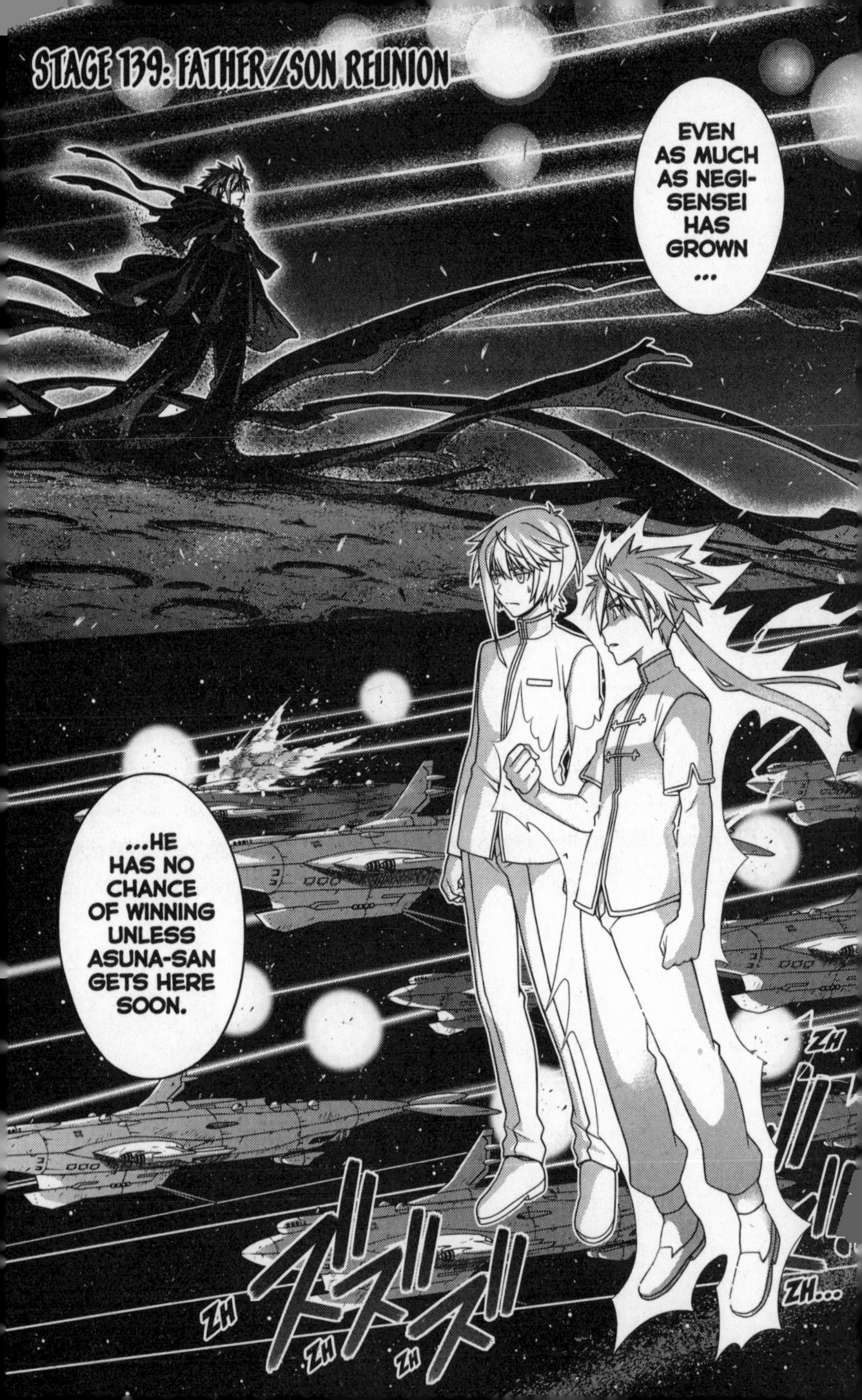
EVEN AS MUCH AS NEGI-SENSEI HAS GROWN ...
...HE HAS NO CHANCE OF WINNING UNLESS ASUNA-SAN GETS HERE SOON.
ZH
ZH...
ZH
ZH
ZH

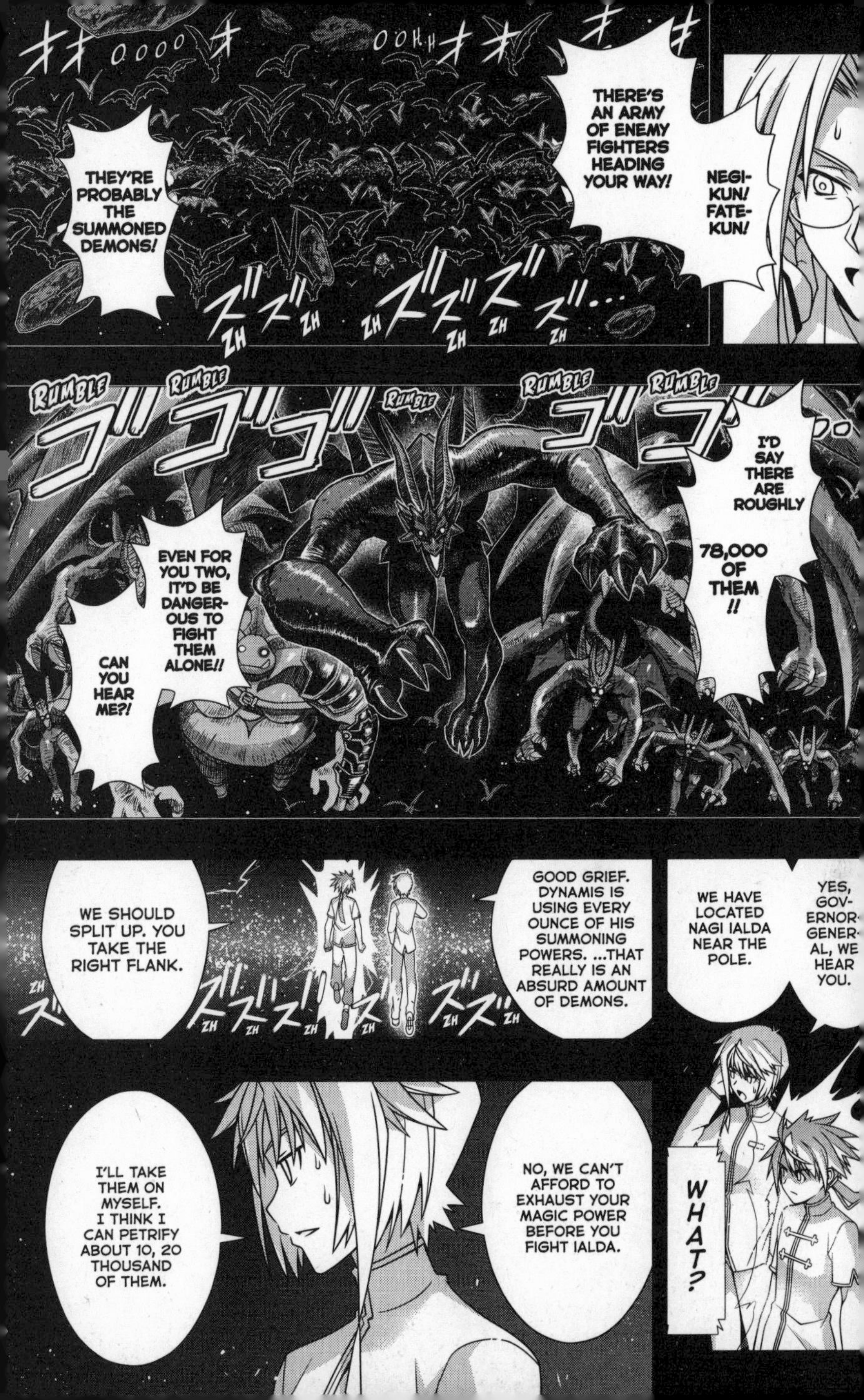
NEGI-KUN! FATE-KUN!
OOHHH
OOOO
THERE'S AN ARMY OF ENEMY FIGHTERS HEADING YOUR WAY!
THEY'RE PROBABLY THE SUMMONED DEMONS!
ZH ZH ZH ZH ZH ZH
RUMBLE RUMBLE RUMBLE RUMBLE RUMBLE
I'D SAY THERE ARE ROUGHLY
78,000 OF THEM!!
EVEN FOR YOU TWO, IT'D BE DANGEROUS TO FIGHT THEM ALONE!!
CAN YOU HEAR ME?!
YES, GOVERNOR-GENERAL, WE HEAR YOU.
WE HAVE LOCATED NAGI IALDA NEAR THE POLE.
GOOD GRIEF. DYNAMIS IS USING EVERY OUNCE OF HIS SUMMONING POWERS. ...THAT REALLY IS AN ABSURD AMOUNT OF DEMONS.
WE SHOULD SPLIT UP. YOU TAKE THE RIGHT FLANK.
ZH ZH ZH ZH ZH ZH
WHAT?
NO, WE CAN'T AFFORD TO EXHAUST YOUR MAGIC POWER BEFORE YOU FIGHT IALDA.
I'LL TAKE THEM ON MYSELF. I THINK I CAN PETRIFY ABOUT 10, 20 THOUSAND OF THEM.

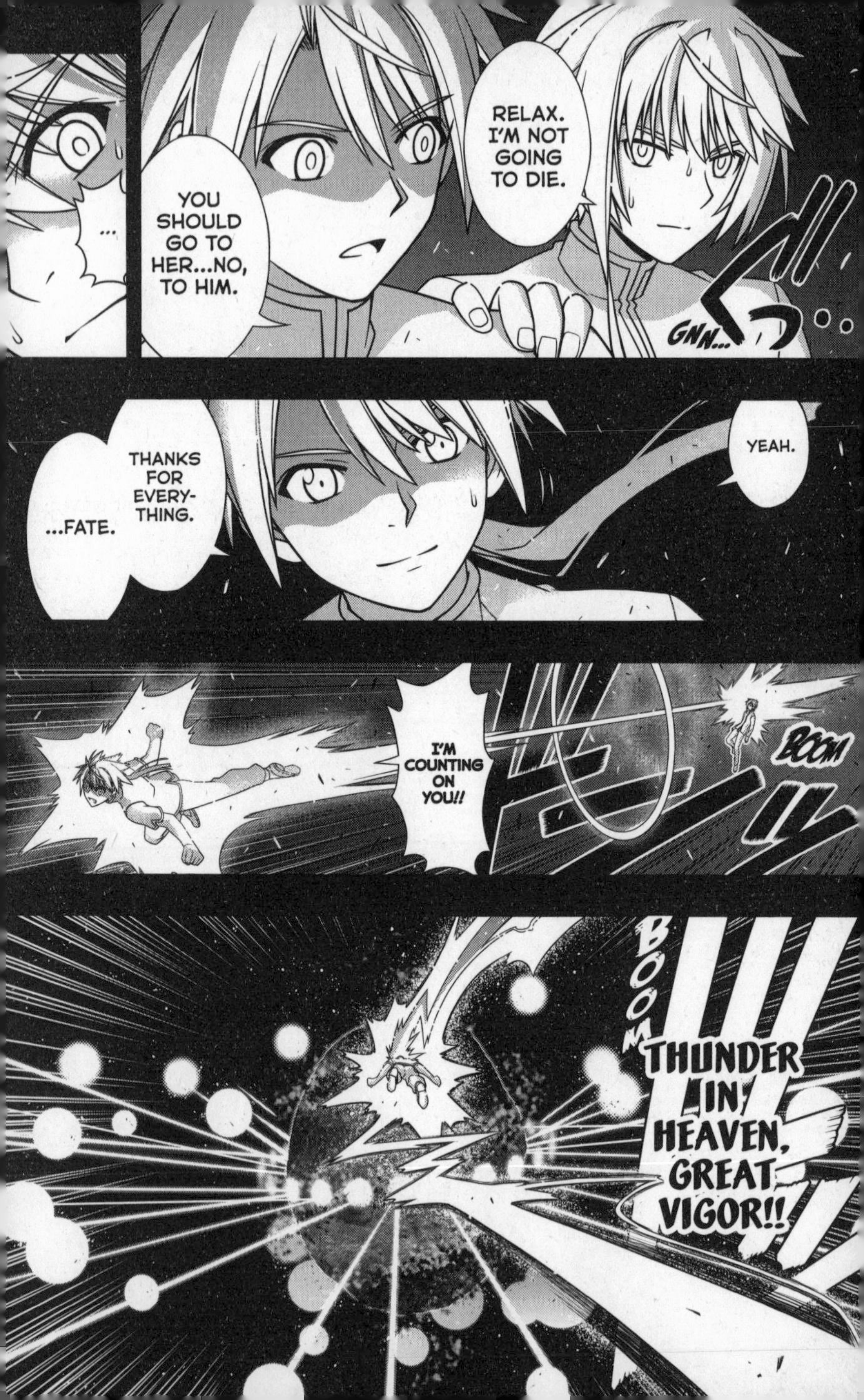
RELAX. I'M NOT GOING TO DIE.
YOU SHOULD GO TO HER...NO, TO HIM.
GNN...
...
YEAH.
THANKS FOR EVERYTHING.
...FATE.
BOOM
I'M COUNTING ON YOU!!
BOOM
THUNDER IN HEAVEN, GREAT VIGOR!!

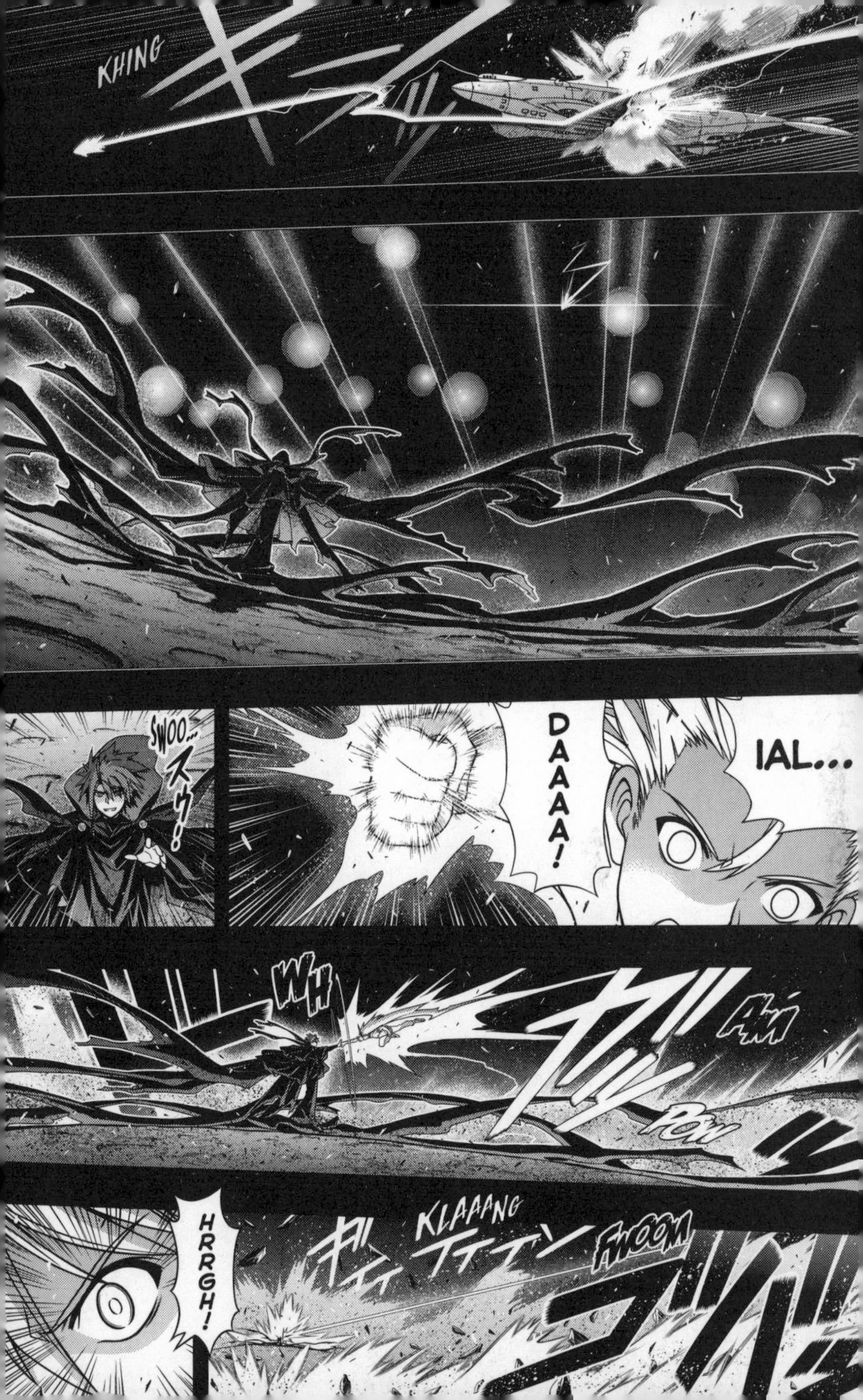
KHING
IAL...
DAAAAA!
SWOO...
スゥ
WH
AM
POW
FWOOM
KLAAANG
HRRGH!

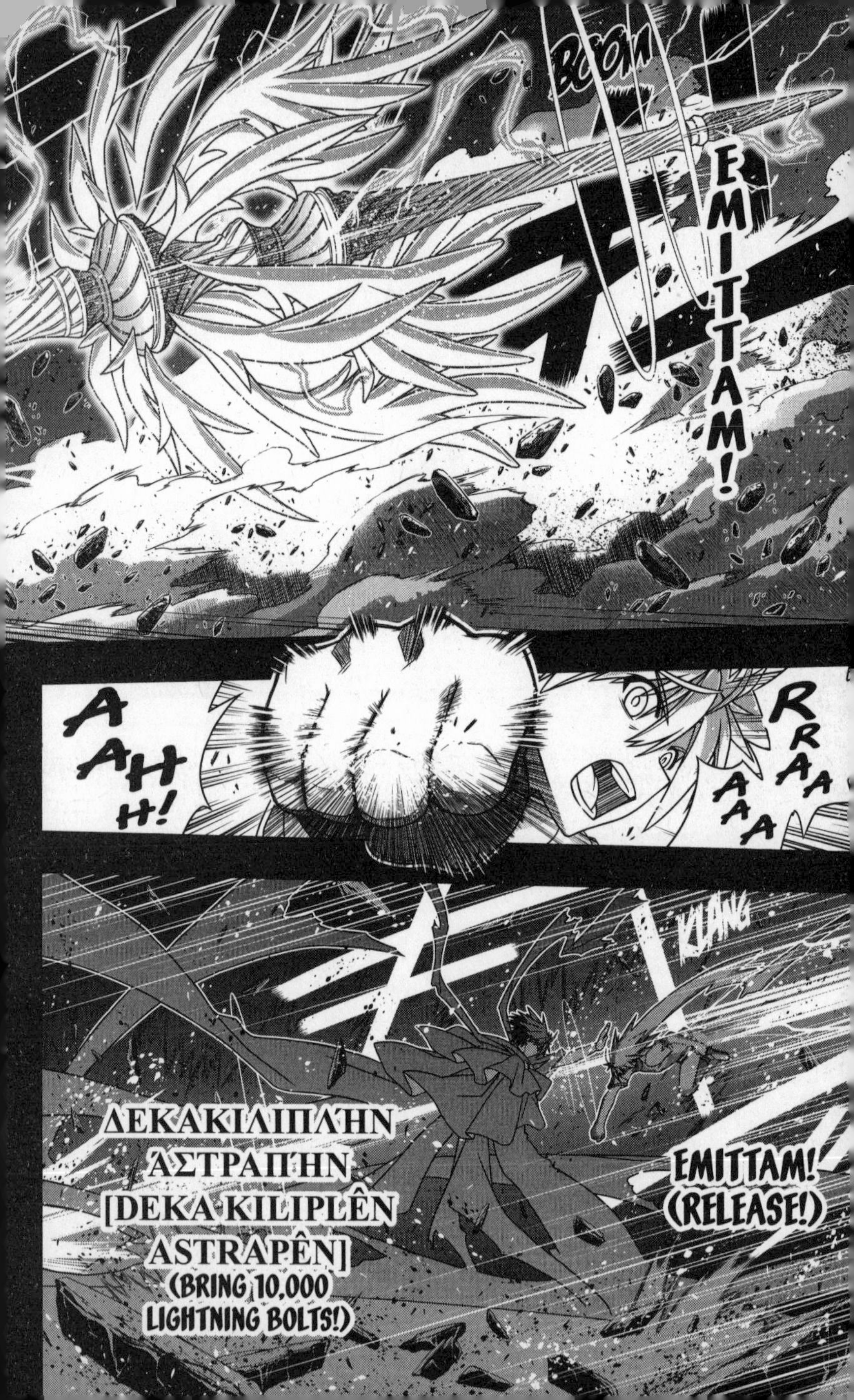
BOOM
EMITTAM!
RRAAAAA
AAHH!
KLANG
EMITTAM! (RELEASE!)
ΔΕΚΑΚΙΛΙΠΛΉΝ ἈΣΤΡΑΠΉΝ [DEKA KILIPLÊN ASTRAPÊN] (BRING 10,000 LIGHTNING BOLTS!)

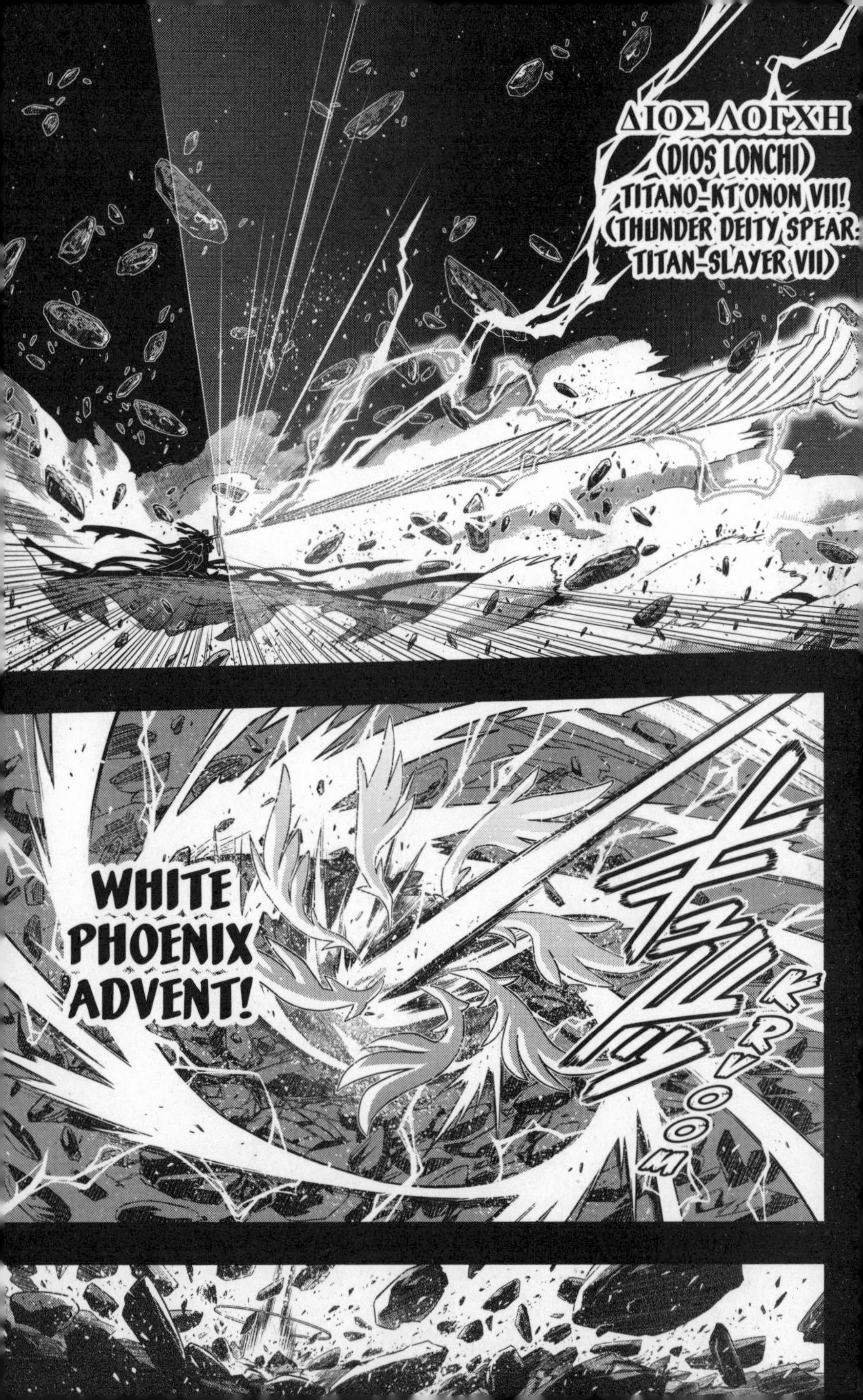
ΔΙΟΣ ΛΟΓΧΗ
(DIOS LONCHI)
TITANO-KT'ONON VII!
(THUNDER DEITY SPEAR:
TITAN-SLAYER VII)
KRVOOOM
WHITE
PHOENIX
ADVENT!

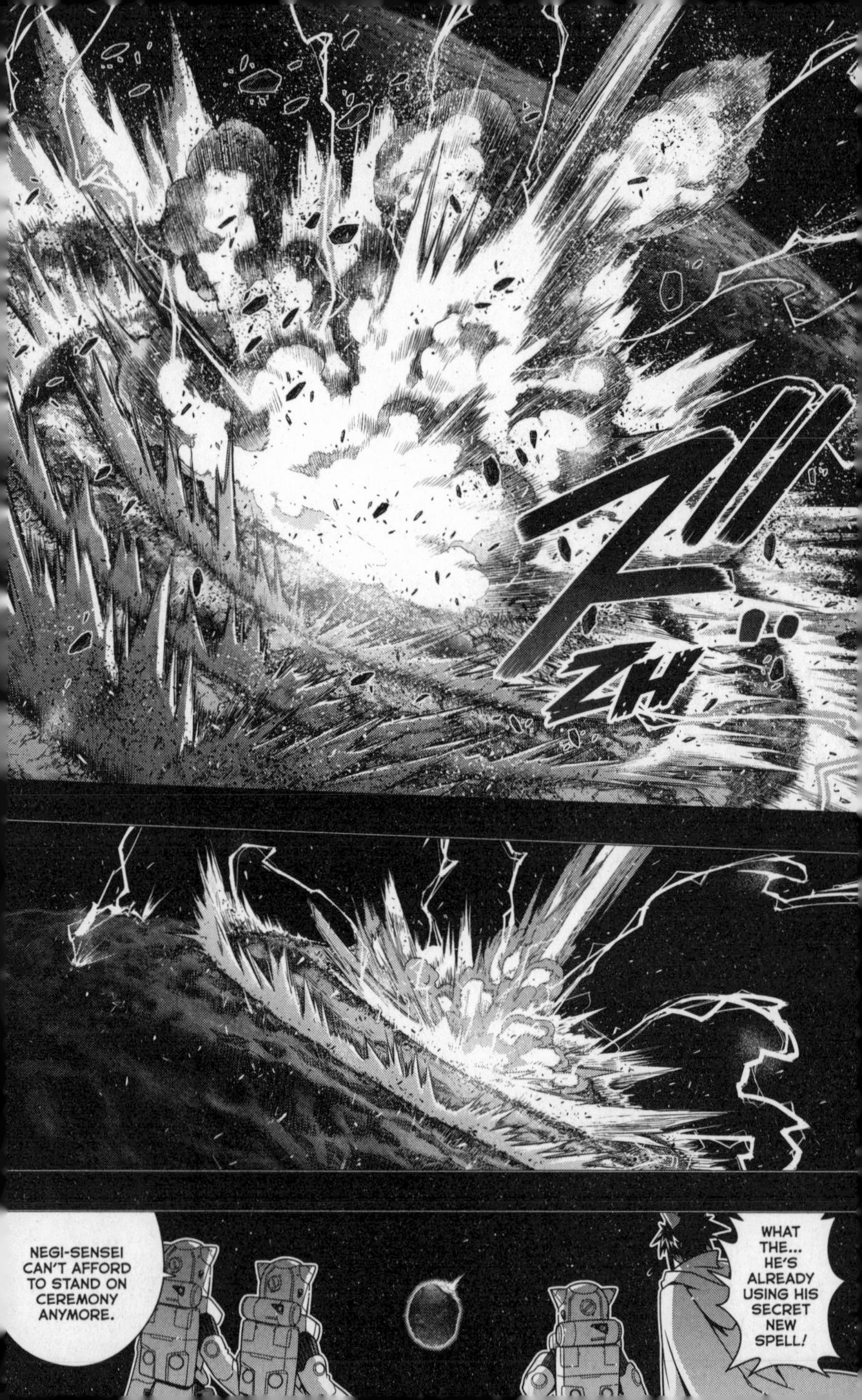
ZH
WHAT THE... HE'S ALREADY USING HIS SECRET NEW SPELL!
NEGI-SENSEI CAN'T AFFORD TO STAND ON CEREMONY ANYMORE.

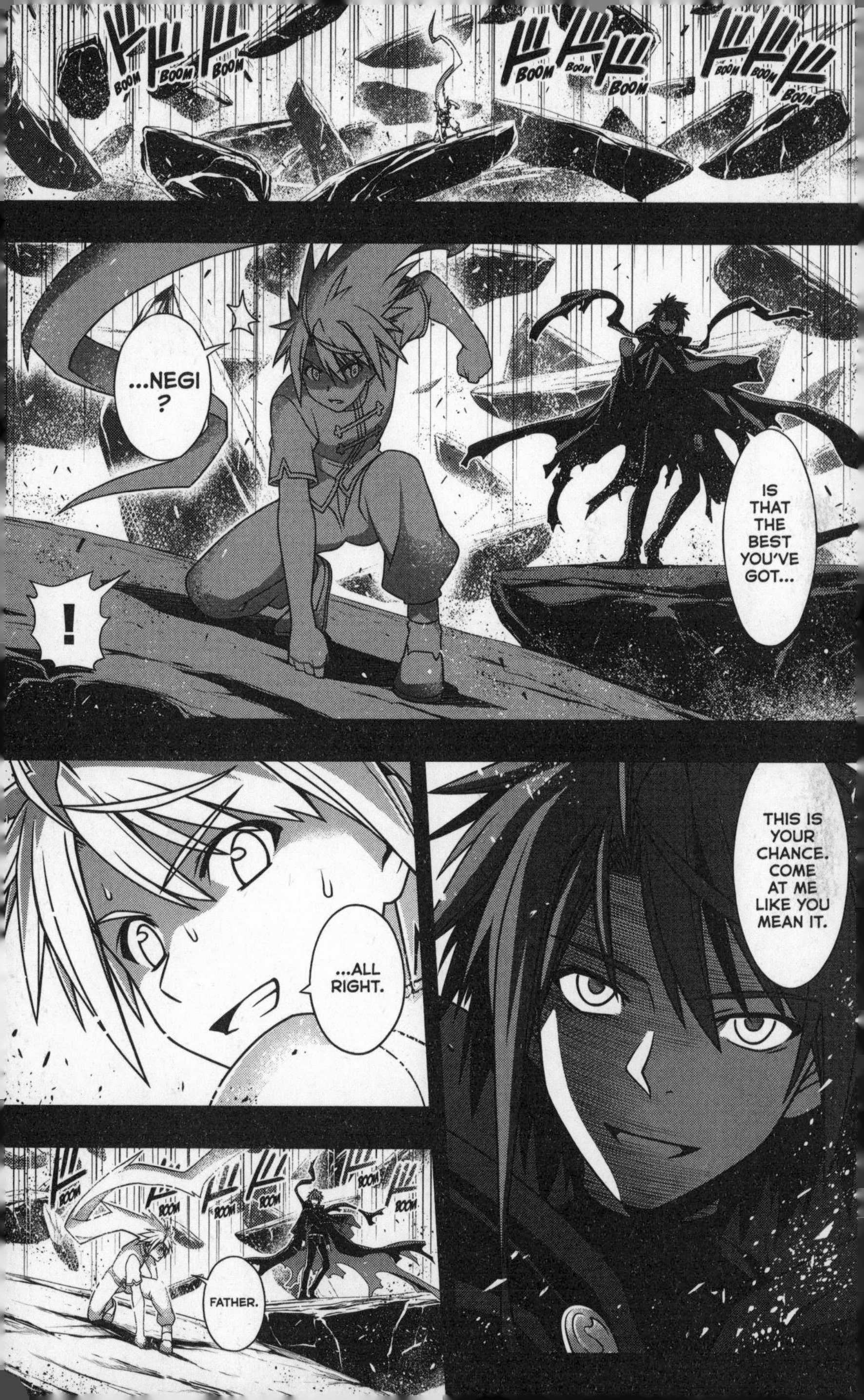

BOOM BOOM BOOM
BOOM BOOM BOOM
BOOM BOOM BOOM
IS THAT THE BEST YOU'VE GOT...
...NEGI?
!
THIS IS YOUR CHANCE. COME AT ME LIKE YOU MEAN IT.
...ALL RIGHT.
BOOM BOOM BOOM BOOM BOOM
FATHER.

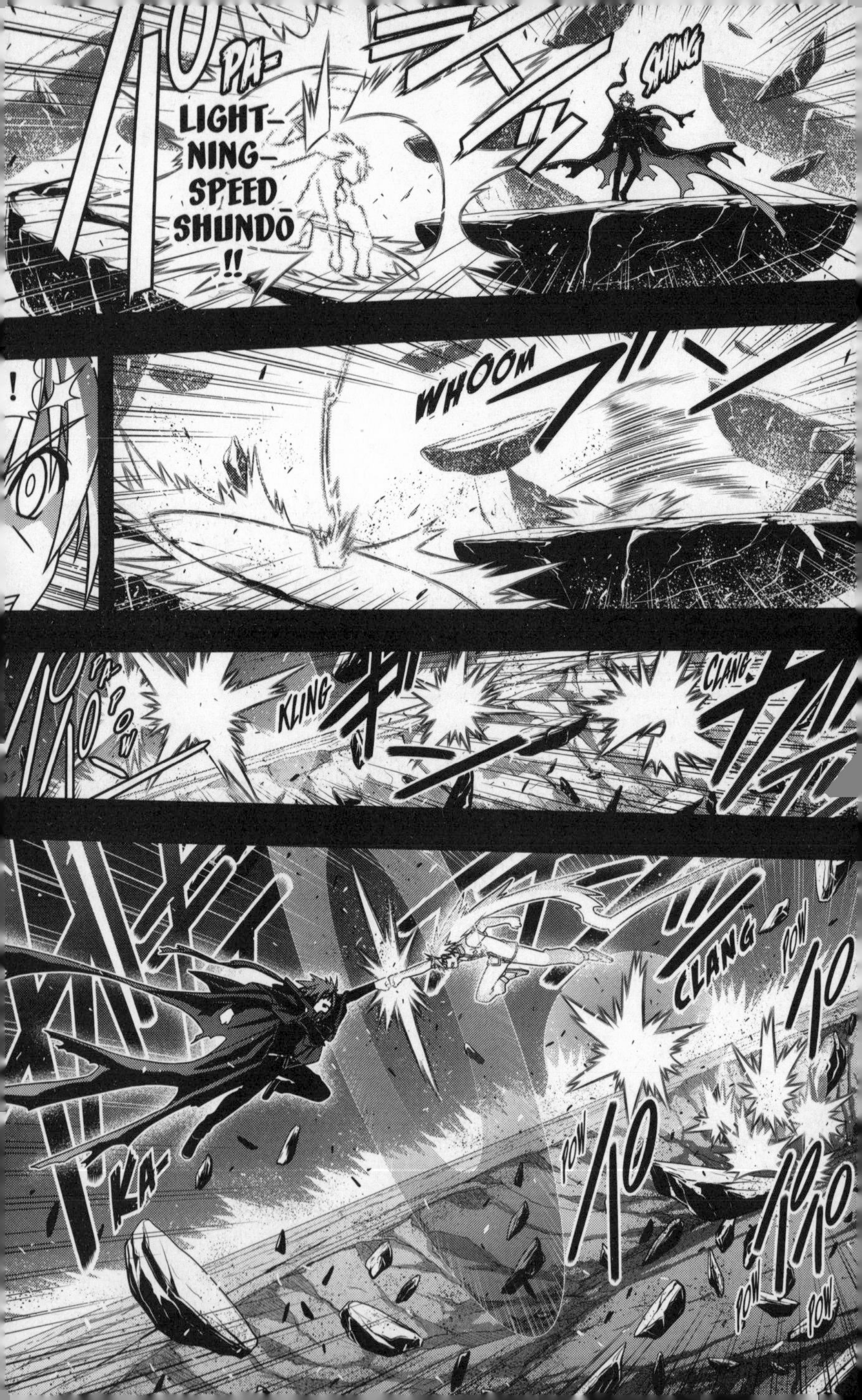
SHING
PA-
LIGHT-
NING-
SPEED
SHUNDŌ
!!
WHOOM
!
CLANG
KLING
PA-
POW
POW
CLANG
POW
POW
POW
POW
KA-

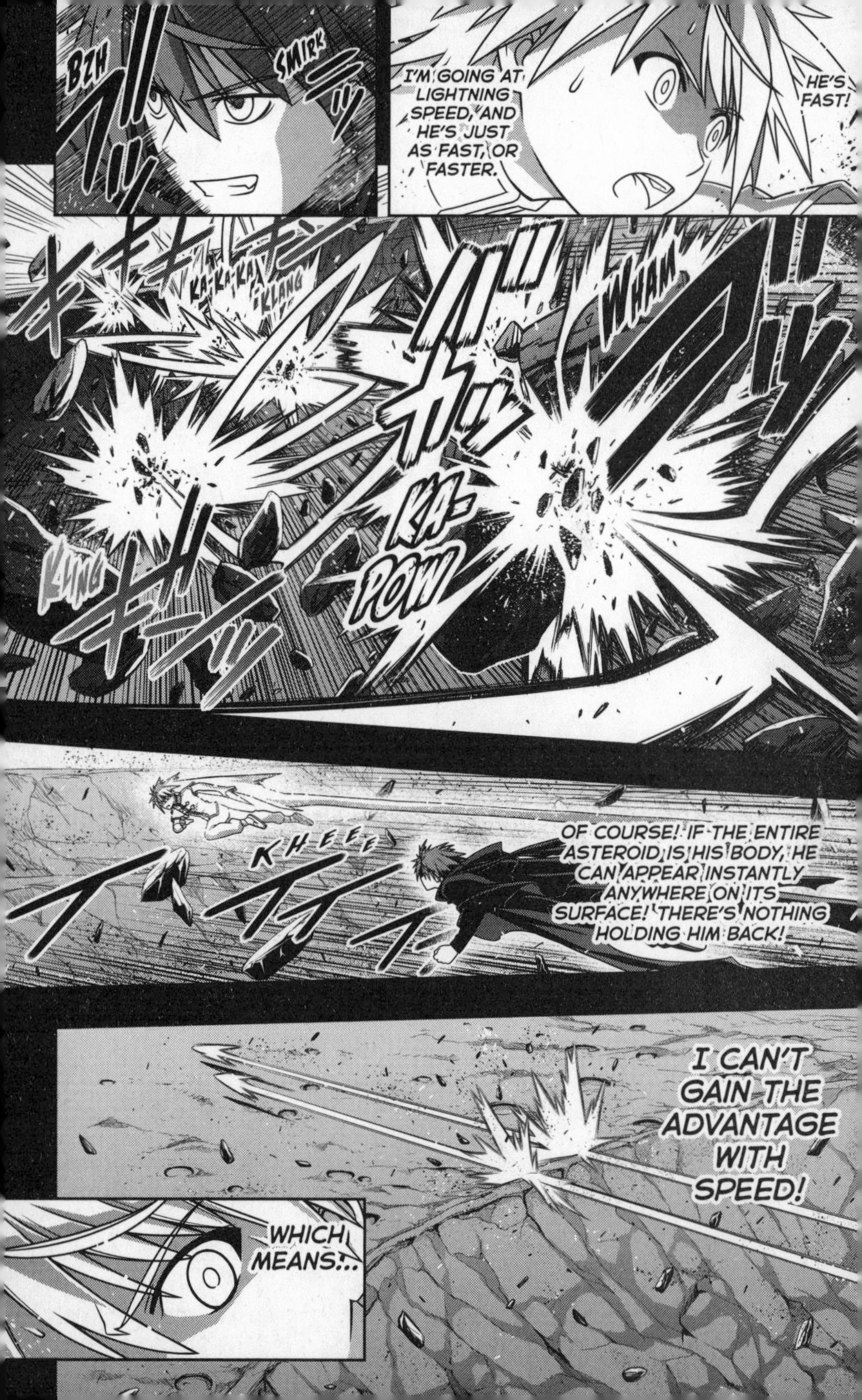
HE'S FAST!
I'M GOING AT LIGHTNING SPEED, AND HE'S JUST AS FAST, OR FASTER.
SMIRK
BZH
WHAM
KLANG
KA-KA-KA
KA-POW
KLING
OF COURSE! IF THE ENTIRE ASTEROID IS HIS BODY, HE CAN APPEAR INSTANTLY ANYWHERE ON ITS SURFACE! THERE'S NOTHING HOLDING HIM BACK!
KHEEE
I CAN'T GAIN THE ADVANTAGE WITH SPEED!
WHICH MEANS...

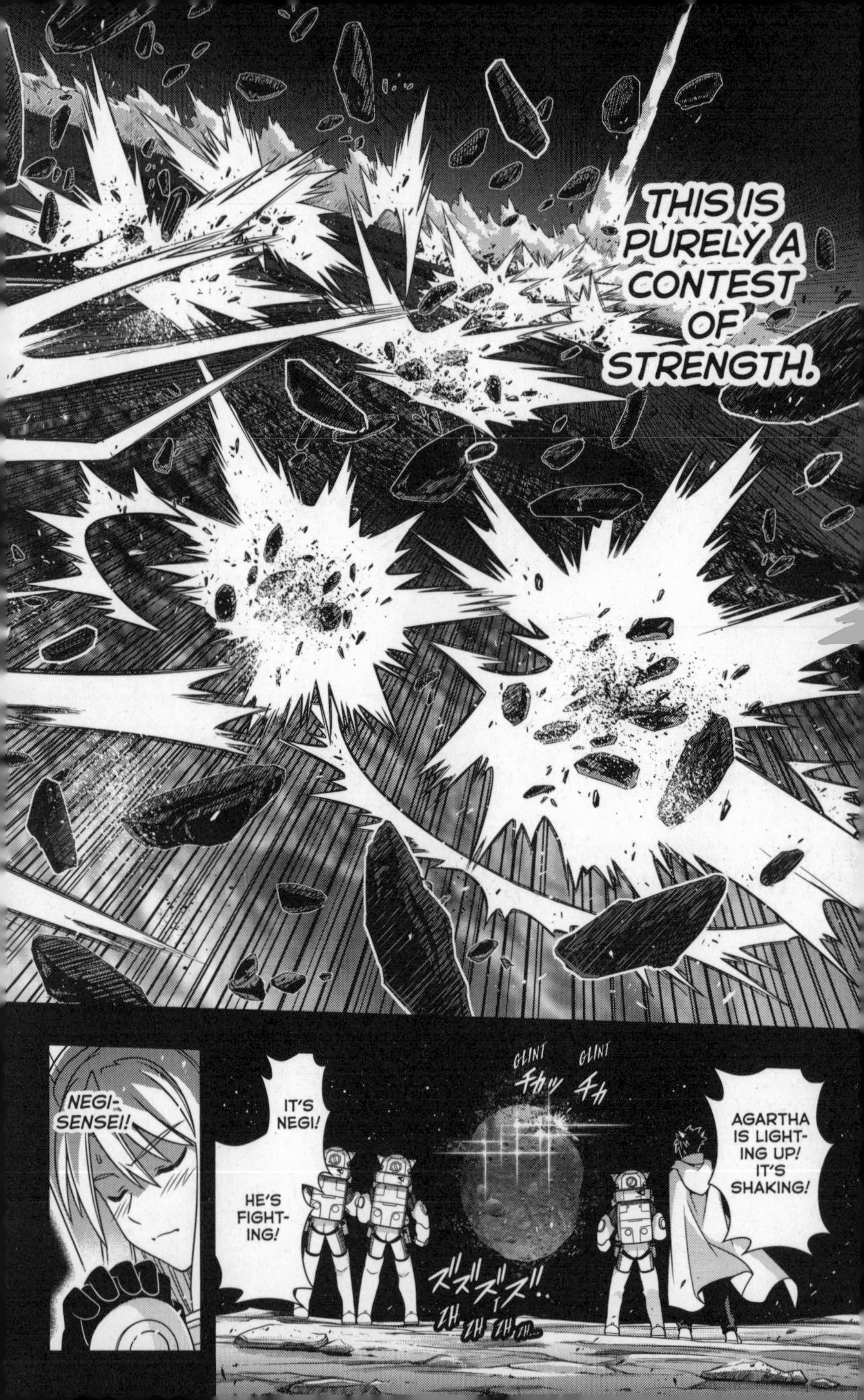

THIS IS PURELY A CONTEST OF STRENGTH.
AGARTHA IS LIGHT-ING UP! IT'S SHAKING!
GLINT チカ
GLINT チカッ
IT'S NEGI!
HE'S FIGHT-ING!
ズズズズ
ZH ZH ZH ZH...
NEGI-SENSEI!

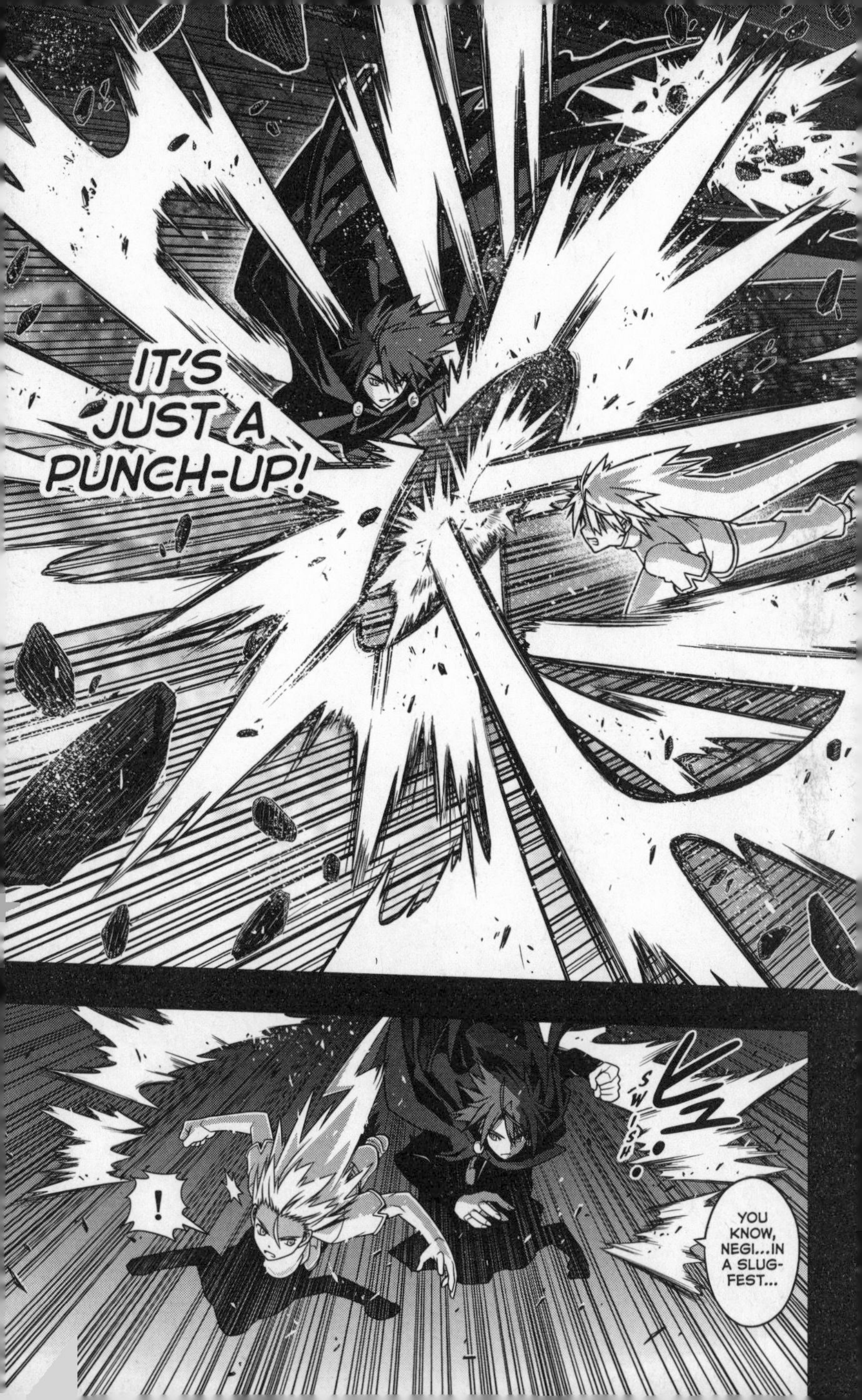
IT'S JUST A PUNCH-UP!
SWISH
YOU KNOW, NEGI...IN A SLUG-FEST...
!

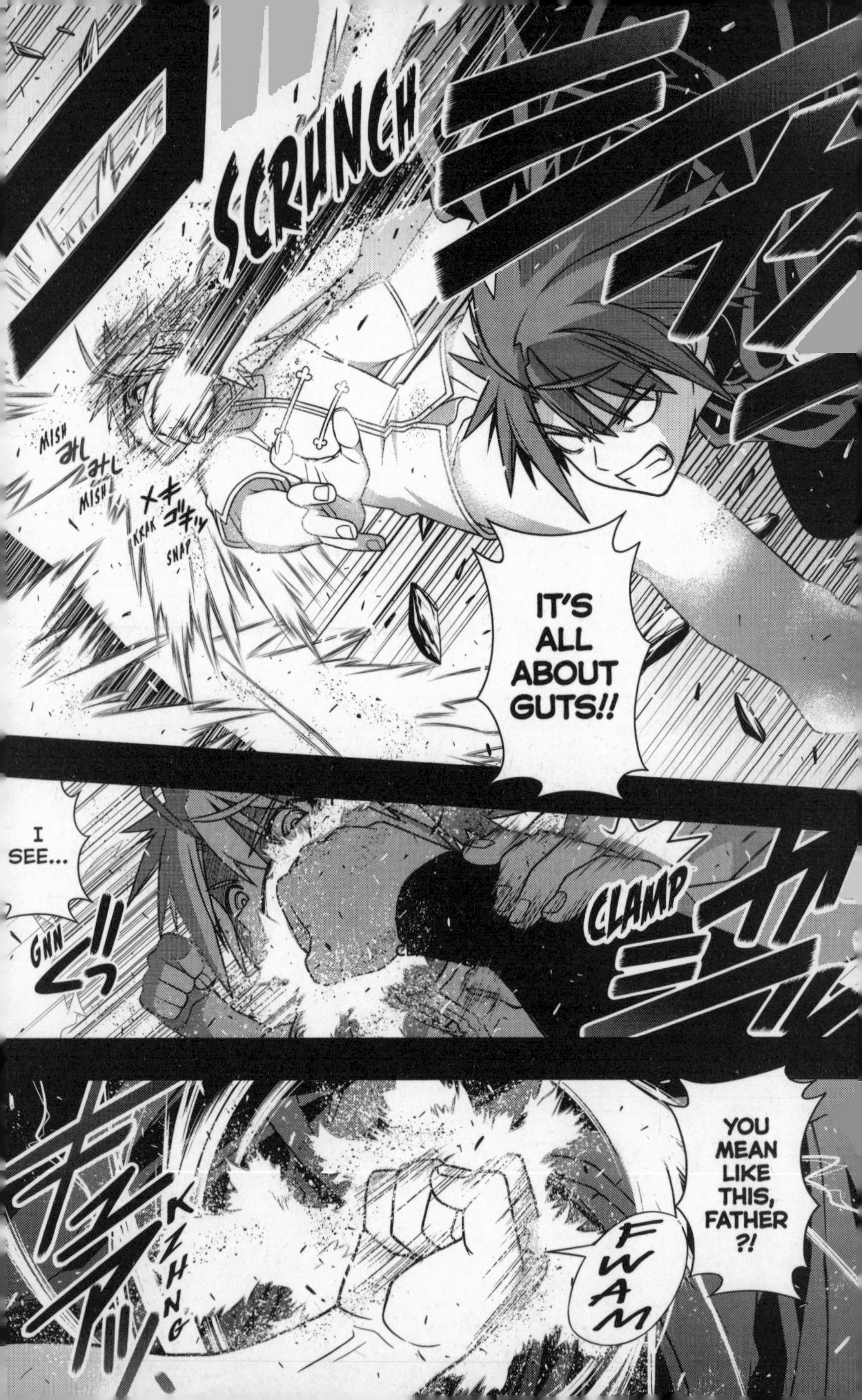
SCRUNCH
MISH みし
みし MISH
メキ KRAK
ゴキッ SNAP
IT'S ALL ABOUT GUTS!!
CLAMP
I SEE...
GNN ぐっ
YOU MEAN LIKE THIS, FATHER?!
FWAM
KZHNG

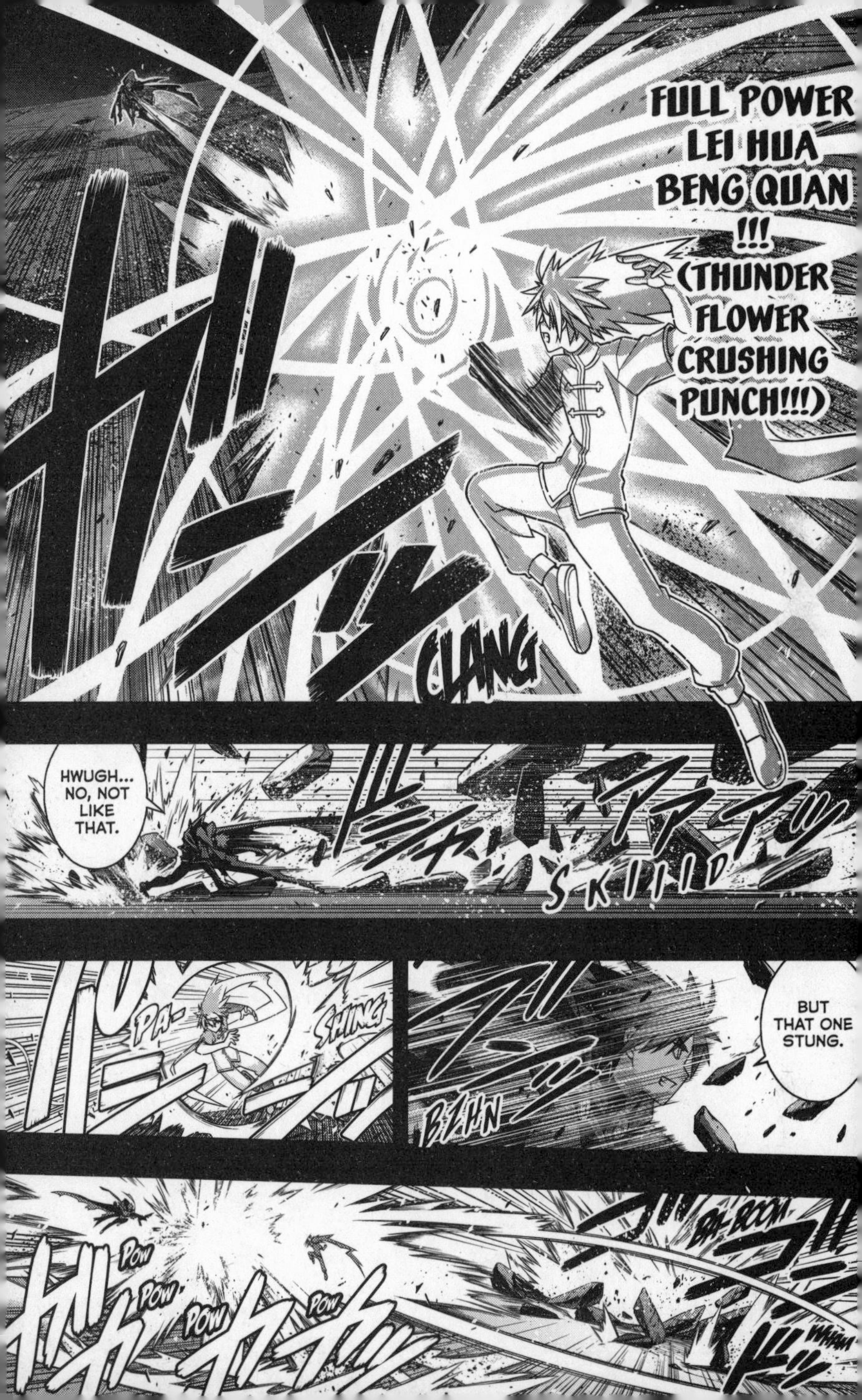
FULL POWER LEI HUA BENG QUAN!!! (THUNDER FLOWER CRUSHING PUNCH!!!)
CLANG
HWUGH... NO, NOT LIKE THAT.
SKIIIID
BUT THAT ONE STUNG.
B'HN
PA-SHING
BA-BOOM
WHAM
POW
POW
POW
POW

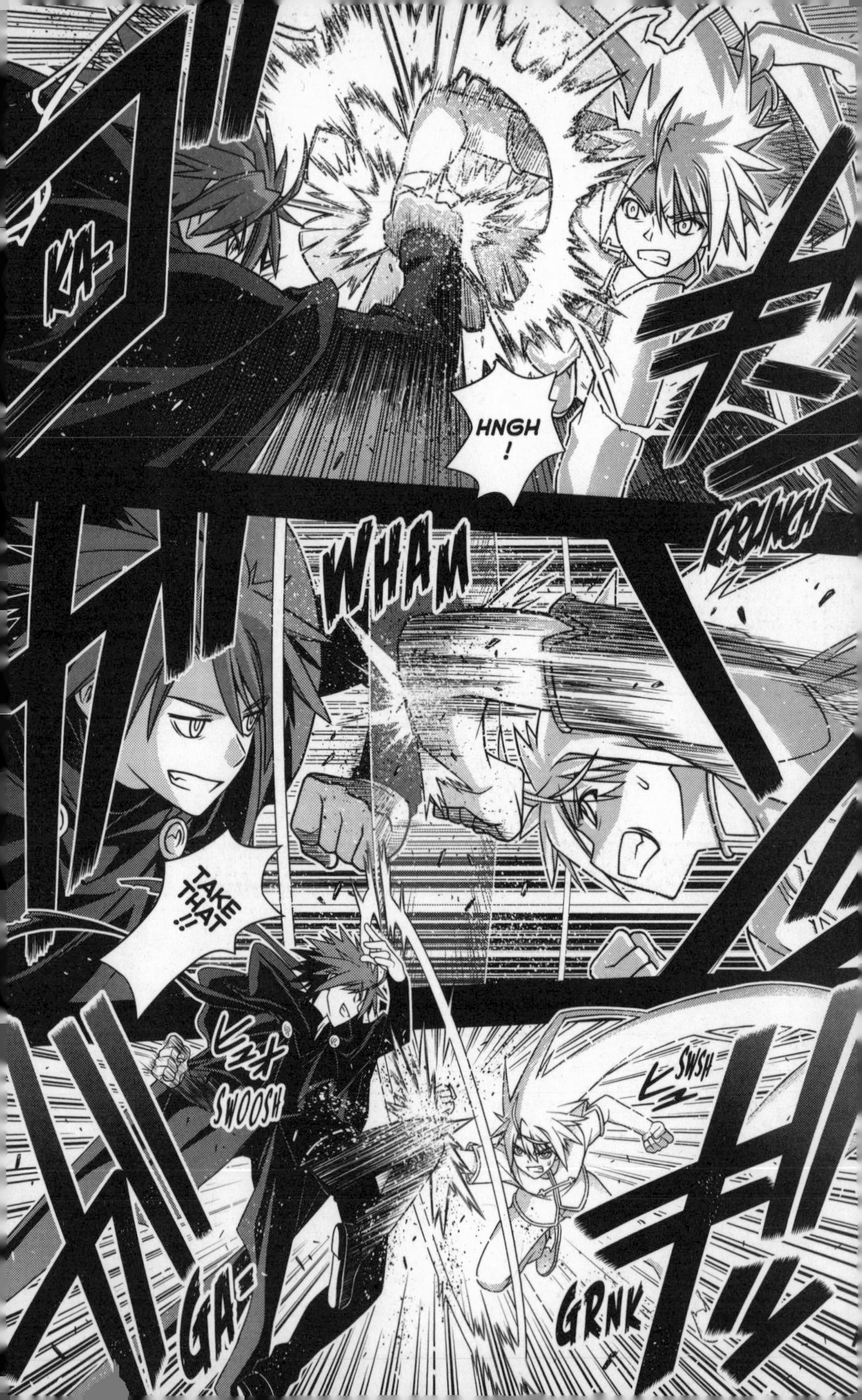
HNGH!
KA-
KRUNCH
WHAM
TAKE THAT!!
SWSH
SWOOSH
GRNK
GA-

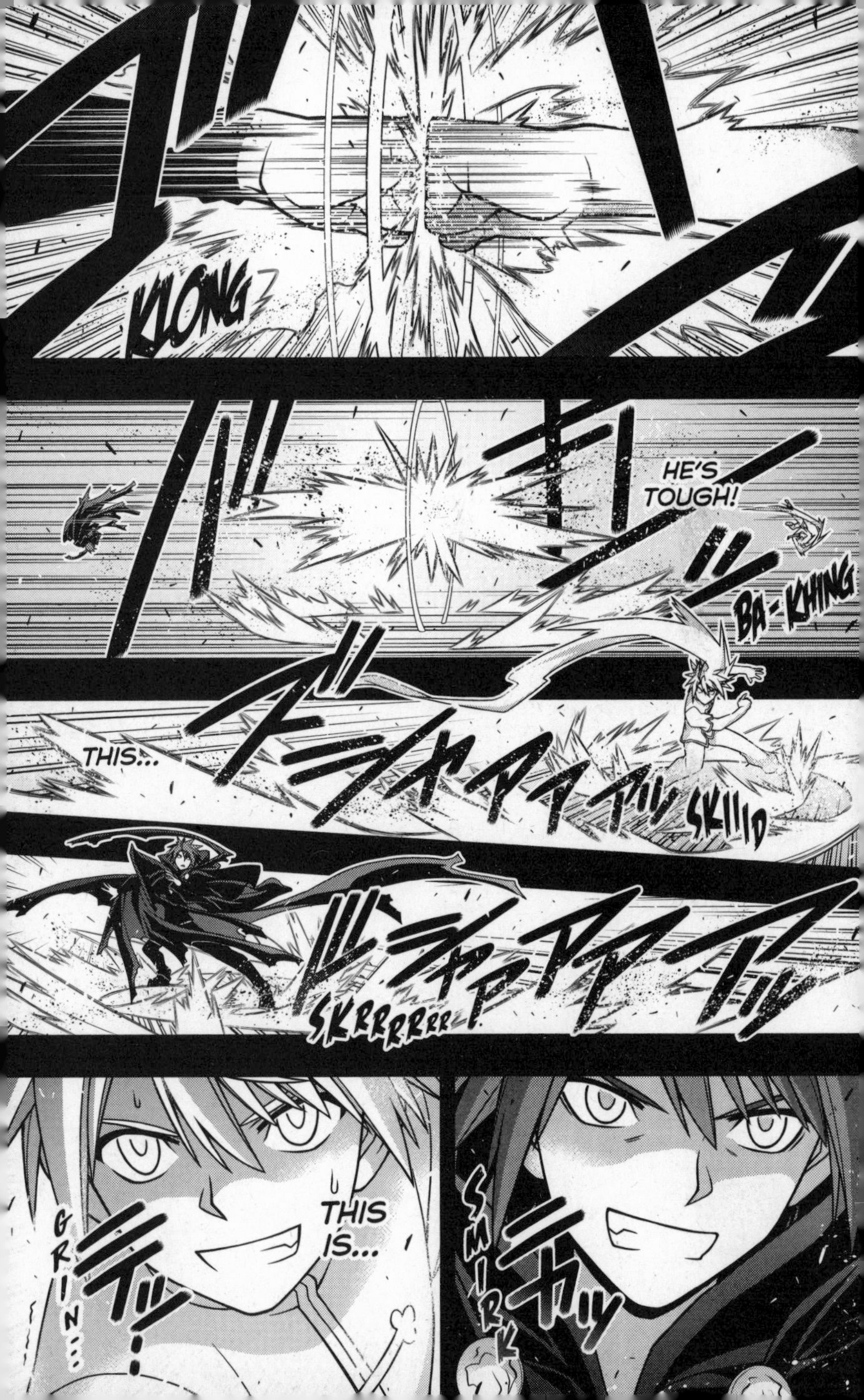
KLONG
HE'S TOUGH!
BA-KHING
THIS...
SKIIID
SKRRRRRRR
SMIRK
THIS IS...
GRIN...

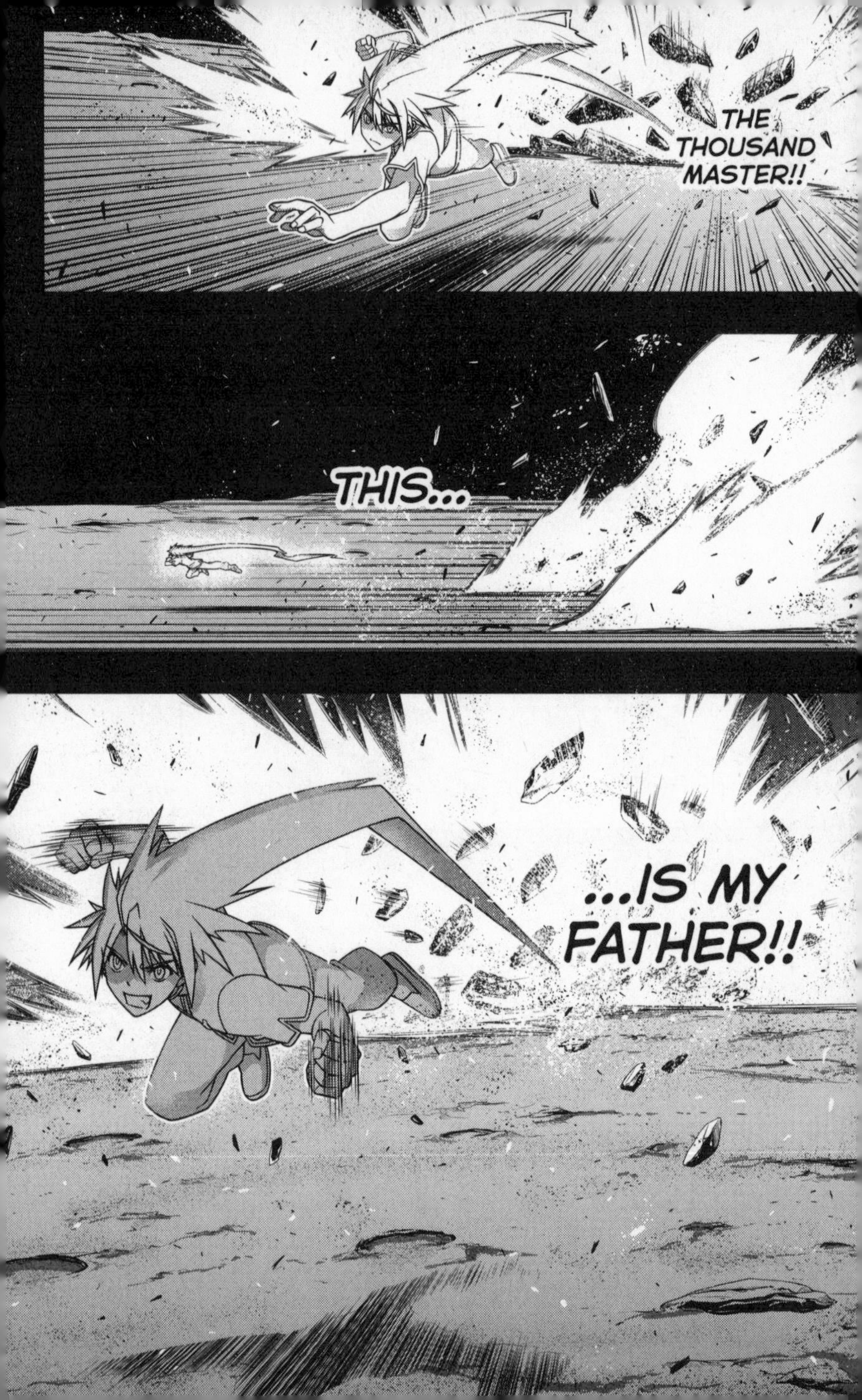
THE THOUSAND MASTER!!
THIS...
...IS MY FATHER!!

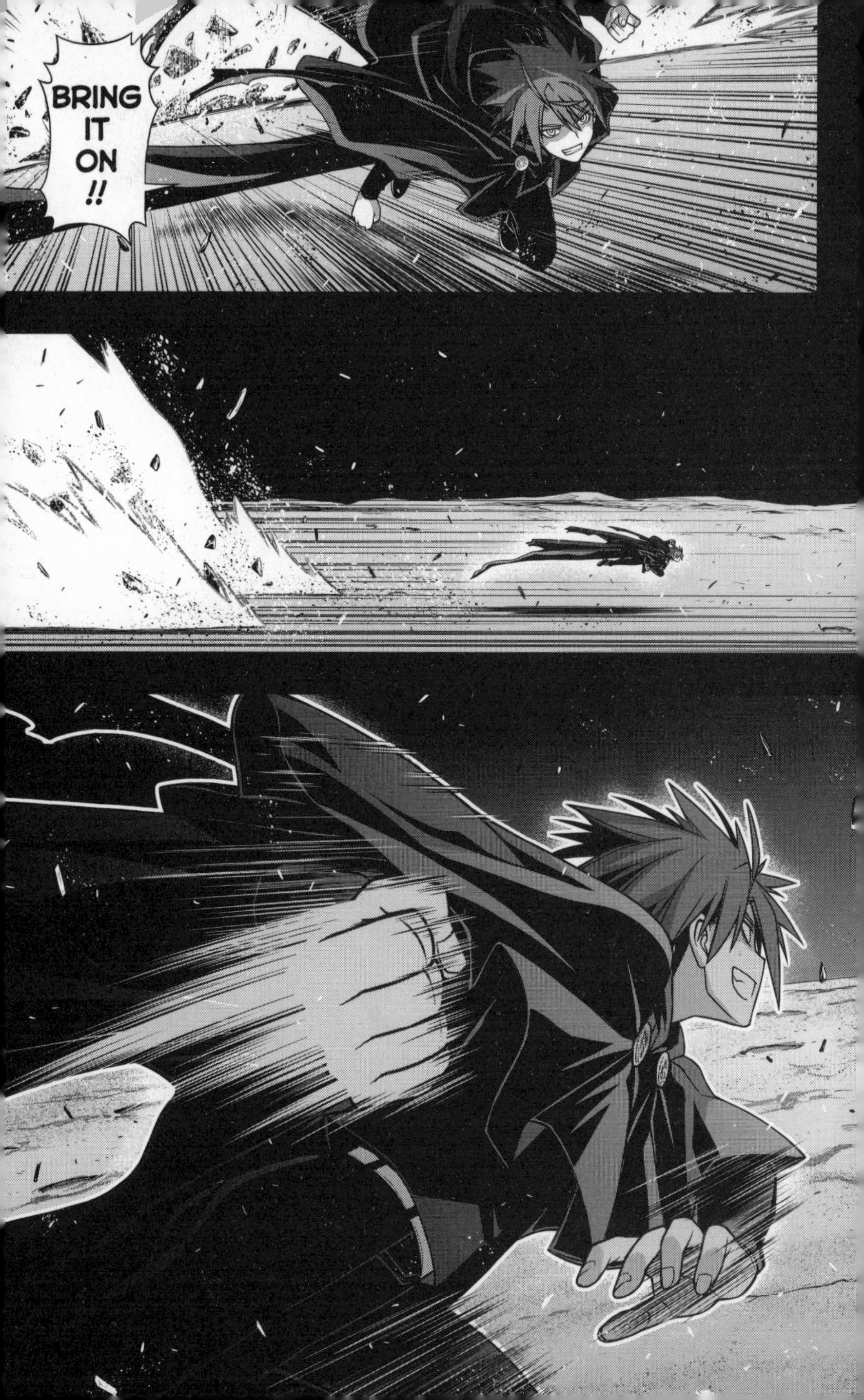
BRING IT ON !!

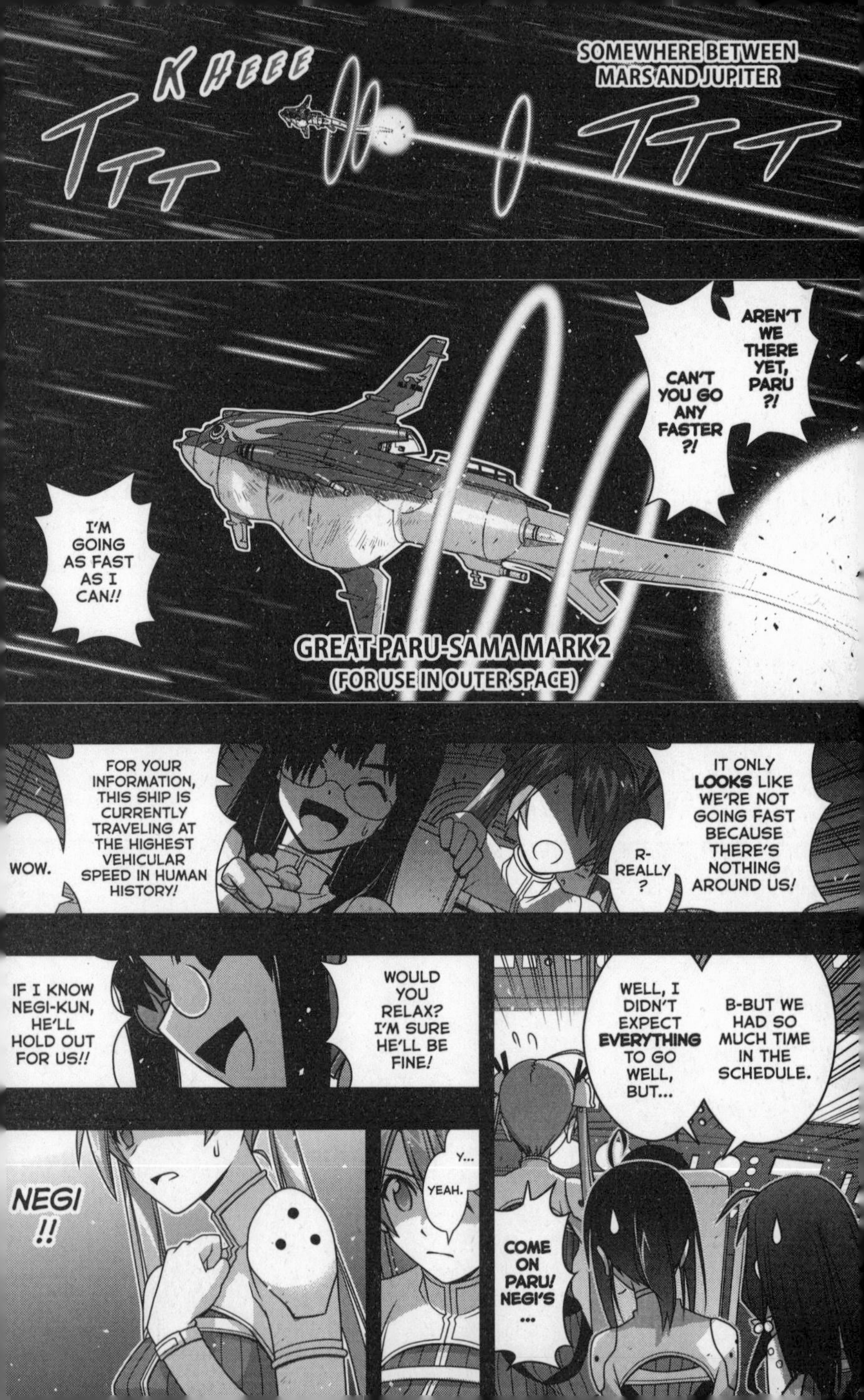
SOMEWHERE BETWEEN MARS AND JUPITER
KHEEE
AREN'T WE THERE YET, PARU?!
CAN'T YOU GO ANY FASTER?!
I'M GOING AS FAST AS I CAN!!
GREAT PARU-SAMA MARK 2
(FOR USE IN OUTER SPACE)
IT ONLY LOOKS LIKE WE'RE NOT GOING FAST BECAUSE THERE'S NOTHING AROUND US!
R-REALLY?
FOR YOUR INFORMATION, THIS SHIP IS CURRENTLY TRAVELING AT THE HIGHEST VEHICULAR SPEED IN HUMAN HISTORY!
WOW.
B-BUT WE HAD SO MUCH TIME IN THE SCHEDULE.
WELL, I DIDN'T EXPECT EVERYTHING TO GO WELL, BUT...
COME ON PARU! NEGI'S...
WOULD YOU RELAX? I'M SURE HE'LL BE FINE!
IF I KNOW NEGI-KUN, HE'LL HOLD OUT FOR US!!
Y... YEAH.
NEGI!!

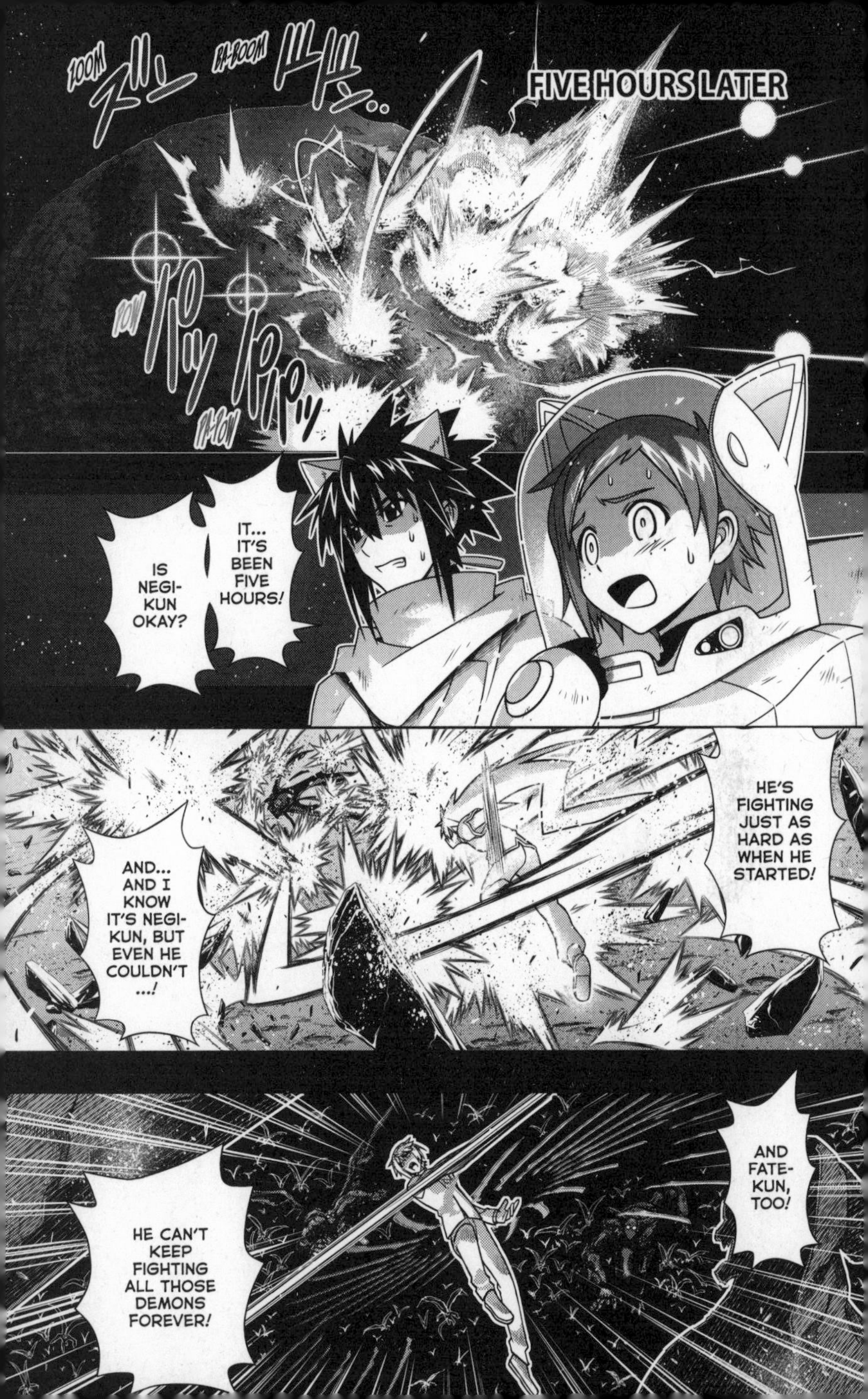
FIVE HOURS LATER
BA-BOOM
ZOOM
POW
PA-POW
IT... IT'S BEEN FIVE HOURS!
IS NEGI-KUN OKAY?
HE'S FIGHTING JUST AS HARD AS WHEN HE STARTED!
AND... AND I KNOW IT'S NEGI-KUN, BUT EVEN HE COULDN'T ...!
AND FATE-KUN, TOO!
HE CAN'T KEEP FIGHTING ALL THOSE DEMONS FOREVER!

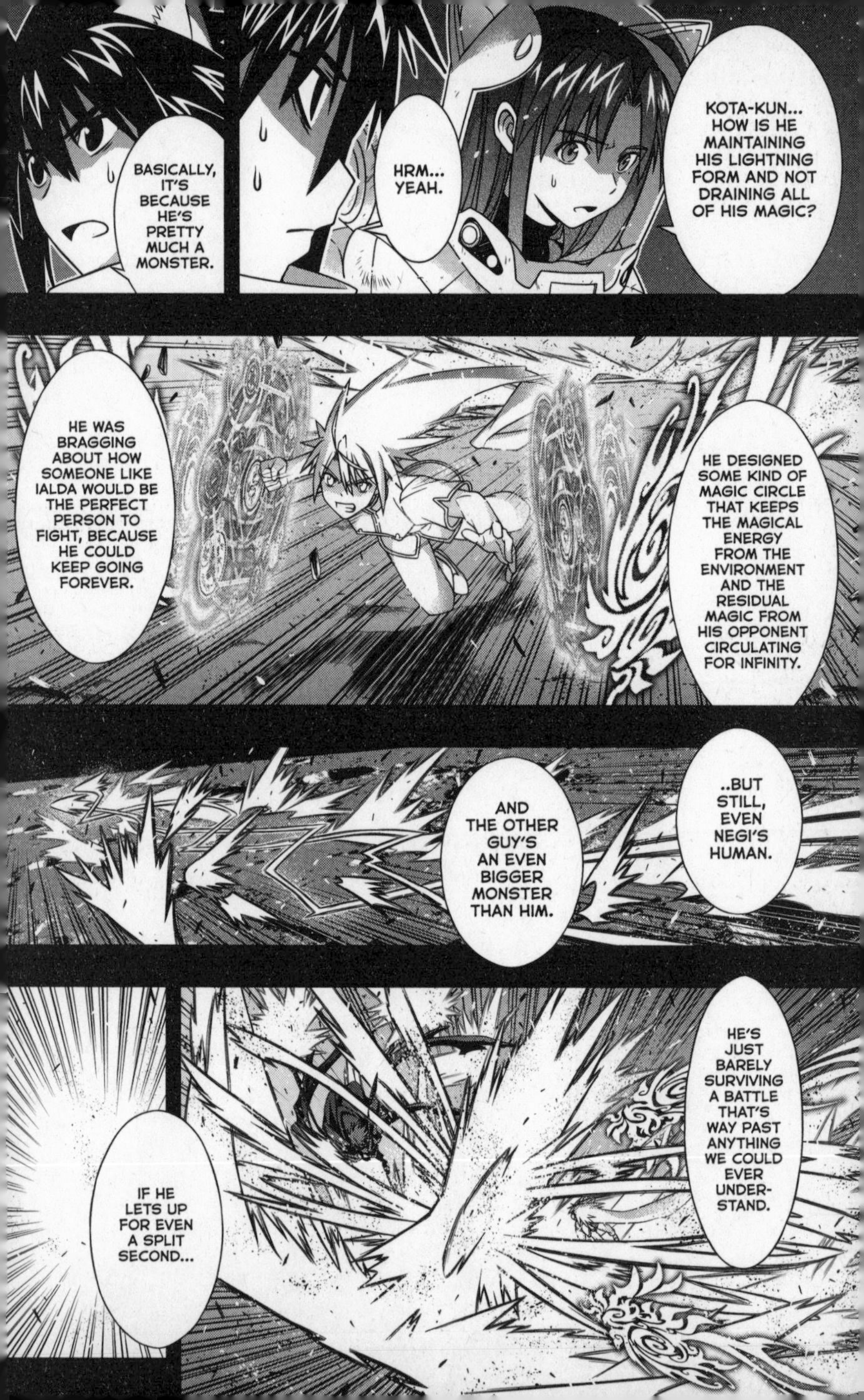
KOTA-KUN... HOW IS HE MAINTAINING HIS LIGHTNING FORM AND NOT DRAINING ALL OF HIS MAGIC?
HRM... YEAH.
BASICALLY, IT'S BECAUSE HE'S PRETTY MUCH A MONSTER.
HE DESIGNED SOME KIND OF MAGIC CIRCLE THAT KEEPS THE MAGICAL ENERGY FROM THE ENVIRONMENT AND THE RESIDUAL MAGIC FROM HIS OPPONENT CIRCULATING FOR INFINITY.
HE WAS BRAGGING ABOUT HOW SOMEONE LIKE IALDA WOULD BE THE PERFECT PERSON TO FIGHT, BECAUSE HE COULD KEEP GOING FOREVER.
..BUT STILL, EVEN NEGI'S HUMAN.
AND THE OTHER GUY'S AN EVEN BIGGER MONSTER THAN HIM.
HE'S JUST BARELY SURVIVING A BATTLE THAT'S WAY PAST ANYTHING WE COULD EVER UNDER-STAND.
IF HE LETS UP FOR EVEN A SPLIT SECOND...

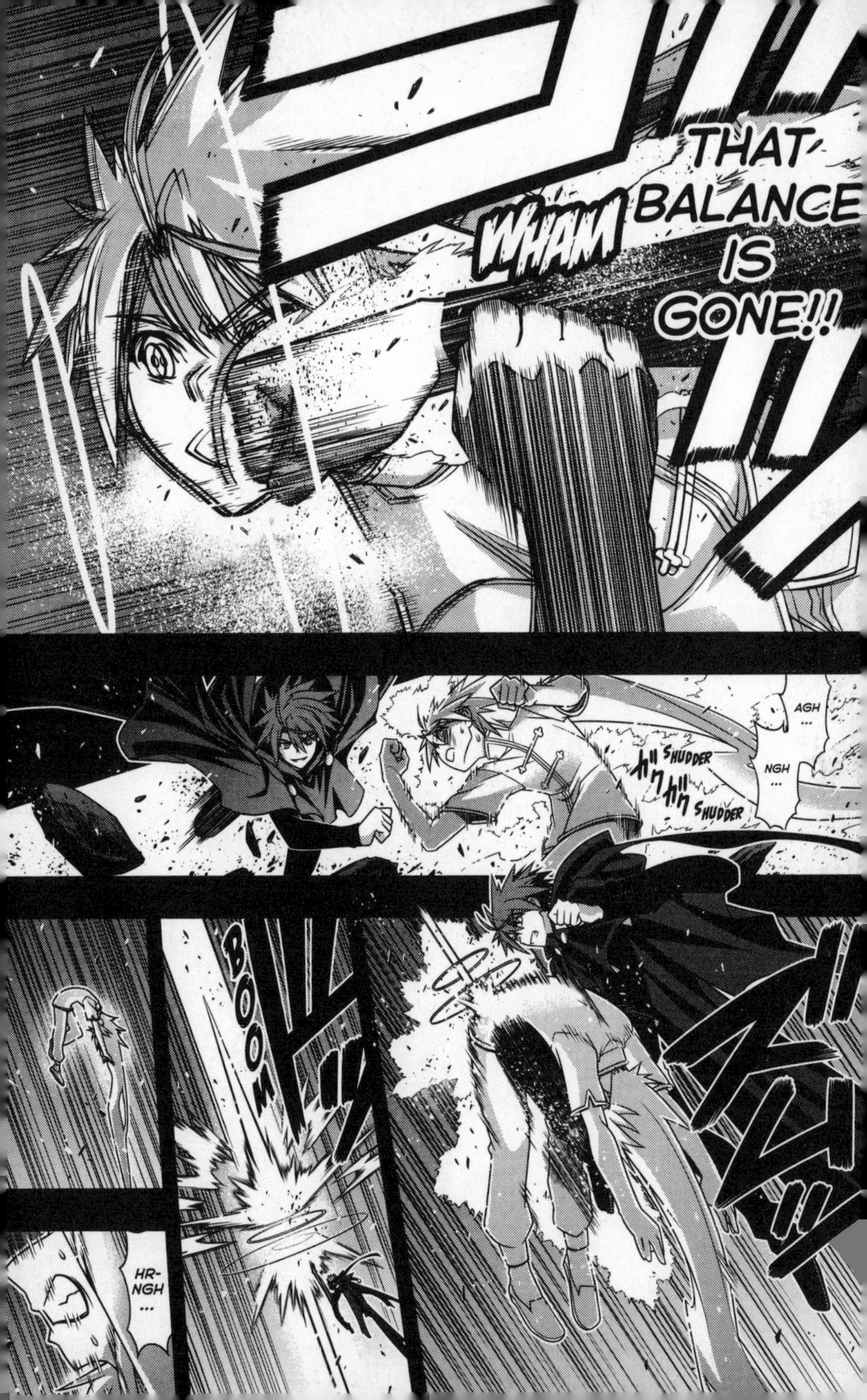

THAT BALANCE IS GONE!!
WHAM
AGH ...
NGH ...
ガク SHUDDER
ガク SHUDDER
BOOM
HR-NGH ...

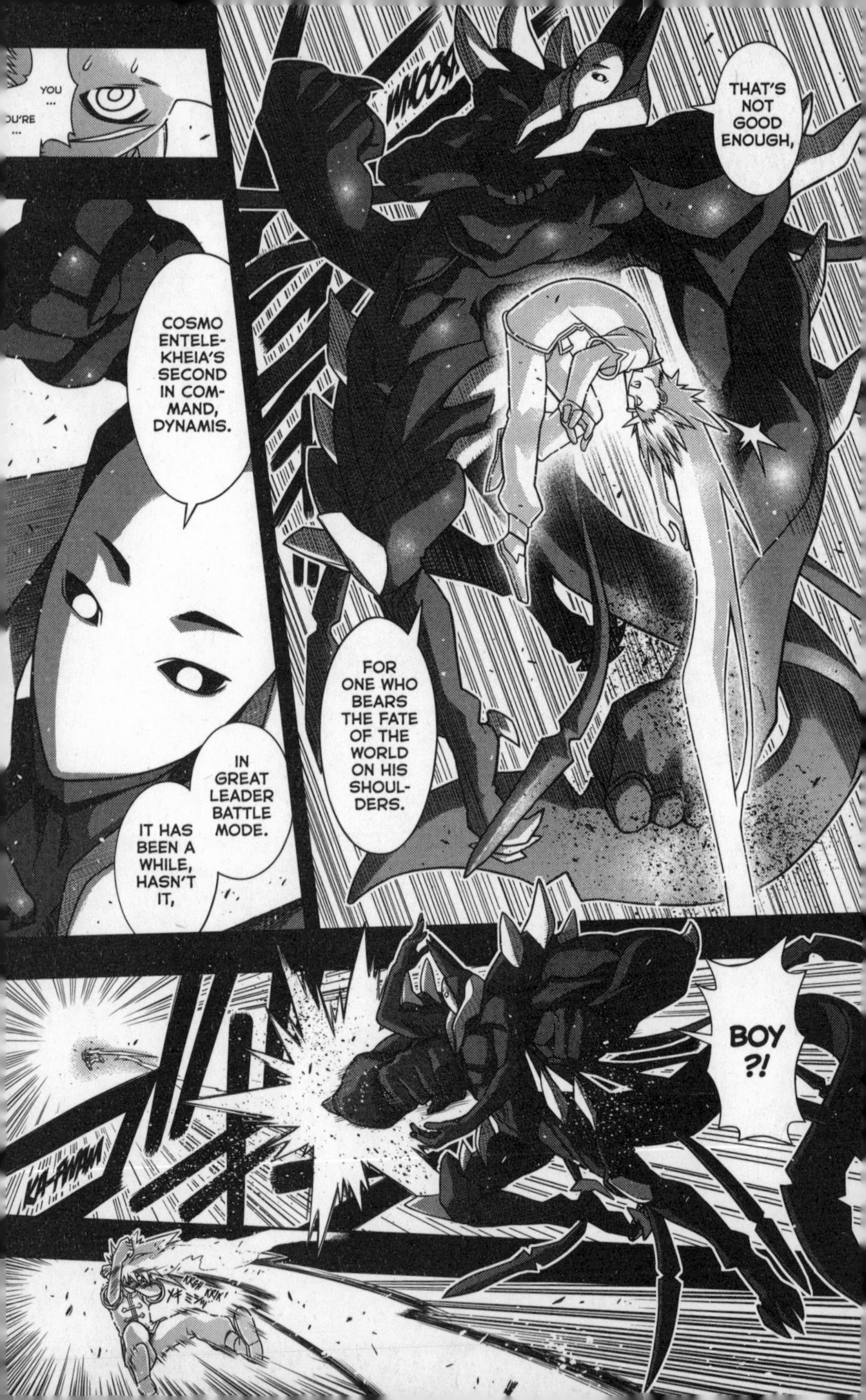
WHOOSH
THAT'S NOT GOOD ENOUGH,
FOR ONE WHO BEARS THE FATE OF THE WORLD ON HIS SHOULDERS.
YOU ...
OU'RE ...
COSMO ENTELEKHEIA'S SECOND IN COMMAND, DYNAMIS.
IN GREAT LEADER BATTLE MODE.
IT HAS BEEN A WHILE, HASN'T IT,
BOY ?!
KA-FWAM
KRIK KRIK!

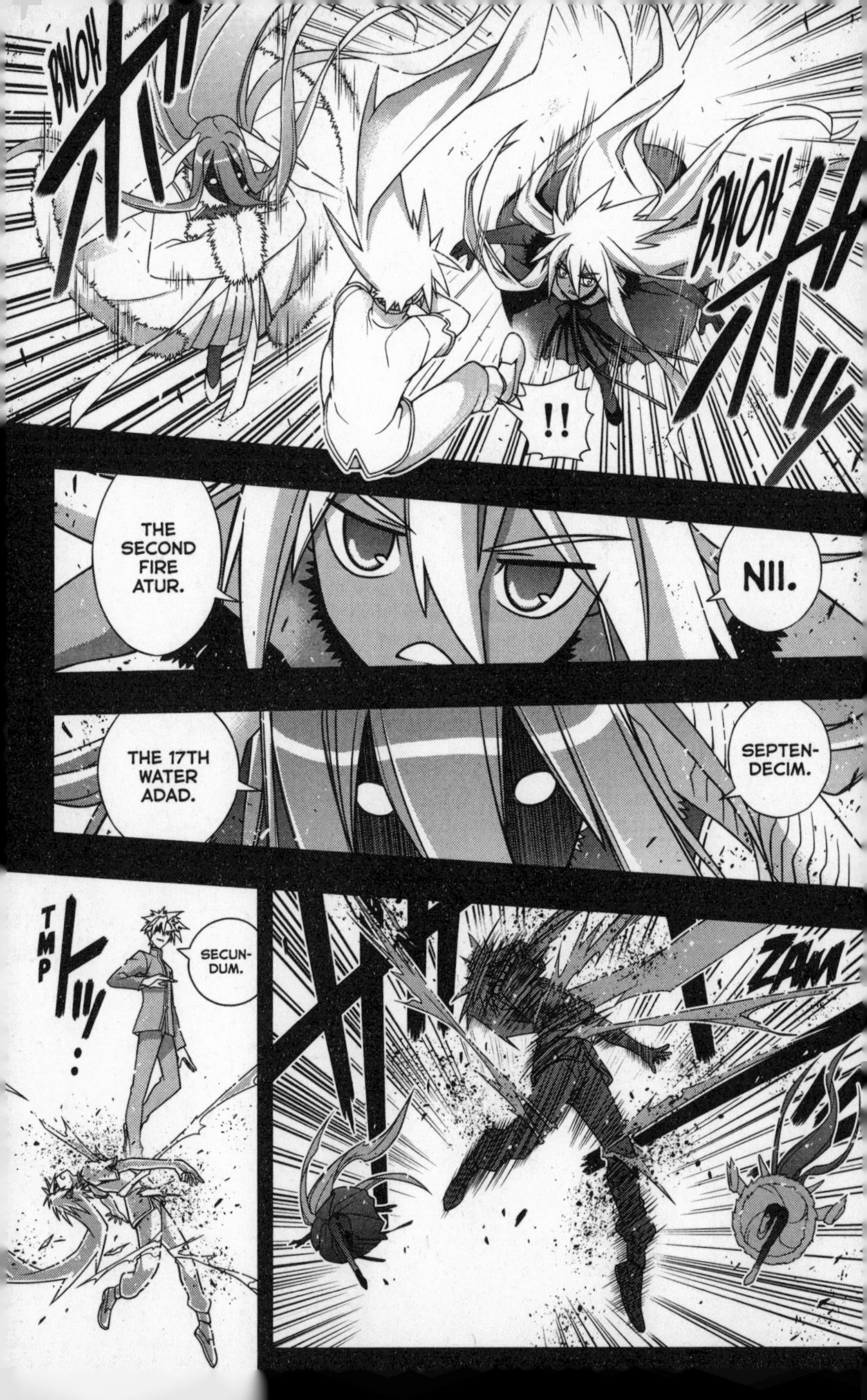
BWOH
!!
BWOH
NII.
THE SECOND FIRE ATUR.
SEPTEN-DECIM.
THE 17TH WATER ADAD.
ZAM
SECUN-DUM.
TMP

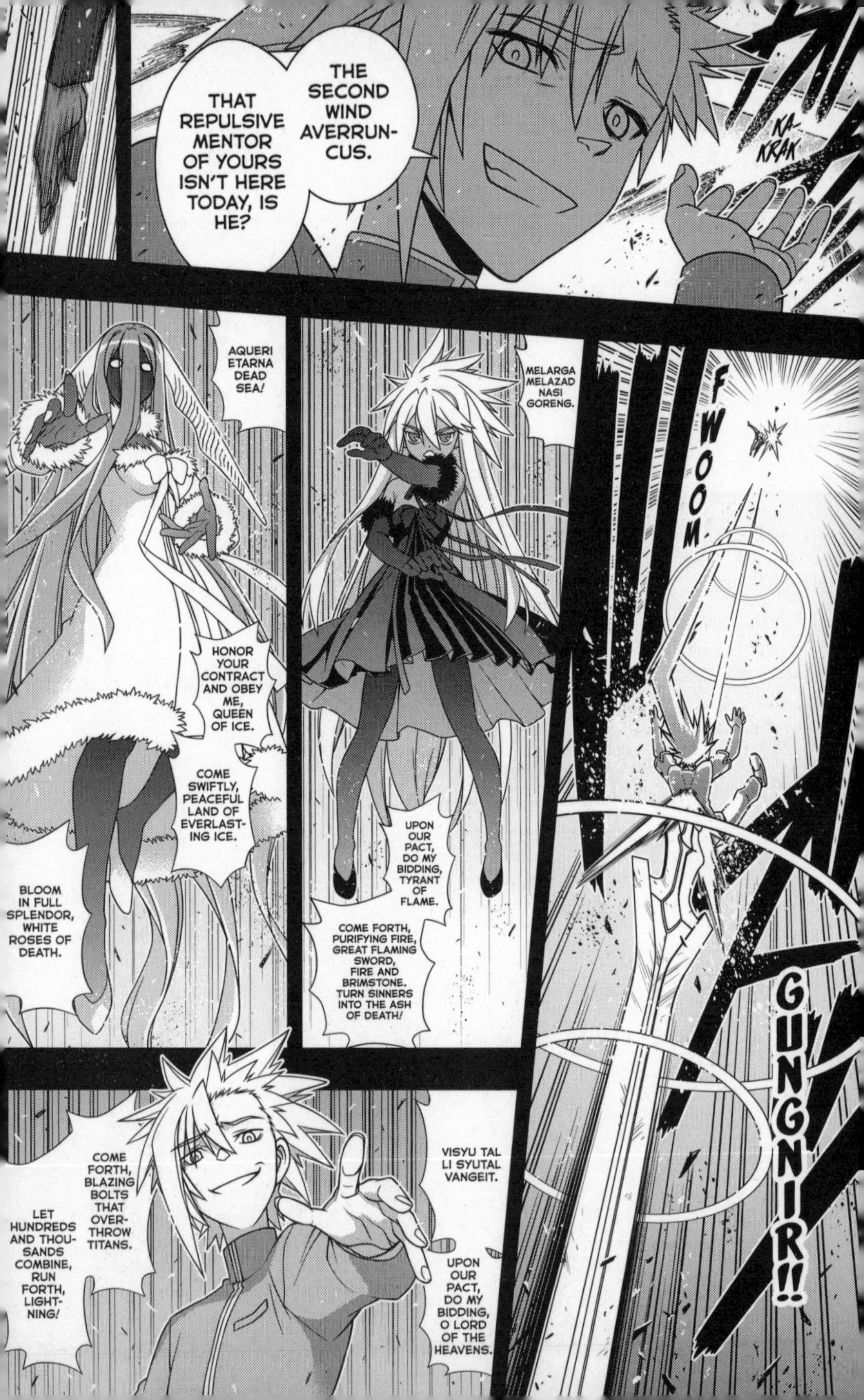

THE SECOND WIND AVERRUNCUS.
THAT REPULSIVE MENTOR OF YOURS ISN'T HERE TODAY, IS HE?
KA-KRAK
FWOOM
GUNGNIR!!
MELARGA MELAZAD NASI GORENG.
UPON OUR PACT, DO MY BIDDING, TYRANT OF FLAME.
COME FORTH, PURIFYING FIRE, GREAT FLAMING SWORD, FIRE AND BRIMSTONE. TURN SINNERS INTO THE ASH OF DEATH!
AQUERI ETARNA DEAD SEA!
HONOR YOUR CONTRACT AND OBEY ME, QUEEN OF ICE.
COME SWIFTLY, PEACEFUL LAND OF EVERLASTING ICE.
BLOOM IN FULL SPLENDOR, WHITE ROSES OF DEATH.
VISYU TAL LI SYUTAL VANGEIT.
UPON OUR PACT, DO MY BIDDING, O LORD OF THE HEAVENS.
COME FORTH, BLAZING BOLTS THAT OVER-THROW TITANS.
LET HUNDREDS AND THOU-SANDS COMBINE, RUN FORTH, LIGHT-NING!

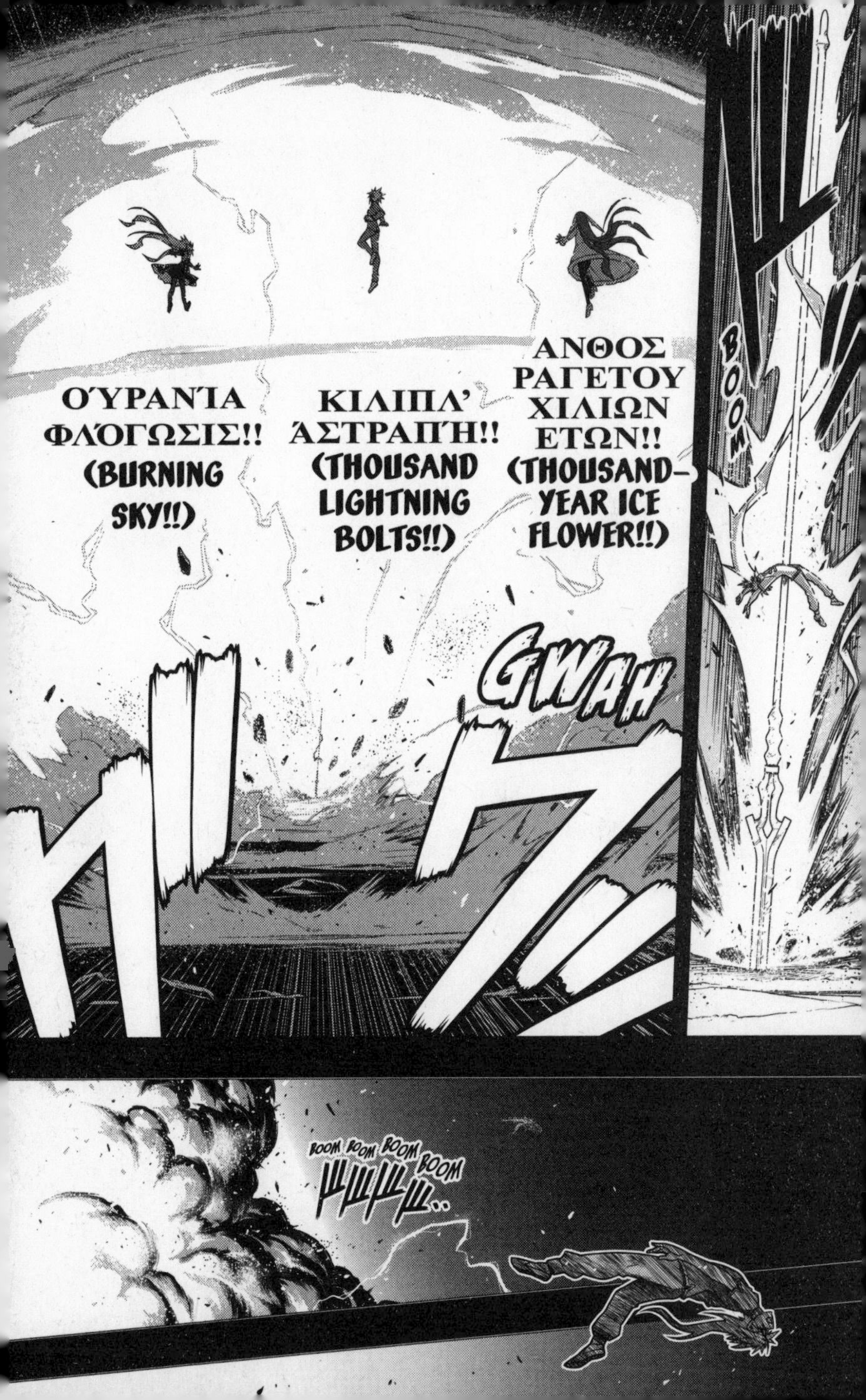
BOOM
ΑΝΘΟΣ ΡΑΓΕΤΟΥ ΧΙΛΙΩΝ ΕΤΩΝ!! (THOUSAND-YEAR ICE FLOWER!!)
ΚΙΛΙΠΛ' ΆΣΤΡΑΠΉ!! (THOUSAND LIGHTNING BOLTS!!)
ΟΎΡΑΝΊΑ ΦΛΌΓΩΣΙΣ!! (BURNING SKY!!)
GWAH
BOOM BOOM BOOM BOOM

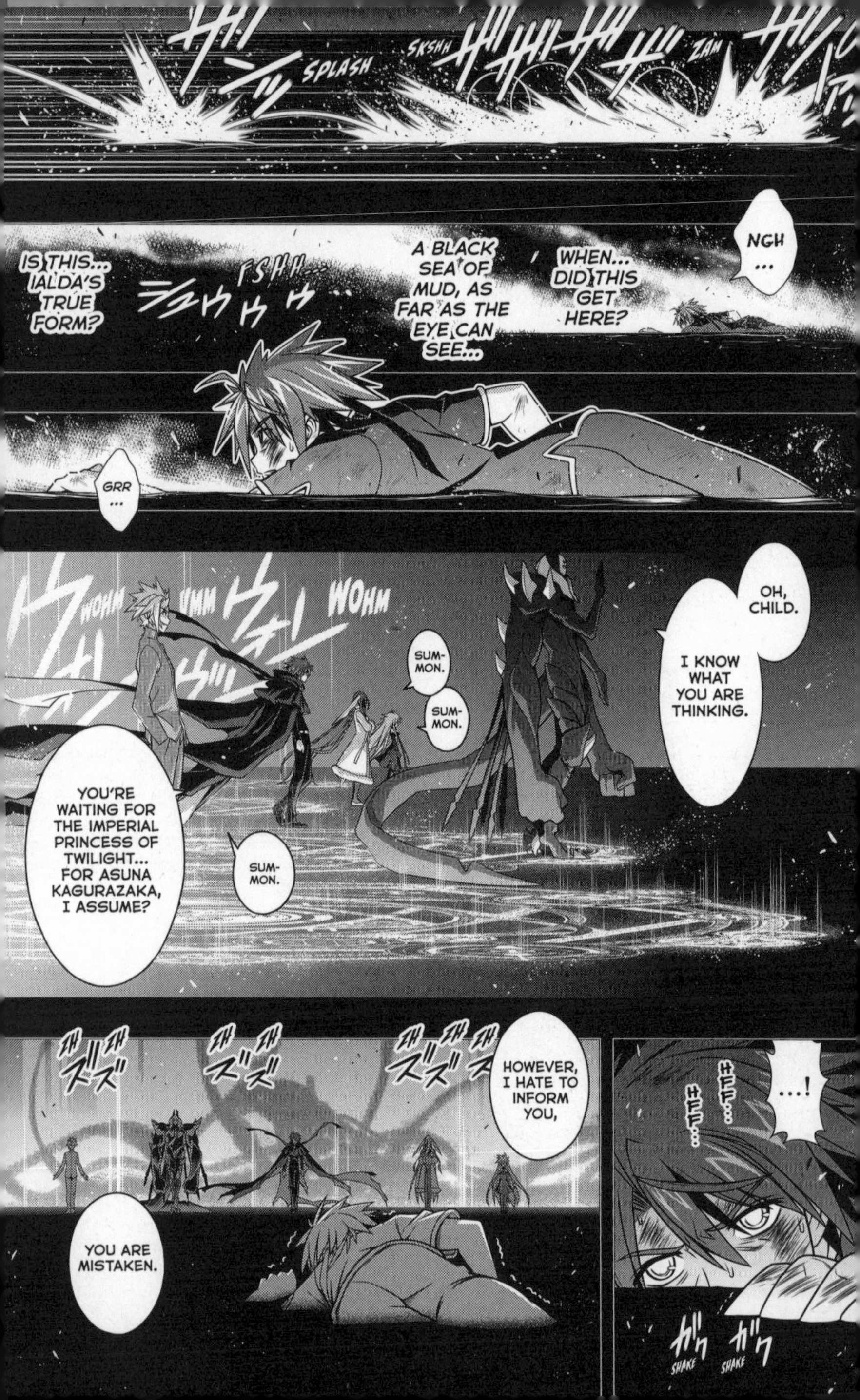
ZAM
SKSHH
SPLASH
NGH ...
WHEN... DID THIS GET HERE?
A BLACK SEA OF MUD, AS FAR AS THE EYE CAN SEE...
FSHH...
IS THIS... IALDA'S TRUE FORM?
GRR ...
OH, CHILD.
I KNOW WHAT YOU ARE THINKING.
SUM-MON.
SUM-MON.
WOHM
VMM
WOHM
YOU'RE WAITING FOR THE IMPERIAL PRINCESS OF TWILIGHT... FOR ASUNA KAGURAZAKA, I ASSUME?
SUM-MON.
...!
HFF... HFF...
SHAKE
SHAKE
ZH ZH
ZH ZH
ZH ZH
HOWEVER, I HATE TO INFORM YOU,
YOU ARE MISTAKEN.

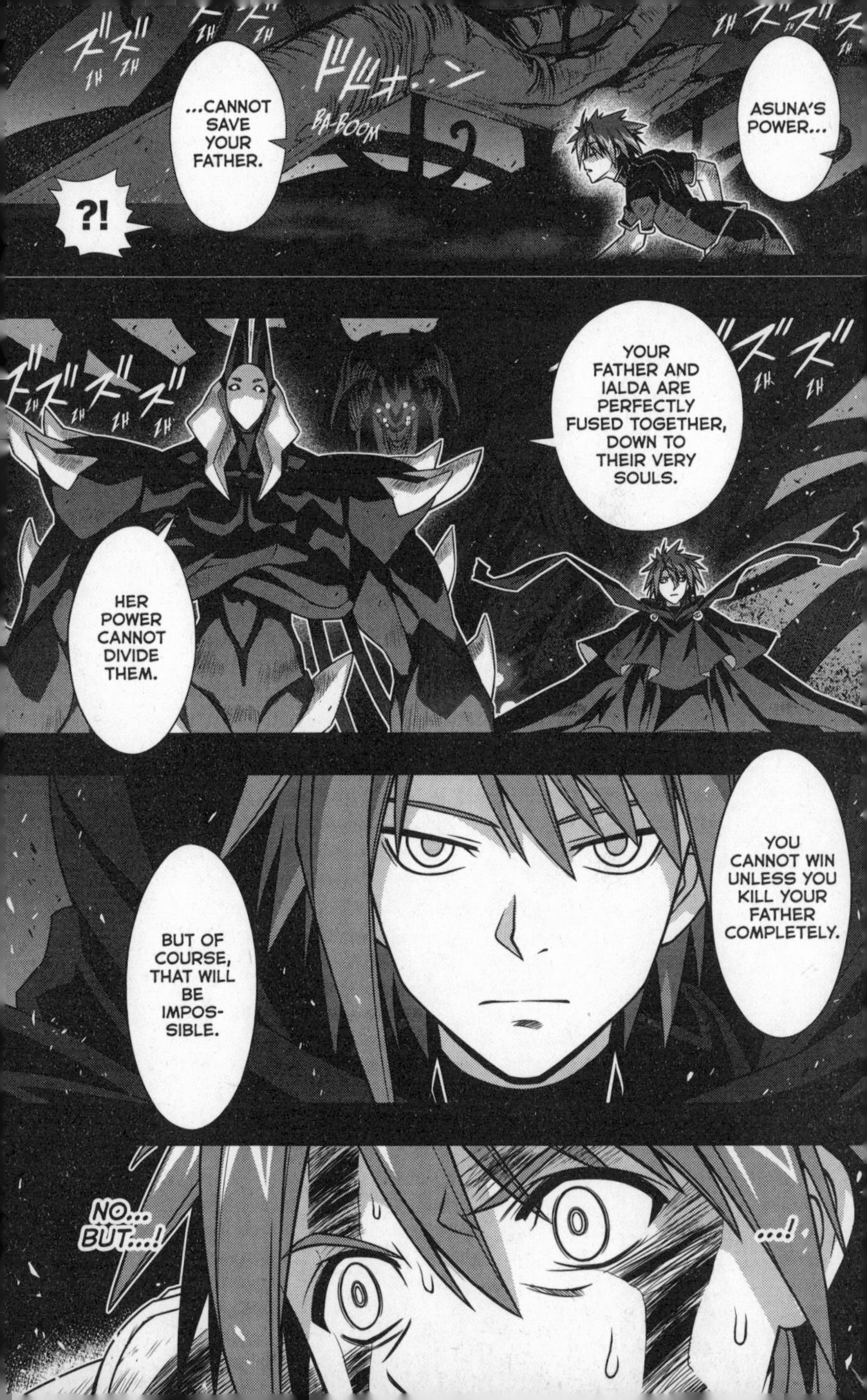
ASUNA'S POWER...
BA-BOOM
...CANNOT SAVE YOUR FATHER.
?!
YOUR FATHER AND IALDA ARE PERFECTLY FUSED TOGETHER, DOWN TO THEIR VERY SOULS.
HER POWER CANNOT DIVIDE THEM.
YOU CANNOT WIN UNLESS YOU KILL YOUR FATHER COMPLETELY.
BUT OF COURSE, THAT WILL BE IMPOSSIBLE.
...!
NO... BUT...!

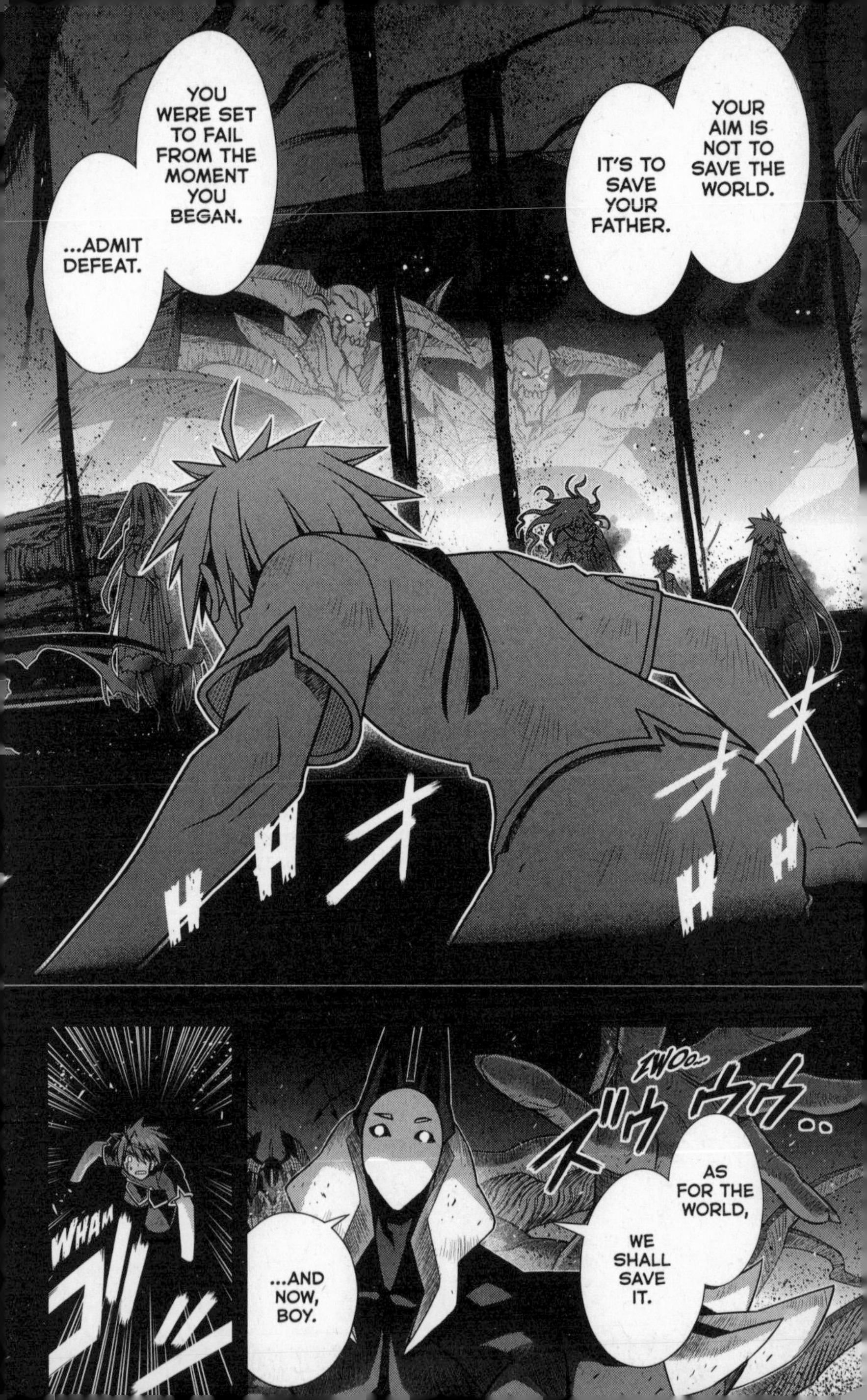
YOUR AIM IS NOT TO SAVE THE WORLD.
IT'S TO SAVE YOUR FATHER.
YOU WERE SET TO FAIL FROM THE MOMENT YOU BEGAN.
...ADMIT DEFEAT.
ZWOO...
ズゥウウ..
AS FOR THE WORLD,
WE SHALL SAVE IT.
...AND NOW, BOY.
WHAM
ゴッ

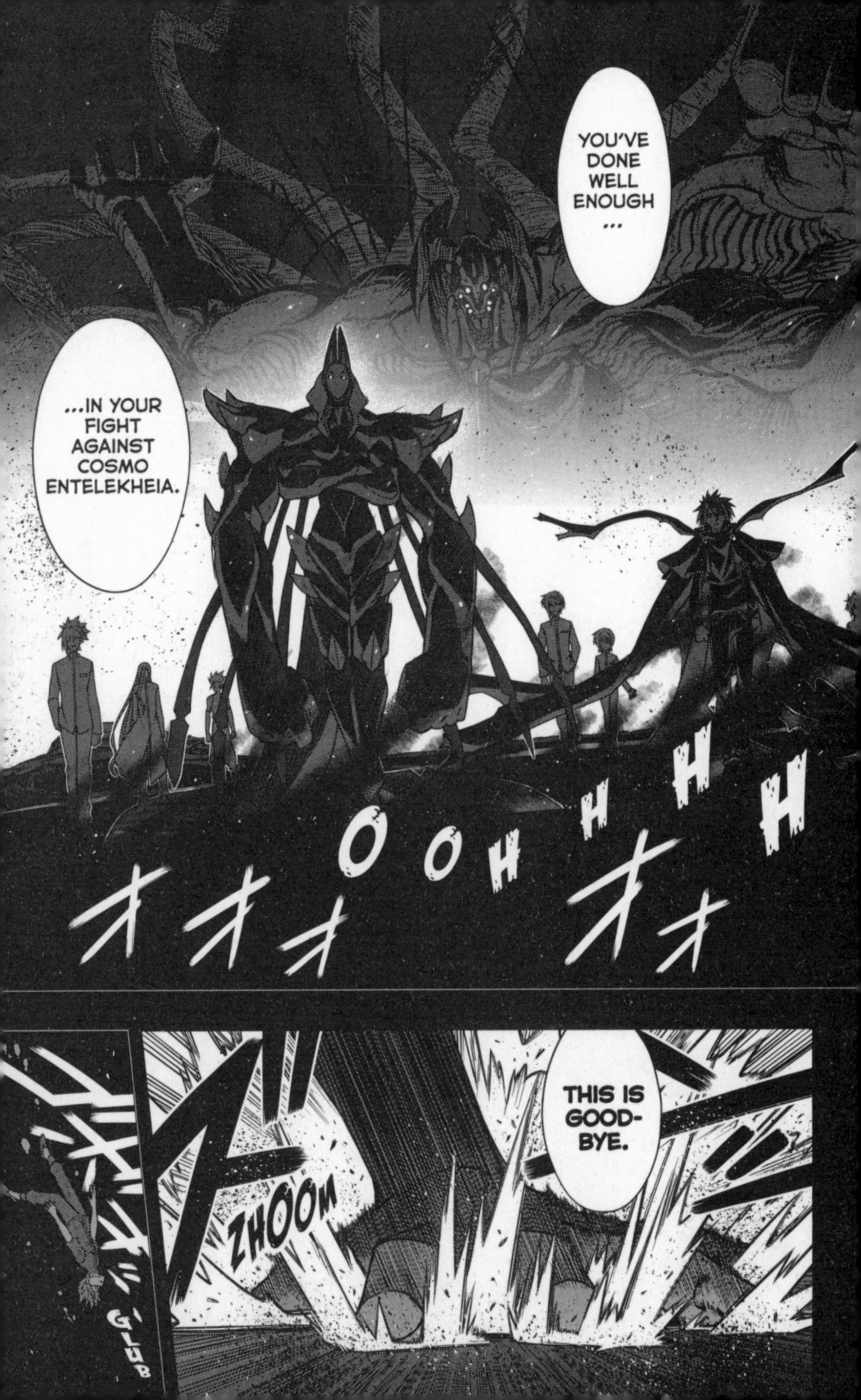
YOU'VE DONE WELL ENOUGH ...
...IN YOUR FIGHT AGAINST COSMO ENTELEKHEIA.
OOHHHH
オオオオオ
THIS IS GOOD-BYE.
ZHOOM
GLUB

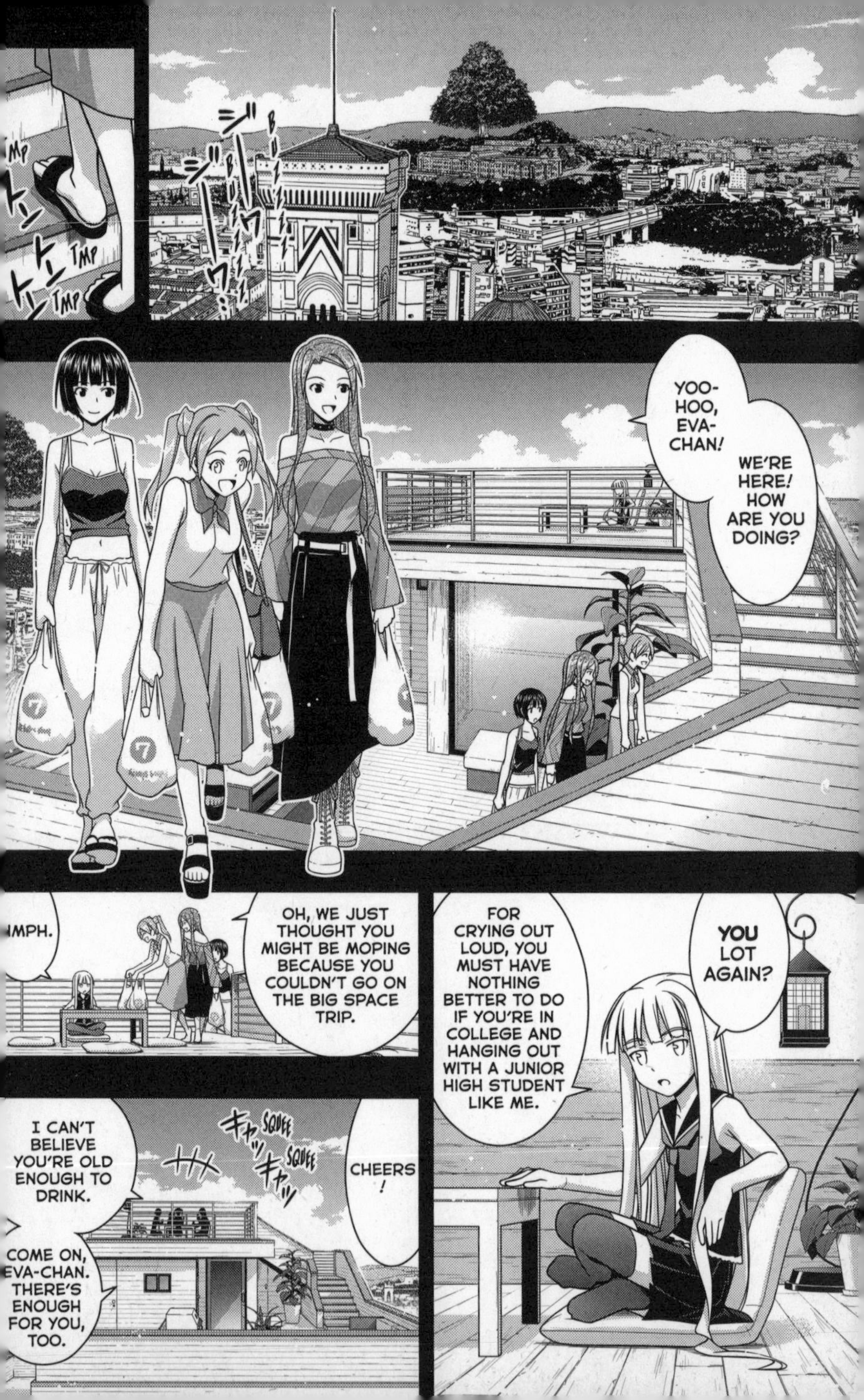
TMP
TMP
TMP
YOO-HOO, EVA-CHAN!
WE'RE HERE! HOW ARE YOU DOING?
YOU LOT AGAIN?
FOR CRYING OUT LOUD, YOU MUST HAVE NOTHING BETTER TO DO IF YOU'RE IN COLLEGE AND HANGING OUT WITH A JUNIOR HIGH STUDENT LIKE ME.
OH, WE JUST THOUGHT YOU MIGHT BE MOPING BECAUSE YOU COULDN'T GO ON THE BIG SPACE TRIP.
MPH.
CHEERS!
SQUEE
SQUEE
I CAN'T BELIEVE YOU'RE OLD ENOUGH TO DRINK.
COME ON, EVA-CHAN. THERE'S ENOUGH FOR YOU, TOO.

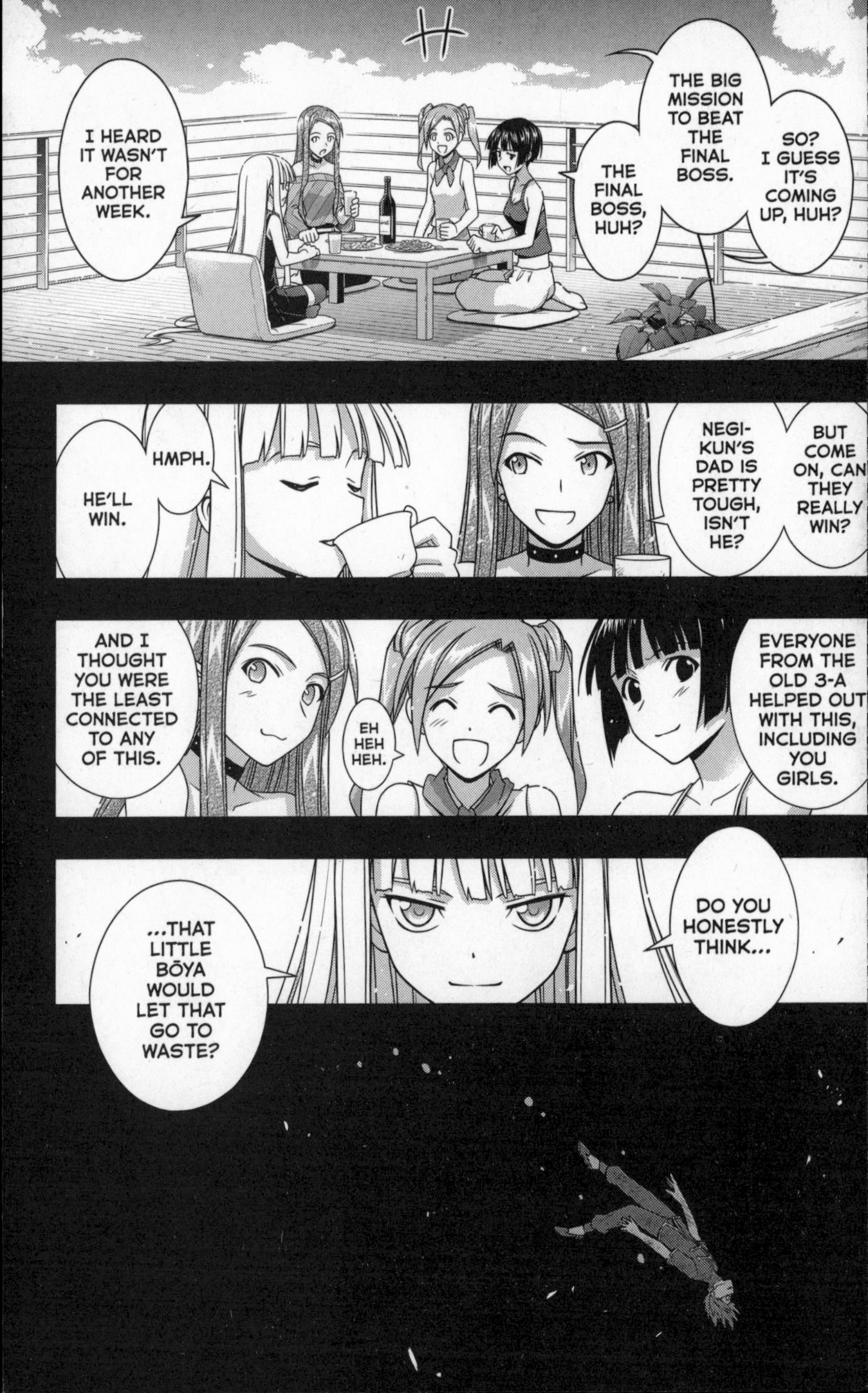
SO? I GUESS IT'S COMING UP, HUH?
THE BIG MISSION TO BEAT THE FINAL BOSS.
THE FINAL BOSS, HUH?
I HEARD IT WASN'T FOR ANOTHER WEEK.
BUT COME ON, CAN THEY REALLY WIN?
NEGI-KUN'S DAD IS PRETTY TOUGH, ISN'T HE?
HMPH.
HE'LL WIN.
EVERYONE FROM THE OLD 3-A HELPED OUT WITH THIS, INCLUDING YOU GIRLS.
EH HEH HEH.
AND I THOUGHT YOU WERE THE LEAST CONNECTED TO ANY OF THIS.
DO YOU HONESTLY THINK...
...THAT LITTLE BŌYA WOULD LET THAT GO TO WASTE?

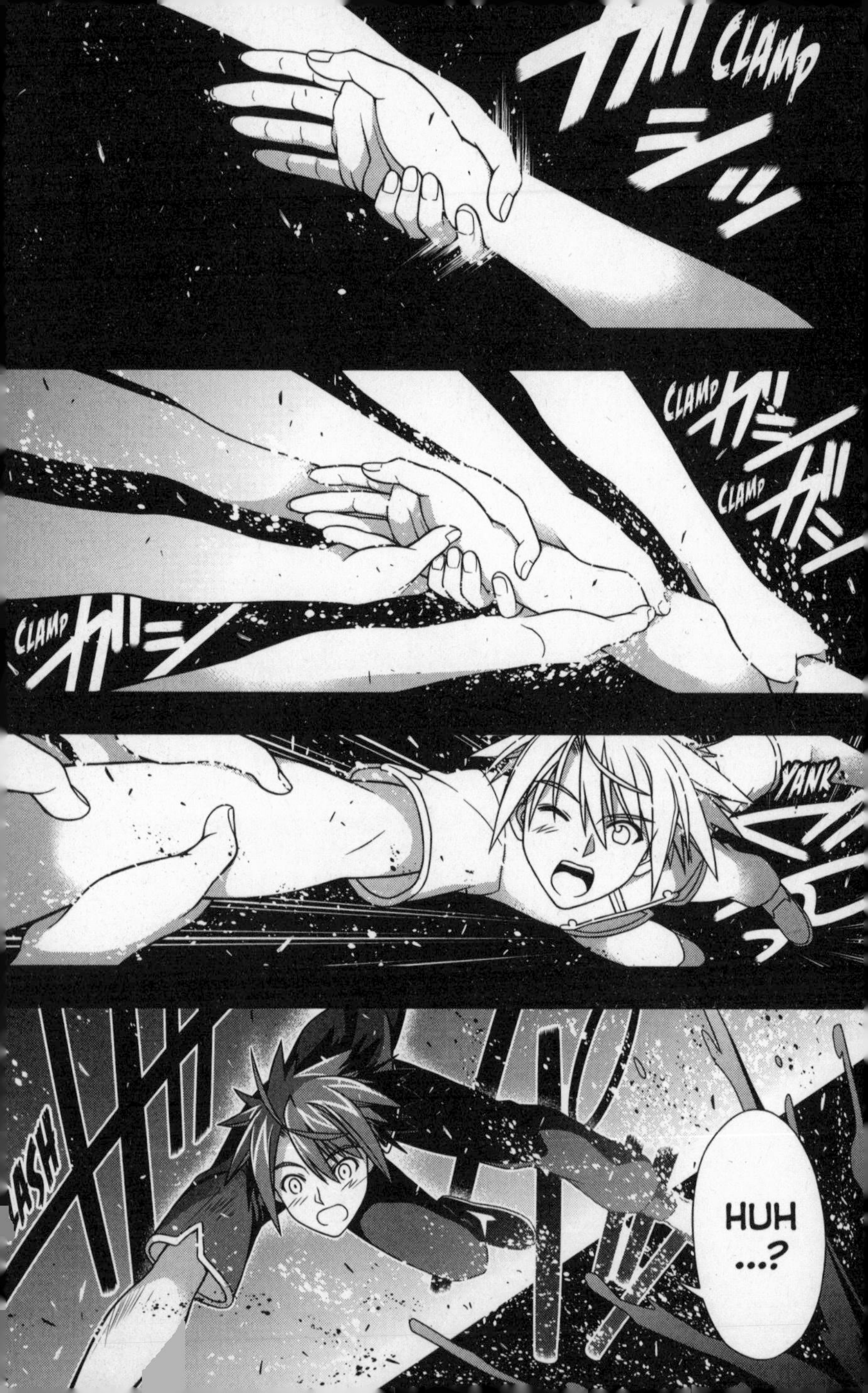
CLAMP
CLAMP
CLAMP
CLAMP
YANK
HUH ...?

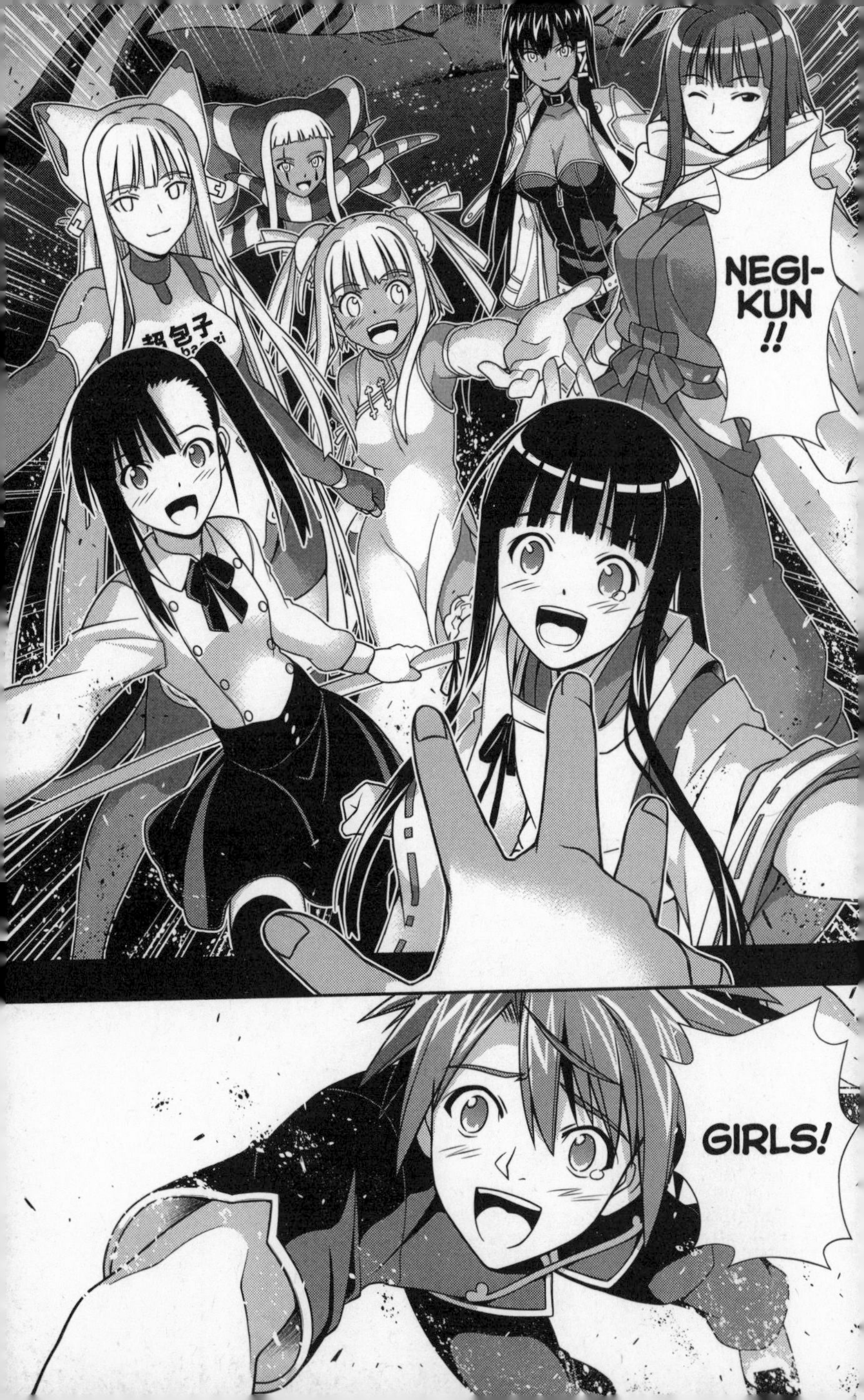
NEGI-
KUN
!!
超包子
GIRLS!

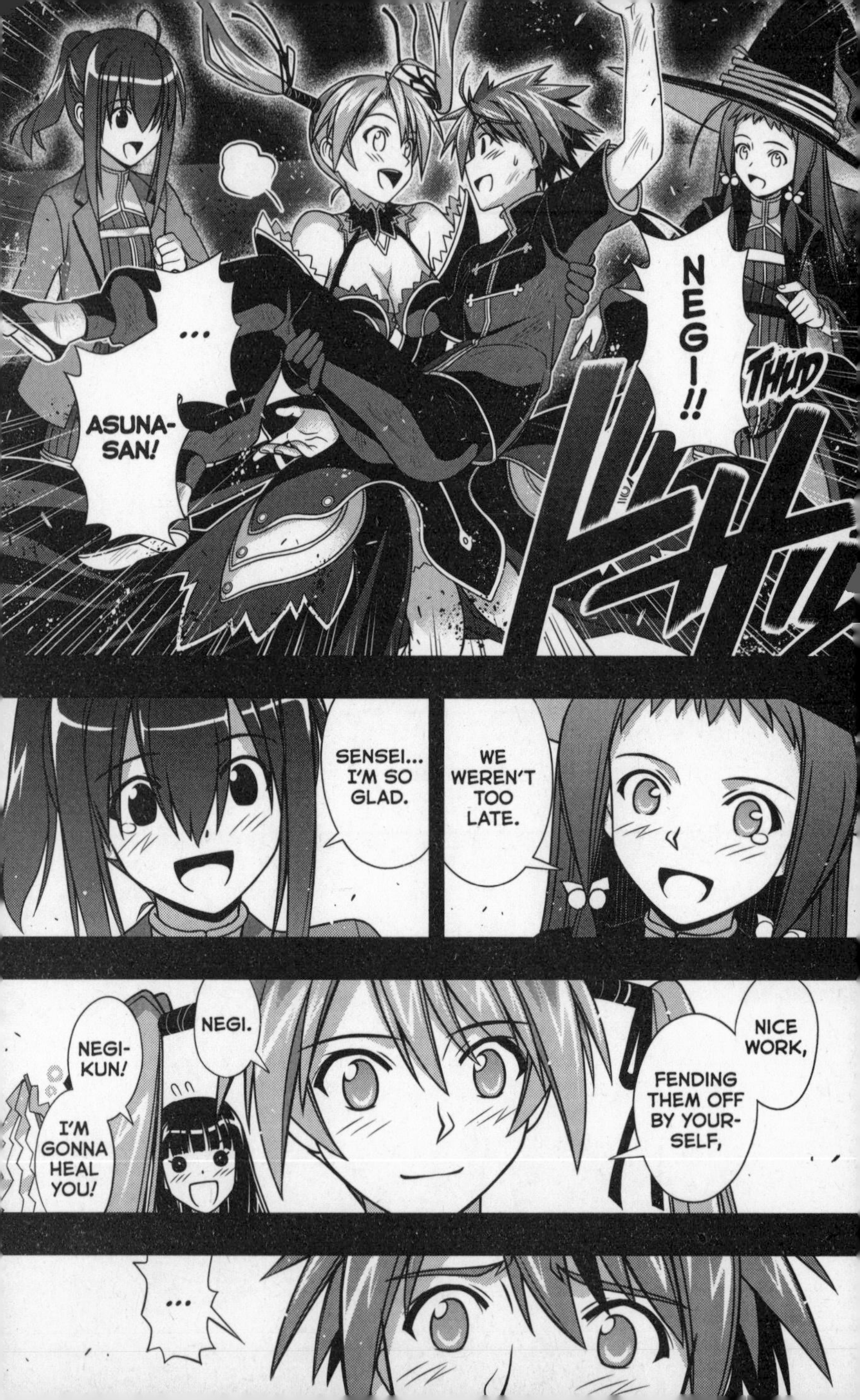
NEGI!!
THUD
... ASUNA-SAN!
WE WEREN'T TOO LATE.
SENSEI... I'M SO GLAD.
NICE WORK, FENDING THEM OFF BY YOURSELF,
NEGI.
NEGI-KUN! I'M GONNA HEAL YOU!
...

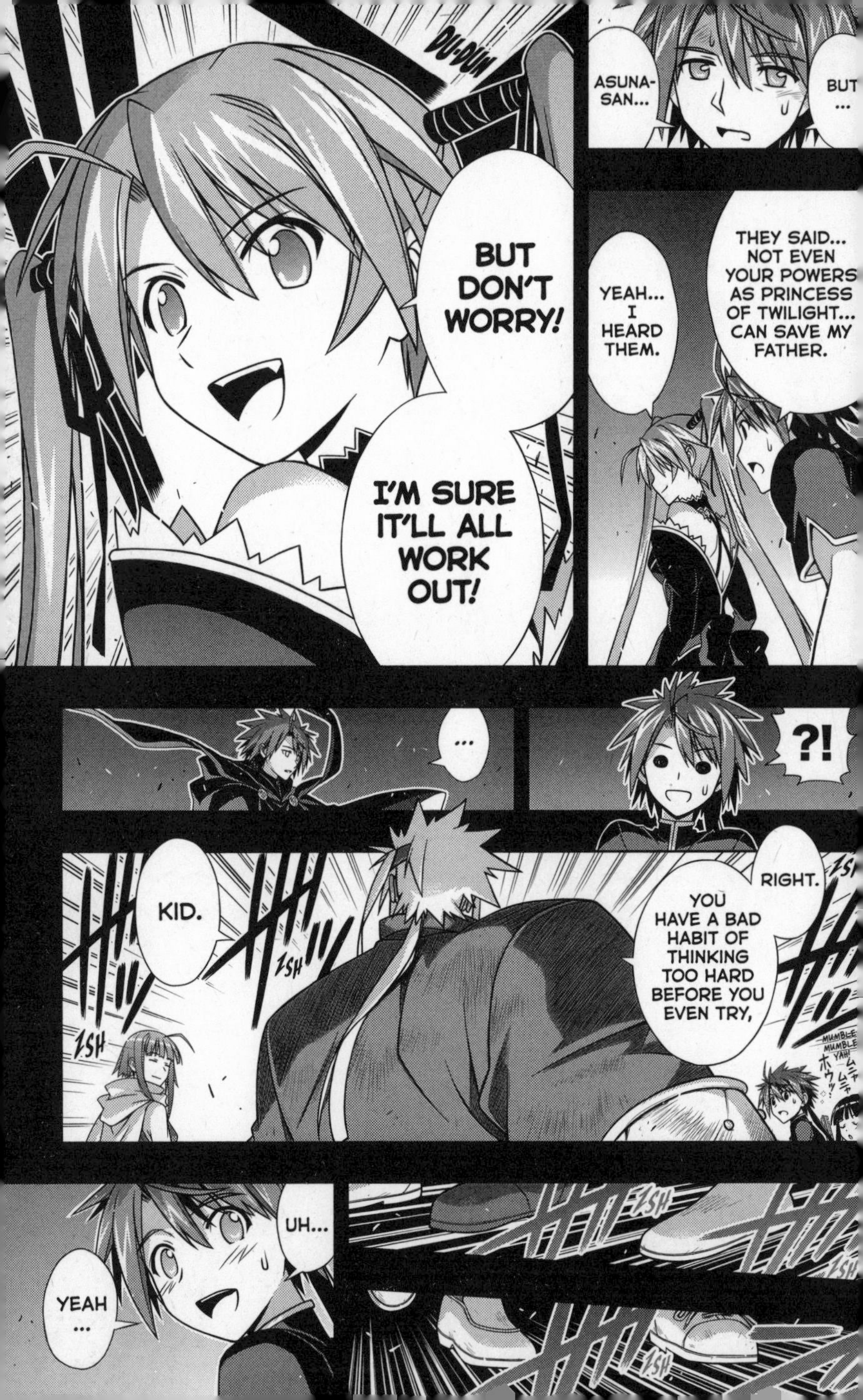
BUT ...
ASUNA-SAN...
THEY SAID... NOT EVEN YOUR POWERS AS PRINCESS OF TWILIGHT... CAN SAVE MY FATHER.
YEAH... I HEARD THEM.
DU-DUN
BUT DON'T WORRY!
I'M SURE IT'LL ALL WORK OUT!
?!
...
RIGHT.
YOU HAVE A BAD HABIT OF THINKING TOO HARD BEFORE YOU EVEN TRY,
ZSH
MUMBLE MUMBLE
YAH
ムニャムニャ
ホウッ
ZSH
KID.
ZSH
ZSH
ZSH
UH...
YEAH ...

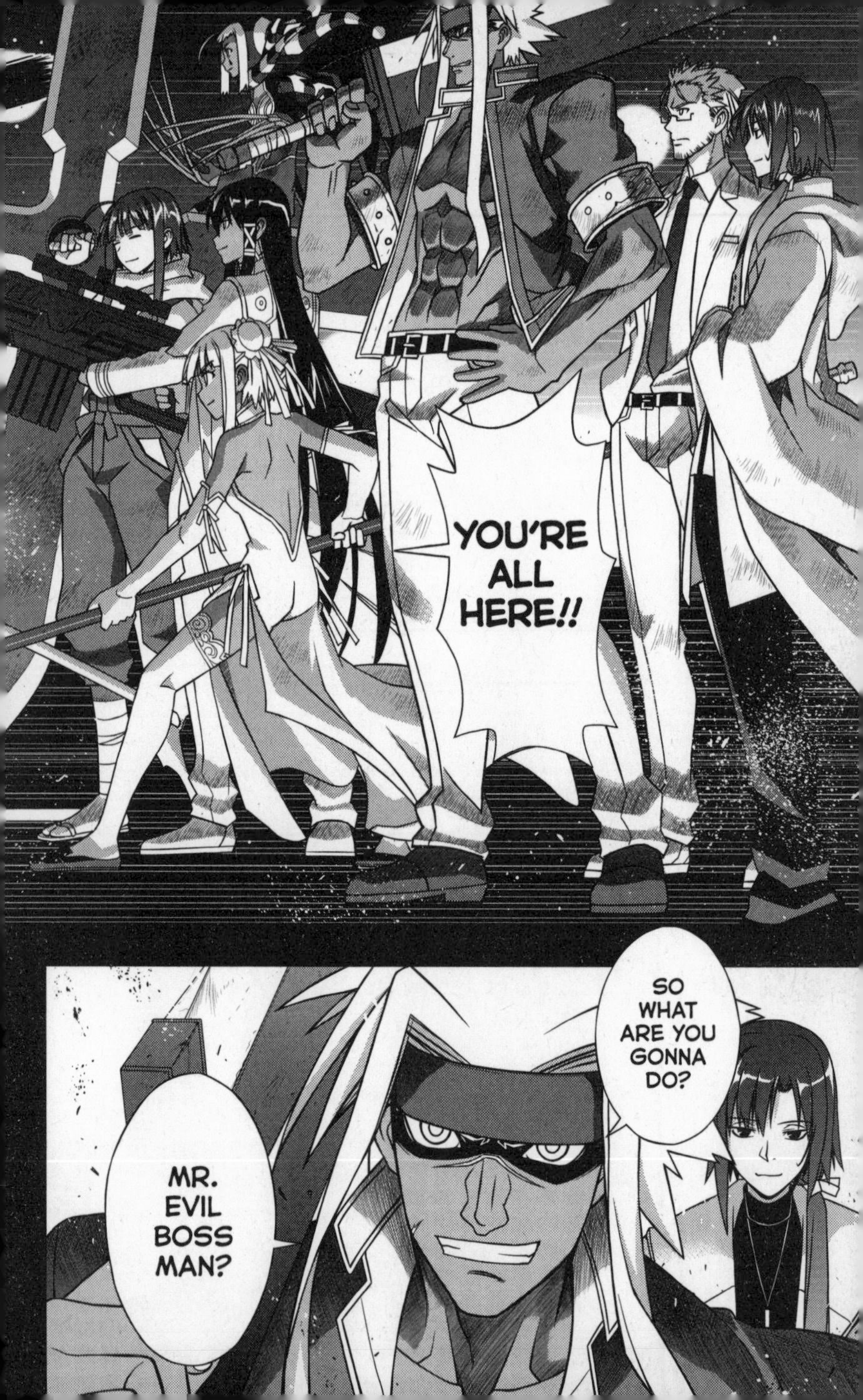
YOU'RE ALL HERE!!
SO WHAT ARE YOU GONNA DO?
MR. EVIL BOSS MAN?

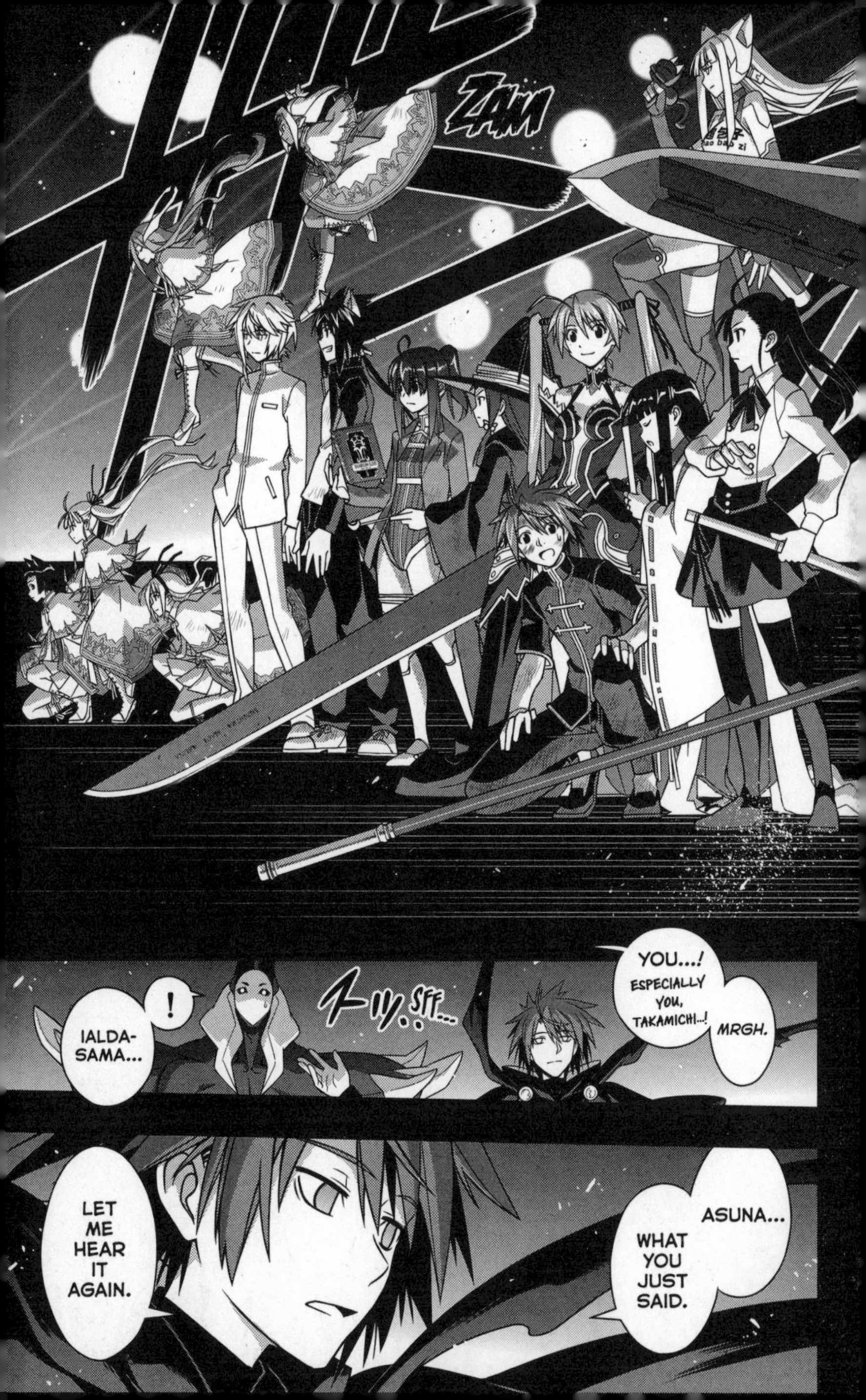
ZAWA
YOU...! ESPECIALLY YOU, TAKAMICHI...!
MRGH.
SFF...
!
IALDA-SAMA...
ASUNA... WHAT YOU JUST SAID.
LET ME HEAR IT AGAIN.

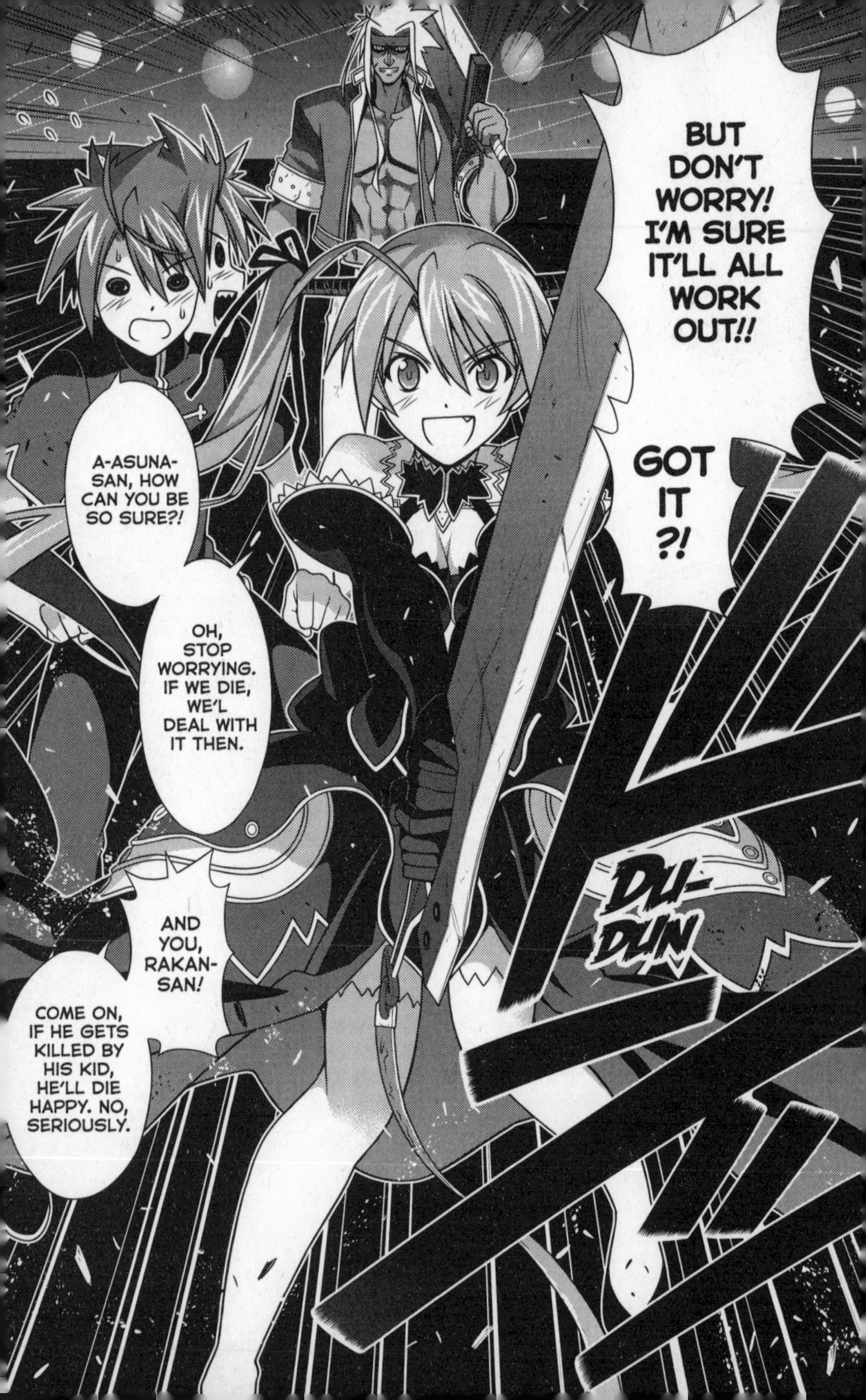
BUT DON'T WORRY! I'M SURE IT'LL ALL WORK OUT!!
GOT IT ?!
A-ASUNA-SAN, HOW CAN YOU BE SO SURE?!
OH, STOP WORRYING. IF WE DIE, WE'L DEAL WITH IT THEN.
DU-DUN
AND YOU, RAKAN-SAN!
COME ON, IF HE GETS KILLED BY HIS KID, HE'LL DIE HAPPY. NO, SERIOUSLY.

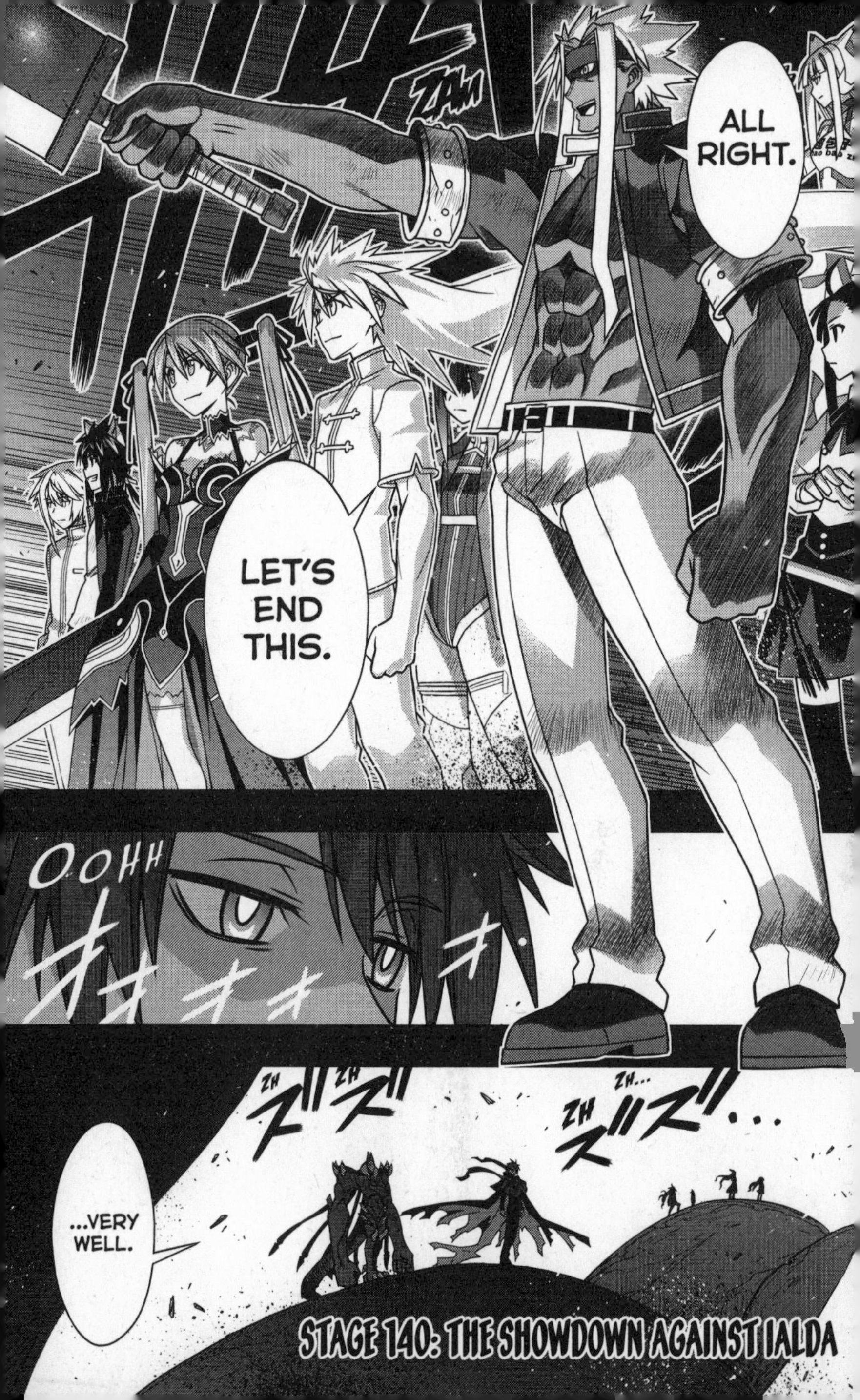

ALL RIGHT.
ZAN
LET'S END THIS.
OOHH
ZH...
ZH
ZH
ZH
...VERY WELL.
STAGE 140: THE SHOWDOWN AGAINST IALDA

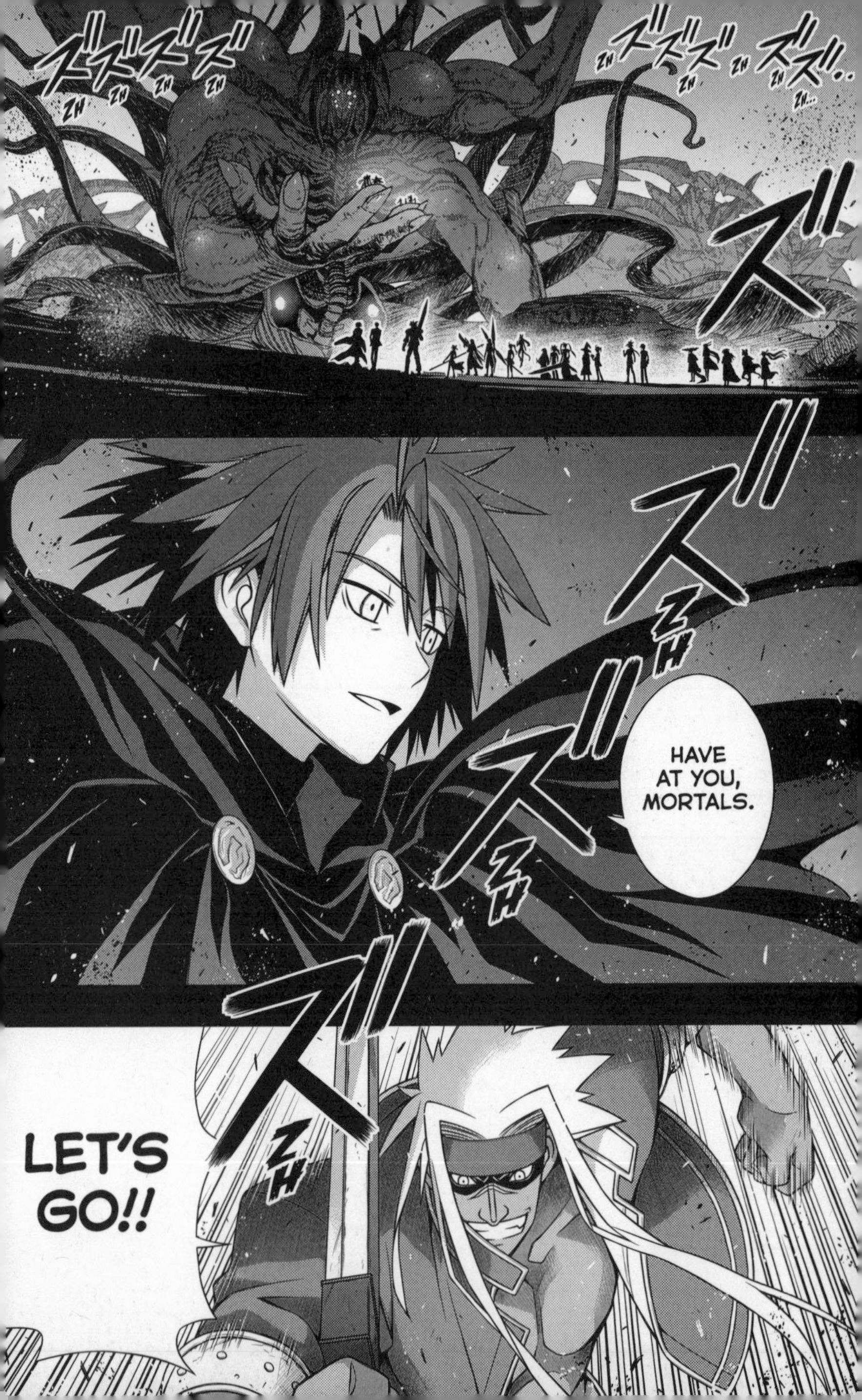
HAVE AT YOU, MORTALS.
LET'S GO!!

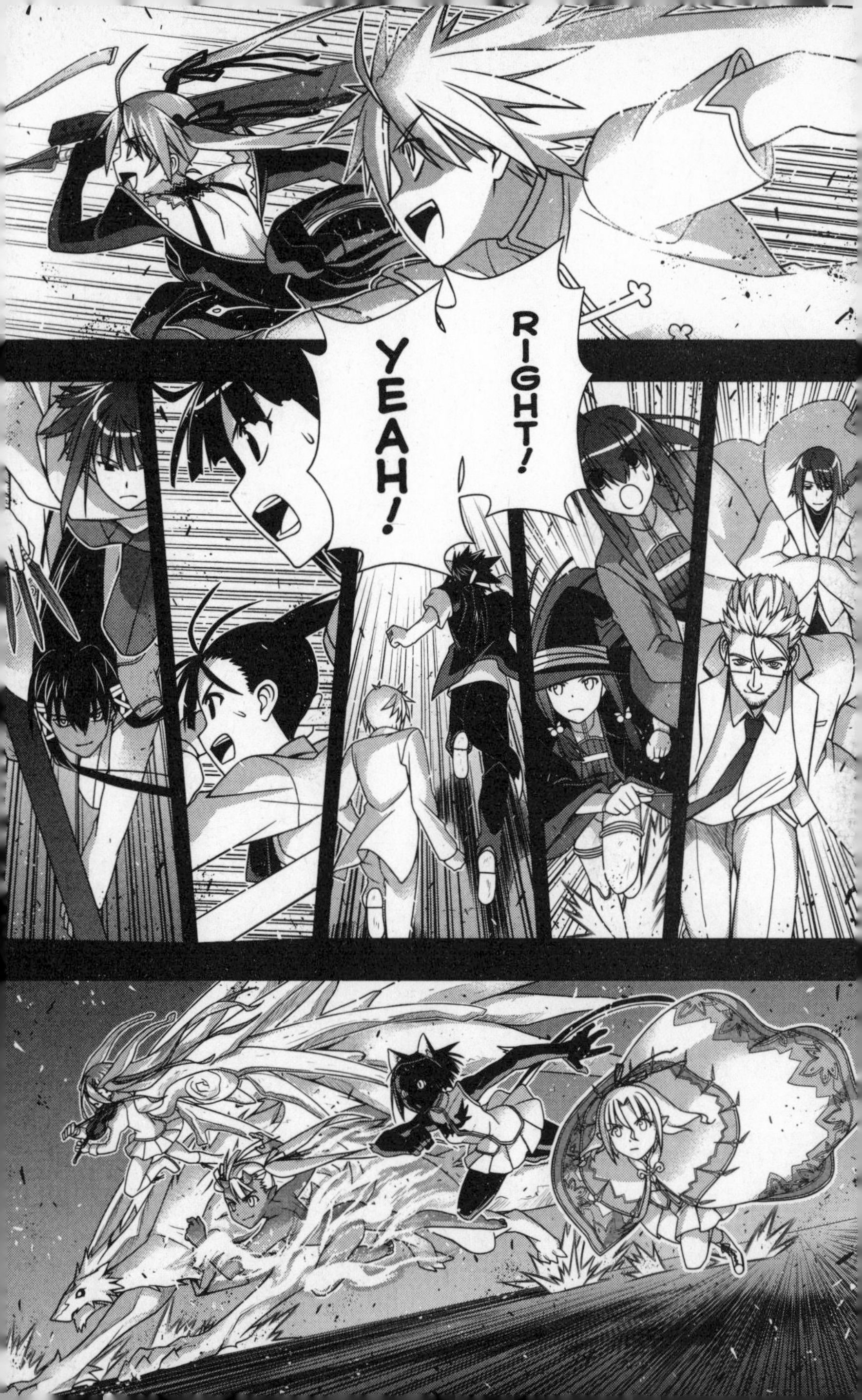
RIGHT!
YEAH!

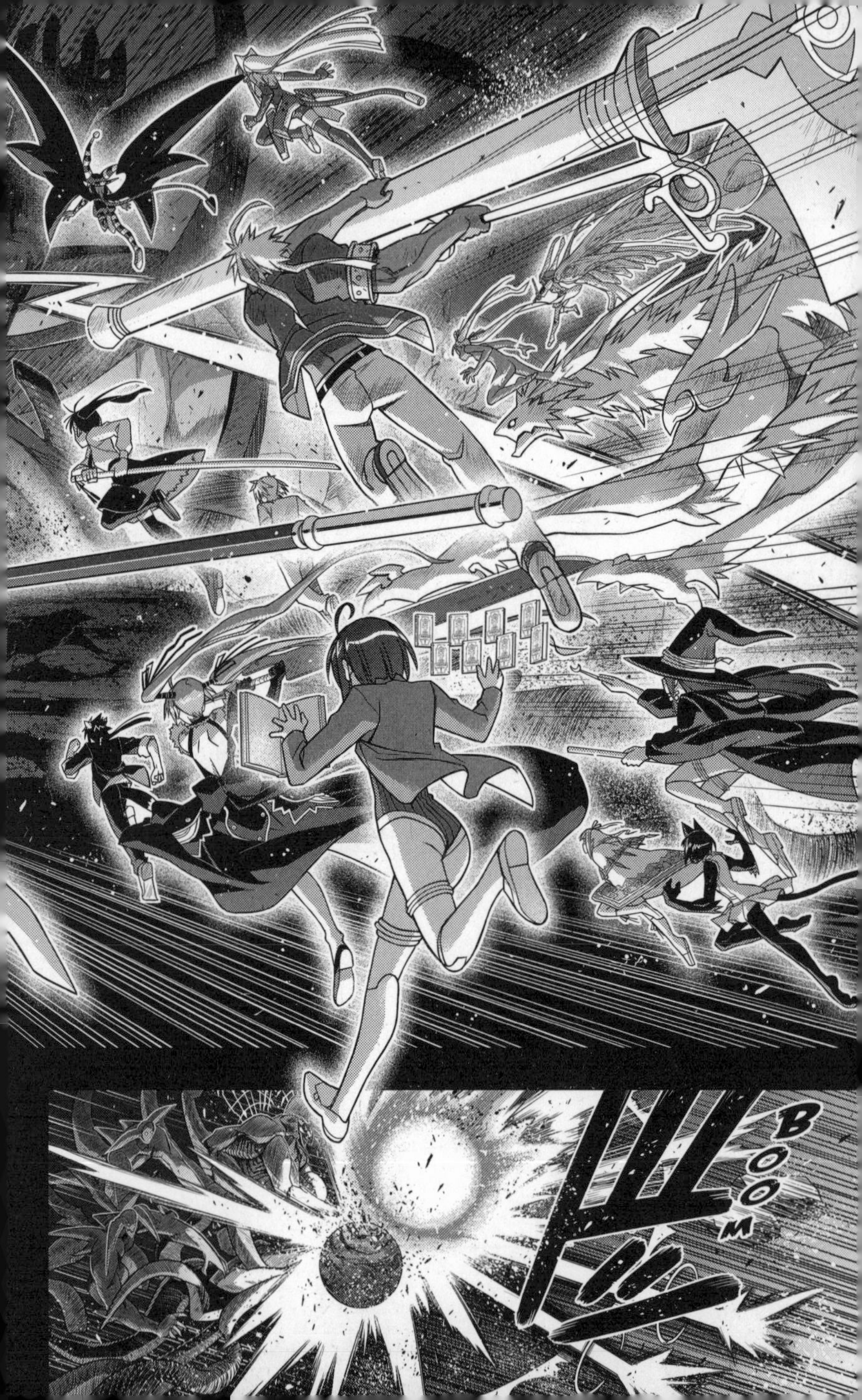
BOOOM

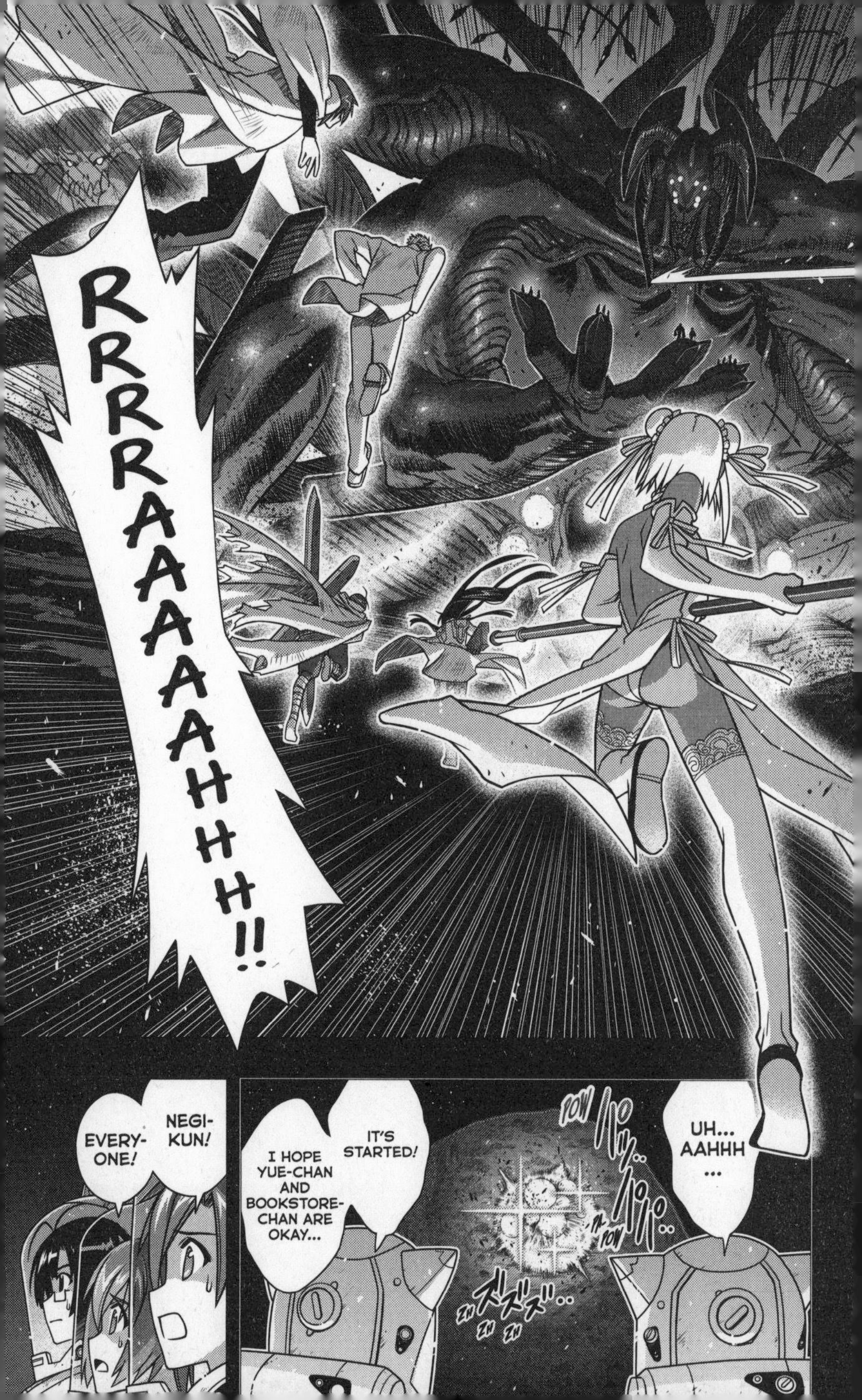
RRRRAAAAAHHHH!!
UH... AAHHH ...
POW
パパ..
パパ
POW
ズズズ..
ZN ZN ZN
IT'S STARTED!
I HOPE YUE-CHAN AND BOOKSTORE-CHAN ARE OKAY...
NEGI-KUN!
EVERY-ONE!

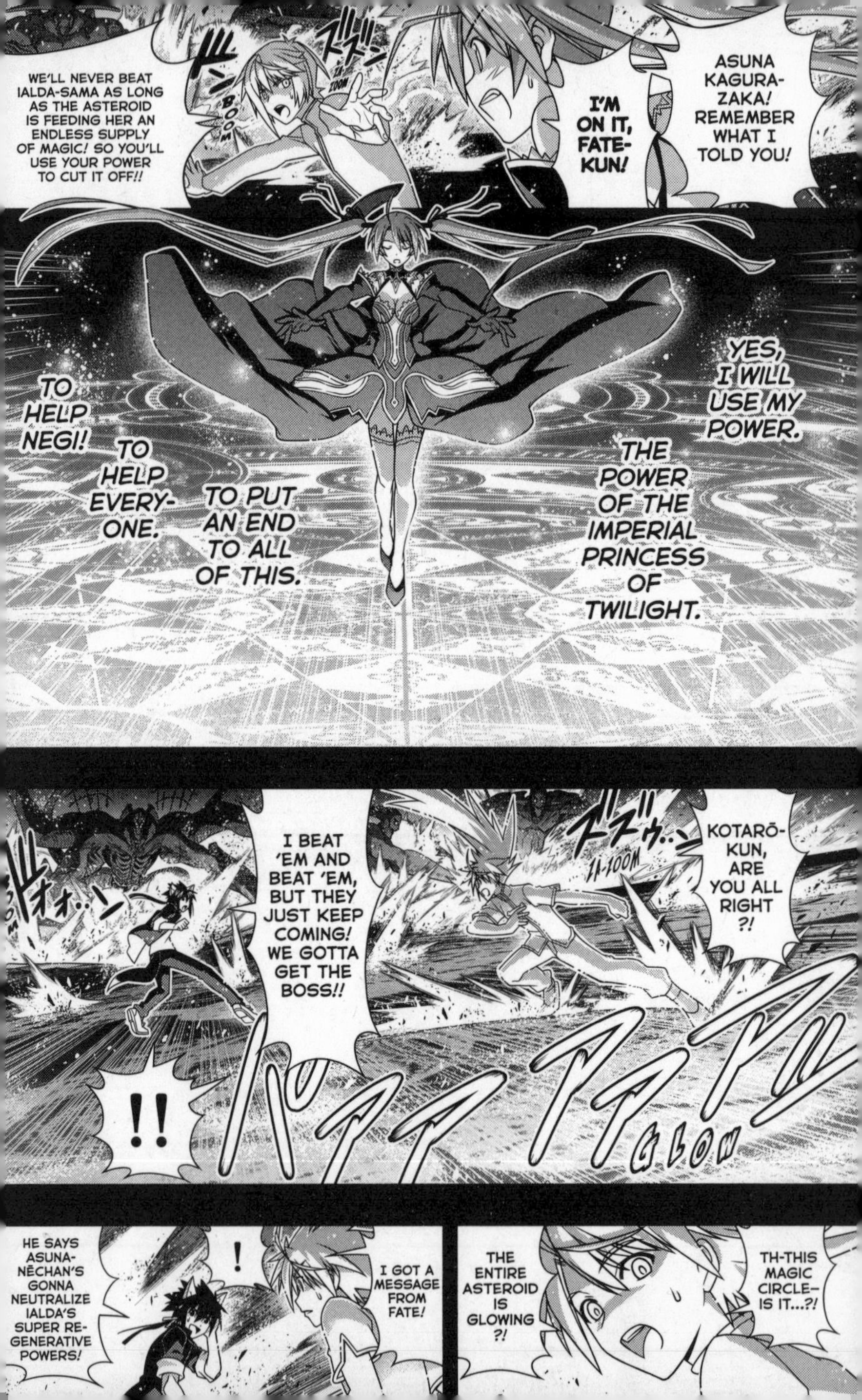
ASUNA KAGURAZAKA! REMEMBER WHAT I TOLD YOU!
I'M ON IT, FATE-KUN!
ZA-ZOOM
BOOM
WE'LL NEVER BEAT IALDA-SAMA AS LONG AS THE ASTEROID IS FEEDING HER AN ENDLESS SUPPLY OF MAGIC! SO YOU'LL USE YOUR POWER TO CUT IT OFF!!
YES, I WILL USE MY POWER.
THE POWER OF THE IMPERIAL PRINCESS OF TWILIGHT.
TO PUT AN END TO ALL OF THIS.
TO HELP EVERYONE.
TO HELP NEGI!
KOTARŌ-KUN, ARE YOU ALL RIGHT?!
I BEAT 'EM AND BEAT 'EM, BUT THEY JUST KEEP COMING! WE GOTTA GET THE BOSS!!
!!
GLOW
TH-THIS MAGIC CIRCLE–IS IT...?!
THE ENTIRE ASTEROID IS GLOWING?!
I GOT A MESSAGE FROM FATE!
!
HE SAYS ASUNA-NĒCHAN'S GONNA NEUTRALIZE IALDA'S SUPER REGENERATIVE POWERS!

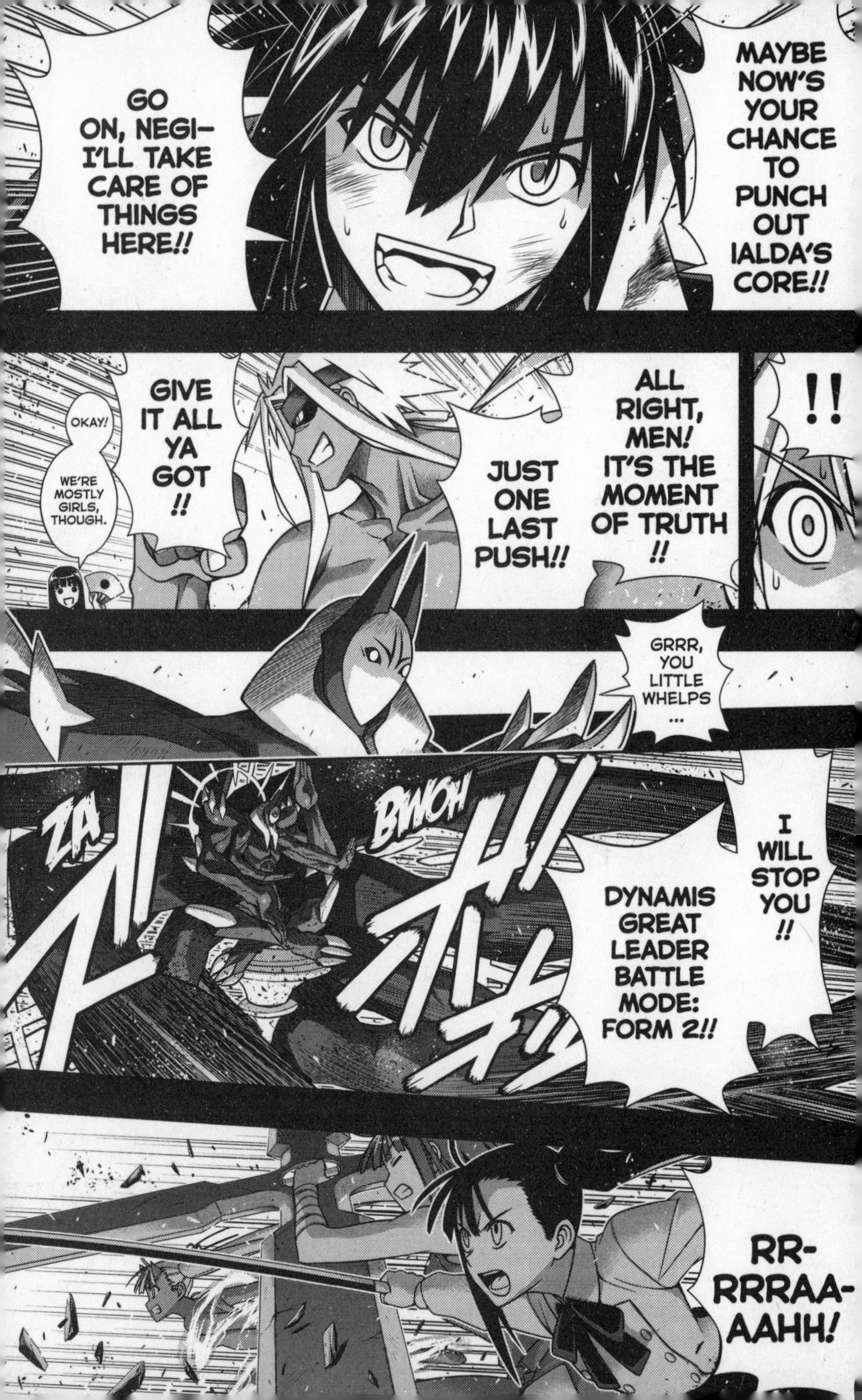
MAYBE NOW'S YOUR CHANCE TO PUNCH OUT IALDA'S CORE!!
GO ON, NEGI— I'LL TAKE CARE OF THINGS HERE!!
!!
ALL RIGHT, MEN! IT'S THE MOMENT OF TRUTH!!
JUST ONE LAST PUSH!!
GIVE IT ALL YA GOT!!
OKAY!
WE'RE MOSTLY GIRLS, THOUGH.
GRRR, YOU LITTLE WHELPS...
I WILL STOP YOU!!
DYNAMIS GREAT LEADER BATTLE MODE: FORM 2!!
BWOH
ZA
RR-RRRAA-AAHH!

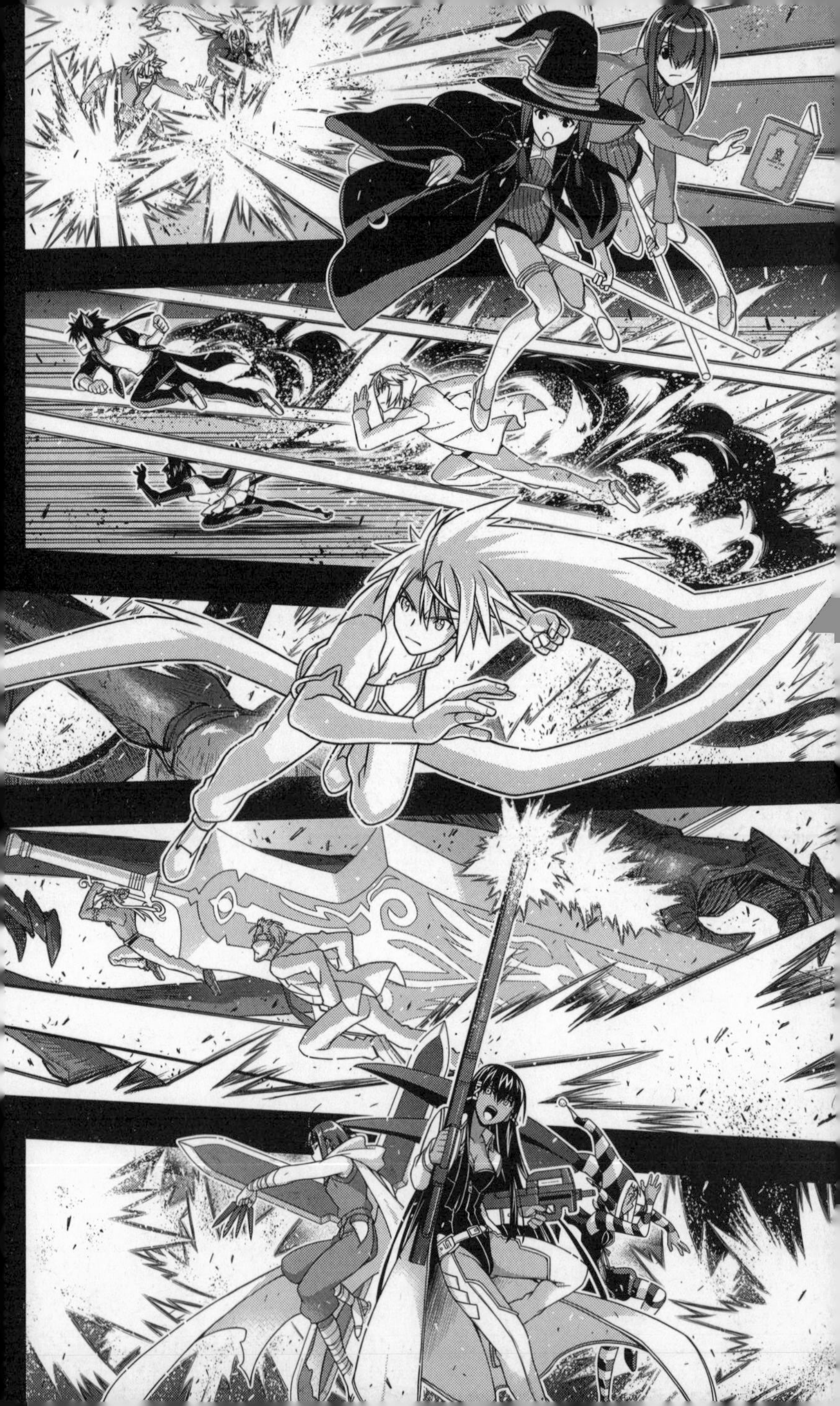

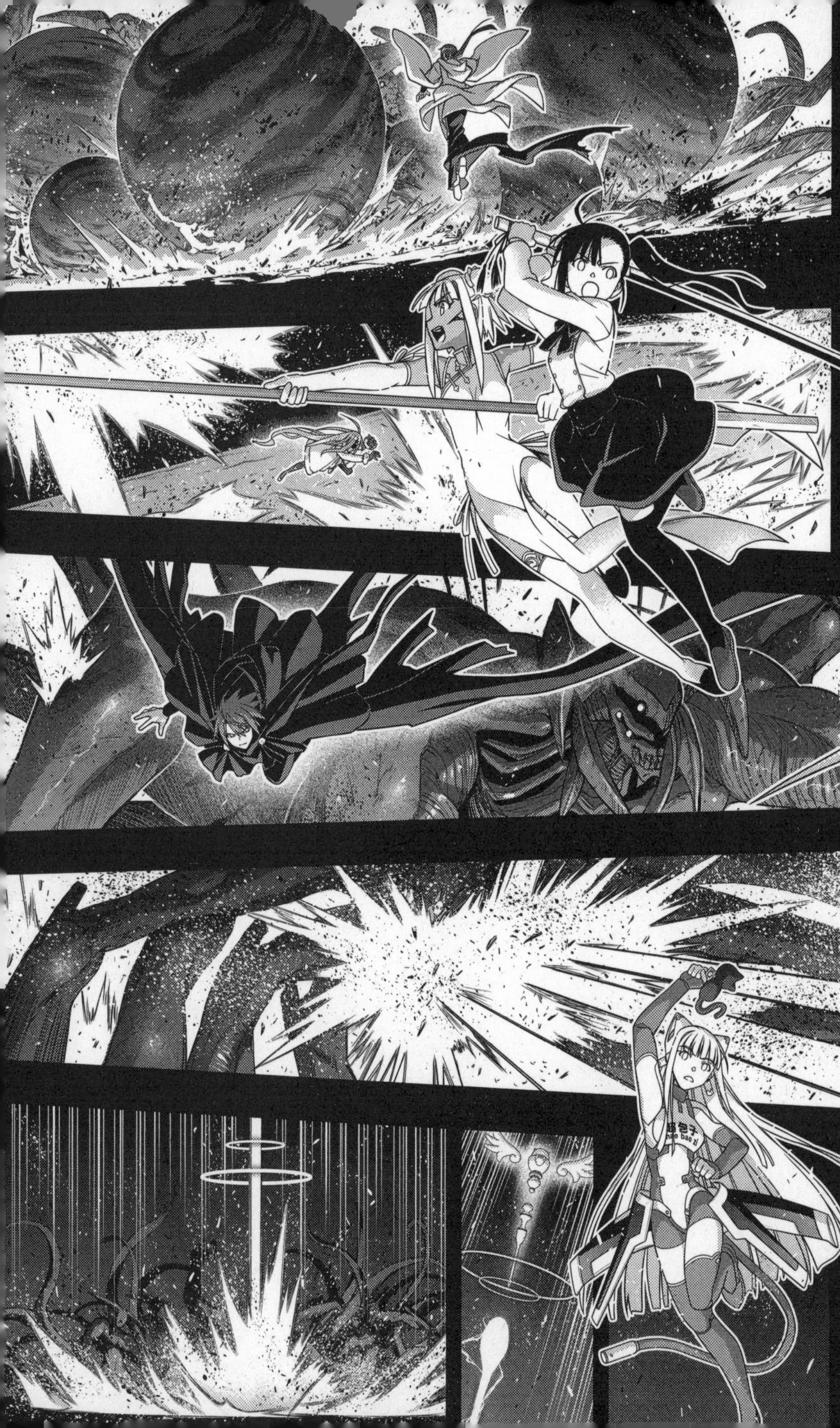
包子
bao zi

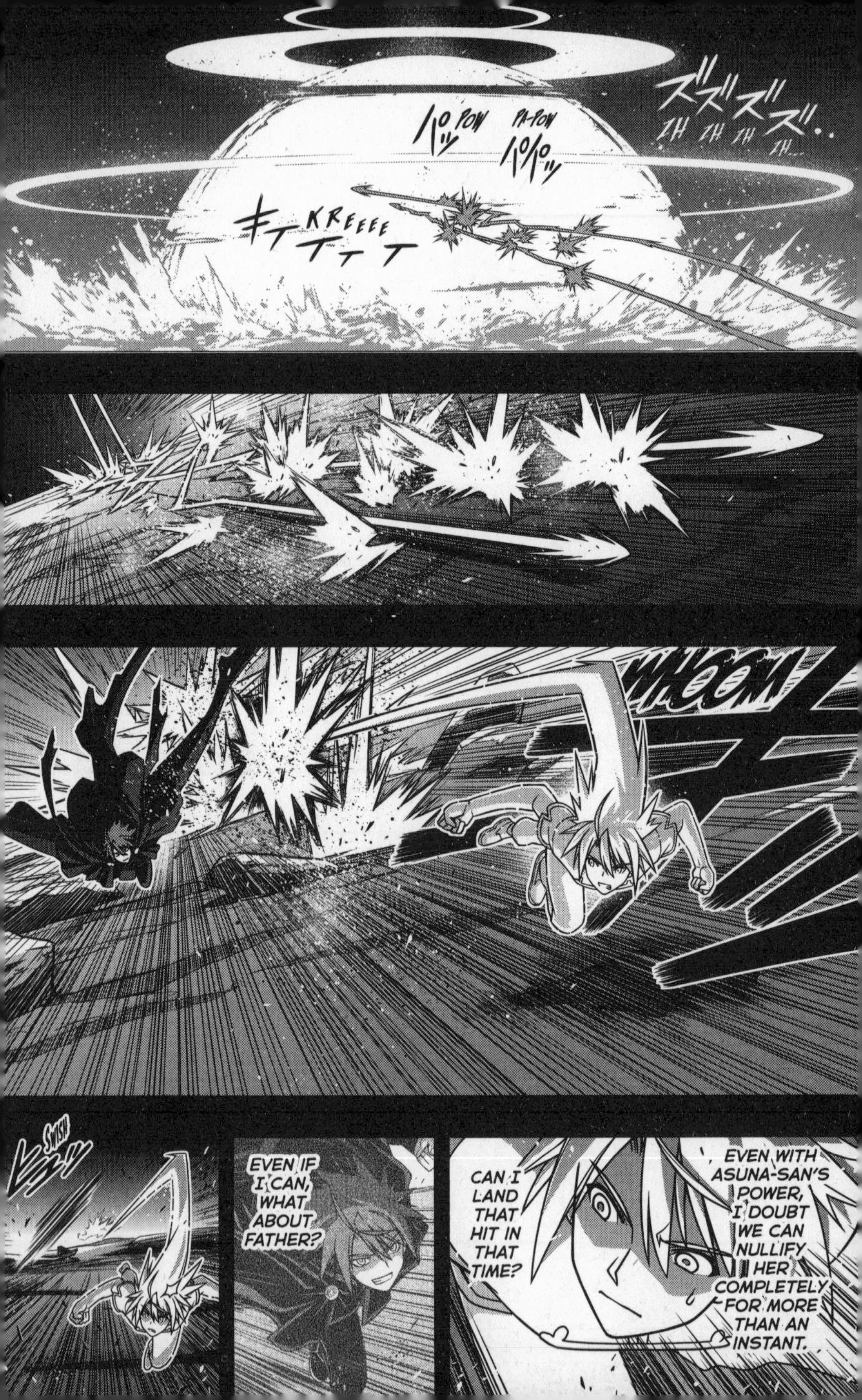

ズズズズ ZH ZH ZH ZH...
パパッ PA-POW
パッ POW
KREEEEE
WHOOOM
EVEN WITH ASUNA-SAN'S POWER, I DOUBT WE CAN NULLIFY HER COMPLETELY FOR MORE THAN AN INSTANT.
CAN I LAND THAT HIT IN THAT TIME?
EVEN IF I CAN, WHAT ABOUT FATHER?
SWISH

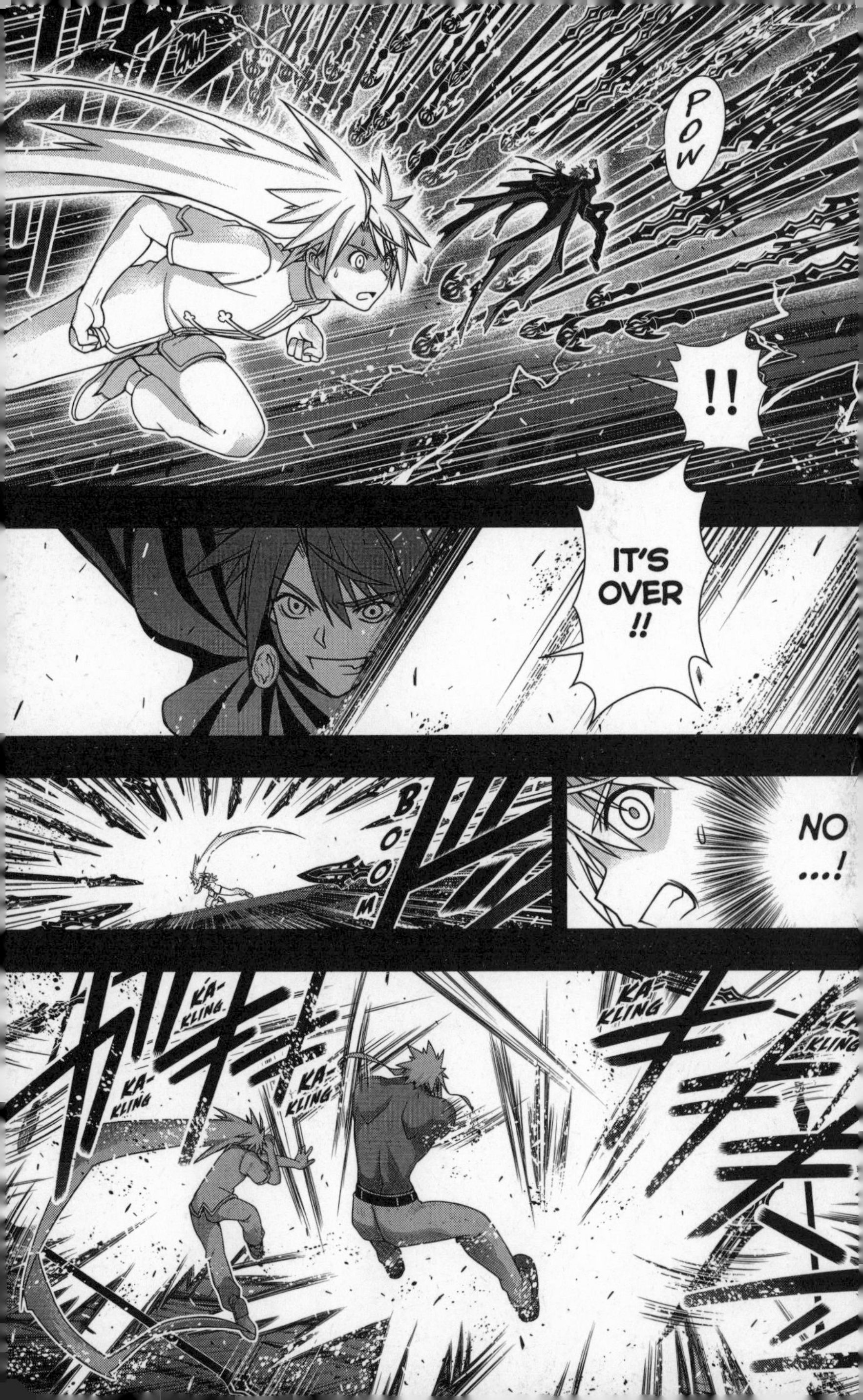
POW
!!
IT'S OVER!!
NO ...!
BOOOM
KA-KLING
KA-KLING
KA-KLING
KA-KLING
KA-KLING

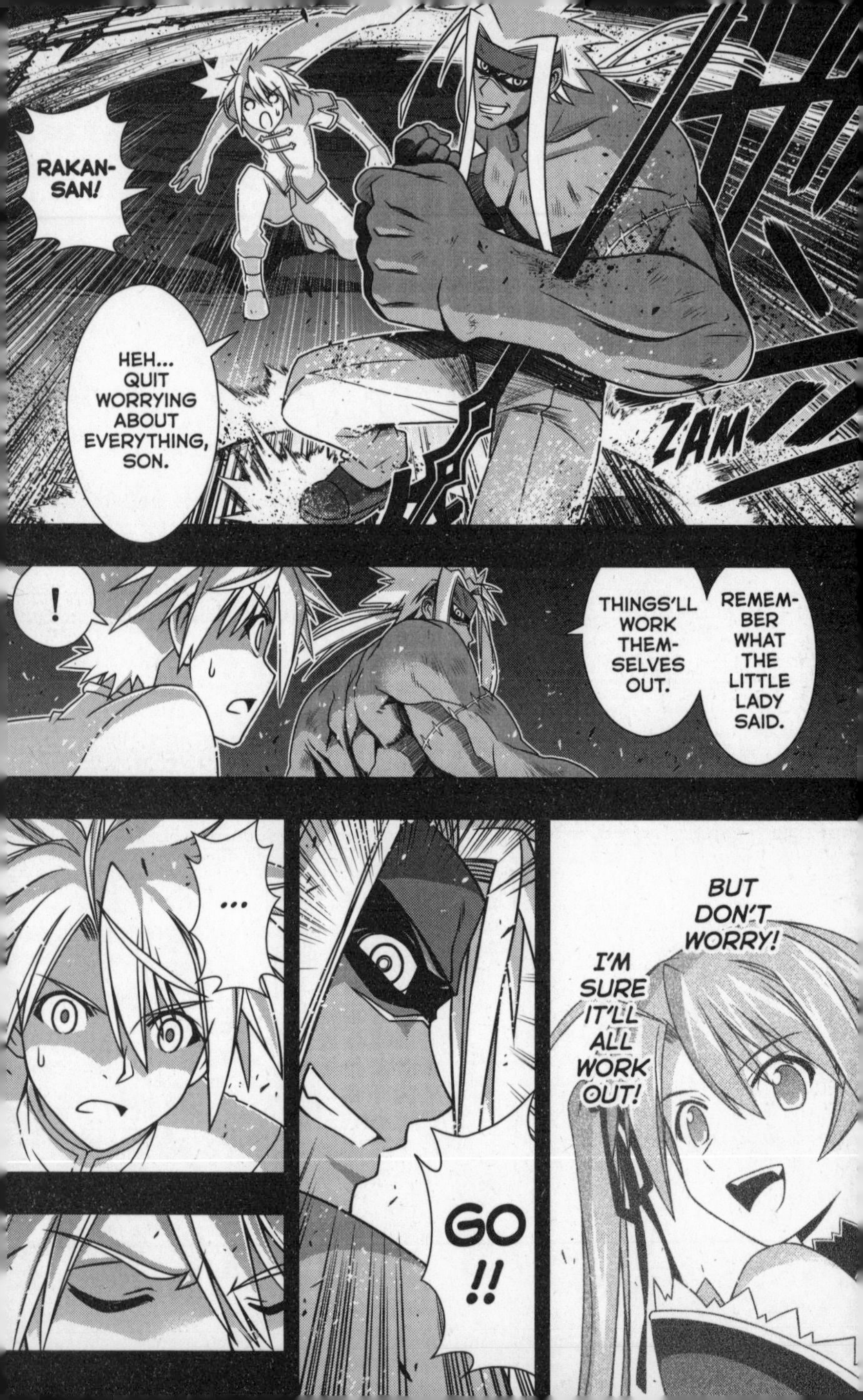
RAKAN-SAN!
HEH... QUIT WORRYING ABOUT EVERYTHING, SON.
ZAM
REMEM-BER WHAT THE LITTLE LADY SAID.
THINGS'LL WORK THEM-SELVES OUT.
!
BUT DON'T WORRY!
I'M SURE IT'LL ALL WORK OUT!
GO !!
...

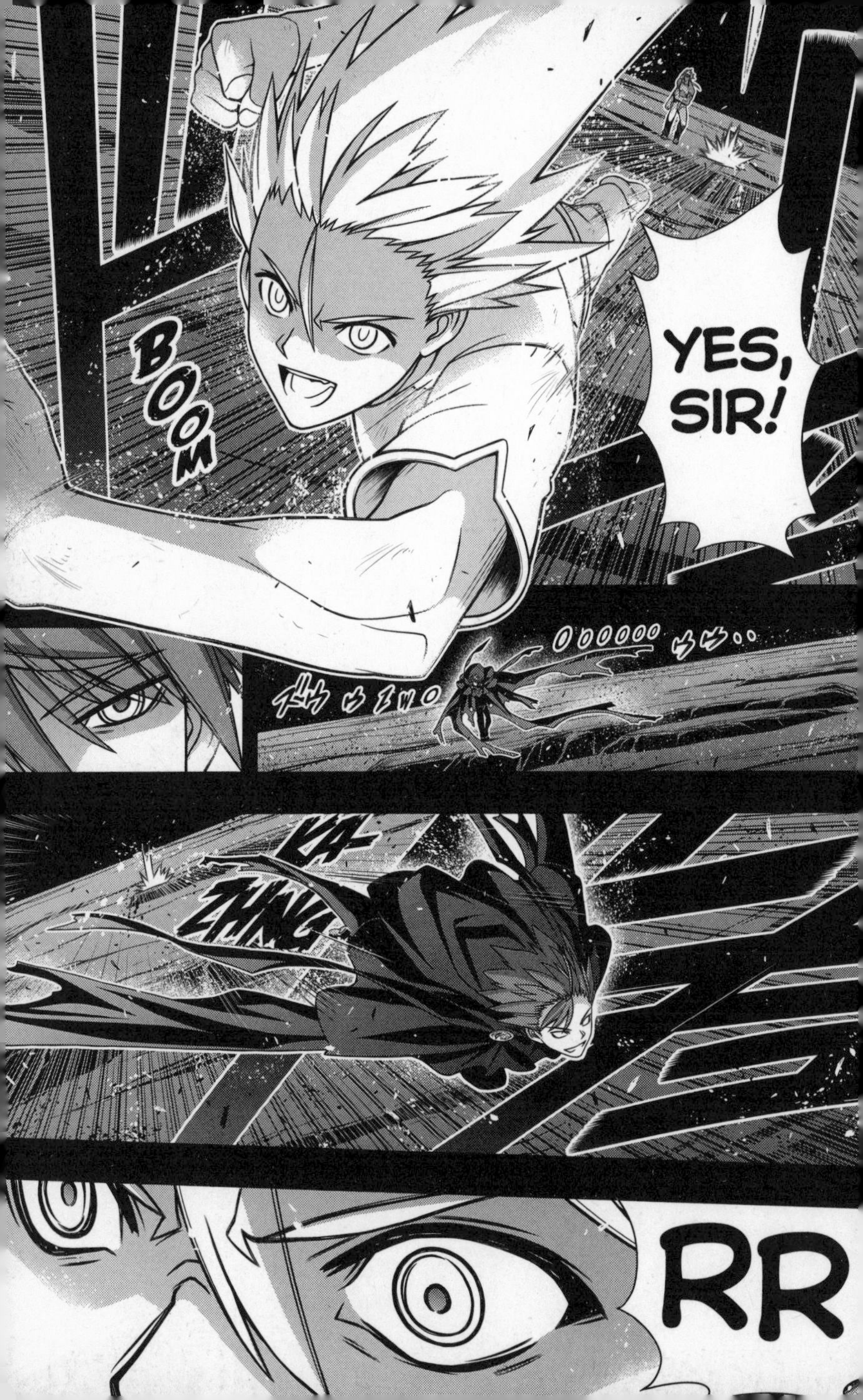
YES, SIR!
BOOM
KA-ZHNG
RR

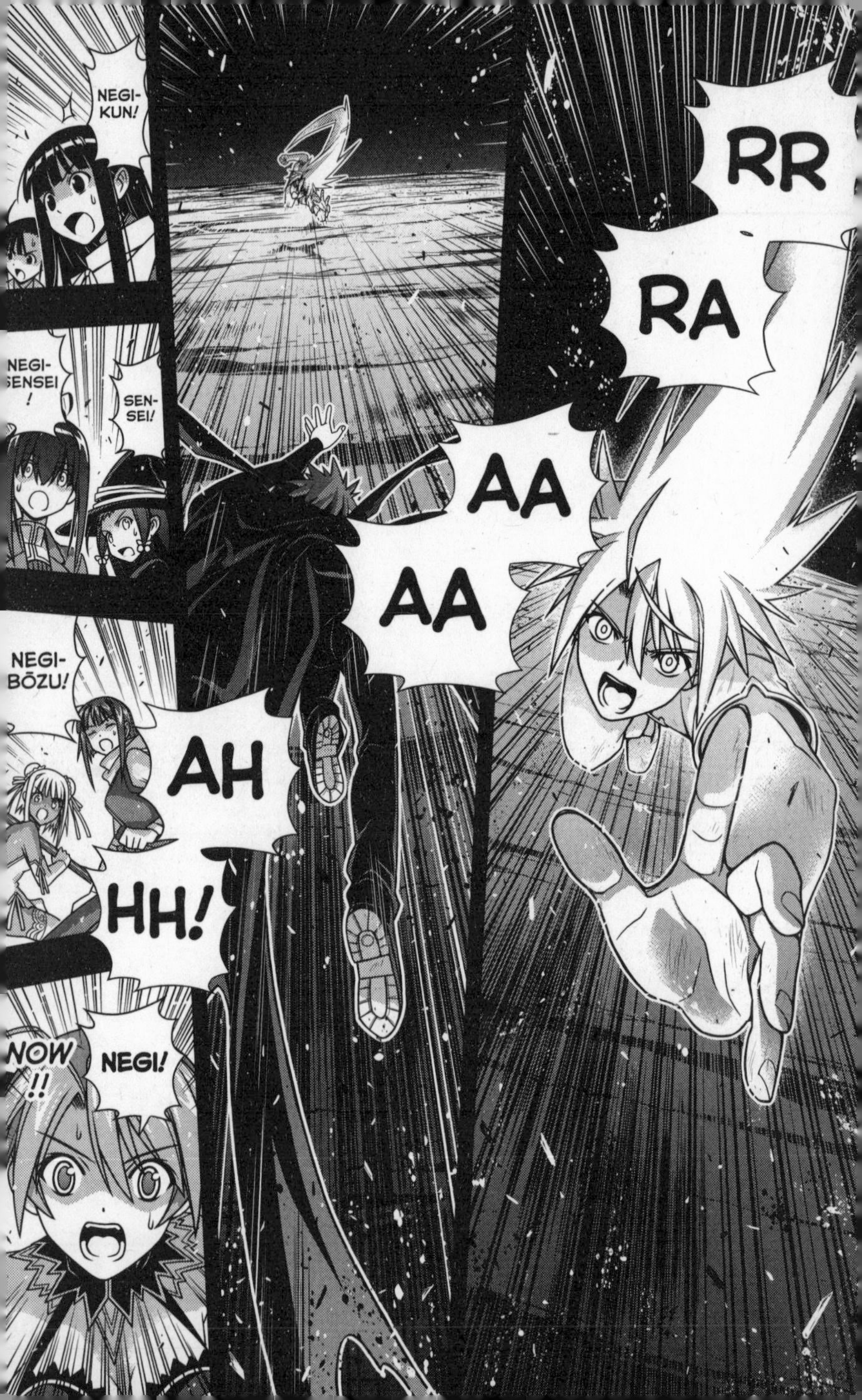
RR
RA
AA
AA
AH
HH!
NEGI-KUN!
SEN-SEI!
NEGI-SENSEI!
NEGI-BŌZU!
NEGI!
NOW!!

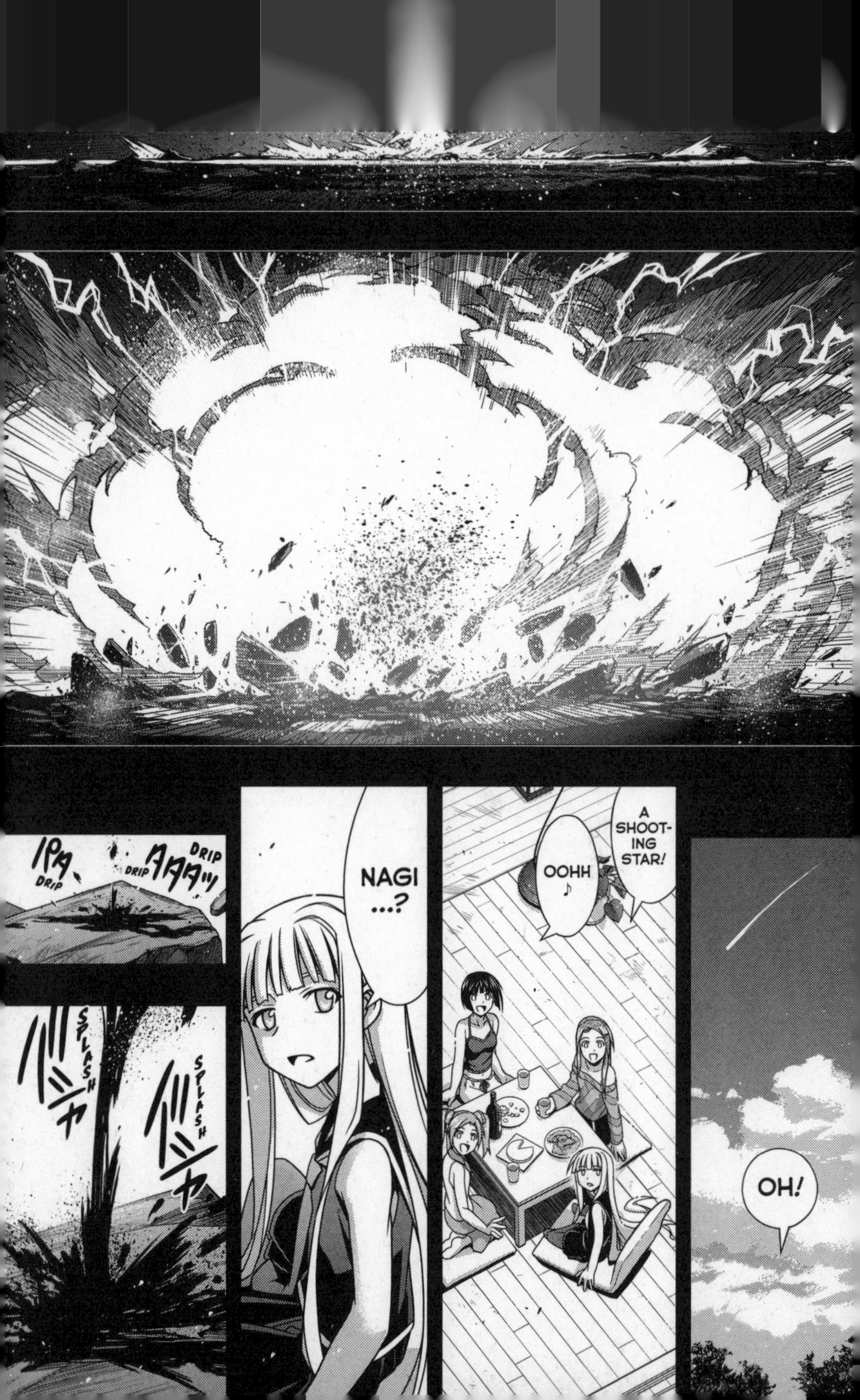
OH!
A SHOOT-ING STAR!
OOHH ♪
NAGI ...?
DRIP
DRIP
DRIP
SPLASH
SPLASH

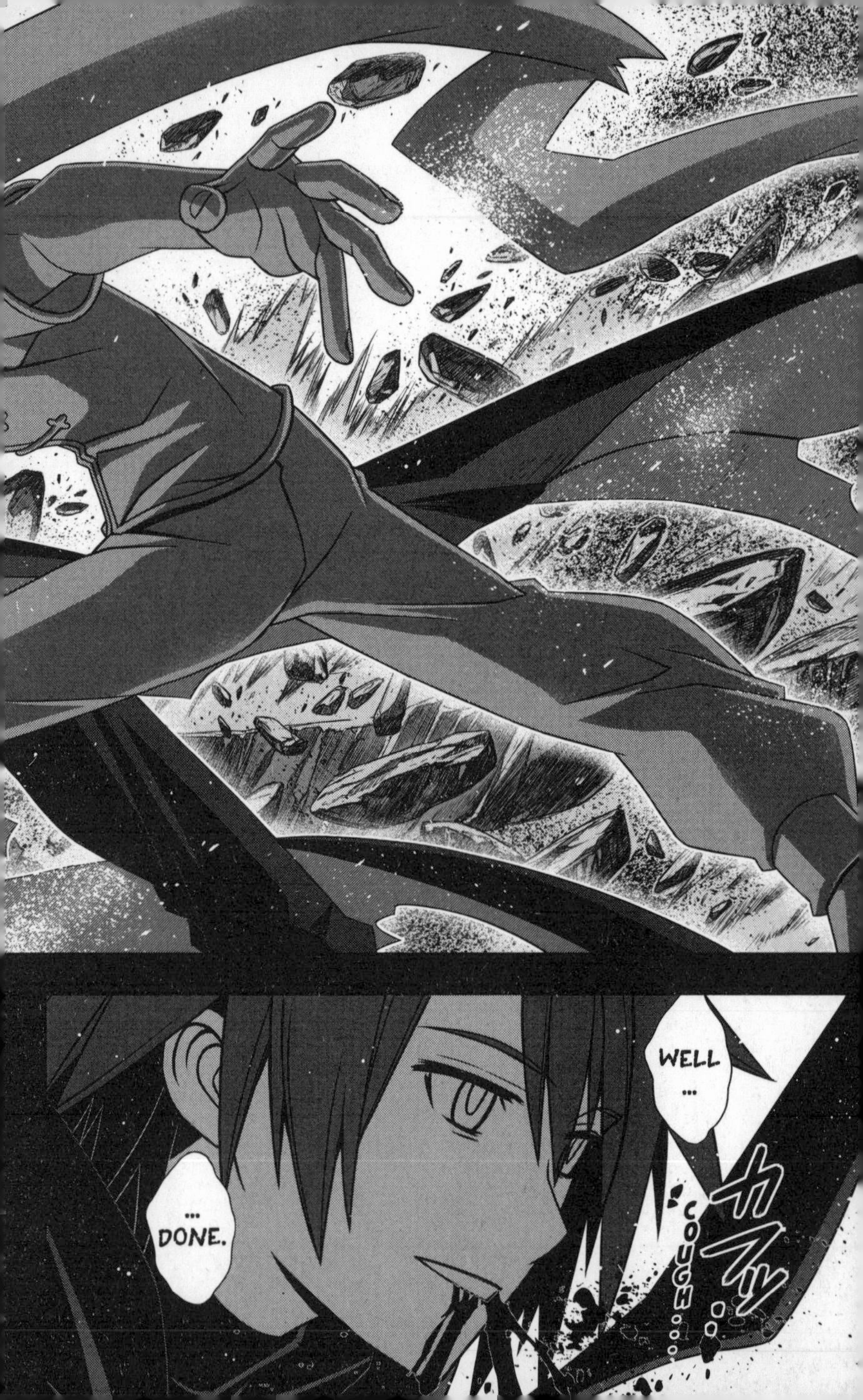
WELL ...
COUGH...
... DONE.

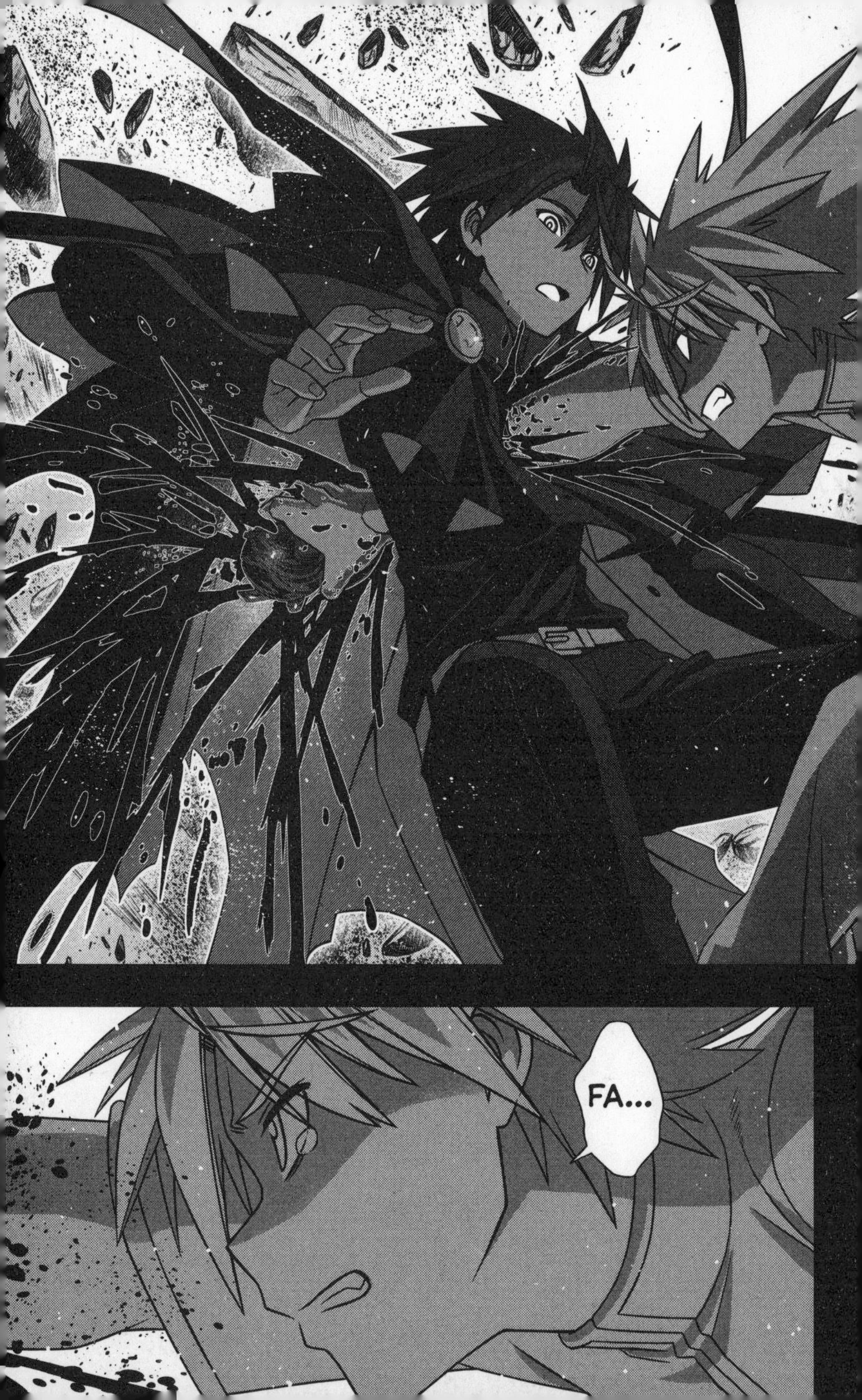
FA...

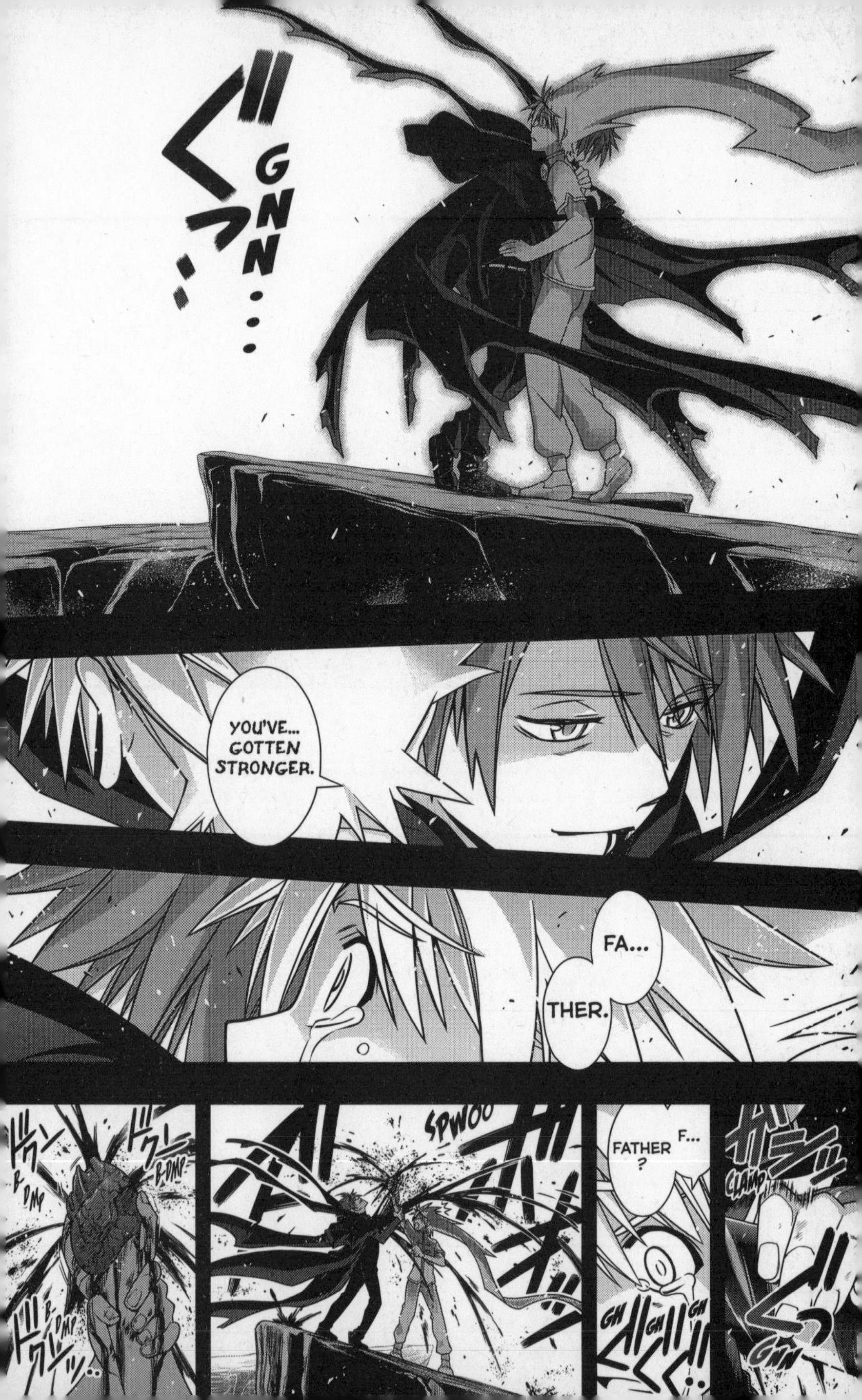
GNN...
YOU'VE... GOTTEN STRONGER.
FA...
THER.
CLAMP
GNN
F...
FATHER ?
GH GH GH
SPWOO
B-DMP
B-DMP
B-DMP

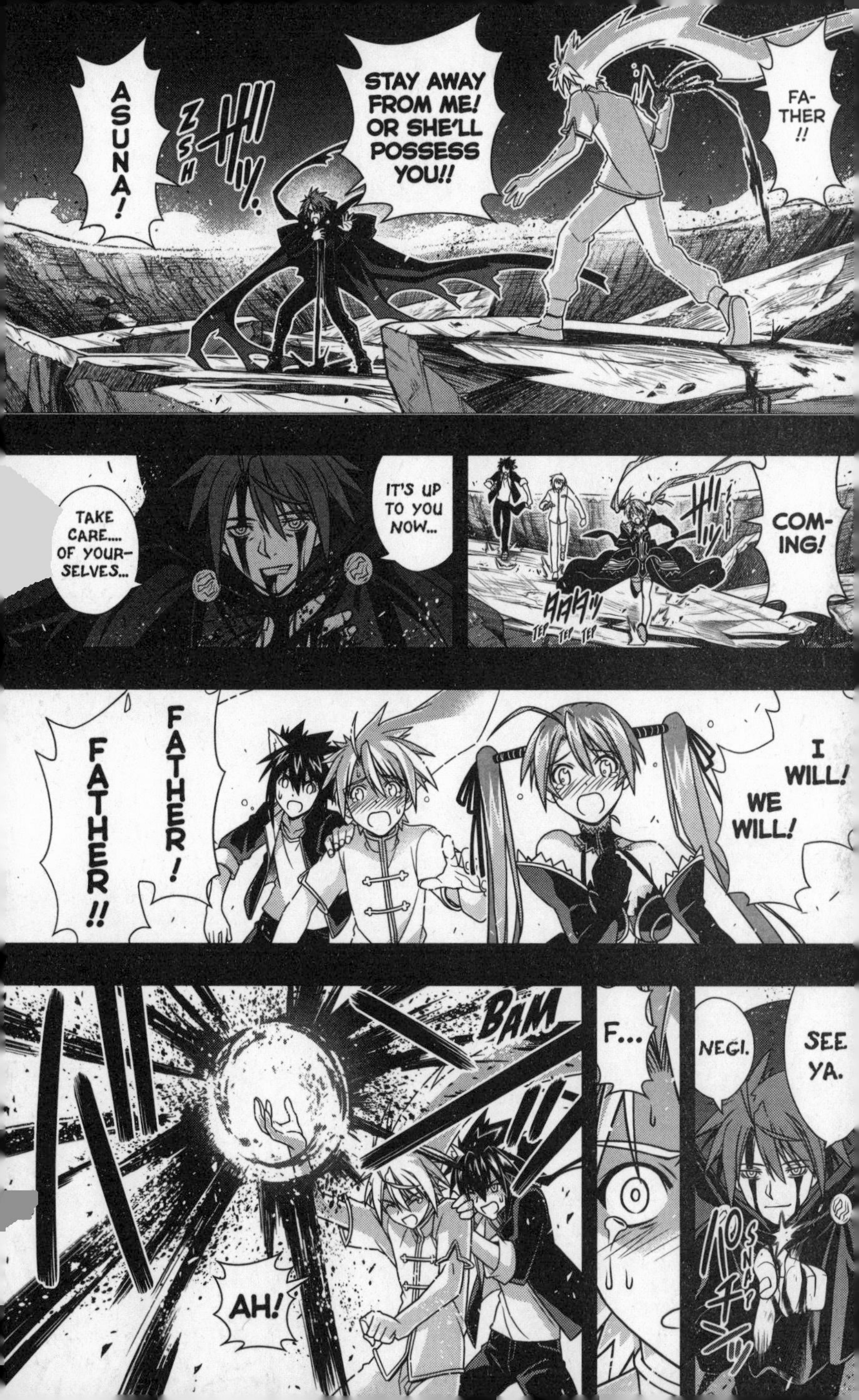
FA-THER!!
STAY AWAY FROM ME! OR SHE'LL POSSESS YOU!!
ZSH
ASUNA!
COMING!
ZSH
TEP TEP TEP
IT'S UP TO YOU NOW...
TAKE CARE.... OF YOUR-SELVES...
I WILL!
WE WILL!
FATHER!
FATHER!!
SEE YA.
NEGI.
SNAP
F...
BAM
AH!

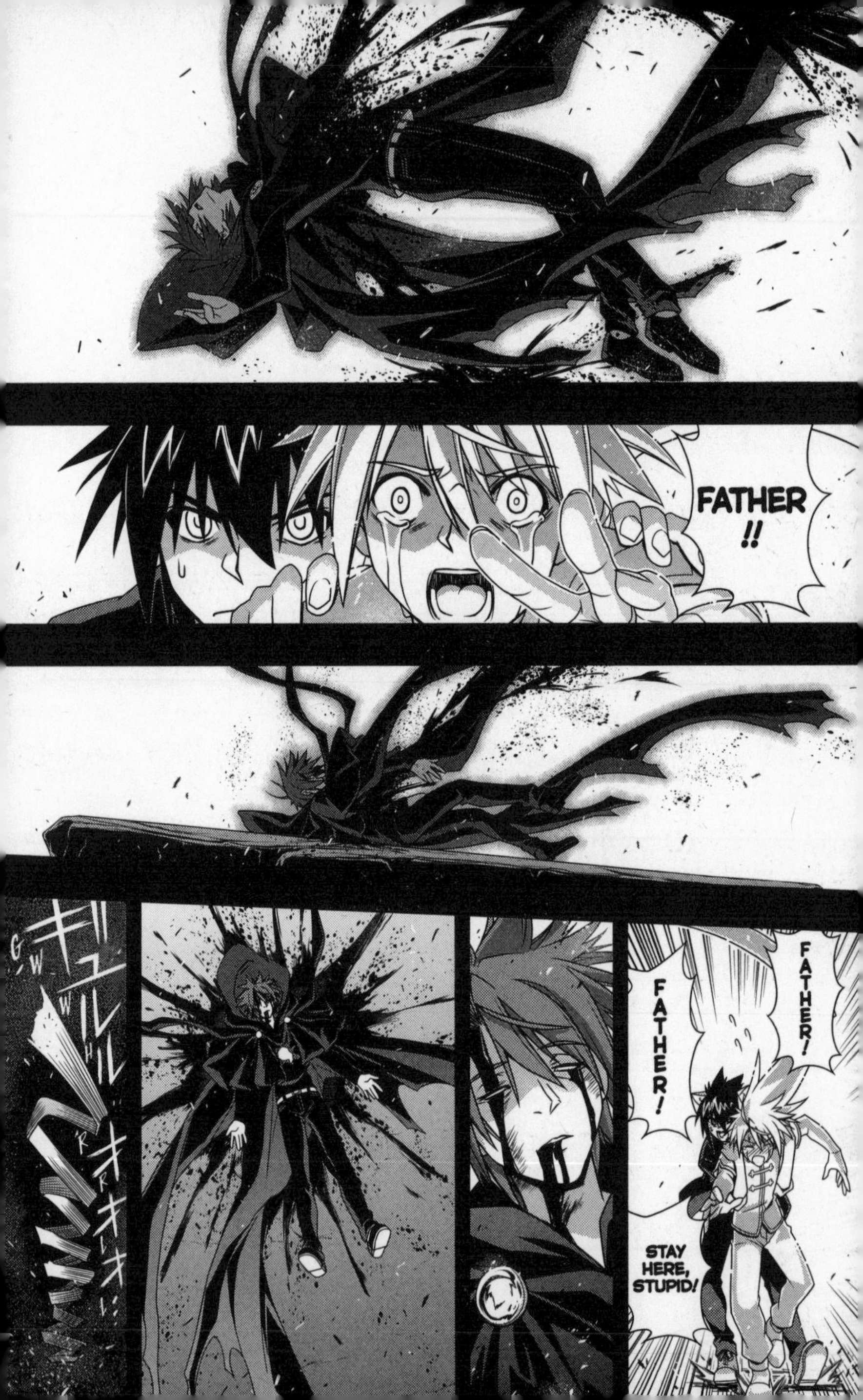
FATHER!!
FATHER!
FATHER!
STAY HERE, STUPID!
ギュルルオオオ
GWWHRRLL!

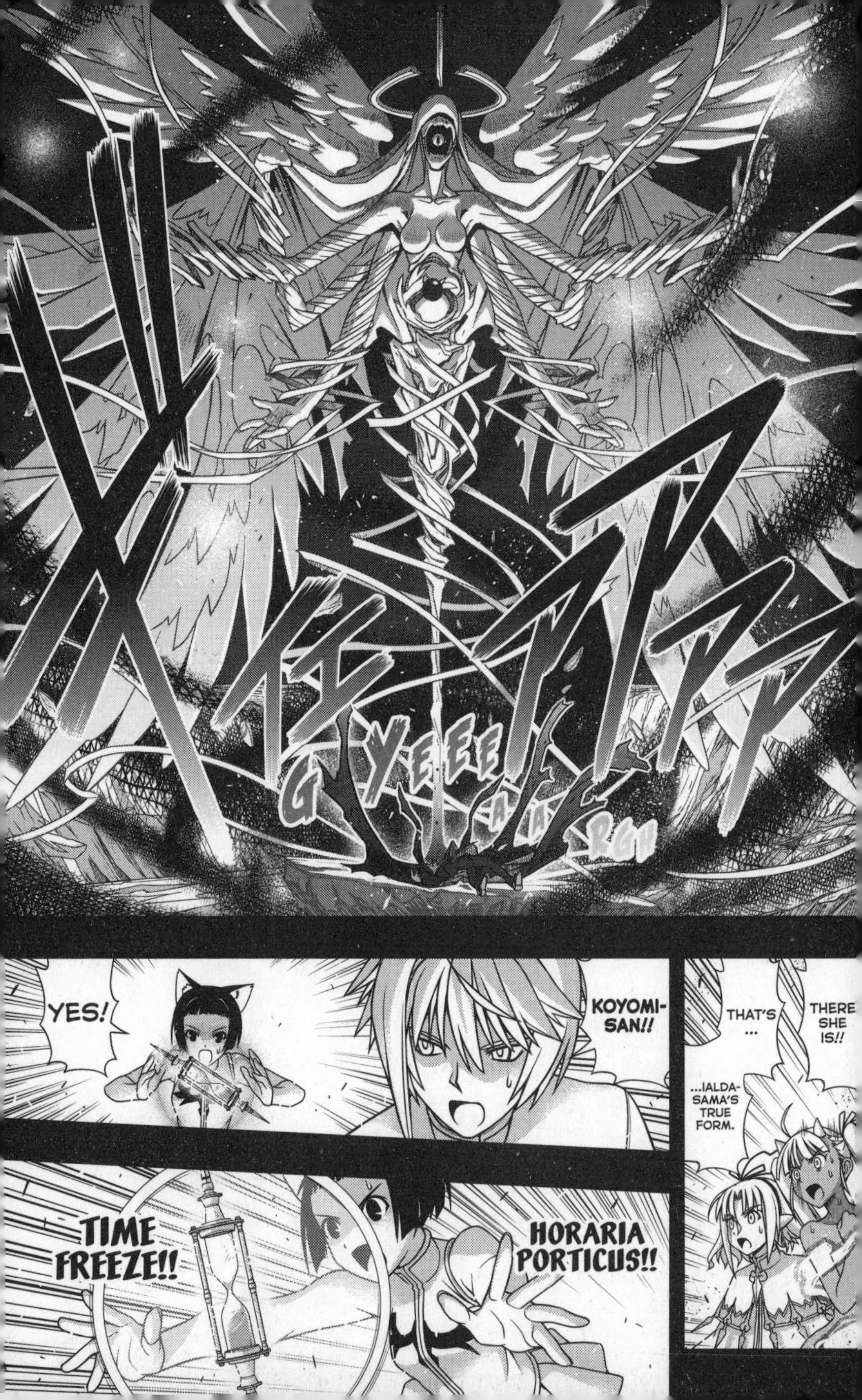
GYEEEAARGH
THERE SHE IS!!
THAT'S ...
...IALDA-SAMA'S TRUE FORM.
KOYOMI-SAN!!
YES!
HORARIA PORTICUS!!
TIME FREEZE!!

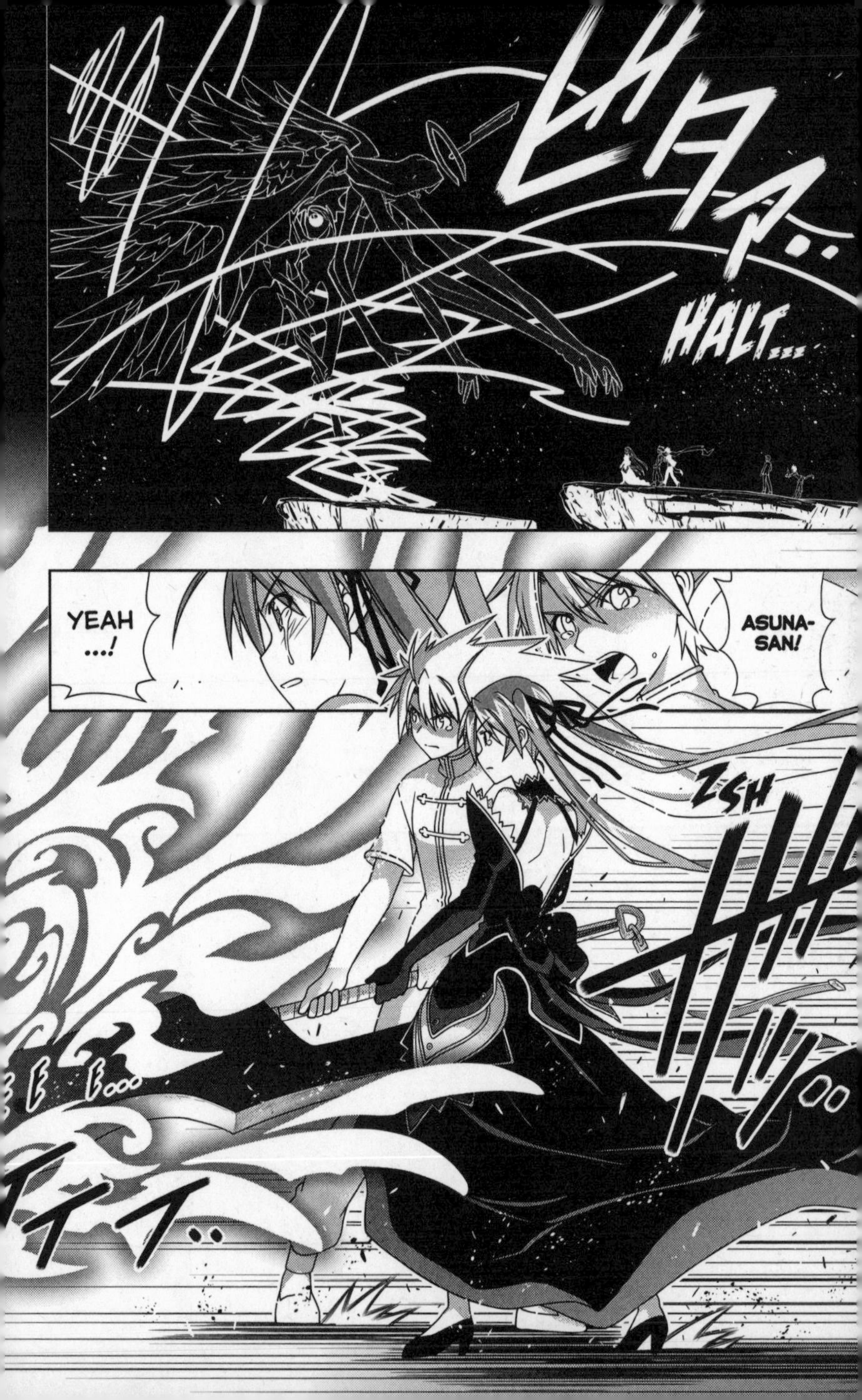
HALT...
ASUNA-SAN!
YEAH ...!
ZSH

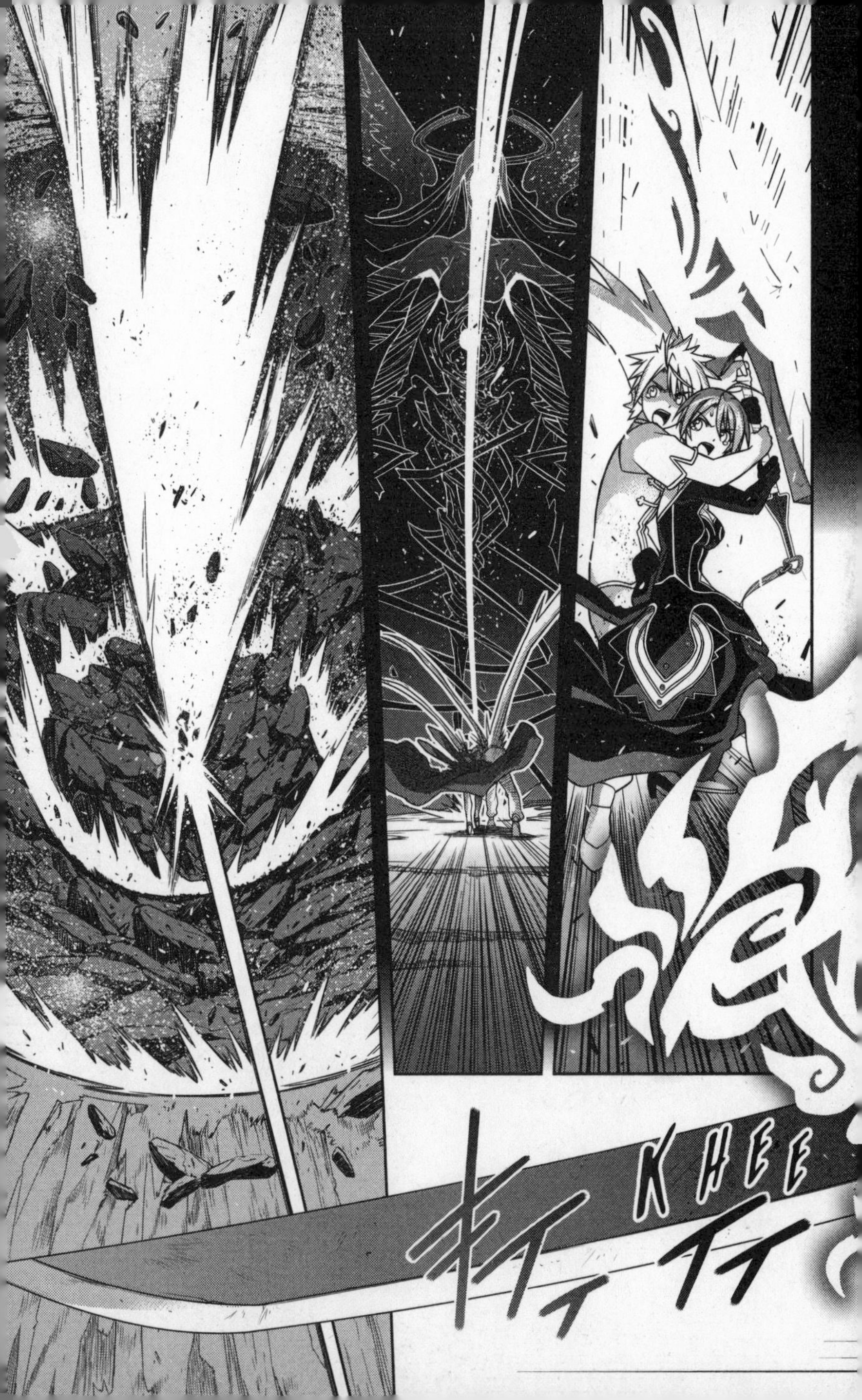
KHEE
キィィィ

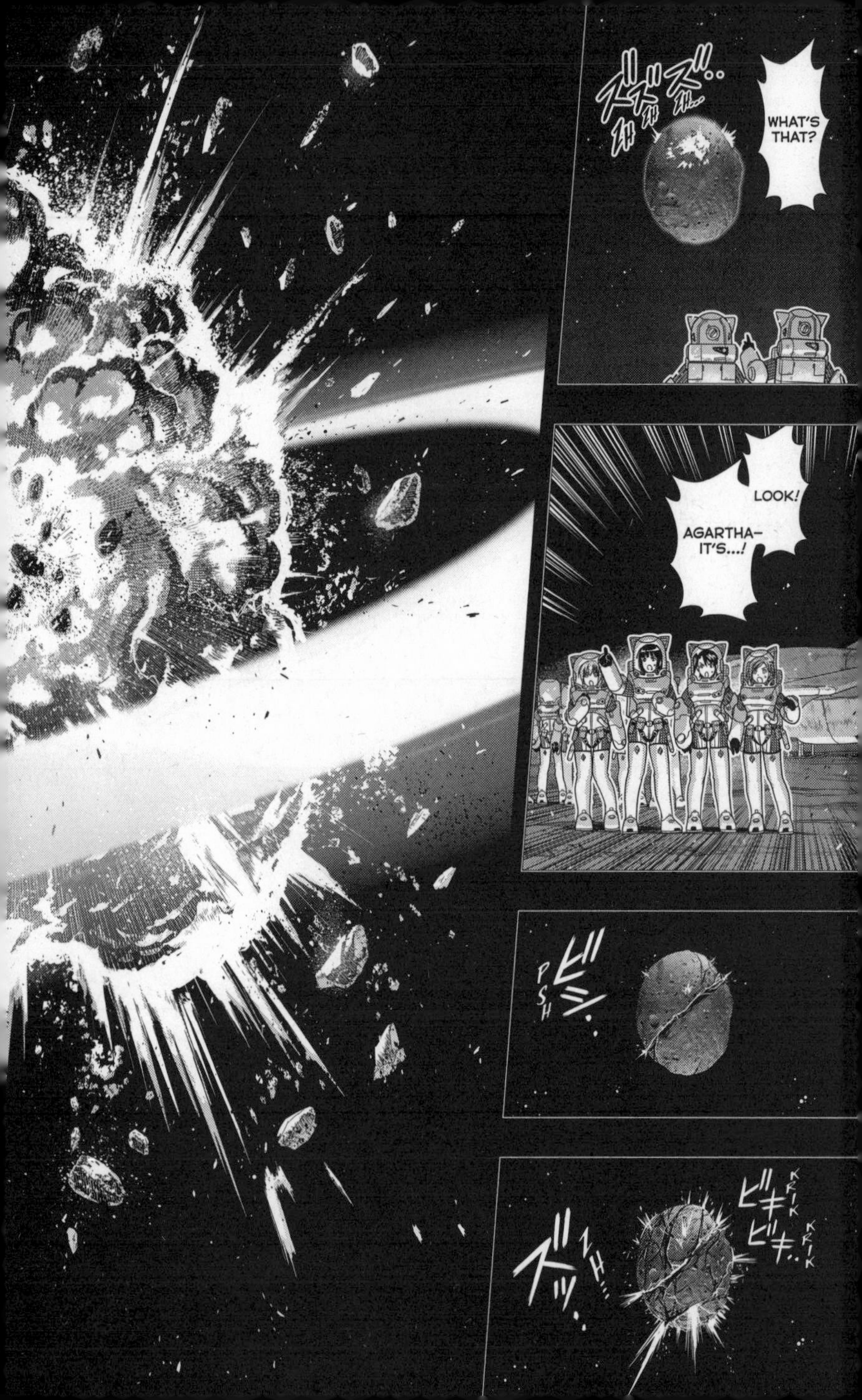
WHAT'S THAT?
ズズズ..
ZH ZH ZH...
LOOK!
AGARTHA— IT'S...!
ビシッ
PSH
KRIK KRIK
ビキビキ..
ズッ..
ZH...

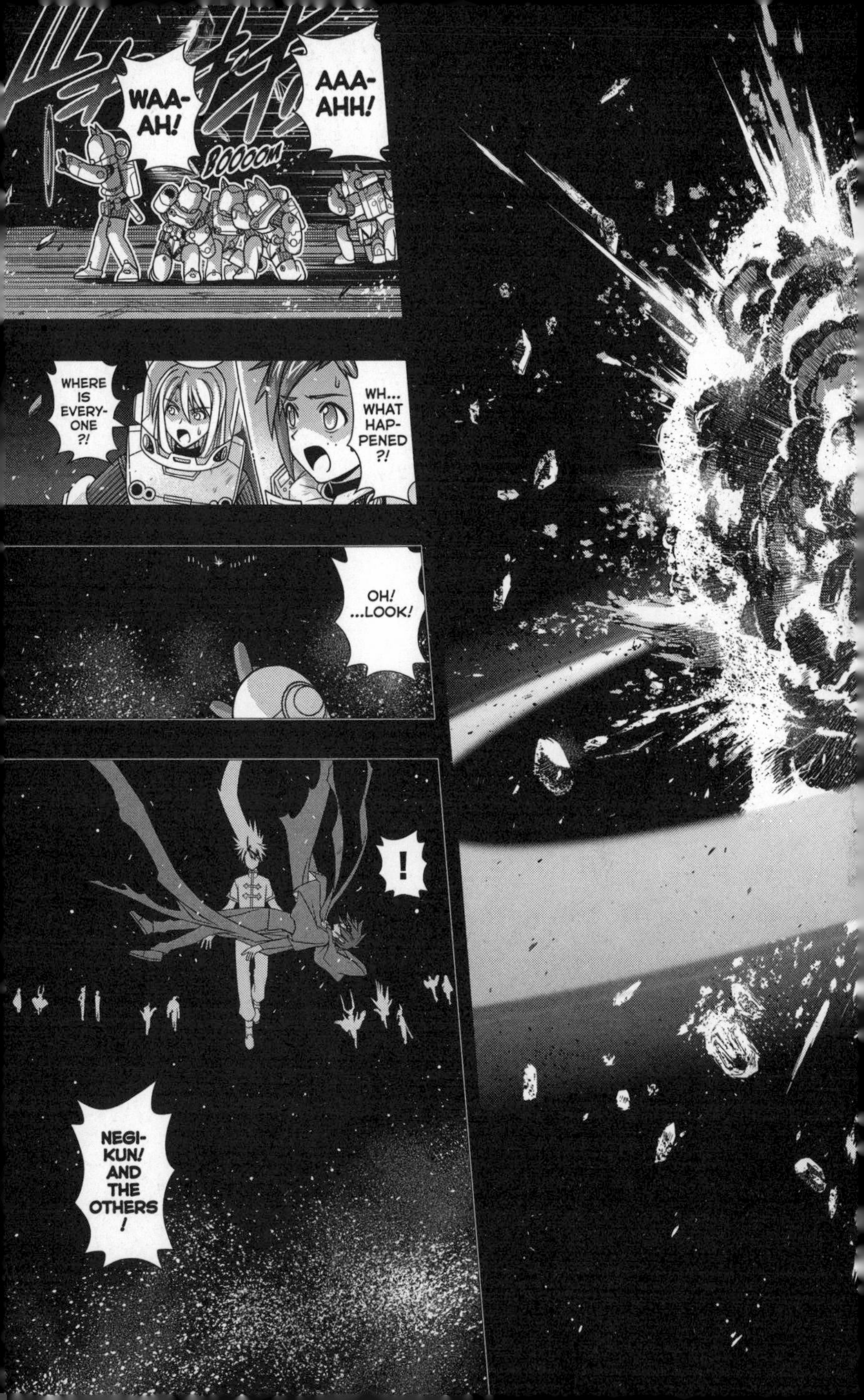
AAA-AHH!
WAA-AH!
BOOOOM
WH... WHAT HAP-PENED ?!
WHERE IS EVERY-ONE ?!
OH! ...LOOK!
!
NEGI-KUN! AND THE OTHERS !

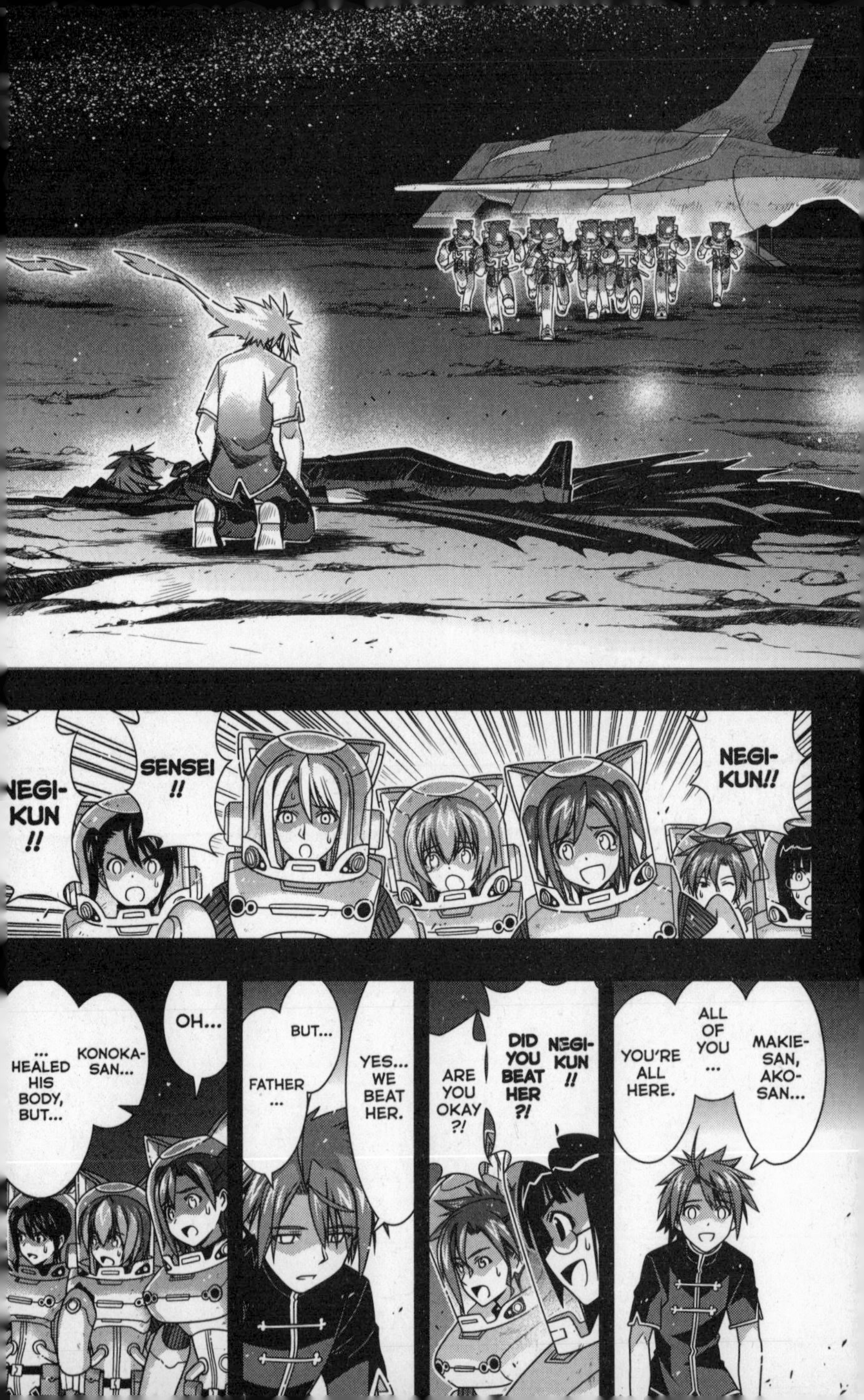
NEGI-KUN!!
SENSEI!!
NEGI-KUN!!
MAKIE-SAN, AKO-SAN...
ALL OF YOU...
YOU'RE ALL HERE.
NEGI-KUN!!
DID YOU BEAT HER?!
ARE YOU OKAY?!
YES... WE BEAT HER.
BUT...
FATHER...
OH...
KONOKA-SAN...
...HEALED HIS BODY, BUT...

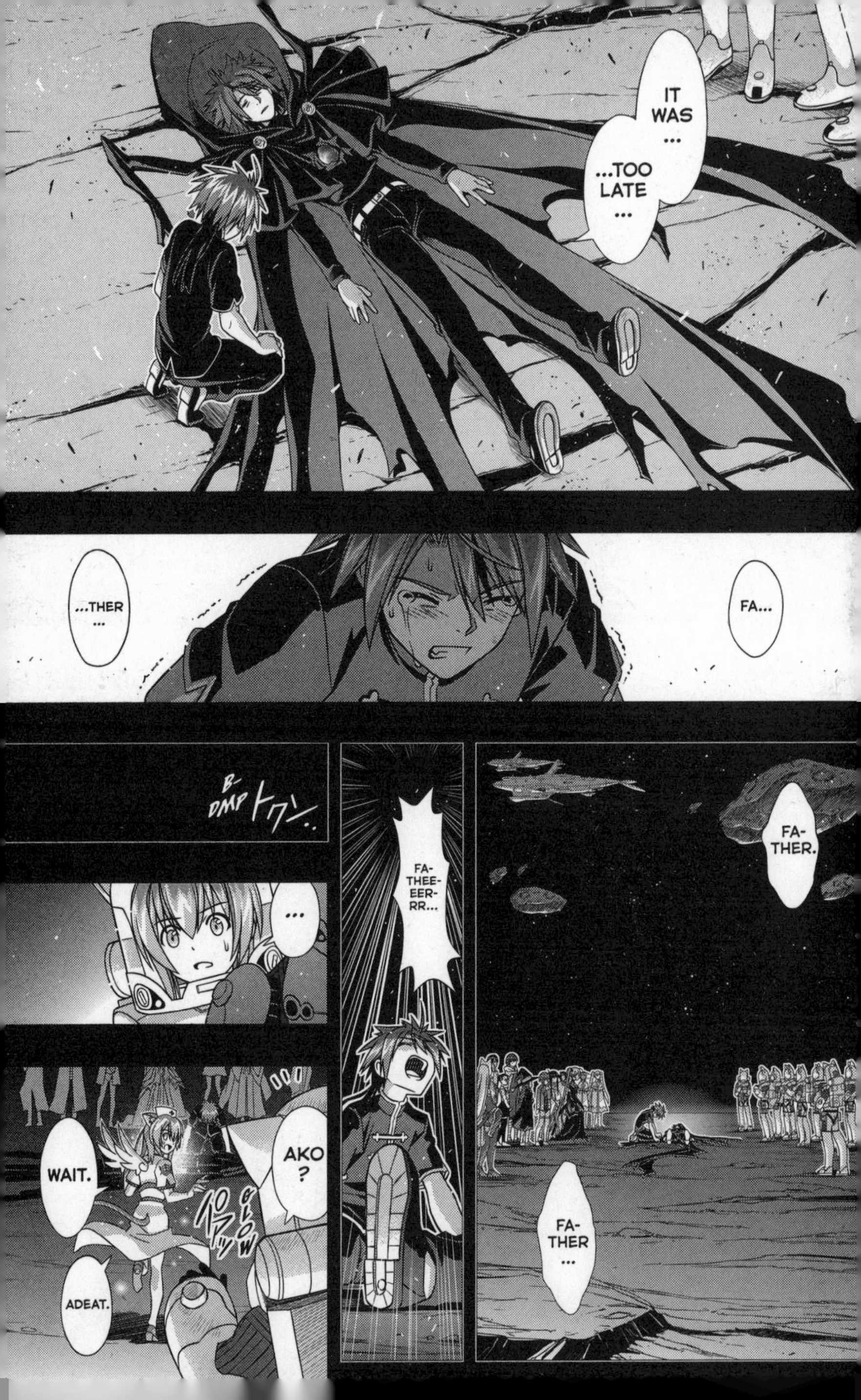
IT WAS ...
...TOO LATE ...
FA...
...THER ...
FA-THER.
FA-THER ...
FA-THEE-EER-RR...
B-DMP トクン..
...
AKO ?
WAIT.
GLOW
ADEAT.

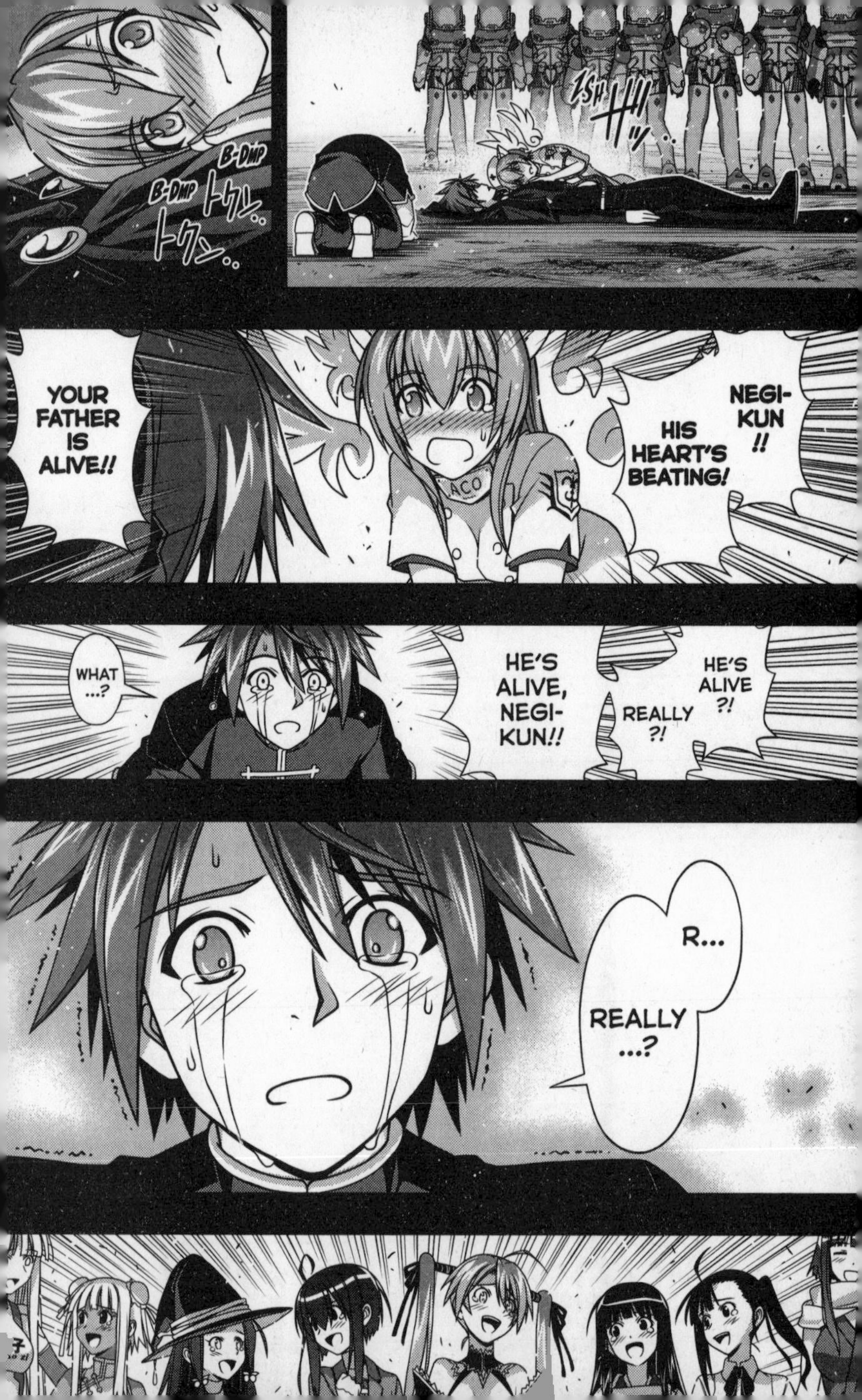
ZSH
B-DMP
B-DMP
トクン..
トクン..
NEGI-KUN!!
HIS HEART'S BEATING!
YOUR FATHER IS ALIVE!!
HE'S ALIVE ?!
REALLY ?!
HE'S ALIVE, NEGI-KUN!!
WHAT ...?
R...
REALLY ...?

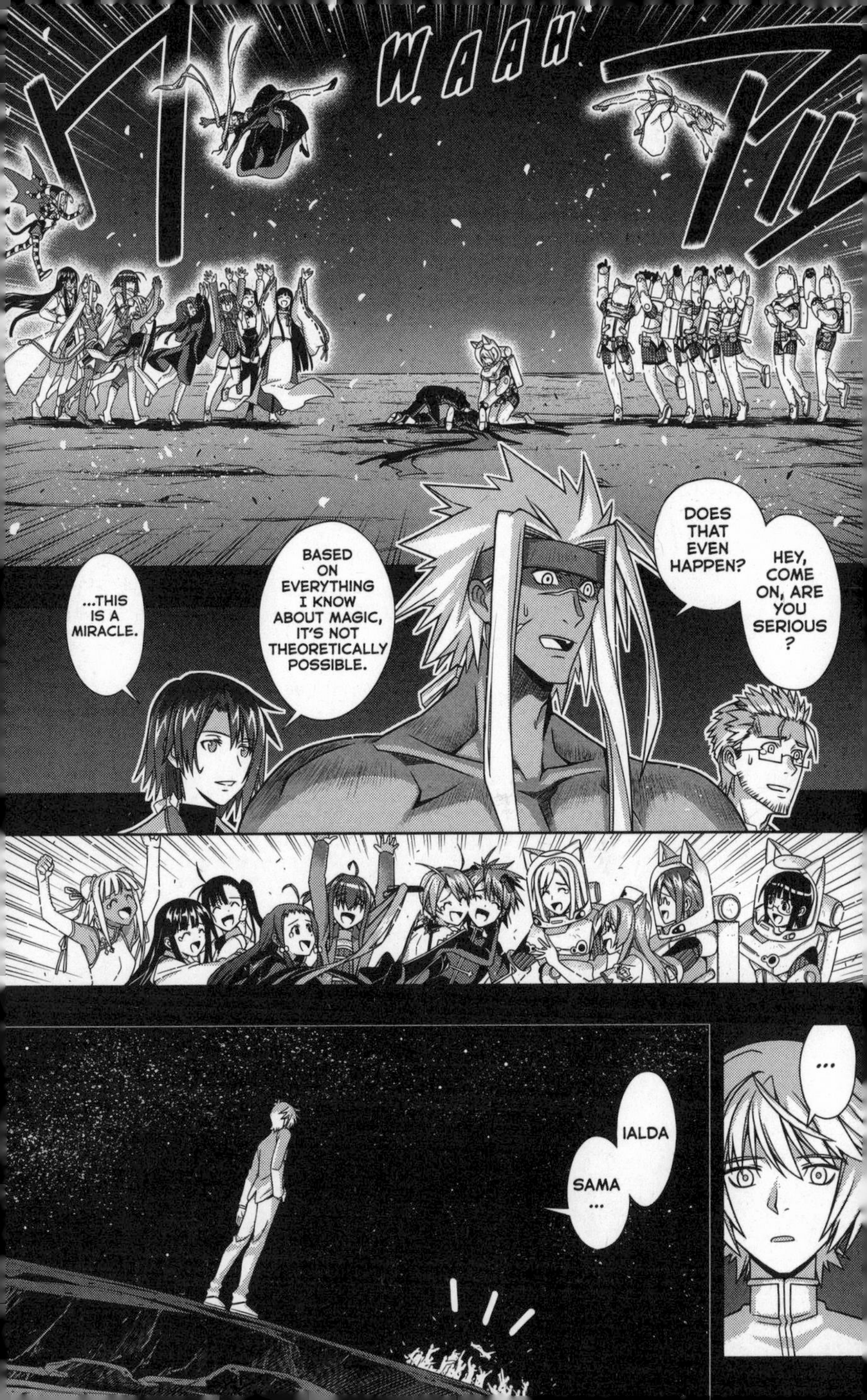
WAAAH
HEY, COME ON, ARE YOU SERIOUS?
DOES THAT EVEN HAPPEN?
BASED ON EVERYTHING I KNOW ABOUT MAGIC, IT'S NOT THEORETICALLY POSSIBLE.
...THIS IS A MIRACLE.
...
IALDA SAMA ...

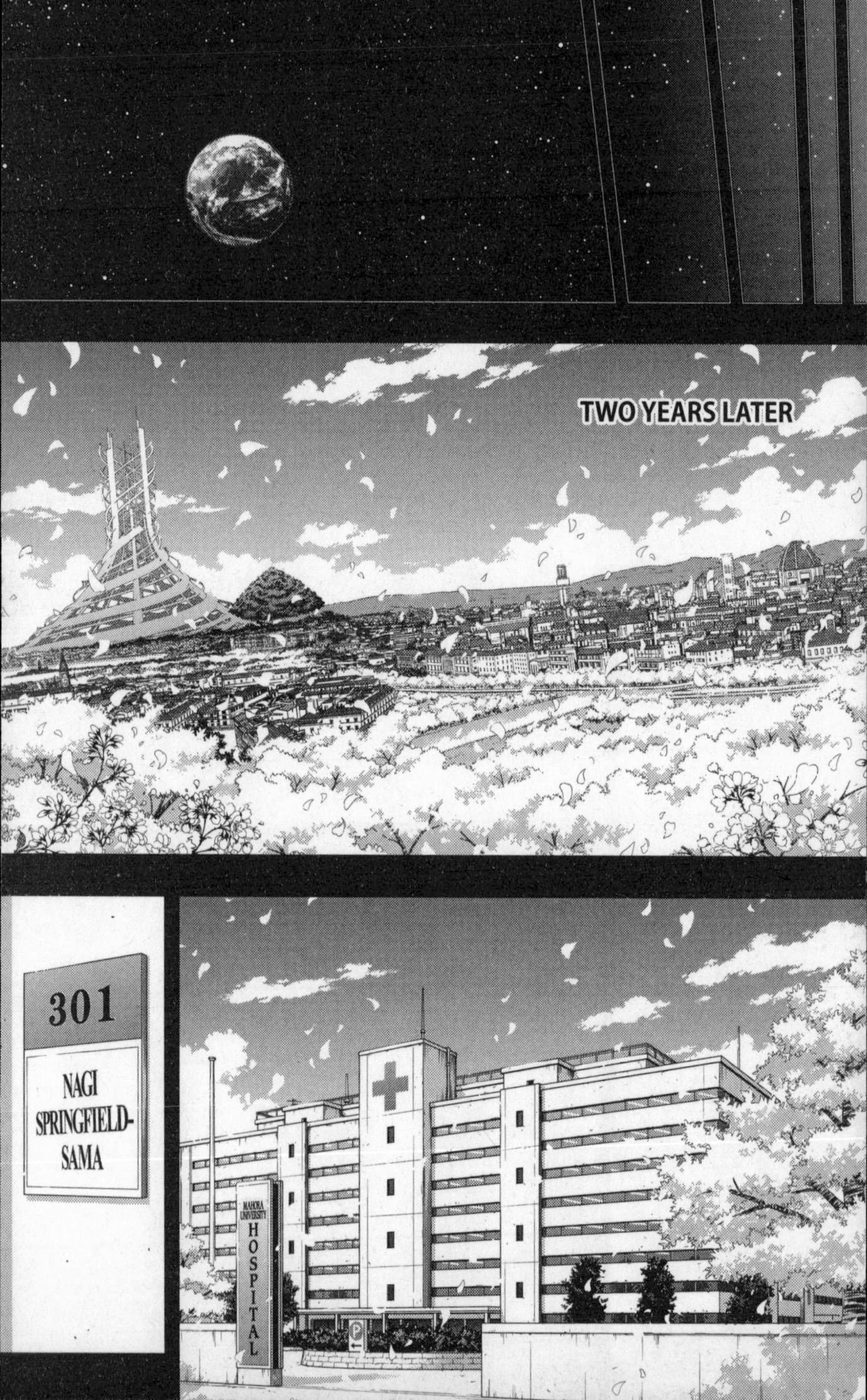
TWO YEARS LATER
MAHORA UNIVERSITY
HOSPITAL
301
NAGI SPRINGFIELD-SAMA

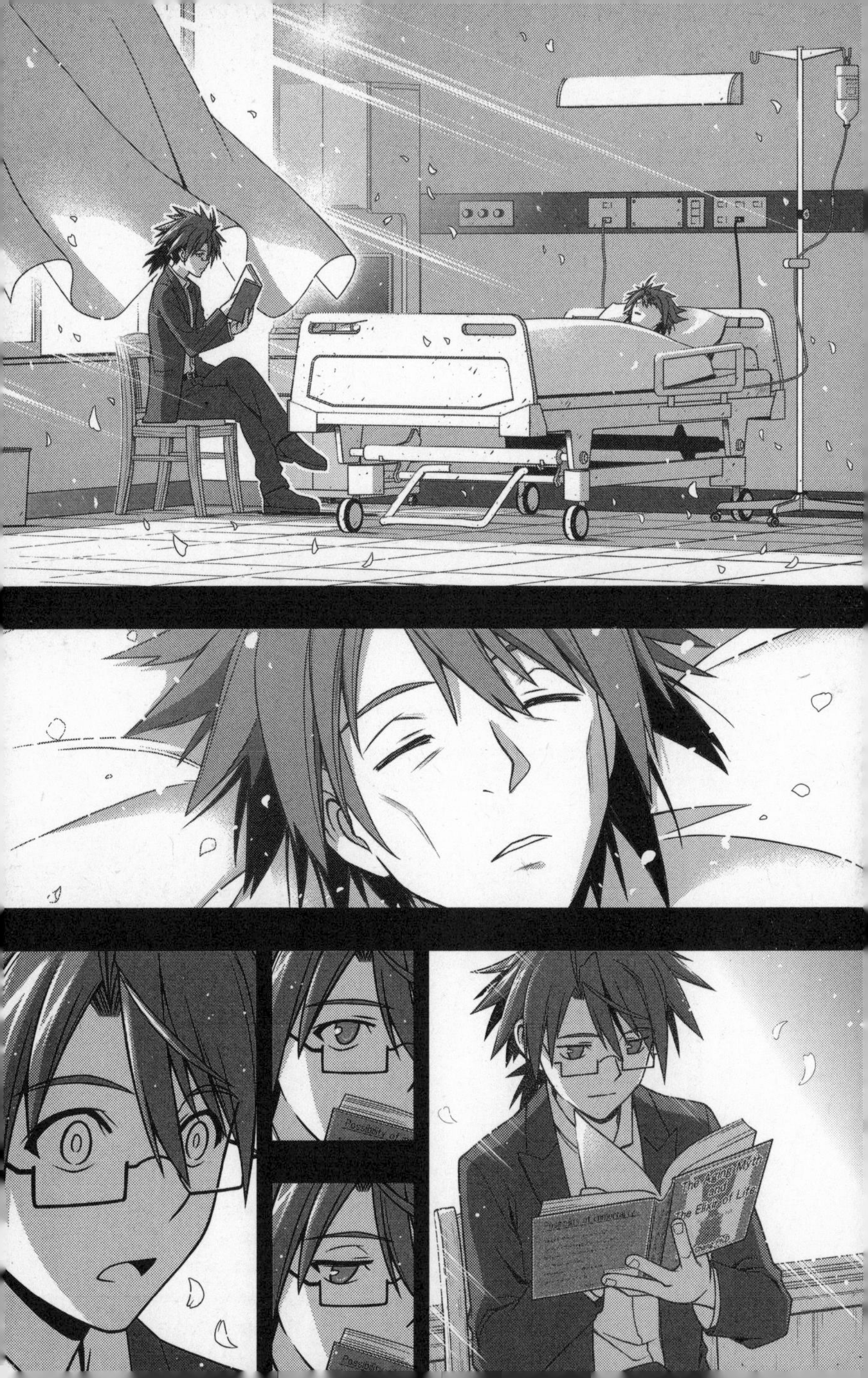
The Aging Myth and The Elixir Of Life

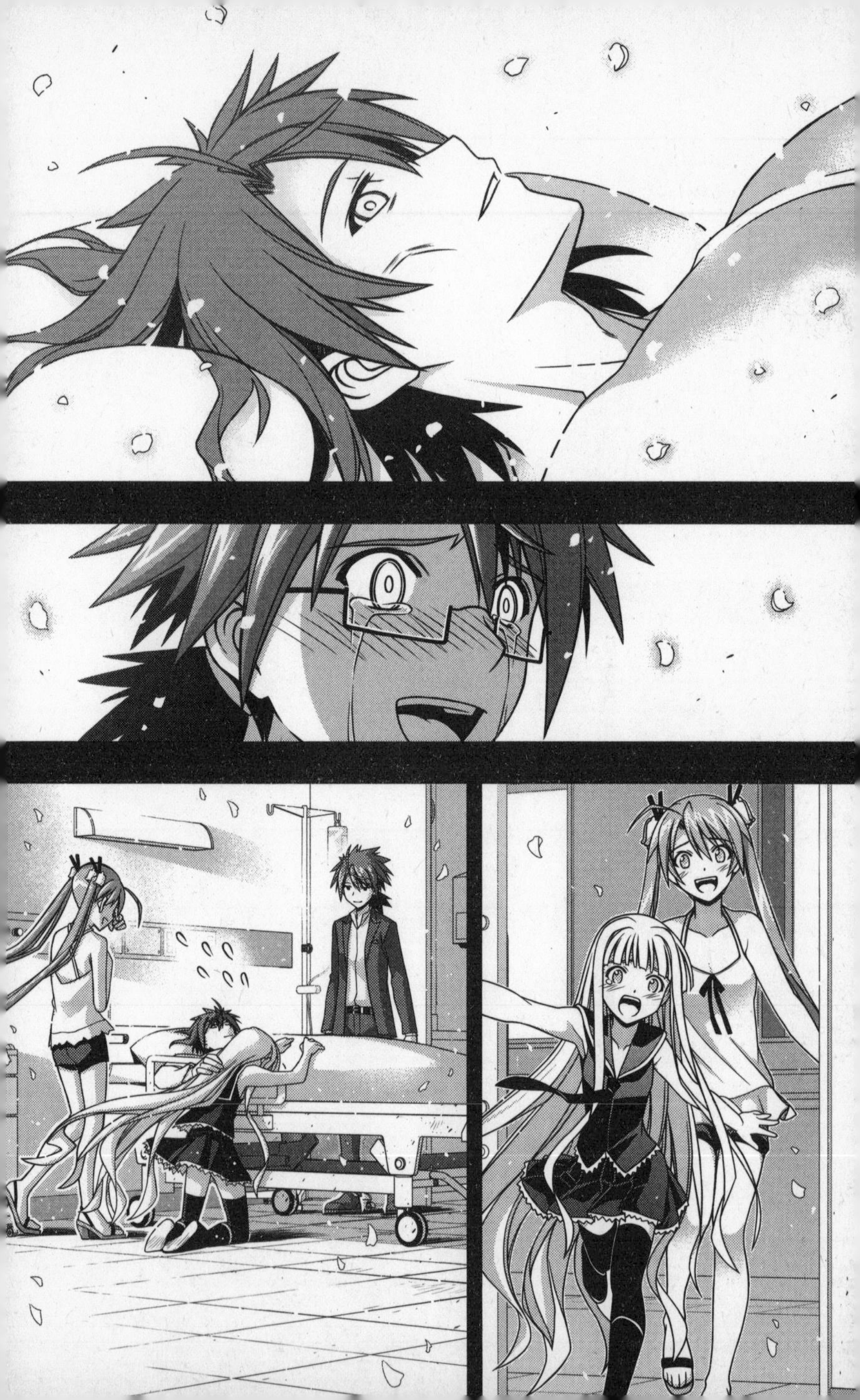

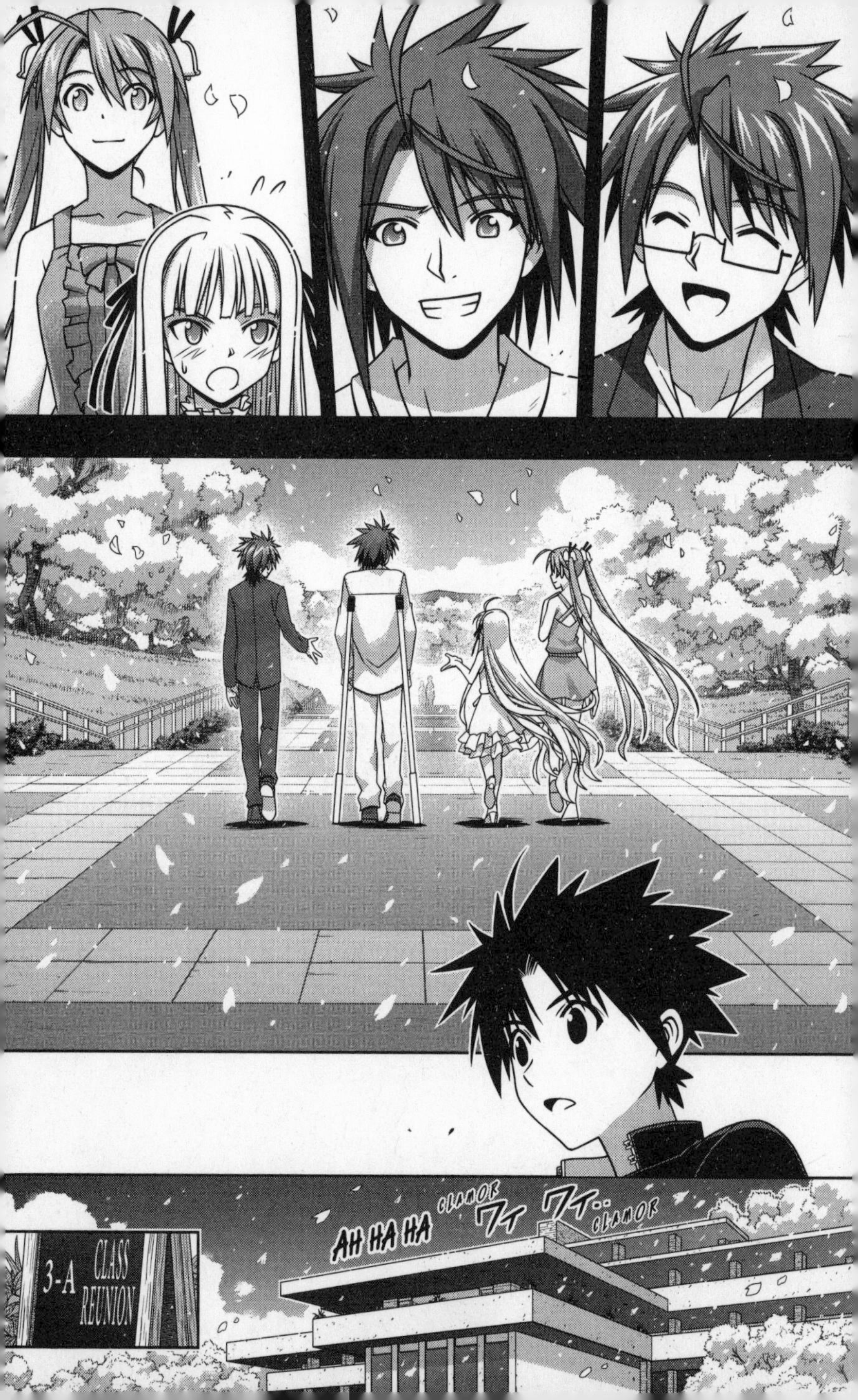
CLAMOR
ワイ ワイ..
CLAMOR
AH HA HA
3-A CLASS REUNION

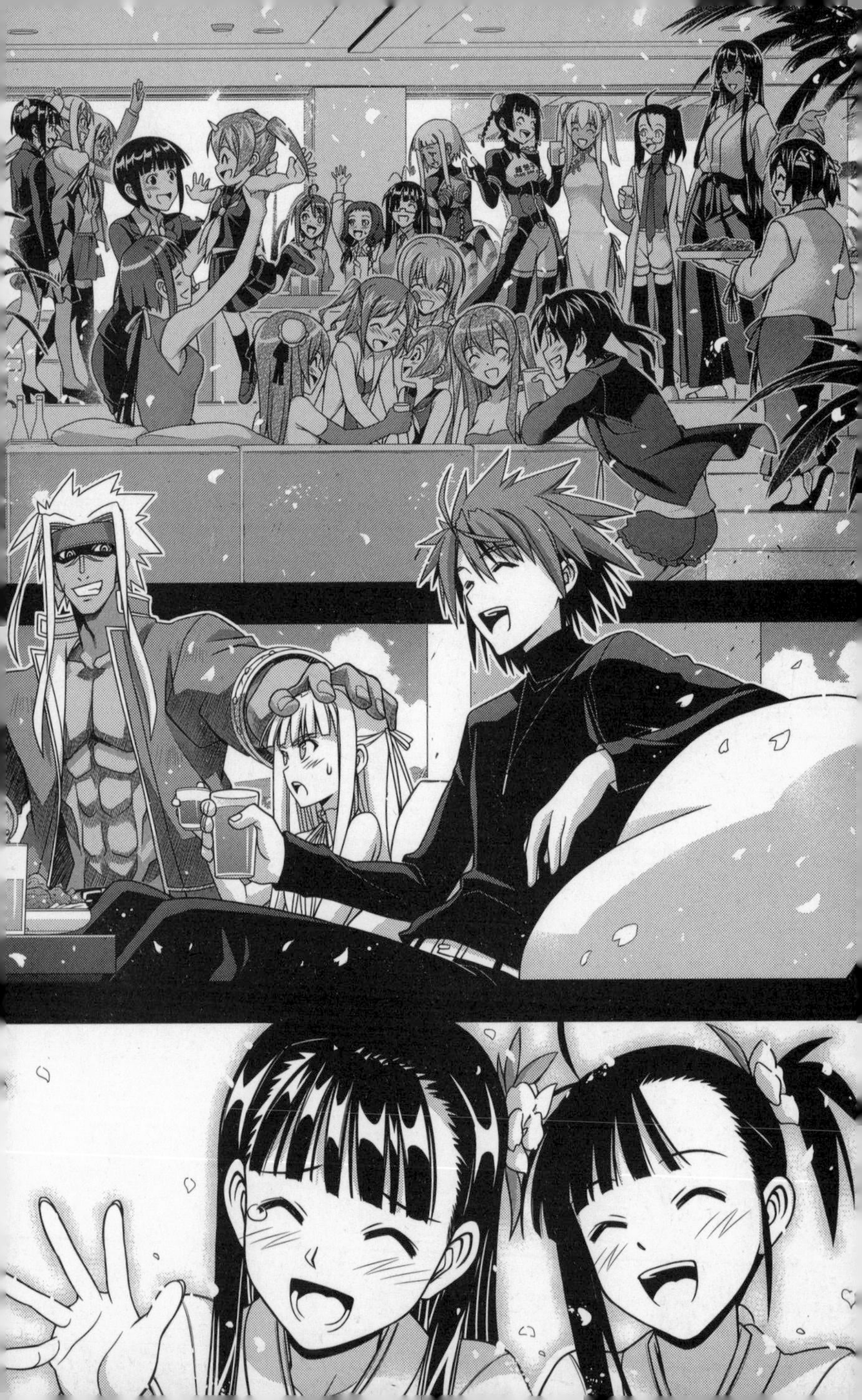

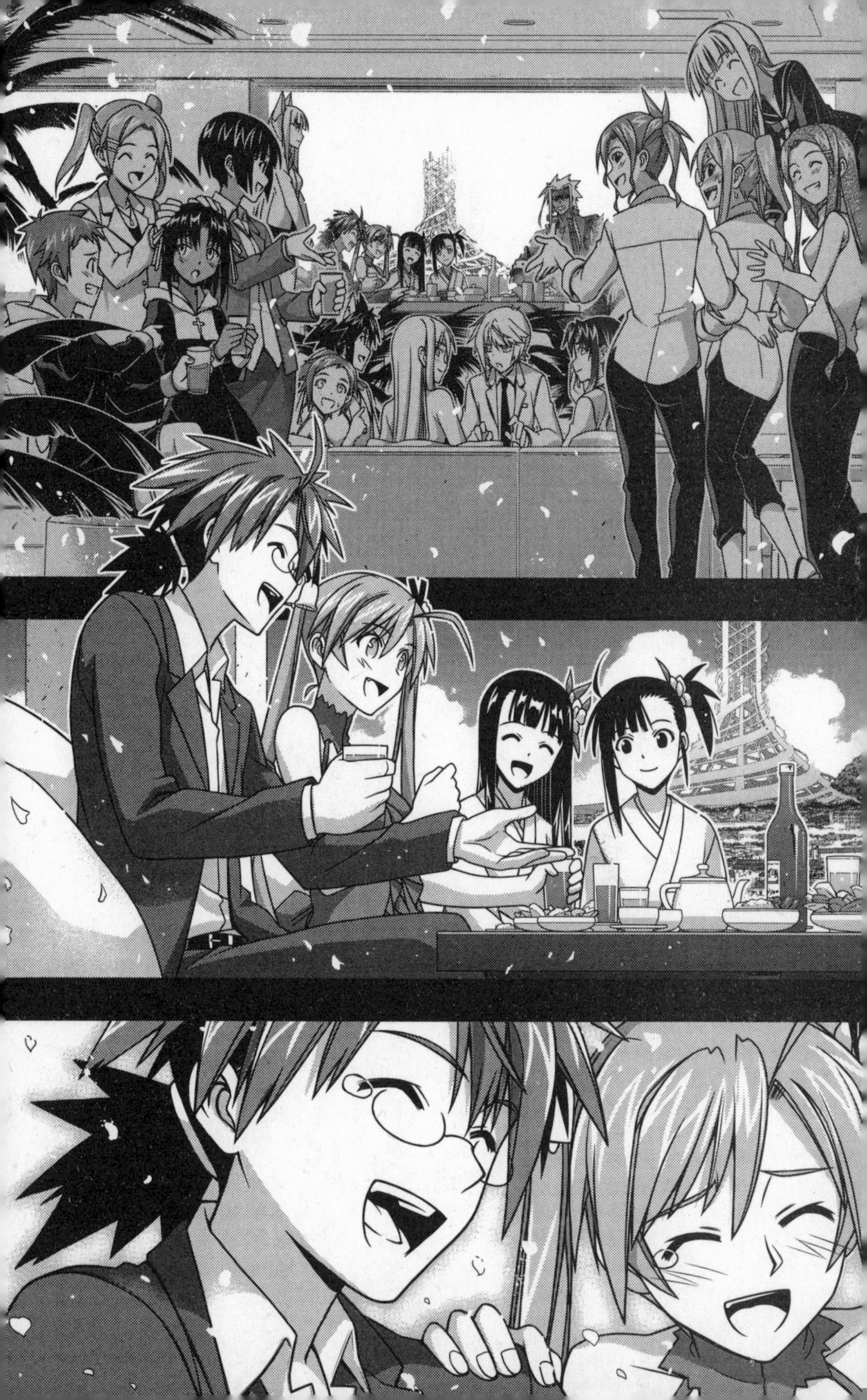

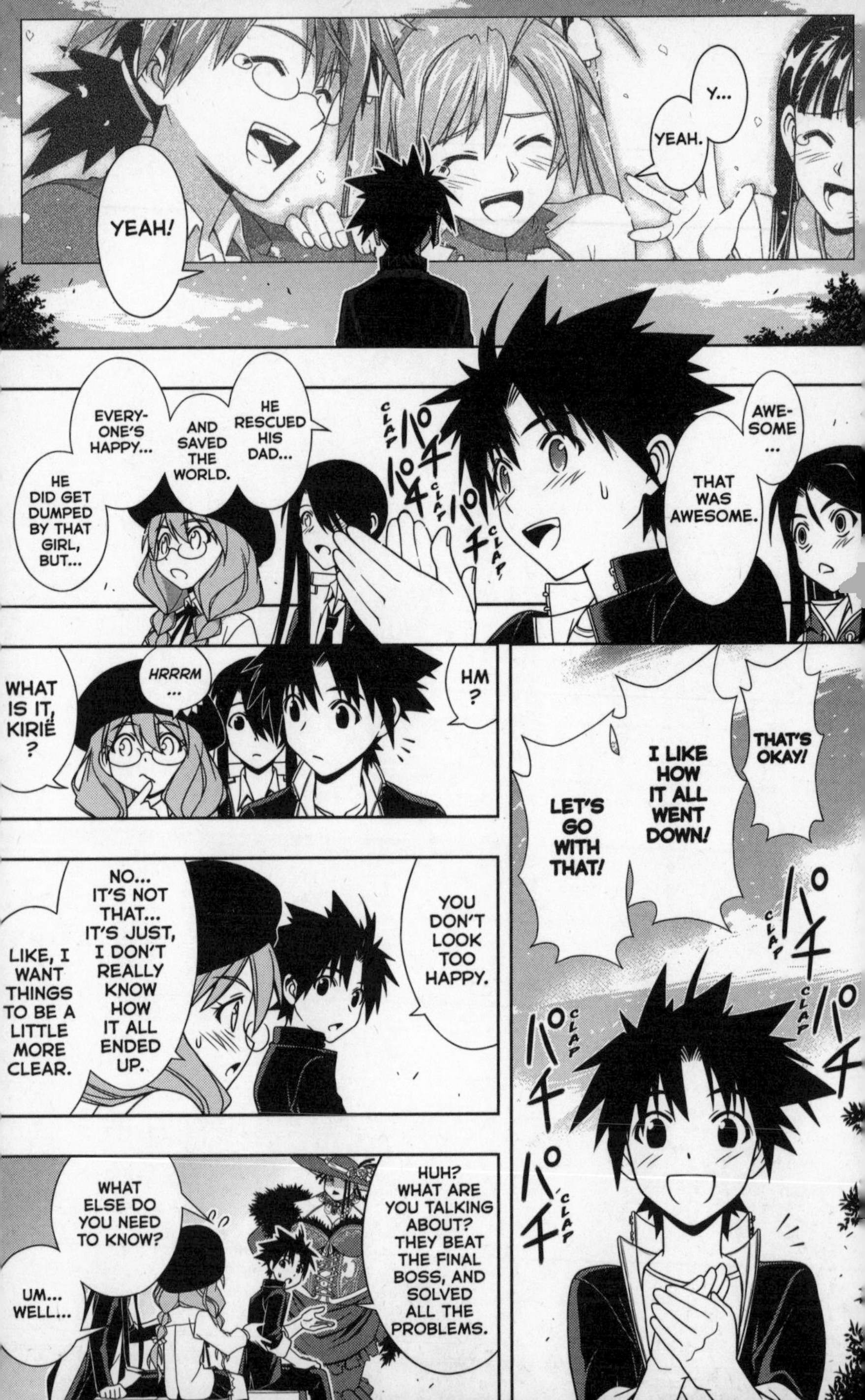
Y...
YEAH.
YEAH!
AWE-SOME...
THAT WAS AWESOME.
パチ CLAP
パチ CLAP
パチ CLAP
HE RESCUED HIS DAD...
AND SAVED THE WORLD.
EVERY-ONE'S HAPPY...
HE DID GET DUMPED BY THAT GIRL, BUT...
THAT'S OKAY!
I LIKE HOW IT ALL WENT DOWN!
LET'S GO WITH THAT!
パチ CLAP
パチ CLAP
パチ CLAP
パチ CLAP
HM?
HRRRM...
WHAT IS IT, KIRIE?
YOU DON'T LOOK TOO HAPPY.
NO... IT'S NOT THAT... IT'S JUST, I DON'T REALLY KNOW HOW IT ALL ENDED UP.
LIKE, I WANT THINGS TO BE A LITTLE MORE CLEAR.
HUH? WHAT ARE YOU TALKING ABOUT? THEY BEAT THE FINAL BOSS, AND SOLVED ALL THE PROBLEMS.
WHAT ELSE DO YOU NEED TO KNOW?
UM... WELL...

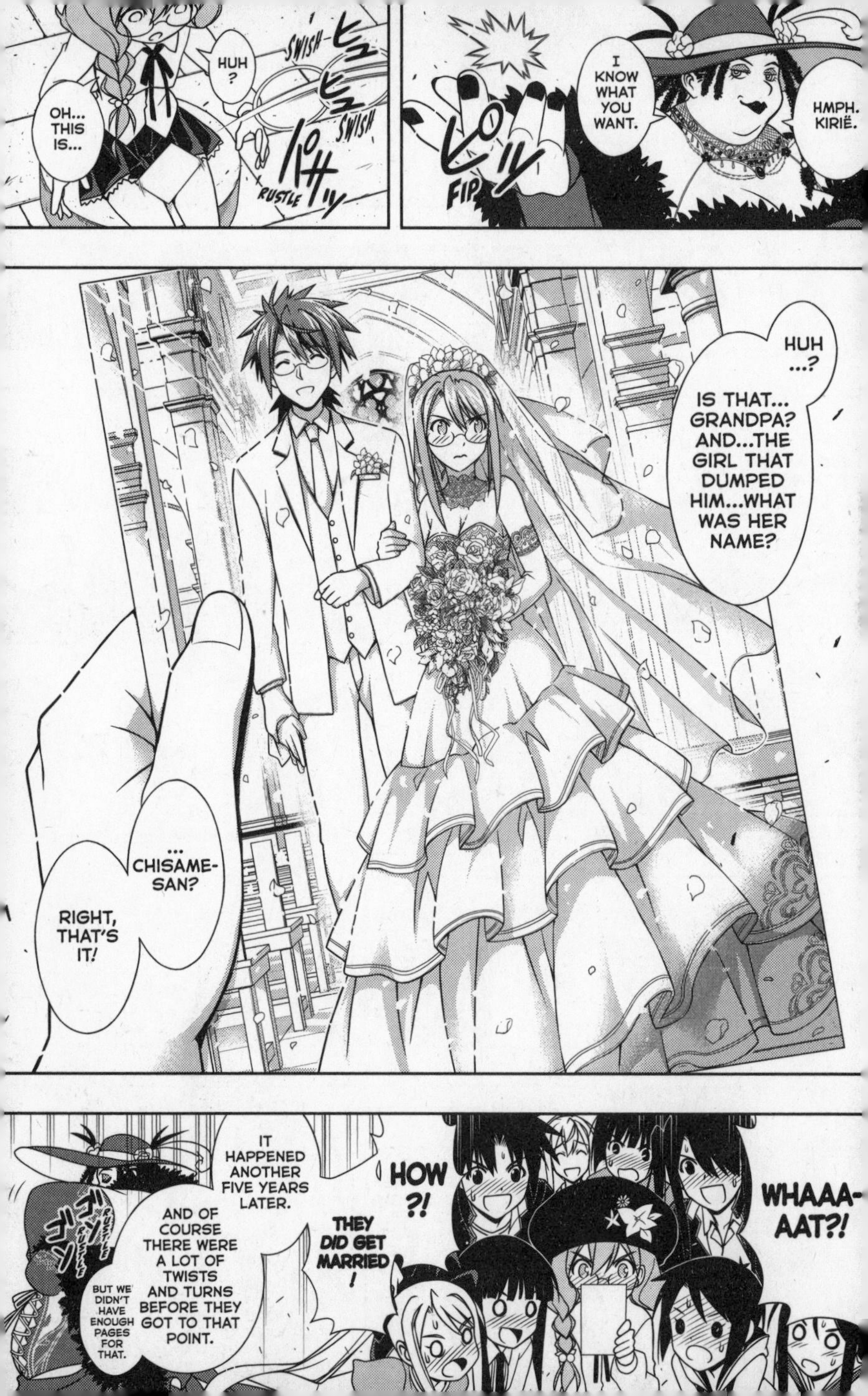
HMPH. KIRIË.
I KNOW WHAT YOU WANT.
ピッ
FIP
SWISH
ヒュ
ヒュ
SWISH
パサッ
RUSTLE
HUH ?
OH... THIS IS...
HUH ...?
IS THAT... GRANDPA? AND...THE GIRL THAT DUMPED HIM...WHAT WAS HER NAME?
... CHISAME-SAN?
RIGHT, THAT'S IT!
WHAAA-AAT?!
HOW ?!
THEY DID GET MARRIED!
IT HAPPENED ANOTHER FIVE YEARS LATER.
AND OF COURSE THERE WERE A LOT OF TWISTS AND TURNS BEFORE THEY GOT TO THAT POINT.
BUT WE DIDN'T HAVE ENOUGH PAGES FOR THAT.
RUSTLE
RUSTLE

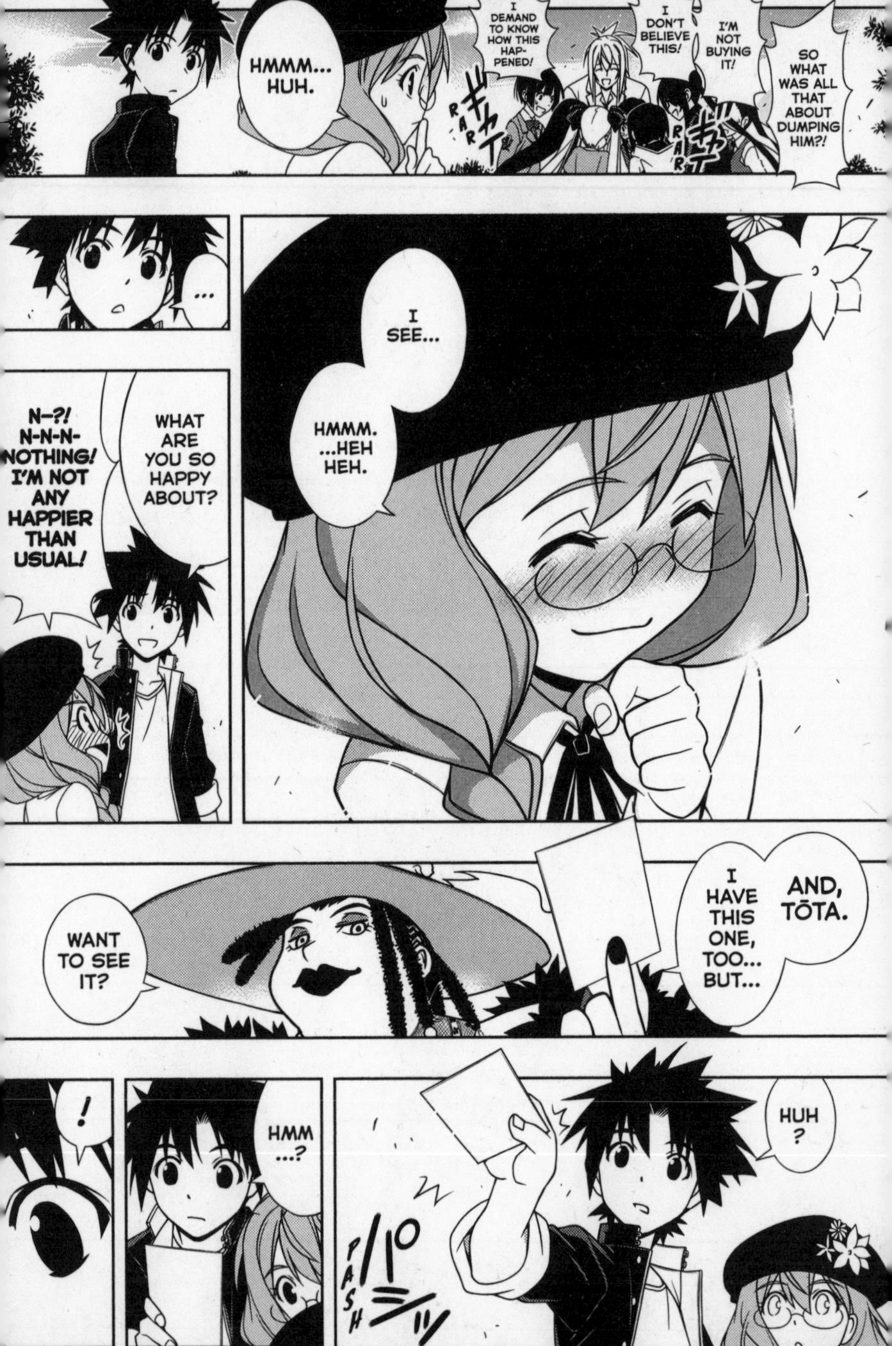
SO WHAT WAS ALL THAT ABOUT DUMPING HIM?!
RAR
I'M NOT BUYING IT!
I DON'T BELIEVE THIS!
I DEMAND TO KNOW HOW THIS HAPPENED!
RAR
HMMM... HUH.
I SEE...
HMMM. ...HEH HEH.
...
WHAT ARE YOU SO HAPPY ABOUT?
N-?! N-N-N-NOTHING! I'M NOT ANY HAPPIER THAN USUAL!
AND, TŌTA.
I HAVE THIS ONE, TOO... BUT...
WANT TO SEE IT?
HUH?
PASH
HMM...?
!

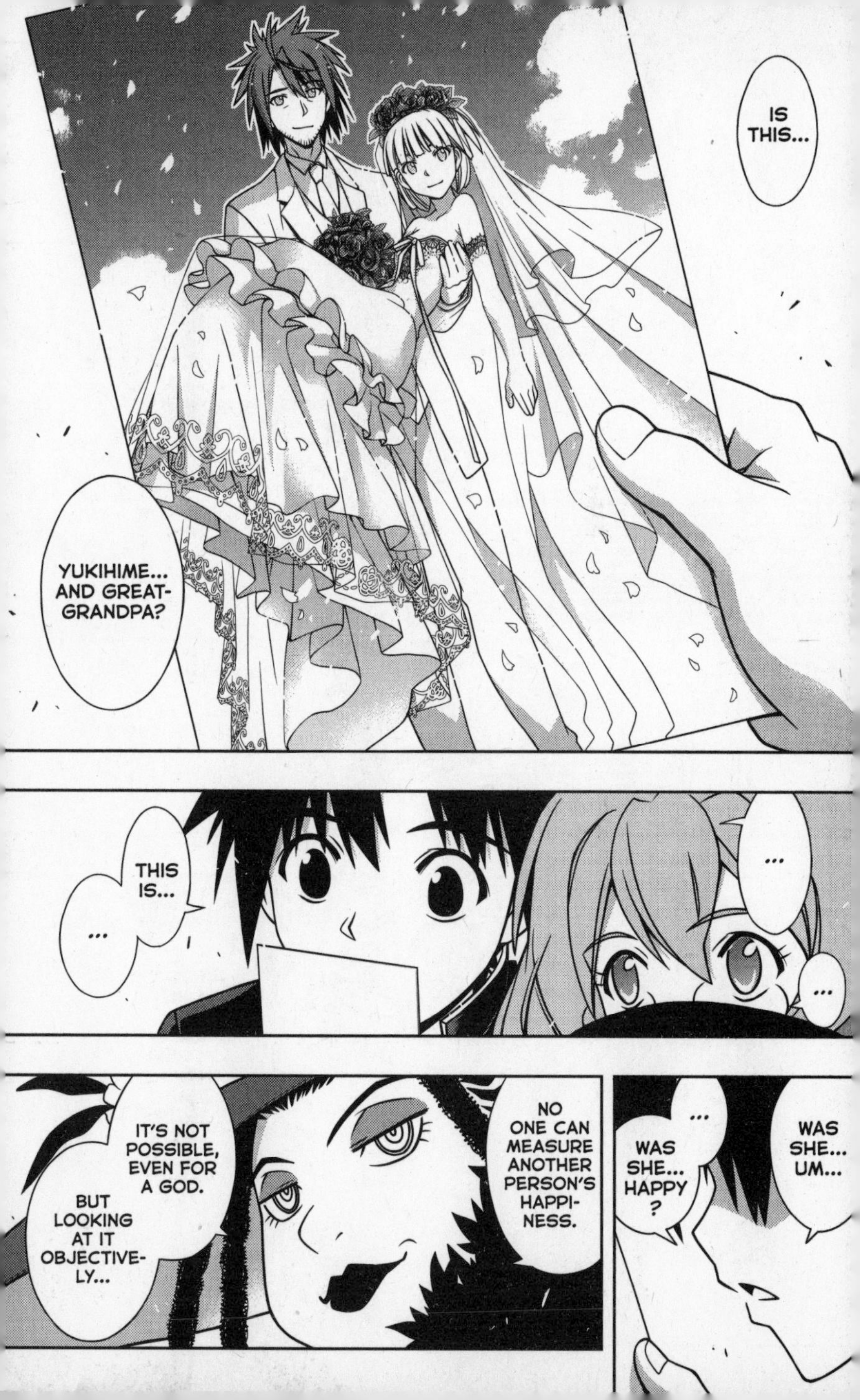
IS THIS...
YUKIHIME... AND GREAT-GRANDPA?
...
...
THIS IS...
...
WAS SHE... UM...
...
WAS SHE... HAPPY?
NO ONE CAN MEASURE ANOTHER PERSON'S HAPPINESS.
IT'S NOT POSSIBLE, EVEN FOR A GOD.
BUT LOOKING AT IT OBJECTIVELY...

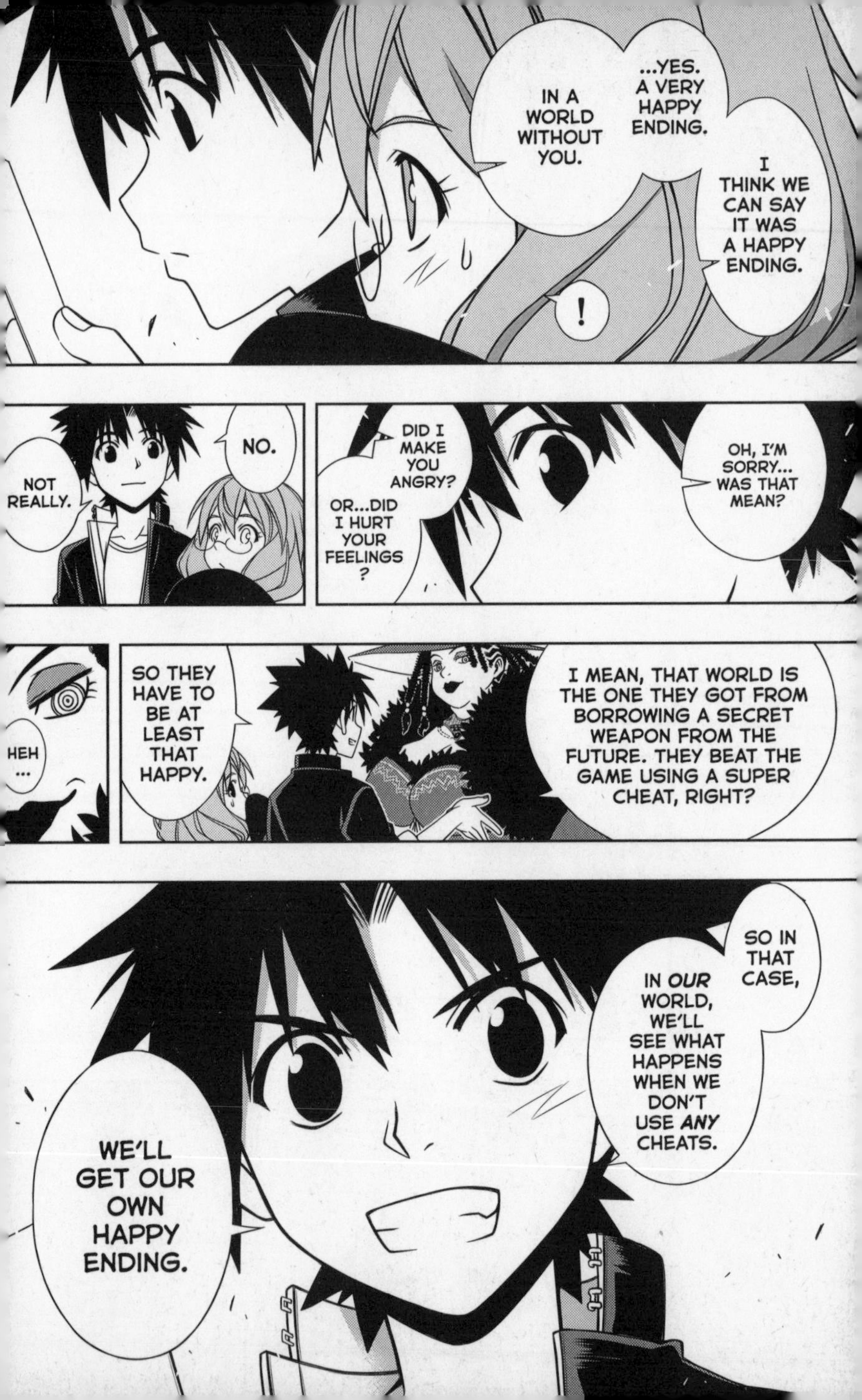
I THINK WE CAN SAY IT WAS A HAPPY ENDING.
!
...YES. A VERY HAPPY ENDING.
IN A WORLD WITHOUT YOU.
OH, I'M SORRY... WAS THAT MEAN?
DID I MAKE YOU ANGRY?
OR...DID I HURT YOUR FEELINGS?
NO.
NOT REALLY.
I MEAN, THAT WORLD IS THE ONE THEY GOT FROM BORROWING A SECRET WEAPON FROM THE FUTURE. THEY BEAT THE GAME USING A SUPER CHEAT, RIGHT?
SO THEY HAVE TO BE AT LEAST THAT HAPPY.
HEH...
SO IN THAT CASE,
IN *OUR* WORLD, WE'LL SEE WHAT HAPPENS WHEN WE DON'T USE *ANY* CHEATS.
WE'LL GET OUR OWN HAPPY ENDING.

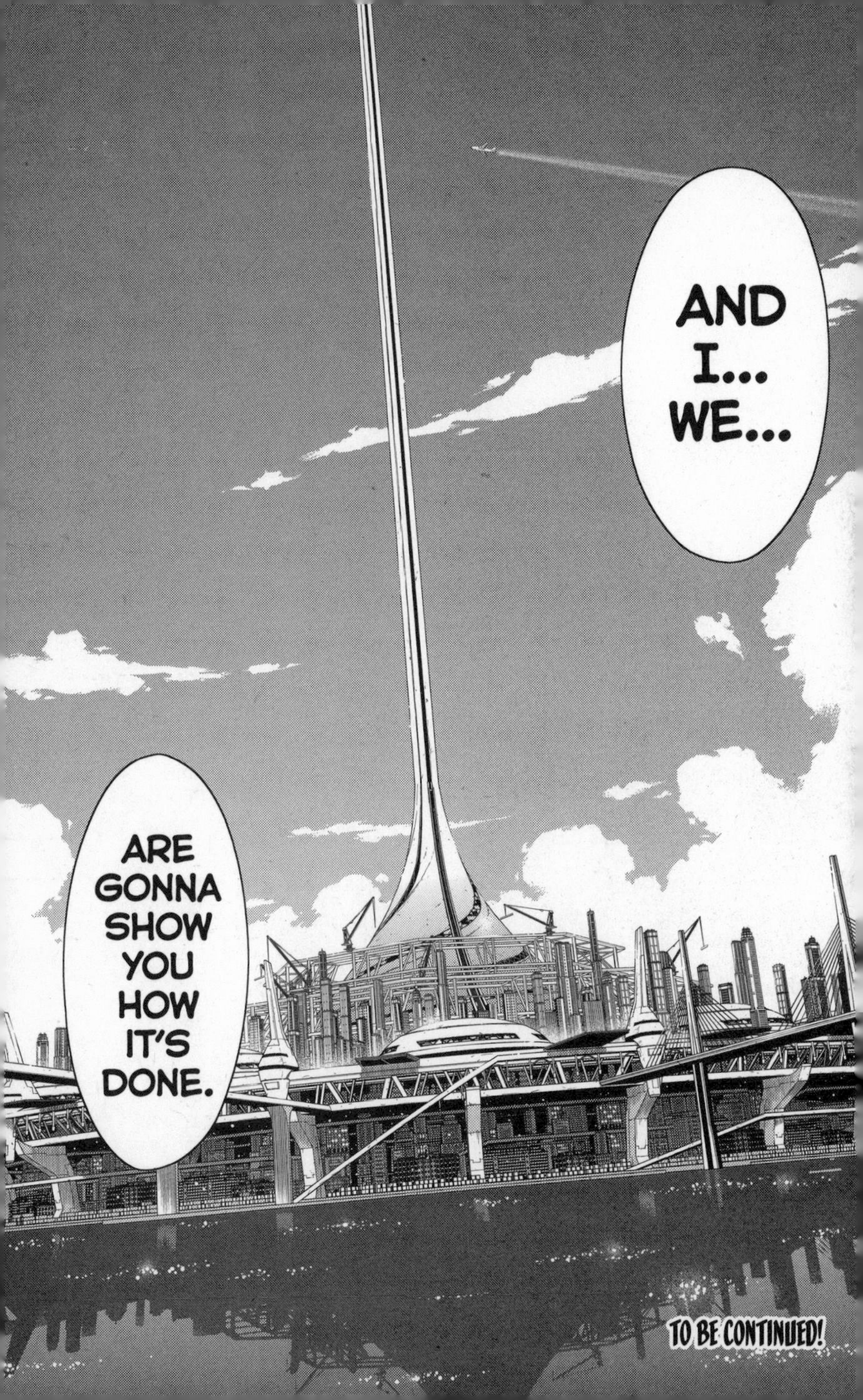
AND I... WE...
ARE GONNA SHOW YOU HOW IT'S DONE.
TO BE CONTINUED!

UQ HOLDER!

STAFF

Ken Akamatsu

Takashi Takemoto

Kenichi Nakamura

Keiichi Yamashita

Yuri Sasaki

Madoka Akanuma

Thanks to Ran Ayanaga

A new series from the creator of *Soul Eater*, the megahit manga and anime seen on Toonami!

"Fun and lively... a great start!"
    -Adventures in
        Poor Taste

FIRE FORCE

By Atsushi Ohkubo

The city of Tokyo is plagued by a deadly phenomenon: spontaneous human combustion! Luckily, a special team is there to quench the inferno: The Fire Force! The fire soldiers at Special Fire Cathedral 8 are about to get a unique addition. Enter Shinra, a boy who possesses the power to run at the speed of a rocket, leaving behind the famous "devil's footprints" (and destroying his shoes in the process). Can Shinra and his colleagues discover the source of this strange epidemic before the city burns to ashes?

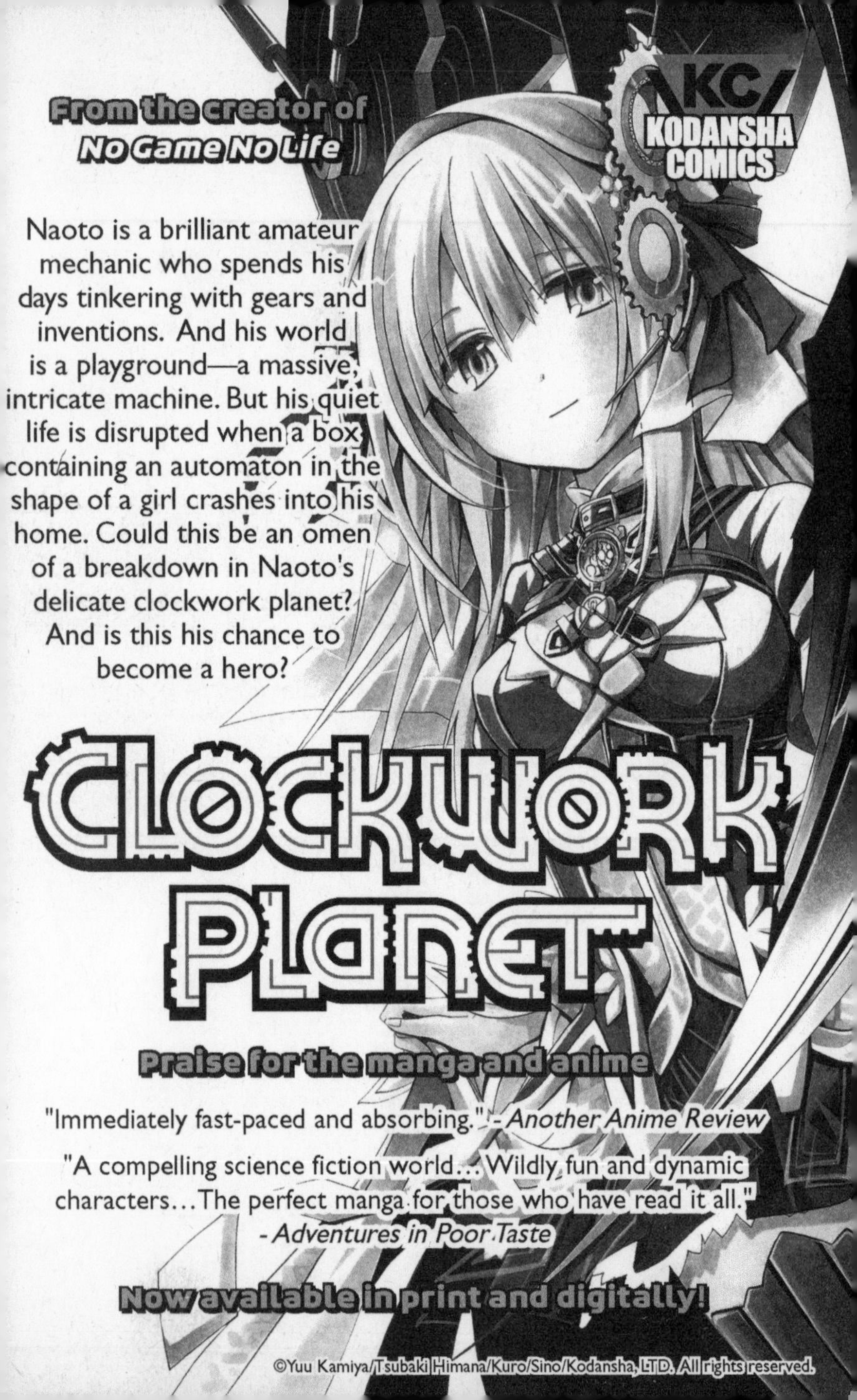
KC KODANSHA COMICS
From the creator of
No Game No Life
Naoto is a brilliant amateur mechanic who spends his days tinkering with gears and inventions. And his world is a playground—a massive, intricate machine. But his quiet life is disrupted when a box containing an automaton in the shape of a girl crashes into his home. Could this be an omen of a breakdown in Naoto's delicate clockwork planet? And is this his chance to become a hero?
Clockwork Planet
Praise for the manga and anime
"Immediately fast-paced and absorbing." - Another Anime Review
"A compelling science fiction world… Wildly fun and dynamic characters…The perfect manga for those who have read it all." - Adventures in Poor Taste
Now available in print and digitally!
©Yuu Kamiya/Tsubaki Himana/Kuro/Sino/Kodansha, LTD. All rights reserved.

THE STORY STARTS **HERE!**

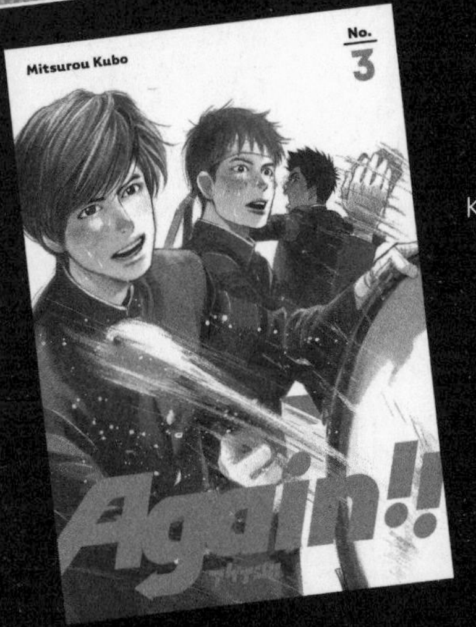
Mitsurou Kubo
No.
3
Again!!

Again!!

アゲイン!!

Kinichiro Imamura isn't a bad guy, really, but on the first day of high school his narrow eyes and bleached blonde hair made him look so shifty that his classmates assumed the worst. Three years later, without any friends or fond memories, he isn't exactly feeling bittersweet about graduation. But after an accidental fall down a flight of stairs, Kinichiro wakes up three years in the past... on the first day of high school! School's starting again—but it's gonna be different this time around!

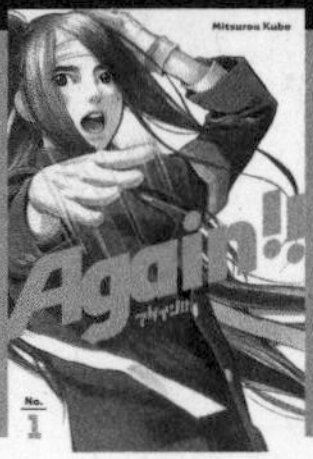
Again!!
No.
1

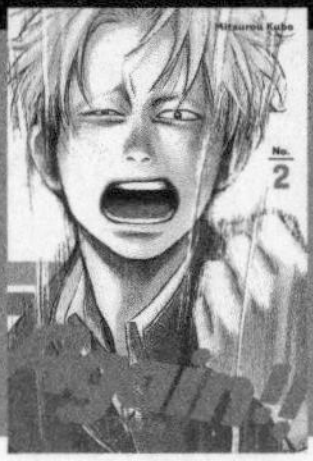
No.
2

Vol. 1-3 now available in **PRINT** and **DIGITAL**!
Vol. 4 coming August 2018!

Find out **MORE** by visiting:
kodanshacomics.com/MitsurouKubo

ABOUT MITSUROU KUBO

Mitsurou Kubo is a manga artist born in Nagasaki prefecture. Her series *3.3.7 Byoshi!!* (2001-2003), *Tokkyu!!* (2004-2008), and *Again!!* (2011-2014) were published in *Weekly Shonen Magazine*, and *Moteki* (2008-2010) was published in the seinen comics magazine *Evening*. After the publication of *Again!!* concluded, she met Sayo Yamamoto, director of the global smash-hit anime ***Yuri!!! on ICE***. Working with Yamamoto, Kubo contributed the original concept, original character designs, and initial script for ***Yuri!!! on ICE***. *Again!!* is her first manga to be published in English.

KC KODANSHA COMICS

Kodansha COMICS

ANIME COMING SUMMER 2018

The award-winning manga about what happens inside you!

"Far more entertaining than it ought to be... What kid doesn't want to think that every time they sneeze, a torpedo shoots out their nose?"

—Anime News Network

Strep throat! Hay fever! Influenza! The world is a dangerous place for a red blood cell just trying to get her deliveries finished. Fortunately, she's not alone. She's got a whole human body's worth of cells ready to help out! The mysterious white blood cell, the buff and brash killer T cell, the nerdy neuron, even the cute little platelets— everyone's got to come together if they want to keep you healthy!

Cells at Work!

はたらく細胞

By Akane Shimizu

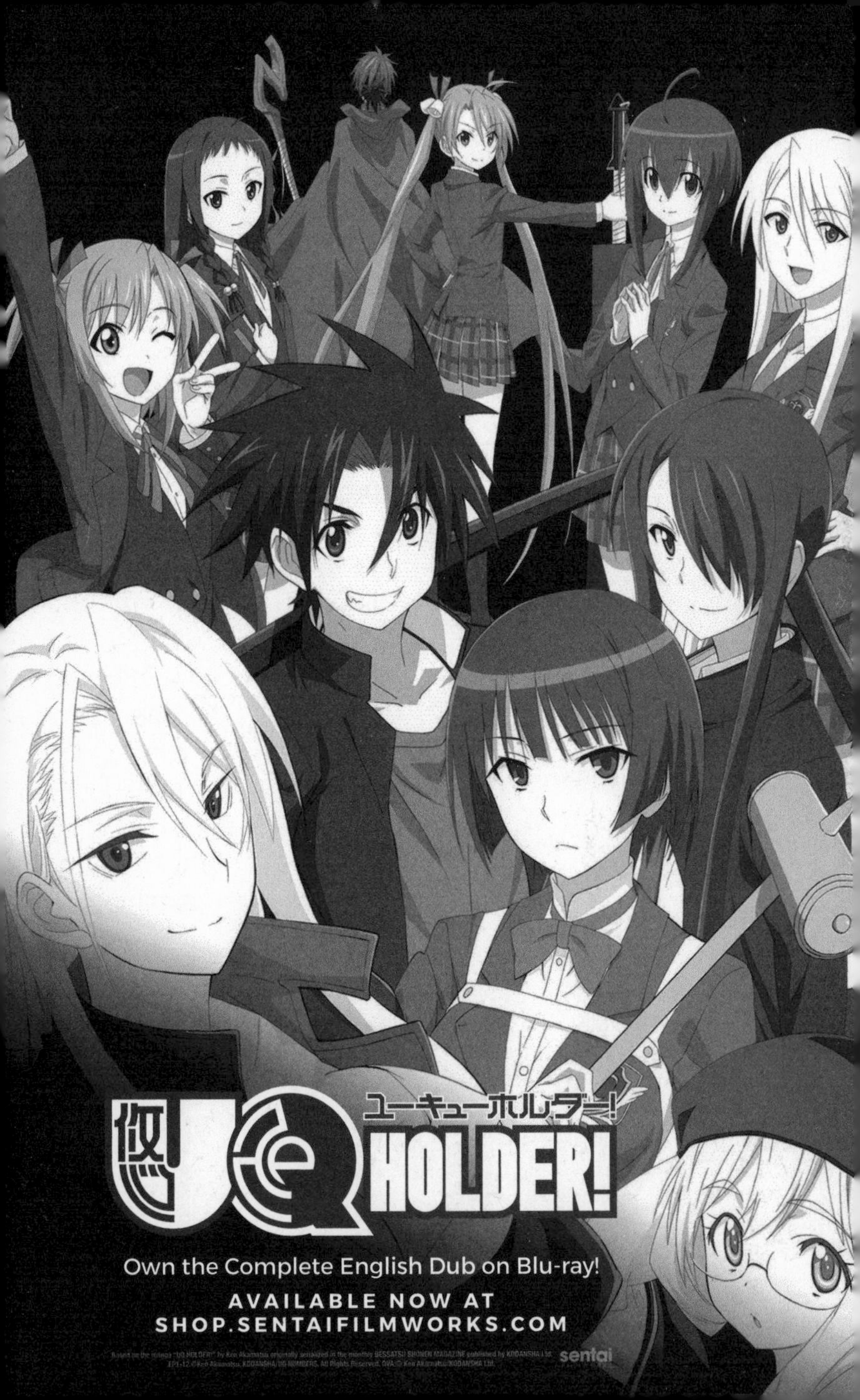
ユーキューホルダー!
UQ HOLDER!
Own the Complete English Dub on Blu-ray!
AVAILABLE NOW AT
SHOP.SENTAIFILMWORKS.COM
sentai

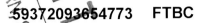

UQ HOLDER! VOLUME 15 IS A WORK OF FICTION. NAMES, CHARACTERS, PLACES, AND INCIDENTS ARE THE PRODUCTS OF THE AUTHOR'S IMAGINATION OR ARE USED FICTITIOUSLY. ANY RESEMBLANCE TO ACTUAL EVENTS, LOCALES, OR PERSONS, LIVING OR DEAD, IS ENTIRELY COINCIDENTAL.

A KODANSHA COMICS TRADE PAPERBACK ORIGINAL

PUBLISHED IN THE UNITED STATES BY KODANSHA COMICS, AN IMPRINT OF KODANSHA USA PUBLISHING, LLC, NEW YORK.

PUBLICATION RIGHTS FOR THIS ENGLISH EDITION ARRANGED THROUGH KODANSHA LTD., TOKYO.

FIRST PUBLISHED IN JAPAN IN 2017 BY KODANSHA LTD., TOKYO.

ISBN 978-1-63236-689-4

PRINTED IN THE UNITED STATES OF AMERICA.

WWW.KODANSHACOMICS.COM

9 8 7 6 5 4 3 2 1

TRANSLATION: ALETHEA NIBLEY AND ATHENA NIBLEY
LETTERING: JAMES DASHIELL
KODANSHA COMICS EDITION COVER DESIGN: PHIL BALSMAN